Register Now for O
to Your B[...]

Your print purchase of *Financial Sustainability for Nonprofit Organizations,* **includes online access to the contents of your book**–increasing accessibility, portability, and searchability!

Access today at:

**http://connect.springerpub.com/content/book/978-0-8261-2986-4
or scan the QR code at the right with your smartphone
and enter the access code below.**

P430NKSA

*Scan here for
quick access.*

SPC

SPRINGER PUBLISHING COMPANY
View all our products at springerpub.com

Financial Sustainability for Nonprofit Organizations

Emmanuel Jean Francois, PhD, is assistant professor of Human Services Leadership and director of the master's program in Transnational Human Services program at the University of Wisconsin, Oshkosh. He earned a doctorate in curriculum and instruction (adult, higher education, and human resources development) from the University of South Florida (USF), a master's degree in human services (organization management and leadership) from Springfield College, a joint postgraduate diploma in population and development from the State University of Haiti and the United Nations Development Program (UNDP), and a joint postgraduate certificate in psychoeducation and social health from the Schools of Cadres in Special Education of Port-au-Prince and Versailles. He studied anthropology and sociology at the State University of Haiti, and pedagogy of secondary education at the University Institute of Educational Sciences. Before coming to the University of Wisconsin, Oshkosh, Dr. Jean Francois taught for 3 years at Springfield College, served as campus coordinator for an international program in youth leadership at the University of South Florida (in collaboration with Georgetown University), and was research coordinator at the Moffitt Cancer Center and Research Institute. Dr. Jean Francois's publications include more than 30 titles in English, French, and Haitian Creole. His most recent books include *Transcultural Blended Learning and Teaching in Postsecondary Education* (2012), *DREAM Model to Start a Small Business* (2011), and *Global Education on Trial by U.S. College Professors* (2010). Dr. Jean Francois is the current president of the Transnational Education and Learning Society (TELS). He has presented at various regional, national, and international conferences about his research on adult and continuing education, nontraditional college students, global education, transnational education, transcultural issues, globalization, international development, study abroad, transformative learning, scholarship of teaching and learning, and community-based participatory research. He is on the editorial board of *Human Services Today* and the *International Interdisciplinary Journal of Education*. He has served as peer reviewer for the *International Journal of Multicultural Education* (IJME), the *American Educational Research Journal* (AERJ), and the Annual Conference of the American Association for Adult and Continuing Education (AAACE).

Financial Sustainability for Nonprofit Organizations

Emmanuel Jean Francois, PhD

SPRINGER PUBLISHING COMPANY
NEW YORK

Springer Publishing Company, LLC
11 West 42nd Street
New York, NY 10036
www.springerpub.com

Acquisitions Editor: Stephanie Drew
Production Editor: Pamela Lankas
Composition: Integra Software Services

ISBN: 978-0-8261-2983-3
e-book ISBN: 978-0-8261-2986-4

14 15 16 17 / 5 4 3 2 1

The author and the publisher of this Work have made every effort to use sources believed to be reliable to provide information that is accurate and compatible with the standards generally accepted at the time of publication. The author and publisher shall not be liable for any special, consequential, or exemplary damages resulting, in whole or in part, from the readers' use of, or reliance on, the information contained in this book. The publisher has no responsibility for the persistence or accuracy of URLs for external or third-party Internet websites referred to in this publication and does not guarantee that any content on such websites is, or will remain, accurate or appropriate.

Library of Congress Cataloging-in-Publication Data

Jean-Francois, Emmanuel, 1971-
Financial sustainability for nonprofit organizations / Emmanuel Jean Francois, PhD.
    pages cm
ISBN 978-0-8261-2983-3
1. Nonprofit organizations—Finance. 2. Nonprofit organizations—Management. 3. Fund raising.
I. Title.
HG4027.65.J43 2014
658.15'9—dc23

2014023228

Printed in the United States of America by Bradford & Bigelow.

This book is dedicated to my adorable wife, Pierrette; my incredible daughters Emmarald and Maellie; and my handsome son, Pierremael.

Contents

Preface

Show me a financially sustainable nonprofit organization, and I will show you an organization that is committed to its vision and mission.

Based on my national and international experience, I can attest that nonprofit organizations serve various purposes, including, but not limited to, providing charity, education, culture, religion, public health and safety, sports, advocacy, politics, philanthropy, fraternity, and civil rights. I also know that some people use the structure of nonprofit organizations to enrich themselves on the backs of disadvantaged people or to fulfill neocolonialist agendas in developing countries. However, this is not the reality of every nonprofit organization. Most nonprofit organizations serve vital functions in societies and communities that neither government agencies nor private corporations are able to tackle. Many nonprofit organizations work and advocate to shed light on abuse, oppression, and exploitation by public and private entities. Many nonprofit organizations implement programs that make a difference in the lives of children, families, and communities. Public charities and other nonprofit entities represent a significant and growing sector not only in the United States, but also around the world.

With greater involvement in addressing social, economic, and environmental issues or challenges in communities, comes greater scrutiny from various stakeholders for accountability and stewardship, especially in times of financial crisis. Consequently, many nonprofit organizations have to face fierce competition to secure funding that will enable them to further their missions over time. The uncertainty of government funding and the decrease of individual contributions in times of financial hardship make financial sustainability more relevant than ever before. Nonprofit organizations must be organizationally and financially sustainable in order to pursue their visions and missions. Furthermore, the ability of the leaders of nonprofit organizations to address the financial sustainability of their agencies has become even more critical. In the context of this book, financial sustainability implies that an organization can financially survive to meet the needs of its constituency as promised by its mission statement, regardless of changes in environments and funding conditions.

This book provides leaders and managers of nonprofit organizations with theoretical and conceptual frameworks, approaches, and strategies that will enable them to manage organizations that are financially sustainable. The book aims to equip students and nonprofit leaders with the information and conceptual frameworks needed to do financial analyses, manage budgets, and conduct various operations for organizational and financial sustainability.

The book may serve as an introductory textbook for future leaders of nonprofit organizations, as well as students in schools or programs of nonprofit leadership, human service leadership, social work, public and community health, organization management, public administration, education, and other similar fields.

More specifically, the book will help the reader:

■ Explore the history, philosophy, and activities of major nonprofit subsectors, including health, education, the arts, environmental advocacy, social services, and others, as well as the context for nonprofit management, the impacts of the nonprofit sector on society, and the unique challenges and opportunities nonprofits encounter in achieving their aims
■ Acquire an understanding of the governance of nonprofit organizations, and the roles and responsibilities of boards, the staff, and volunteers and what makes boards and individual board members effective
■ Explore administrative issues that affect the management of nonprofit organizations
■ Explore the various theories, attributes, concepts, and components pertaining to nonprofit management
■ Discuss the philosophy, approaches, principles, strategies, and conceptual frameworks that may help a nonprofit organization become financially sustainable or take a path toward financial sustainability
■ Explore business models that can foster the financial viability of a nonprofit organization
■ Explore the relationship between theories and practices of nonprofit leadership and management and financial sustainability
■ Identify areas of concern in nonprofit leadership and management and how such concerns relate to governing, accountability, and stewardship responsibilities of nonprofit organizations

People have a tendency to think of financial sustainability almost exclusively in financial terms. This book argues that financial sustainability involves both financial and nonfinancial facets. To that end it provides a systemic conceptual framework. The chapters are articulated around four sections. The first part introduces the concepts of nonprofit organizations and financial sustainability. The second part, "Organization and Planning," is about key aspects of organization and planning for sustainability in a nonprofit organization. The third part, "Financial Sustainability," discusses issues that are vital to the financial sustainability of a nonprofit organization. The last part, "Management and Leadership," emphasizes the contributions of management and leadership practices to the financial sustainability of nonprofit organizations.

Chapter 1, "The Nonprofit Organization Universe," introduces the concept of nonprofit organizations in the United States. The chapter addresses the role that nonprofit organizations play in their countries and how sociocultural imperatives determine their missions. The chapter investigates the size and activities of major nonprofit subsectors, including health, education, the arts, environmental advocacy, social services, and others. It sets the context for nonprofit management by exploring the impact of the nonprofit sector on society and thinking about the unique challenges and opportunities nonprofits encounter in achieving their aims.

Chapter 2, "Financial Sustainability," explores the dimensions of financial sustainability, as well as the principles needed to manage a nonprofit organization and generate continuous funding through diverse sources in order to support its vision and mission in a way that is socially and environmentally sustainable.

Chapter 3, "Governance and Financial Sustainability," discusses the legal and organizational roles of the board of directors and special committees in the governance and financial viability of a nonprofit organization. The chapter explores strategies that foster financial sustainability through effective governance.

Chapter 4, "Needs Assessment and Financial Sustainability," emphasizes how financial sustainability is rooted in the investigation and analysis of the needs of a target community. The chapter discusses theories about the needs-assessment process, as well as action steps needed for the development of a community needs-assessment report. The chapter explores facets of financial needs assessment of a nonprofit that can help chart a course to further the vision and mission statements. The chapter argues that needs assessment is linked to the financial sustainability of nonprofit organizations.

Chapter 5, "Asset Mapping and Financial Sustainability," introduces the theories, concepts, and approaches of asset mapping as a strategy to help nonprofit organizations identify obvious and hidden assets within their communities, mobilize them to connect issues and needs with assets, and foster the financial sustainability of a nonprofit organization. Also, the chapter examines the community context of nonprofit organizations in relation to community groups, neighborhoods, and larger social systems that influence quality of life. The chapter includes the concept and theory of community capacity, models of asset-based development for building community capacity, empowering individuals and groups, generating funding from new sources, and creating additional paths toward financial sustainability.

Chapter 6, "Strategic Planning and Financial Sustainability," focuses on the principles, approaches, and processes of long-term strategic planning, the relationship of strategic management and program effectiveness, and the interrelations between strategic planning and financial sustainability. The chapter introduces various approaches of effective strategic planning that are geared to the financial sustainability of a nonprofit organization. The chapter includes a step-by-step development of a strategic plan that flows logically from the mission of the organization, the external environment, and organizational goals and objectives.

Chapter 7, "Budget and Financial Sustainability," introduces the budgeting process as a key component of a financially sustainable nonprofit organization. The chapter further explains the essential role played by budget approaches and techniques in the successful and sustainable operations of a nonprofit organization.

Chapter 8, "Financial Management," examines the financial and accounting principles and procedures related to the management of a nonprofit organization. The chapter addresses frameworks and organizational structures involved in cash-flow management, cost analysis, investment management, the analysis of new programmatic investments, and strategic financial analysis.

Chapter 9, "Financial Statements," introduces the generic structures or formats of three main financial statements: the income statement, the balance sheet, and the statement of cash flow. This chapter explores principles and procedures used to develop various financial statements and links them to the legal financial reporting requirements of a nonprofit organization.

Chapter 10, "Financial Sustainability Analysis," is a study of the tools and techniques of financial statement analysis, which are necessary in order to make a judgment about the financial sustainability status of a nonprofit organization. The chapter includes a systemic framework to analyze the financial sustainability of a nonprofit organization.

Chapter 11, "Financial Sustainability Plan," suggests approaches and best practices in developing a financial sustainability plan for a nonprofit organization. The chapter includes a conceptual framework and a step-by-step process used to develop a financial sustainability plan for a nonprofit organization.

Chapter 12, "Fund-Raising and Financial Sustainability," provides conceptual frameworks and approaches employed to organize fund-raising activities that can generate alternative funding for financial sustainability. The chapter includes an overview of various types of fund-raising strategies, existing sources of funding for nonprofit organizations, and planning of fund-raising activities.

Chapter 13, "Social Enterprise and Financial Sustainability," emphasizes social entrepreneurship as a mission-driven enterprise and a strategy for financial sustainability in nonprofit organizations. The chapter provides introductory information on the field of social entrepreneurship, social entrepreneurship models, and frameworks used to develop a business plan for a social enterprise.

Chapter 14 "Investment and Financial Sustainability," suggests selected investment options that nonprofit organizations can use to strengthen their financial sustainability. The roles of governance structures, accountability, ethics, and stewardship are explored in relation to investment for financial sustainability.

Chapter 15, "Grant Seeking and Financial Sustainability," focuses on how grant seeking can serve as a strategy to generate revenues that may ultimately contribute to the financial sustainability of a nonprofit organization. The chapter discusses the grant-searching and proposal-development process, criteria for writing effective grant proposals, and the best way to use grant awards and contracts to further the financial sustainability goals of a nonprofit organization.

Chapter 16, "Risk Management and Financial Sustainability," introduces the theories and practices of "integrated risk management," in relation to its contributions to the financial sustainability of a nonprofit organization. Topics include, but are not limited to, analytical frameworks for risk assessment and risk management plans.

Chapter 17, "Human Resources, Job Satisfaction, and Financial Sustainability," discusses various concepts related to human resources management, as well as approaches and theories on job satisfaction. The chapter further explains the key roles human resources management and job satisfaction play in the financial sustainability of a nonprofit organization.

Chapter 18, "Service Delivery and Financial Sustainability," is designed to help understand how service delivery and financial sustainability are interconnected. The chapter discusses the roles of client-centeredness, decision making, scheduling, priority setting, effective and efficient flow of services or activities, quality assurance, and continuing quality improvement, and how these factors contribute in their own context to influence positively or negatively the financial sustainability of a nonprofit organization.

Chapter 19, "Program Evaluation and Financial Sustainability," focuses on the role played by program evaluation and performance measurement in influencing the financial sustainability of a nonprofit organization. Topics in this chapter include theories, concepts, and principles of program evaluation, logic models, performance measurement, basic research skills related to program evaluation, development of program evaluation plans for quality assurance, and continuing quality improvement.

Chapter 20, "Community Relations and Financial Sustainability," introduces the institutions and processes that constitute the external environment of nonprofit organizations. The chapter discusses outreach, partnership, advocacy, and public relations as facets of community relations for nonprofit organizations. The chapter examines the role of a culture of accountability, communication, trust, and credibility in the financial sustainability of a nonprofit organization.

Chapter 21, "Information Technology and Financial Sustainability," emphasizes the role of information technology as support for financial sustainability in a nonprofit organization. The chapter discusses the relationships among various aspects of nonprofit management, including financial sustainability.

Chapter 22, "Social Marketing and Financial Sustainability," is designed to provide an introduction to the principles and practices of social marketing and their applicability to nonprofit organizations. It emphasizes the need for strategic planning in the marketing of not only products, but also programs and services. It is intended to enable nonprofit managers to manage their social marketing efforts strategically.

Chapter 23, "Leadership and Financial Sustainability," examines various leadership theories and approaches related to nonprofit organizations. The chapter emphasizes the relationship between leadership and strategic planning, with an emphasis on the influence of leadership on the financial sustainability of a nonprofit organization.

Chapter 24, "Organizational Transformation and Financial Sustainability," argues in favor of organizational transformation as a strategy for financial sustainability. The chapter discusses the context and applications of organizational development, adaptation to change, resistance to change, and transition management.

Each chapter in this book starts with learning objectives. Chapters include boxes that provide additional facts (e.g., history, story, cases, or data) and practical tips. The chapter contents are followed by Questions and Activities that serve as review questions and reflective or application exercises. The Questions and Activities are suitable for self-directed learning and online and face-to-face courses. The book provides ready-to-use frameworks and templates that are easily customizable by leaders and managers of nonprofit organizations.

I hope this book will empower leaders and managers of nonprofit organizations in making decisions that may contribute to the financial sustainability of their organizations.

Emmanuel Jean Francois, PhD
University of Wisconsin, Oshkosh

Acknowledgments

This book was inspired by the resilience of the victims of the earthquake that hit the country of Haiti on January 12, 2010, and all the nonprofit organizations that dedicated themselves to assist its victims. I also would like to acknowledge the victims of all the recent tragic natural disasters in New Orleans, Chile, Japan, and the Philippines, just to name a few. I am grateful for all the nonprofit organizations and volunteers in the United States and around the world who wake up every day, thinking and doing things to contribute to making the world a better place for the neediest citizens. My hope is that they can use the contents of this book to strive for the financial sustainability of their nonprofit enterprises.

A special "thank you!" to Stephanie Drew, acquisitions editor at Springer Publishing Company. Her support was simply invaluable.

Finally, I owe special thanks to several cohorts of students from Springfield College and the University of Wisconsin, Oshkosh, who provided their input in various aspects of this book through their interactions in my class.

Financial Sustainability for Nonprofit Organizations

The Nonprofit Organization Universe

At the completion of this chapter the reader will be able to:

1. Define the concept of a nonprofit organization.
2. Describe the differences between a nonprofit and a for-profit corporation.
3. Identify the different types of nonprofit organizations in the United States.
4. Summarize the scope of the nonprofit sector in the United States.
5. Identify the basic principles related to the starting of a nonprofit organization in the United States.

Nonprofit organizations have existed for many centuries, especially through religious groups or religious-based activities. During the early American colonial period, the churches were basically the first nonprofit organizations. They played key roles in the health, well-being, education, culture, artistic diversity, and community-service areas. Talking about his travels throughout the United States, the French sociologist Alexis de Tocqueville (1966) noted in his book *Democracy in America*,

> Americans of all ages, all conditions, and all dispositions, constantly form associations. . . . The Americans make associations to give entertainments, to found establishments for education, to build inns, to construct churches, to diffuse books, to send missionaries to the antipodes; and in this manner they found hospitals, prisons, and schools. (p. 114)

Tocqueville's comments represent an acknowledgment that nonprofit organizations are part of the American tradition and are used as a strategy to address community issues. Until the late 18th century, corporations were considered public entities and included churches and institutions of higher education (Scavoy, 1982; Whitehead, 1976). Lubove (1975) reported that most U.S. nonprofit organizations had offices in most American cities by 1900. It is important to underscore that they were self-governing groups, associations, or agencies that had no owners and were exempt from taxation. Nonprofit organizations faced suspicion in some conservative states, because of the social aspect of their activities. Miller (1961) and Dabney (1981) explained that while the New England states encouraged the creation of charitable organizations during the 19th century, the Southern states were very suspicious and even discouraged private charity activities. However, the post-Depression era facilitated the emergence of new nonprofit organizations. Despite some historical challenges, nonprofit organizations continue to provide services to those in need, advocate on behalf of the disadvantaged, and enrich and empower the lives of children, families, and communities throughout the United States.

ABOUT THE TERM "NONPROFIT ORGANIZATION"

The concept "nonprofit" includes the prefix "non" and thus may refer to what is "not for profit" or what is "not profitable." Does the term "nonprofit organization" imply one of these two meanings or both? Consider first the meaning of "not for profit." A not-for-profit organization is an organization whose purpose is not to make a profit from the activities that it conducts. This is in contrast to a "for-profit" organization, whose purpose is to make a profit for the owner(s). On the other hand, a "not profitable" organization is an entity (organization) whose activities do not generate a profit. In that context, profit refers to a positive balance when subtracting total expenses from total revenues or income.

Because many nonprofit organizations indicate they exist for educational, cultural, and charitable purposes, they can be labeled certainly as "not-for-profit organizations." However, many of these organizations that are called "not for-profit" or "nonprofit" generate a profit that they report on their annual financial reports. Therefore, they will not fit the definition that considers them "not profitable" organizations. A question emerges: Is "profit" incompatible with the status of a nonprofit organization? If the answer is "yes," there are no real nonprofit organizations, because most effective nonprofit organizations report a profit. If the answer is "no," one may ask, "Why do many nonprofit organizations make a profit?" In fact, the answer is "no," which means profit is not incompatible with the status of nonprofit organizations. In other words, nonprofit organizations do exist, and they do a lot of good for people and communities around the world. To the question, "Why do many nonprofit organizations make a profit?" the answer is simple: Effective nonprofit organizations must generate a continuing profit to be sustainable. Profit helps maintain appropriate resources that enable them to continue to serve their target population in unforeseen financial hardship. The question is not whether nonprofit organizations can generate profit, because they can. The Internal Revenue Service (IRS) recognizes 28 types of tax-exempt organizations, which is another label for nonprofit organizations. This categorization does not distinguish whether an organization makes a profit or not. These organizations are exempt from taxation of their profit, except for "unrelated business income," which is "income from a trade or business, regularly carried on, that is not substantially related to the charitable, educational, or other purpose that is the basis of the organization's exemption" (IRS, 2014b, para 1).

NONPROFIT AND FOR-PROFIT CORPORATIONS

Modern societies are organized into local and national or federal governmental entities that are primarily funded by taxpayers' money in order to provide public services to citizens and residents. Consequently, governmental entities are owned by the taxpayers. These entities do not pay taxes, because their revenue comes from taxes.

On the other hand, individuals in society, especially in capitalist societies, can use their money to engage in entrepreneurial activities by creating businesses. Usually, businesses take several forms, such as a sole proprietorship (owned by one single individual), partnership (usually owned by two or more partner investors), or corporation defined by a U.S. Supreme Court decision as "an artificial being, invisible, intangible, and existing only in the contemplation of the law" (Schneeman, 1997, p. 159) A corporation is an entity separated from its owners or managers. It is liable for any debts and obligations. The requirements necessary to start a corporation vary from one state to another in the United States and from one country to another throughout the world.

A corporation can be for profit or not for profit, as indicated previously. A for-profit corporation is organized by a group of owners (or equity holders or shareholders) in order to generate profit (net earnings) that can be distributed to shareholders in the form of dividends. A for-profit corporation pays federal taxes. The dividends are also taxable wealth. This is what is called the principle of double taxation: The corporation is taxed as an entity, and the individual shareholder is taxed when the dividend is received.

Contrary to a for-profit corporation, a nonprofit corporation is organized to provide community services that a government agency would have had to provide and that a for-profit corporation may have no interest in providing (Box 1.1). As a result, nonprofit corporations are exempt from taxation. A nonprofit corporation has no owner, but it is controlled by the members and a board. Unlike a for-profit corporation, a nonprofit corporation cannot distribute profit to those who control and/or financially support it. The profit generated by a nonprofit organization must go to bettering services, motivating staff, upgrading equipment, providing staff training, and implementing other activities to further the vision and mission of such organizations.

Sometimes it can be difficult to distinguish a for-profit corporation from a nonprofit corporation just based on the services provided. A corporation may provide a service that looks like a nonprofit activity, but is nevertheless a for-profit business entity. For example, let us consider a fictitious corporation called Loving Companion Care, Inc. (LCC), which is owned by a group of registered nurses and is located in Appleton, Wisconsin. The mission of LCC is to provide quality companion care to elderly individuals in Appleton. Despite the financial crisis, LCC has done well. In fact, LCC has been making regular contributions to cultural events organized by some civic associations. The LCC's shareholders were very

BOX 1.1			
Comparison	**Government Agency**	**Nonprofit Corporation**	**For-Profit Corporation**
Purpose	Provides public services to members of a society.	Provides community services.	Exists to generate profit for shareholders or owners.
Ownership	Owned by tax payers.	Does not have owners, but is controlled by members and board.	Owned by shareholders; ownership is transferable.
Profit	Belongs to tax payers.	Used to support activities and expand the organization's mission.	Distributed to shareholders as dividends.
Taxation	Tax exempt.	Tax exempt.	Double taxation.

happy with the dividends they received at the end of the fiscal year. Would you say that LLC is a nonprofit corporation, a for-profit corporation, a sole proprietorship, or none of the above? Yes, LCC provides an important community service. Also, LCC contributes to cultural events in its community. However, LCC belongs to a group of nurses and distributes dividends to its shareholders. A corporation that belongs to a group of individuals and distributes dividends to shareholders cannot be a nonprofit organization. A nonprofit organization belongs to the public, because it receives public financial support through tax exemption and various donations. The members or board members of a nonprofit corporation act on behalf of the community.

NONPROFIT CORPORATION AS NONPROFIT ORGANIZATION

A nonprofit corporation exists based on the model of the for-profit corporation. It is also referred to as a nonprofit organization. The Internal Revenue Service defines a charitable organization as follows:

> To be tax-exempt under section 501(c)(3) of the Internal Revenue Code, an organization must be organized and operated exclusively for exempt purposes set forth in section 501(c)(3), and none of its earnings may inure to any private shareholder or individual. In addition, it may not be an *action organization, i.e.,* it may not attempt to influence legislation as a substantial part of its activities and it may not participate in any campaign activity for or against political candidates.
>
> Organizations described in section 501(c)(3) are commonly referred to as *charitable organizations*. Organizations described in section 501(c)(3), other than testing for public safety organizations, are eligible to receive tax-deductible contributions in accordance with Code section 170. The organization must not be organized or operated for the benefit of private interests, and no part of a section 501(c)(3) organization's net earnings may inure to the benefit of any private shareholder or individual. If the organization engages in an excess benefit transaction with a person having substantial influence over the organization, an excise tax may be imposed on the person and any organization managers agreeing to the transaction. (IRS, 2014a, para 1)

As the IRS definition indicates, nonprofit organizations are "charitable organizations," and are exempt from federal taxation under section 501(c) of the IRS Tax Code. There are various other terms used in the United States and around the world to refer to nonprofit organizations. Equivalent terms include, but are not limited to "charities," "voluntary associations," "independent sector organizations," "civil society organizations," "civic sector organizations," "social sector organizations," "tax-exempt organizations," "philanthropic sector," "third sector organizations," or "nongovernment organizations." According to Willets (2012), a nongovernment or nonprofit organization is "an independent voluntary association of people acting together on a continuous basis for some common purpose other than achieving government office, making money or illegal activities." This definition has similarities with the IRS determination of a nonprofit organization, in the sense that there must be a social community purpose, and the organization must not exist to further a partisan political agenda. The United Nations (UN) provides a definition that considers a nonprofit organization on a larger scale as "a not-for-profit group, principally independent from government, which is organized on a local, national or international level to address issues in support of the public good" (United Nations Rule of Laws, 2014).

NONPROFIT ORGANIZATION AS ORGANIZATION

Nonprofit organizations exit as corporations in the eyes of the law and in the context of legal and financial transactions. However, as social entities, nonprofit corporations are nonprofit organizations created by collectives of people who share common goals that they want to achieve through a formal structure. Max Weber (Handel, 2002) conceptualized the formal structure of organization or bureaucracy as encompassing key elements such as (a) a division of labor or assignment of tasks to members, (b) empowerment of people through training that enables them to develop expertise in their assignment, (c) a formal hierarchy of decision making, and (d) rules of communication. By contrast, Etzioni (1975) categorized formal organizations as normative, coercive, and utilitarian. Normative organizations are created by people to pursue common goals. People join such organizations voluntarily. Coercive organizations are created to perform functions of social coercion (e.g., prisons). Individuals are forced to join coercive organizations. Finally, utilitarian organizations exist to provide opportunities to people. Members join utilitarian organizations (e.g., school, work) to gain a reward that they would not receive otherwise. A nonprofit organization is fundamentally a normative organization, because it is supposed to be a membership-based or open social or community entity. However, there are nonprofit organizations that are partially or completely coercive (e.g., a mental health residential agency) or utilitarian (e.g., a nonprofit college or university).

Various organizational theories have implications for nonprofit organizations. For example, the rational choice perspective argues that a rational bureaucracy or organizational structure is essential to achieving the goals of the collective that created an organization (Morgan, 2006; Shafritz & Ott, 2005). The system perspective counter-argues that formal structures in organizations do not guarantee efficiency and effectiveness if an organization does not account for the multiple social, political, economic, cultural, and technology factors that constitute its environment and affect its efficiency and effectiveness (Morgan, 2006; Northouse, 2004). Furthermore, an organization is subject to the dynamics of conflict of interests and perspectives in a society. Consequently, the conflict perspective theorizes that an organization can reproduce patterns of inequality in society by prioritizing the interests of the owners and managers over the interests of the workers (Morgan, 2006; Shafritz & Ott, 2005). In the context of a nonprofit organization, the conflict would be between the interests of leaders and managers and the interests of clients and communities. It is not always easy to avoid such conflict dynamics in organizations, including nonprofit organizations. As the interpretive perspective explains, organizations are social constructions of reality that reflect the human consciousness and worldview of the founders (Hutchison, 2008). To sum up, although formal structures and common goals are important for the efficiency and effectiveness of a nonprofit organization, they are not enough. In addition, a nonprofit organization must account for factors in its external environment, and have safeguards to avoid conflict of interests, as well as to ensure inclusion and responsiveness to multiple worldviews or viewpoints.

SCOPE OF THE NONPROFIT SECTOR IN THE UNITED STATES

The scope of the nonprofit sector in the United States is very significant in all aspects of social, economic, cultural, and political life. As of 2012, there were 1.6 million registered nonprofit organizations in the United States. The registered nonprofit organizations include 973,961 public charities; 98,785 private foundations; and 495,169 other types of nonprofit organizations, including chambers of commerce, fraternal organizations, and civic leagues (NCCS, 2012). Registered nonprofit organizations in the United States receive their funding from (a) contributions, gifts, grants, and contracts from the government; (b) individual volunteering and charitable giving; (c) foundation giving; and (d) revenues generated from their programs (e.g., fees for services). Roeger, Blackwood, and Pettijohn (2012) estimated that nonprofit organizations accounted for 9.2% of all wages and salaries paid in the United States in 2010, and a share of 5.5% of the U.S. gross domestic product (GDP) in 2012. Registered nonprofit organizations in the United States reported more than $2 trillion in revenue on their Forms 990, and more than $6 trillion in assets. Form 990 is a mandatory report that registered nonprofit organizations with revenues over $5,000 must submit to the Internal Revenue Service. The numbers, total revenues, and assets reported by U.S. registered nonprofit organizations on their Forms 990 are described in Table 1.1.

TYPES OF NONPROFIT ORGANIZATIONS IN THE UNITED STATES

There is a variety of nonprofit organizations in the United States that are based on their function in the nonprofit sector. The main types of nonprofit organizations functionally include, but are not limited to:

1. **Direct-service providers**, which provide direct human or social services (e.g., health, community education, referrals, counseling, and economic assistance) to clients through programs managed by their staff and volunteers. Nonprofit hospitals, community clinics, and community organizations are examples of direct-service providers.
2. **Social clubs and organizations**, which conduct activities to further the social interests of their members. Examples of social clubs and organizations include fraternities, lodges, sporting clubs, women's associations, gay and lesbian rights groups, and unions and professional associations.
3. **Religious and cultural organizations**, which exist to profess and practice activities to advance and promote a particular religious or cultural belief. Churches, synagogues, mosques, artistic associations, and musical associations are examples of religious and cultural organizations.
4. **Information and knowledge providers**, which accumulate and manage information and knowledge to provide to their users. This category includes colleges and universities, advocacy groups, think tanks, trade associations, and research institutes.
5. **Development and support providers**, which furnish resources and support to other nonprofit organizations. Organization and management support groups are examples of development and support providers.
6. **Funding providers**, which award grants or funding to other nonprofit organizations. Private foundations are example of funding providers.

TABLE 1.1 The Number, Total Revenue, and Assets Reported by U.S. Registered Nonprofit Organizations on Form 990

National Taxonomy of Exempt Entities	Count	Total Revenue Reported on Form 990 (in U.S. Dollars)	Assets Reported on Form 990 (in U.S. Dollars)
A—Arts, Culture & Humanities	105,893	36,118,532,387	124,958,259,362
B—Education	191,341	275,465,458,178	955,772,039,806
C—Environment	33,183	10,903,364,784	32,842,032,224
D—Animal Related	22,782	6,695,594,399	15,427,980,428
E—Health Care	42,289	969,582,740,536	1,186,965,550,705
F—Mental Health & Crisis Intervention	15,734	28,368,089,408	23,893,394,079
G—Voluntary Health Associations & Medical Disciplines	25,042	16,701,313,870	22,941,378,975
H—Medical Research	4,005	10,965,845,510	39,988,685,232
I—Crime & Legal Issues	19,115	8,856,467,171	9,106,072,193
J—Employment	39,232	34,177,502,134	41,177,954,238
K—Food, Agriculture, & Nutrition	15,586	12,184,541,497	10,897,536,117
L—Housing & Shelter	31,428	23,921,818,969	80,914,754,979
M—Public Safety, Disaster Preparedness, & Relief	21,573	3,614,599,650	9,579,696,316
N—Recreation & Sports	103,097	29,578,570,307	52,542,765,412
O—Youth Development	38,698	7,192,996,044	14,172,539,359
P—Human Services	88,692	125,808,903,915	172,500,851,333
Q—International, Foreign Affairs, & National Security	18,642	32,403,574,660	38,241,823,790
R—Civil Rights, Social Action, & Advocacy	8,368	4,156,674,135	5,366,722,543
S—Community Improvement & Capacity Building	120,810	38,478,732,573	119,946,373,533
T—Philanthropy, Voluntarism, & Grant-Making Foundations	207,700	83,137,058,191	2,332,740,669,689
U—Science & Technology	7,356	20,344,788,156	22,869,962,528
V—Social Science	2,050	2,598,061,730	4,350,679,096
W—Public & Societal Benefit	67,455	91,839,987,304	562,506,042,744
X—Religion Related	252,953	14,767,743,466	41,100,965,563
Y—Mutual & Membership Benefit	75,394	158,853,258,729	309,765,547,235
Z—Unknown	7,079	2,668,846,979	2,580,924,936
Total	1,565,497	2,049,385,064,682	6,233,151,202,415

Source: Internal Revenue Service, Exempt Organizations Business Master File (2012).

Notes: Includes organizations that filed a Form 990, 990-EZ, 990-PF, and, since 2008, 990-N ePostcard within 24 months of the BMF (business master file) release date, as reported in National Center for Charitable Statistics Core Files and IRS Business Master Files. Organizations based in the U.S. Territories and Puerto Rico and other "out-of-scope" organizations (see NCCS Data Guide, p. 21) are excluded.

According to the National Taxonomy of Exempt Entities (NTEE), there are 9 major types of nonprofit organizations in the United States, including 26 categories and over 400 subcategories. The nine major categories are as follows (with important subcategories listed):

1. Arts, Culture, and Humanities—A (e.g., historical societies, museums)
2. Education—B (e.g., schools, colleges, and universities)
3. Environment and Animals—C, D (e.g., humane societies)
4. Health—E, F, G, H (e.g., nonprofit hospitals)
5. Human Services—I, J, K, L, M, N, O, P (e.g., family services, child protection agencies)
6. International, Foreign Affairs—Q (e.g., the Salvation Army, ACTIONAID USA)
7. Public, Societal Benefit—R, S, T, U, V, W (e.g., United Way)
8. Religion Related—X (e.g., churches, mosques, synagogues)
9. Mutual/Membership Benefit—Y (e.g., credit unions)

As previously indicated, nonprofit organization can apply for 501(c) status through the International Revenue Service. The IRS classifies 32 categories of nonprofit organizations under sections 501(c)(1) through 501(c)(27) and sections 501(d) through 501(n), including several subcategories. Table 1.2 describes the major nonprofit organization categories of the IRS Code of 1986.

STARTING A NONPROFIT ORGANIZATION

Starting a nonprofit organization requires three key factors: (1) a vision and mission, (2) satisfaction of legal requirements, and (3) organization and management practices.

Vision and Mission

The Industrial Revolution in England (1750–1850) facilitated the birth of big cities where people (pickpockets, beggars, drunks, thugs, and abandoned children) lived in very poor economic and social conditions. Also, there were many young men who left the countryside to work in urban jobs that became available as a result of the Industrial Revolution. These young men worked about 12 hours per day, 6 days a week. In June 1844, George Williams, a young British sales assistant in a London shop, and a group of his coworkers started a group to bring hope and comfort using a Christian perspective to young men living in unhealthy conditions in London. The group was called the Young Men's Christian Association or the YMCA. Today, the YMCA operates in many countries in the world, serving people from all social, political, and economic backgrounds.

In June 1859, a Swiss businessman named Jean-Henri Dunant traveled to Italy, then occupied by France, in order to lobby before the French emperor about his difficulties in doing business in Algeria, which was also occupied by France. While in Italy, Dunant witnessed an important battle of the Austro-Sardinian war in a small Italian town called Solferino. In *A Memory of Solferino*, Dunant reported that about 40,000 soldiers from both sides died or were left wounded in just 1 day. The tragedy was that there was little to no basic medical care for the wounded. Dunant abandoned the business mission of his trip,

TABLE 1.2 Sections of 1986 Tax Code Relative to Tax-Exempt Organizations in the United States

Section of 1986 Tax Code	Description of Organization	General Nature of Activities
501(c)(1)	Corporations organized under Acts of Congress (including federal credit unions)	Instrumentalities of the United States
501(c)(2)	Title-holding corporation for exempt organization	Holding title to property of an exempt organization
501(c)(3)	Religious, educational, charitable, scientific, literary, testing for public safety, to foster national or international amateur sports competition, or prevention of cruelty to children or animals organizations	Activities of a nature implied by description of class of organization Further classified as: private foundations or public charity organizations
501(c)(4)	Civic leagues, social welfare organizations, and local associations of employees	Promotion of community welfare; charitable, educational, or recreational
501(c)(5)	Labor, agricultural, and horticultural organizations	Educational or instructive, the purpose being to improve working conditions and to improve products and efficiency
501(c)(6)	Business leagues, chambers of commerce, real estate boards, etc.	Improvement of business conditions of one or more lines of business
501(c)(7)	Social and recreation clubs	Pleasure, recreation, social activities
501(c)(8)	Fraternal beneficiary societies and associations	Lodges that provide payment of life, sickness, accident, or other benefits to members
501(c)(9)	Voluntary employees' beneficiary associations	Provide payment of life, sickness, accident, or other benefits to members
501(c)(10)	Domestic fraternal societies and associations	Lodge devoting its net earnings to charitable, fraternal, and other specified purposes; no life, sickness, or accident benefits to members
501(c)(11)	Teachers' retirement fund associations	Teachers' association for payment of retirement benefits
501(c)(12)	Benevolent life insurance associations, mutual ditch or irrigation companies, mutual or cooperative telephone companies, etc.	Activities of a mutually beneficial nature similar to those implied by the description of class of organization
501(c)(13)	Cemetery companies	Burials and incidental activities
501(c)(14)	State-chartered credit unions, mutual reserve funds	Loans to members

(continued)

TABLE 1.2 Sections of 1986 Tax Code Relative to Tax Exempt Organizations in the United States (*continued*)

Section of 1986 Tax Code	Description of Organization	General Nature of Activities
501(c)(15)	Mutual insurance companies or associations	Provide insurance to members substantially at cost
501(c)(16)	Cooperative organizations to finance crop operations	Financing crop operations in conjunction with activities of a marketing or purchasing association
501(c)(17)	Supplemental unemployment benefit trusts	Provide payment of supplemental unemployment compensation benefits
501(c)(18)	Employee-funded pension trust (created before June 25, 1959)	Payment of benefits under a pension plan funded by employees
501(c)(19)	Post or organization of past or present members of the armed forces	Activities implied by nature of organization
501(c)(20)	Group legal services plan organizations	n/a
501(c)(21)	Black lung benefit trusts	Funded by coal mine operators to satisfy their liability for disability or death due to black lung diseases
501(c)(22)	Withdrawal liability payment fund	To provide funds to meet the liability of employers withdrawing from a multiemployer pension fund
501(c)(23)	Veterans organization (created before 1880)	To provide insurance and other benefits to veterans
501(c)(25)	Title-holding corporations or trusts with multiple Parents	Holding title and paying income from property to 35 or fewer parents or beneficiaries
501(c)(26)	State-sponsored organization providing health coverage for high-risk individuals	Provide health care coverage to high-risk individuals
501(c)(27)	State-sponsored workers' compensation reinsurance organization	Reimburse members for losses under workers' compensation acts
501(d)	Religious and apostolic associations	Regular business activities; communal, religious community
501(e)	Cooperative hospital service organizations	Perform cooperative services for hospitals
501(f)	Cooperative service organizations of operating educational organizations	Perform collective investment services for educational organizations
501(k)	Child care organization	Provide care for children
501(n)	Charitable risk pools	Pool certain insurance risks of 501(c)(3)

Source: Internal Revenue Service (2013).

and devoted himself to helping with treatment and care for the wounded. Also, he orga- nized and motivated the local community to help care for the wounded of both sides, with no discrimination. Then he advocated before powerful political and military figures in Europe for the creation of a voluntary relief organization that could assist nurses in caring for the wounded. He also argued for an international treaty to guarantee the protection of neutral medical professionals and volunteers caring for the wounded on a battlefield. The commitment and determination of Dunant and other people whom he won to his cause led to the creation of the International Committee of the Red Cross. Today, every country in the world has its version of the Red Cross, which provides assistance not only during wars, but also in times of natural disaster.

In 1860, three women in Hartford, Connecticut—Mary Goodwin, Alice Goodwin, and Elizabeth Hammersley—saw young boys in the streets who seemed to be a lost cause. These women felt the need to take action and provide an alternative way of life for these children. They created a club to provide hope to these young boys. The Boys Club was born. Later, other people bought into the vision and created Boys Clubs throughout the United States. They created Boys Clubs of America, which received a U.S. congressional charter in 1956. Later, in 1990, Boys Clubs of America integrated young girls, and the orga- nization renewed its charter to become what is known today as "Boys and Girls Clubs of America."

Mary, Alice, and Elizabeth saw a situation that probably broke their hearts. They formed a vision from that situation. They acted on that vision, and created an organization that rescued the lives of many people. George saw a need, responded to a call for action, and made a difference through a nonprofit organization called the YMCA. Like George Williams and the women of Hartford, Jean Henry Dunant saw a need. He claimed a vision and a mission from that need. He persuaded others to espouse his vision, and created a nonprofit organization that positively changed the world forever. In all three examples, there was a need identified by one person or a group of people. Then, there was a vision. The vision was translated into a mission to act, to create a nonprofit organization that transcends times and makes a difference in the lives of people. The point is that serious nonprofit organizations start with a vision, and from the vision emerges a mission to drive the call for action. Organizations, including nonprofit organizations, express their drive through their vision and mission statements.

Vision Statement: Haines (2000) refers to vision statements as "shared hopes, dreams, and shared image of the future" (p. 25). Allison and Kaye (2005) define a vision state- ment as "a guiding image of success" and "the pursuit of this shared image of success that inspires and motivates people to work together" (p. 68). Although the above defini- tions inform us about what a vision statement is, they fail to provide specific indicators that would enable us to tell a well-written organizational vision statement from one that is not.

Jean Francois (2011) asserts that in the vision statement of most organizations, there are:

- A strategic intent *(where the organization will be at some future time)*
- A statement of value *(the values that the organization will be recognized for)*
- A statement of quality *(the quality of its operations and products or services)*
- One or more indicators of change in a broader community, nation-state, or world perspective

According to Jean Francois (2011), a vision is "an ideal picture of what an individual, organization, or a business strives to be at some future time. This is an overall direction, something to be pursued" (p. 7). The focus can be on the organization or the client or a community, a society, or the world.

Example 1: Save The Children's Vision Statement

Our vision is a world in which every child attains the right to survival, protection, development and participation.

This vision statement includes:

- ■ **A strategic intent:** ... *a world in which every child attains* ...
- ■ **A statement of value:** *every child = inclusion, children's rights and protection*
- ■ **A statement of quality:** *child survival, protection, development, and participation*

Example 2: Mississippi Library Commission's Vision Statement

All Mississippians have access to quality library services in order to achieve their greatest potential, participate in a global society, and enrich their daily lives.

This vision statement includes:

- ■ **A strategic intent:** *All Mississippians have access to quality library services* ...
- ■ **A statement of value:** ... *achievement, participation in globalization, life enrichment*
- ■ **A statement of quality:** ... *access to quality library services*

Mission Statement: Most textbooks on for-profit or nonprofit organizations introduce the concept of the mission statement as a mandatory ingredient of the organization's strategic-planning process (Allison & Kaye, 2005; Haines, 2000; Holland & Ritvo, 2008; Jean Francois, 2011; Smith, 2005). Almost all scholars agree that a mission statement answers the following questions: (a) Why does organization "X" exist? (b) What does it want to accomplish? (c) For whom? (d) What are the guiding principles in the process? Jean Francois (2011, p. 9) indicates that a mission statement should include:

- ■ A statement of purpose (*Why does organization "X" exist?*)
- ■ The specification of the clients (*Whom does the organization serve?*)
- ■ The business (*What are the services, products ... offered by the organization?*)
- ■ The philosophy (*What are the values, beliefs, or guiding principles of servicing, producing...?*)
- ■ And possibly a self-concept (*Is there some concept of pride that the organization values in a unique way?*)

Example 3: Big Brothers Big Sisters of America's Mission Statement

The mission of Big Brothers Big Sisters of America is to make a positive difference in the lives of children and youth, primarily through a professionally supported one-to-one relationship with a caring adult, and to assist them in achieving their highest potential as they grow to become confident, competent and caring individuals.

This mission statement includes:

■ **A statement of purpose:** ... *make a positive difference*
■ **The specification of the clients***: ... children and youth*
■ **The business:** ... *professionally supported one-to-one relationship with a caring adult*
■ **The philosophy:** ... *assist them in achieving their highest potential*
■ And possibly **a self-concept:** ... *confident, competent and caring*

Example 4: The Gazelle Trust's Mission Statement

Provide essential financial and material assistance, in terms of education, shelter and healthcare to orphans and vulnerable children in developing countries.

This mission statement includes:

■ **A statement of purpose:** ... *provide essential financial and material assistance*
■ **The specification of the clients:** ... *orphans and vulnerable children in developing countries*
■ **The business:** ... *education, shelter and healthcare*
■ **The philosophy:** ... *humanitarian assistance*
■ **Self-concept:** *None!*

Satisfaction of Legal Requirements

As indicated earlier, a nonprofit organization starts with a vision and a mission. Vision and mission statements can be written in formal styles to share with others who might be interested in espousing them. Having a vision and a mission can be an important factor in helping to meet the requirements related to the creation of a nonprofit organization in the United States. One of the requirements is to have a board of at least three members in order to incorporate a nonprofit organization. The specific requirements, including incorporation fees, vary from one state to another. However, in every U.S. state, there is a division of corporations that receives applications from U.S. legal residents or citizens who want to either start an American or a foreign for-profit or nonprofit corporation. Articles of incorporation and other documents may be required to incorporate depending on the state. Articles of incorporation are usually provided in the form of a template that will help a state record the name of the nonprofit organization, the purpose, the names and physical addresses of the board members, the incorporator, and the registered agent.

As a corporation, a nonprofit organization must apply for an Employer Identification Number (EIN) through the IRS. The EIN is the equivalent of the Social Security Number of a nonprofit organization. It is especially necessary for future financial transactions of the organization. For example, it is mandatory to provide a copy of the EIN along with the proof of nonprofit incorporation in order to open a bank account for a nonprofit organization.

In the United States, incorporation is done at the state level. However, there is another layer of requirements to meet in order for a nonprofit organization to become exempt from federal taxes. The IRS considers every corporation a taxable entity until such corporation proves otherwise by applying for tax-exempt status. To that end, a nonprofit organization can apply for 501(c) status through the IRS. One of the most popular 501(c) tax-exempt organizations is the 501(c)(3) type. An applicant organization must complete IRS Form 1023 to apply for 501(c)(3) status. If the application is approved, the IRS issues a 501(c)(3) determination letter, which will serve as proof that the organization enjoys federally tax-exempt status. In addition, a nonprofit organization must file for exemptions at the local and state levels, depending on the state. Finally, a nonprofit organization must comply with charitable solicitation laws that may exist at the state, county, or municipal levels. This is especially important for fund-raising purposes.

Organization and Management Practices

The overall organization and management of a nonprofit organization is the responsibility of the board of directors. However, the board of directors must delegate the management and administration of regular activities to an executive or administrative body (chief executive officer, chief financial officer, development officer, program managers, project managers, program assistants, and other similar staff), which will vary from one organization to another. A compelling vision alone is not enough for a successful nonprofit organization. Strategic planning and implementation of activities are very important to fulfill the vision and mission of a nonprofit organization. A nonprofit organization must have bylaws, which set the principles and procedures to make decisions within the organization. The adoption of the bylaws is the responsibility of the board members. The board must also work with managers to develop budget, fund-raising plans, development plans, record-keeping and accounting systems, and to maintain insurance policies for risk prevention and management.

A nonprofit organization must conduct a community needs assessment to ensure that future programs will take into account the needs of the target population. Simply put, a community needs assessment consists of process and research activities for identifying the available resources of a community and the unmet needs of its people. A community needs assessment can involve extensive data collection through surveys and/or- interviews. It can also be a review of secondary data that are available online or in libraries. It can be a nominal group technique with key informants from a target population. The approach adopted depends on what an organization wants to accomplish.

A needs assessment is important because it provides a baseline of information for strategic planning. A nonprofit organization must translate its mission statement into more specific strategic goals that can be achieved within a reasonable period of time, usually 5, 7, or 10 years. The document that outlines the strategic goals and activities and resources to achieve such goals is called a strategic plan.

As the name implies, strategic goals are designed to provide the big picture to an organization. Strategic goals cannot be achieved overnight. They may never be achieved at all if there is no effort to follow through on their implementation. Specific objectives and activities, as well as appropriate strategies, must be defined into a more short-term (annual, quarterly) document called an action plan. The action plan determines the regular decisions that must be made in order for the organization to fulfill its mission and vision. In other words, the fulfillment of the vision and the mission of a nonprofit organization is an ongoing endeavor, which can succeed only if the strategic plan is translated into operational or short-term action plans. Obviously, organization and management require continuous assessment and monitoring to ensure that a nonprofit organization is on a viable or sustainable path.

CONCLUSION

This chapter provided an overview of the nonprofit organization in the United States, the main characteristics of nonprofit organizations, and the reality of the nonprofit sector today. Nonprofit organizations and human service agencies employ nearly 11 million full-time equivalent (FTE) employees, representing the third-largest U.S. industry (Salamon, Sokolowski, & Geller, 2012). The nongovernmental sector is growing throughout the world. Increasingly, these organizations are playing key roles in the economic and social contexts of their countries. Unlike private-sector organizations concerned primarily with making a profit, nonprofit organizations are focused on carrying out a specific public-service mission. Successful nonprofit organizations require substantial capability in key areas of management: developing strong boards of directors, recruiting and motivating talented staff and volunteers, creating plans to focus resources on relevant goals and innovative programs, winning the support of diverse stakeholders, raising funds, and wisely managing fiscal and human resources.

QUESTIONS AND ACTIVITIES

1. The Association for Special Children and Families (ASCF) is based in Cleveland, Ohio. The Association was created in 2001 by a group of professionals who wanted to help special needs children and their families. According to the official document of the Association, the vision of ASCF is to *"help people realize their dream."* Their mission is to *"provide opportunities to the community."* The ASCF provides the following services:
   - Guidance and support to parents with special needs children
   - Free information through a newsletter and the ASCF website
   - Training and advocacy assistance at no cost
   - Recreation programs for children and their families
   - Campaigns for acceptance of children and adults with disabilities
   - Education and information for parents and professionals about disability issues

   a. Would you say that the vision and mission statements of the Association for Special Children and Families are well crafted? Explain.
   b. Based on the information provided, how would you rewrite the mission and vision statements of the Association?
2. Find the vision and mission statements of an existing nonprofit organization.
   a. Write a critique of the selected vision and mission statements.
   b. Conclude whether or not the vision and mission statements are effective.
   c. If not effective, how would you rewrite the vision and/or the mission statement?
3. Go to the website of the Division of Corporations for your state of residence. What are the requirements to incorporate a nonprofit organization?
4. Go to the website of your state, county, or city of residence.
   a. What are the requirements to obtain tax-exempt status for a nonprofit organization?
   b. What are the requirements to obtain authorization to make charitable solicitations?

5. Describe an issue that breaks your heart or bothers you every time you witness it or think about it. What do you think you can do to address that issue or solve that problem? Identify at least two other people you think might be interested in addressing that problem. What would you say to convince them to partner with you and start a nonprofit organization?

REFERENCES

Allison, M., & Kaye, J. (2005). *Strategic planning for nonprofit organizations: A practical guide and workbook.* New York, NY: John Wiley.

Dabney, V. (1981). *Mr. Jefferson's university: A history.* Charlottesville, VA: University Press of Virginia.

Etzioni, A. (1975). *A comparative analysis of complex organizations: On power, involvement, and their correlates* (rev. ed.). New York, NY: Free Press.

Haines, S. G. (2000). *The systems thinking approach to strategic planning and management.* Boca Raton, FL: St. Lucie Press.

Handel, M. J. (2002). *The sociology of organizations: Classic, contemporary, and critical readings.* Thousand Oaks, CA: Sage.

Holland, T. P., & Ritvo, R. A. (2008). *Nonprofit organizations: Principles and practices.* New York, NY: Columbia University Press.

Hutchison, E. D. (2008). *Dimensions of human behavior: Person and environment* (3rd ed.). Thousand Oaks, CA: Sage.

Internal Revenue Service. (2013). *Tax-exempt status for your organization.* Retrieved from http://www.irs.gov/publications/p557/ar02.html

International Revenue Service. (2014a). *Exemption requirements—501(c)(3): Organization.* Retrieved from http://www.irs.gov/Charities-&-Non-Profits/Charitable-Organizations/Exemption-Requirements-Section-501(c)(3)-Organizations

Internal Revenue Service. (2014b). *Unrelated business income tax.* Retrieved from http://www.irs.gov/Charities-&-Non-Profits/Unrelated-Business-Income-Tax

Jean Francois, E. (2011). *Dream model to start a small business.* Bloomington, IN: iUniverse.

Lubove, R. (1975). *The professional altruist: The emergence of social work as a career, 1880–1930.* Cambridge, MA: Harvard University Press.

Miller, H. S. (1961). *The legal foundation of American philanthropy, 1776–1844.* Madison, WI: Wisconsin Historical Society.

Morgan, G. (2006). *Images of organizations* (rev. ed.). Thousand Oaks, CA: Sage.

NCCS. (2012). *Quick facts about nonprofits.* Retrieved from http://nccs.urban.org/statistics/quickfacts.cfm

Northouse, P. G. (2004). *Leadership: Theory and practice* (3rd ed.). Thousand Oaks, CA: Sage.

Roeger, K. L., Blackwood, A. S., & Pettijohn, S. (2012). *The nonprofit almanac 201.* Washington, DC: Urban Institute Press.

Salamon, L., Sokolwski, S. W., & Geller, S. (2012). *Holding the fort: Nonprofit employment during a decade of turmoil.* Baltimore, MD: Johns Hopkins University, Center for Civil Society Studies.

Scavoy, R. E. (1982). *The origins of the American business corporation 1784–1855: Broadening the concept of public service during industrialization.* Westport, CT: Greenwood Press.

Schneeman, A. (1997). *The law of corporations, partnership, and sole proprietorships* (2nd ed). Albany, NY: Delmar Publishers.

Shafritz, J., & Ott, J. (2005). *Classics of organization theories* (6th ed.). Belmont, CA: Thomson Wadsworth.

Smith, R. D. (2005). *Strategic planning for public relations.* Mahwah, NJ: Lawrence Erlbaum Associates.

Tocqueville, A. (2004). In A. Goldhammer (Trans.) & O. Zunz (Ed.), *Democracy in America.* New York, NY: Library of America.

United Nations Rule of Laws. (2014). *Non-governmental organizations.* Retrieved from http://unrol.org/article.aspx?article_id=23

Whitehead, J. S. (1976). *The separation of college and state: Columbia, Dartmouth, Harvard, and Yale, 1776–1876.* New Haven, CT: Yale University Press.

Willetts, P. (2012). *What is a non-governmental organization? UNESCO encyclopaedia of life support systems.* London, UK: City University.

Financial Sustainability

At the completion of the chapter the reader will be able to:

1. Define the concept of sustainability.
2. Define "financial sustainability."
3. Describe some factors affecting the financial sustainability of nonprofit organizations.
4. Discuss indicators of financial sustainability for nonprofit organizations.
5. Reflect on the practical implications of financial sustainability for nonprofit organizations.

This chapter explores the dimensions of financial sustainability as well as the principles needed to manage a nonprofit organization that can generate continuous funding through diverse sources in order to support its vision and mission in a way that is socially and environmentally sustainable. The chapter discusses the inherent, collateral, and environmental factors of financial sustainability in nonprofit organizations. Further, the chapter describes key indicators that can reveal whether an organization is financially sustainable or is on the path for financial sustainability.

ABOUT SUSTAINABILITY

Sustainability is the ability of a business, an organization, or a project to fulfill its vision and mission, meet its goals, and serve its stakeholders over time. In that context, sustainability can be assessed in terms of the organization itself, the services provided, and its finances. *Organizational sustainability* refers to the capacity of an organization to (a) develop a strategic plan, (b) secure, (c) and maintain resources that enable it to provide services over time. *Service sustainability* concerns the ability to provide quality services to clients independent of cycles of funding. Hart and Milstein (2003) developed the sustainable value framework as a strategy to assure business shareholders about the value of global sustainability. The framework addresses two major challenges represented by two axes:

1. *A vertical axis*, which is related to the challenges for businesses to be proactive regarding the creation of future technology and markets while managing today's business.

2. *A horizontal axis,* which represents the challenge for businesses to infuse external per-spectives and knowledge without jeopardizing organizational growth, skills, and capabilities.

The interrelations between the vertical and horizontal axes create four quadrants or strate-gies for business sustainability:

1. *Quadrant 1:* Pollution prevention intended for cost and risk reduction
2. *Quadrant 2:* Product stewardship to secure reputation and legitimacy
3. *Quadrant 3:* Clean technology for innovation and repositioning
4. *Quadrant 4:* Sustainability vision as growth trajectory

Hart and Milstein's (2003) framework is based on sustainability for businesses and for-profit corporations. Therefore, it has limited application to nonprofit organizations. However, it is insightful about the relevance of sustainability for all organizations.

SUSTAINABLE BUSINESS

A sustainable business strives to have minimal negative impact on its global and local environments by linking all business decisions and operations to sustainability principles, supplying environmentally friendly products or services, and doing everything possible to adequately address the current environment in the process of making a profit. Sustainable business works to reduce or possibly eliminate environmental harms caused by produc-tion and consumption of goods and services. Environmental harms are measured by the carbon footprint or the amount of carbon dioxide necessary to support the consumption of products. To reduce environmental harms, sustainable businesses use various strategies such as:

■ Innovation and technology that eliminate products and services with potential environ-mental harms
■ Collaboration or partnership with other sustainable businesses
■ Continuing quality improvement in evidence-based sustainable practices
■ Sustainable reporting to document benchmarks, progress, and ensure greater accountability

Financial Sustainability

Nonprofit organizations not only provide goods and services, but also contribute to the economies of their communities and societies. Nonprofit organizations are involved in community development, informal, nonformal, and formal education activities and pro-grams. They develop talents and human capital that benefit communities and societies in all aspects of life. They employ millions of people who contribute payroll taxes to their govern-ments. Their employees are consumers who contribute to their local, regional, and national economies. Most of the services that they provide would not have been offered by for-profit businesses, because such services are simply not profitable. However, their contributions to communities and societies are linked to the challenges that they face in competing for resources, especially financial resources, that are necessary to continue to operate effectively.

Kingsley (2012) reported on the closing of various nonprofit organizations in southern Nevada. These organizations used to provide vital services to the chronically homeless and to clients with severe mental illness. For example, the Salvation Army of Southern Nevada had 80 clients with severe mental illness that they referred to a coalition of service providers. The Nevada Treatment Center closed its doors and transferred its indigent clients to human services agencies. Further, the Nevada Association of Latin Americans shut its doors and ceased to provide much-needed services, such as low-cost day care, HIV/AIDS treatment, and job training. Kingsley (2012) interviewed various nonprofit leaders who expressed their concerns about long waits for services, and increases in the unemployment rate and numbers of food stamp recipients in the area, because no group has filled the void left by the nonprofit organizations that closed their doors. There is no doubt that these organizations were very helpful to the neediest citizens in their communities. However, they could not continue to provide these services, which had constituted a great safety net for their clients. The question one may ask is, "Why did they have to close their doors?" Throughout the article, Kingsley (2012) provided the reason, which can be summarized in three words: *lack of funding*. For example, Kingsley (2012) asserted: "The Salvation Army had been losing money for years"; "Nevada Treatment Center ... shut its doors due to lack of funding"; "the founder of Nevada Treatment Center ... struggled to raise money"; and "the Association of Latin Americans ... filed for bankruptcy." As you may have noticed, lack of funding may have various explanations. In the case of the Salvation Army, they could not afford the expenses of providing intensive care for their severely mentally ill homeless clients. The Nevada Treatment Center relied mostly on state funding and could not raise enough money from other sources. The Association of Latin Americans filed for bankruptcy over possible allegations of mismanagement or fraud. Regardless of the explanation, the outcome is the same for these nonprofit organizations: They dissolved and could not continue to provide services to their clients. They were not financially sustainable. What could they have done differently as nonprofit organizations?

Bassett and Mitchell (2006) suggested six steps related to the financial sustainability of schools:

1. *Trend analysis*: The purpose is to identify key financial trends that can help make financial projections. Trends can be identified through internal financial data and in comparison to other similar organizations.
2. *Ratio analysis*: Ratio analysis is performed to obtain a snapshot of current key ratios that will help in strategic financial planning. Key ratios can be compared against comparable institutions to observe variance, similarities, and differences.
3. *Evaluating financial planning assumptions*: This step aims to help an institution identify objective assumptions that will enable it to make policy decisions and strategic choices related to financial growth and stability to achieve a stronger long-term financial position.
4. *Establishing markers of school success*: This step consists of identifying and setting goals that can ensure anticipated positive outcomes and financial equilibrium. This implies that the institution must develop a budget that is adequate to ensure success, as well as to serve as a benchmark to measure continuing progress.
5. *Re-engineering strategies*: This fifth step relates to adopting strategies that are the most likely to help achieve key financial objectives. Part of developing re-engineering strategies includes taking into account potential financial vulnerabilities and strategies to overcome them.
6. *Projecting multiple scenarios*: The final step is to test various financial scenarios through projection and plans for the envisioned financial future.

The Basset and Mitchell (2006) model is sequential, although I would argue that financial sustainability is a multifaceted process, not a finite project. In addition, the model is similar to a classic strategic-planning process. Obviously, the model was developed for independent schools. Therefore, other types of nonprofit organizations might need to consider additional factors when planning for financial sustainability. However, the model has the merit of outlining specific strategic initiatives and actions that may help nonprofit organizations maintain better financial management practices and take them on path toward financial sustainability.

What is financial sustainability for nonprofit organizations? For for-profit businesses, financial sustainability is easy to define because the bottom line is money. A business achieves financial sustainability once it is able to deliver products and services to customers at a price that covers all its investment and operating expenses and generates sustained profit for its owners. It is different for nonprofit organization, because the bottom line is not money, but vision, mission, and values. In other words, although financial sustainability is inherent to finance, it must also account for the ability of a nonprofit organization to further its mission. Financial sustainability for nonprofit organizations is the ability of an organization to maintain a diverse source of revenue that enables it to continue to provide ongoing quality services regardless of changes in funding sources, in target population, and other changes among its internal and external stakeholders. Financial sustainability is the ability of a project, a program, or an organization to maintain broader sources of funding in order to provide standard services to its clients over time. Financial sustainability is a process, not an end. It can be evaluated through

(a) **Profitability** or the surplus of revenue over expenses
(b) **Liquidity** or the ability to meet cash requirements (e.g., paying bills)
(c) **Solvency** or the ability to pay all debts if the business were sold tomorrow
(d) **Efficiency** or the ability of an organization to deliver the maximum service possible with the lowest amount of human, material, and financial resources
(e) **Effectiveness** or the extent to which an organization uses its resources adequately to fulfill its mission and vision

FACTORS AFFECTING FINANCIAL SUSTAINABILITY

There are three major factors related to the financial sustainability of a nonprofit organization (Figure 2.1):

1. The inherent factors
2. The collateral factors
3. The environmental factors

Inherent Factors

The inherent factors are directly linked to financial sustainability. They determine whether an organization is financially sustainable or not. Inherent factors of financial sustainability include, but are not limited to:

■ Financial management
■ Budget

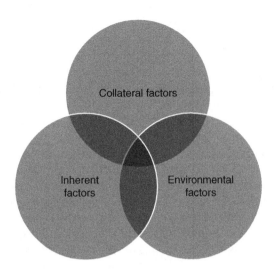

FIGURE 2.1 Factors affecting financial sustainability.

■ Financial statement analysis
■ Financial sustainability plan
■ Social enterprise
■ Fund-raising
■ Grant seeking
■ Investment
■ Risk management

FINANCIAL MANAGEMENT

Roseland Community Hospital of Chicago provides an interesting illustration of the impact of financial management on the financial sustainability of a nonprofit organization. Roseland is a 162-bed community hospital that provides health care services to 28,000 people per year, mostly poor patients without health insurance coverage. Thomas (2013) reported that Roseland was on the brink of closing, partly because of $7 million of debt that was more than 90 days delinquent, but also because of poor financial management decisions. For example, Thomas (2013) explained that management used its operations money to build an adolescent behavioral health unit, which could have waited until the hospital received $7 million in funding from the state of Illinois, which eventually materialized. There is nothing wrong with building an adolescent behavioral health unit. The building project may be in response to a need identified by the agency. However, if building that new unit will jeopardize the entire agency, it is very unwise to build it. Regardless of the justification, this was not an effective financial management decision. Effective financial management enables a nonprofit organization to continue to provide services to clients within the limits of its capacities. Ineffective financial management will lead to the opposite, which is an organization that is unable to fulfill its mission and is forced to stop core services or even close its doors. Sound financial management can help a nonprofit organization anticipate and mitigate risks, reduce costs, build reserves, and put financing strategies in place in order to continue to provide core services, even if external donors withdraw their funding.

BUDGET

The budget allows nonprofit organizations to anticipate sources of revenue, make proper appropriation of funds, plan for contingencies, and monitor expenses to ensure that they are being executed according to plan. The budget is one the best financial tools available to shape the path of nonprofit organizations toward financial sustainability. The budgeting process, which includes forecasting, provides clarity about what the financial future may look like. This puts an organization in a better position to make decisions in advance to meet challenges that could constitute an existential threat to an organization.

FINANCIAL STATEMENT ANALYSIS

Financial statement analysis is an effective tool used to understand the financial health and conditions of an organization in relation to its financial strengths and weaknesses. It helps assess financial management effectiveness and make judgments about whether the organization is financially sustainable, on a path to financial sustainability, or near a crisis of financial sustainability. Findings from financial statement analysis can be used for strategic planning, budgeting, fund-raising, investment, and/or organizational transformation decisions and operations.

FINANCIAL SUSTAINABILITY PLAN

A financial sustainability plan results from financial sustainability analysis. Therefore, it is based on changing a current situation into a desired situation. A financial sustainability plan creates an increased focus on financial sustainability in relation to the vision and mission of an organization. A financial sustainability plan provides criteria to monitor progress toward financial sustainability and thus serves as a basis to take corrective actions that can help an organization maintain core programs in the event of financial stress.

SOCIAL ENTERPRISE

Social enterprise is a great strategy used to generate consistent and reliable revenues to support programs and services that help fulfill the vision and mission of a nonprofit organization. Income generated from social enterprise is unrestricted and can be relied on if the social enterprise is managed efficiently.

FUND-RAISING

Overturf (2013) has written about the Leon County Community Coalition, a Texas-based nonprofit organization that is likely to close its doors because "government funding dried up." Overturf explained that the organization provided after-school programs for students, drug and alcohol abuse prevention, community-service activities for juveniles involved in the courts, and purchased equipment for law enforcement officers. According to the executive director of that organization, 97% of their budget was provided by the government. Then, the organization received a 30-day notice informing it of the loss of its funding. Fund-raising gives a nonprofit organization the option to diversify its funding sources. Having all income coming from one source is a threat to financial sustainability. Diversifying funding sources enables an organization to remain stable or continue to provide core services or maintain core programs, even if external donors completely or partially withdraw their funding.

GRANT SEEKING

Grants bring additional money to a nonprofit organization. Therefore, they automatically help a nonprofit organization provide services. However, grants should be used with caution so that they do not transform a nonprofit organization into a sand castle. The reality is that grant funding is an opportunity for an organization to use restricted resources that can help fulfill its mission and vision while managing unrestricted money to make financial decisions that can help sustain it in an unforeseen time of financial hardship.

INVESTMENT

Investment is the use of an organization's money to create an asset with the expectation of receiving a return from such a transaction. Many nonprofit organizations maintain portfolios that are managed in the investment market and from which they receive regular income to support their activities while the capital invested remains secure. Further, nonprofit organizations can identify opportunities for innovation and creation of new income-generation services, within the limits of the law, that aim to provide more efficient services or expand programs in a cost-effective manner. This can help nonprofit organizations differentiate themselves from competing agencies and attract social and community support, as well as new donors.

RISK MANAGEMENT

To ensure sustainability, nonprofit organizations should perform systematic evaluation of environmental, social, and financial risks in order to minimize financial liabilities, which can endanger their financial sustainability. Fraud, corruption, financial mismanagement, or a lawsuit can drive a nonprofit organization out of business.

COLLATERAL FACTORS

Collateral factors are indirectly related to financial sustainability. The collateral factors either (a) influence the planning, implementation, or monitoring of financial sustainability; (b) facilitate greater long-term viability; (c) help create an external or external environment that fosters financial sustainability initiatives or activities; or (d) help maintain a path toward financial sustainability. Collateral factors of financial sustainability include, but are not limited to:

- Governance
- Leadership
- Strategic planning
- Human resources and job satisfaction
- Needs assessment
- Asset mapping
- Community relations
- Service delivery
- Technology
- Program evaluation
- Social marketing
- Organizational transformation

Governance

Governance resides in the power entrusted to the board of directors of a nonprofit organization to oversee activities and operations on behalf of the target population. Board members must ensure that a nonprofit organization generates enough revenue to support its mission and that funds are used to provide the maximum units of services possible to beneficiaries. Effective governance fosters conditions that anticipate risks and plan for reserves, in order to protect the organization from financial downturns and liabilities, which have direct impact on financial sustainability. Financial sustainability depends on the strength of governance practices within a nonprofit organization. A nonprofit organization can manage its way toward financial sustainability based on its ability to govern, lead, and manage itself in a manner that can always gather public support and create its own metabolism to manage and resolve conflicts, take decisive corrective actions on mistakes, and anticipate and neutralize systemic crises.

Leadership

Leadership helps make sound financial management decisions in ways that can produce the best return on investment possible. Leadership can make a difference in addressing chronic financial issues that can negatively affect the financial sustainability of a nonprofit organization. In one example, Barbour (2013) wrote, "Chronic money problems have led officials with Norfolk's Associated Marine Institute, a nonprofit education organization, to close its doors after nearly 20 years of teaching troubled teenagers." The organization was serving a target population that really needed help: troubled teenagers. However, it was faced with "chronic money problems." When an organization is dealing with a chronic lack of financial resources, it is not a question of whether it will survive, but only how long it will survive. Effective leadership can help turn around such issues through organizational redesigning, streamlining of operations, mobilizing monetary and in-kind support, deferring or eliminating discretionary costs, developing collaborations for cost sharing, changing fund-raising and spending patterns, and other similar initiatives.

Strategic Planning

With strategic planning, a nonprofit organization develops strategic clarity for internal and external stakeholders through organizational mandates and adoption of strategic priorities or key programmatic areas. Having a clear focus helps identify more reliable funding sources and provides arguments to convince donors and the public to support the vision and mission of a nonprofit organization. Strategic planning is an antecedent to financial sustainability. A nonprofit organization that does not have a culture of strategic planning cannot be on a path for financial sustainability or become financially sustainable.

Human Resources and Job Satisfaction

Personnel are one of the greatest assets of a nonprofit organization. To hire and retain efficient and committed employees costs money. Effective human resource management can help with job satisfaction and staff motivation and retention, and can save money for a nonprofit organization. Lack of employee satisfaction can lead to lower productivity and high staff turnover, which can affect the efficiency and effectiveness of a nonprofit organization. On the other hand, a nurturing work environment can contribute to employee commitment, cost reduction, saving, and income generation.

Needs Assessment

When organizations develop strategic plans, programs, and services based on needs-assessment results, they are more likely to secure community support because activities are rooted in targeted needs that are being met by such organizations. Needs assessment provides nonprofit organizations with information that can help them adapt to change in their external environment. The ability to adapt to changing demographic conditions and other factors is essential for the financial sustainability of a nonprofit organization.

Asset Mapping

Through asset mapping, a nonprofit organization can identify community resources that can be used to further financial sustainability strategies and plans. Asset mapping helps gather information to initiate and develop strategic partnerships that can help reduce risks, save money, and generate both monetary and nonmonetary contributions, which can strengthen the financial sustainability of a nonprofit organization.

Community Relations

Sometimes organizations provide services that are no longer perceived as critical by their community or funders. This was the situation of Rosehedge/Multifaith Works, a nonprofit organization in Seattle that has been providing housing and services for 25 years to people living with HIV/AIDS. The organization lost a substantial amount of government and corporate support. Bauman (2013, para 1) cited the executive director, who said that, "many funders no longer see HIV/AIDS as the pressing concern it once was." Once funders do not believe there is a pressing need to support the activities of a nonprofit organization, they will stop providing their financial assistance. As a result, the board of directors decided to dissolve the organization. Effective community relations are a contributing factor to the financial sustainability of a nonprofit organization. Nonprofit organizations can develop better, stronger, and smarter collaborations or partnerships with various community stakeholders to obtain additional funding and in-kind contributions to help reduce cost, improve the reputation of the organization, and facilitate greater community commitment to its mission.

Service Delivery

Donors support a nonprofit organization because they believe, support, or understand the value of services offered and programs implemented by such a nonprofit organization. They also want to have evidence that the service is of great or at least acceptable quality. If quality is lacking, organizations may lose public support, donors may withdraw their funding, and the organization may not be able to continue to operate.

Technology

Technology helps streamline job processes and reduce costs in personnel and time needed to complete tasks. Cost reduction through technology contributes to financial sustainability. Saving through investment in technology frees up additional funds that can be invested in programs.

Social Marketing

Social marketing is an effective strategy used to help supporters, funders, and the public at large understand the effectiveness and value of programs and services offered by a nonprofit organization. This in turn contributes to increased monetary and nonmonetary support for the organization. Further, social marketing can be used as a cost recovery strategy for a nonprofit organization. Cost-recovery programs strengthen the commitment of clients to key services and help ensure that such services continue to exist regardless of changes in funding sources.

Program Evaluation

Program evaluation helps measure performance outcomes. Program evaluation provides data or information about outcomes, productivity, efficiency, and effectiveness, as well as suggestions of strategies for continuous quality improvement. Performance outcomes are related to efficiency, quality, and effectiveness. As previously indicated, the financial sustainability of nonprofit organizations depends not only on financial conditions, but also on organizational efficiency and effectiveness. Program evaluation helps show which programs have the best possible rate of return on investment. Therefore, program evaluation is a contributor to financial sustainability.

Organizational Transformation

Sometimes organizational transformation can be the only option that organizations have to become financial sustainable. They may operate, for instance, on a business model that must be changed radically. Organizational transformation is rooted in the ability of an entity to assess its strengths and weaknesses, threats, and opportunities, and make decisions to reverse negative trends by changing the way it operates. Organizational transformation can help bring new energy that helps a nonprofit organization take a path toward financial sustainability.

ENVIRONMENTAL FACTORS

Environmental factors are social, economic, and political (SEP) issues that may affect funding, support, and operations of a nonprofit organization in ways that determine whether such organization will survive.

Social Issues

Social issues can create an environmental that is hostile to a nonprofit organization and lead to its closing. The closing of many Planned Parenthood clinics is a great example. Feminist Wire (2013) reported the closing of several Planned Parenthood clinics in Texas. Planned Parenthood is a national nonprofit organization that maintains local health clinics, which provide various women's health services that some women may not be able to find elsewhere. Therefore, the beneficiaries to these services may rely solely on Planned Parenthood to receive services that can be a matter of life or death. I use the closing of Planned Parenthood clinics in Texas as a random example. However, this is representative of a larger trend, which has seen the closing of Planned Parenthood clinics in many other U.S. states. The closing resulted from the controversial social issue of abortion, which is one of the many services available at Planned Parenthood clinics. When the clinics are forced to close, this affects not only the beneficiaries, but also the overall financial conditions of that agency. In more specific terms, the funding that used to come as a result of fee-based services from such clinics is no longer available.

Economics

Economic or financial crises can affect donor abilities to contribute to nonprofit organizations and affect their financial sustainability. The Nonprofit Finance Fund (2011) conducted a survey on the impact of the 2008 financial crisis on nonprofit organizations in the United States.

About 50% of respondents identified themselves as nonprofit organizations that provide services that are critical to the health and safety of those in need. More than 70% of them saw increases in demand for services and significant decreases in the financial contributions they used to receive. As a result, some of them had to use their reserve funds, reduce the amount of services, and maintain accumulated deficits that may lead them to bankruptcy.

Politics

Changes in government and legislatures can be a threat to the financial sustainability of a nonprofit organization. Hulse (2009) reported in the *New York Times* that the U.S. House of Representatives voted to ban federal funds for the nonprofit organization Association of Community Organizations for Reform Now (ACORN) over a controversial video. ACORN was a collection of community-based, nonprofit organizations with about 500,000 members at its peak, which used to advocate for low- and moderate-income families on various social issues, such as health care, voter registration, affordable housing, neighborhood safety, and other similar issues. Later, the video that was the basis for cutting funding for ACORN was found to be edited and baseless (Rovzar, 2013). Although ACORN used to receive about 10% of its funding from the federal government, all the other streams of income evaporated as a result of a political action by the U.S. House of Representatives. The organization had no choice but to dissolve.

INDICATORS OF FINANCIAL SUSTAINABILITY

Financial sustainability is an ongoing process. It is difficult to say in absolute terms that a nonprofit organization is financially sustainable, given all the factors that are not exclusively financial, which affect the financial sustainability of nonprofit organizations. However, there are key indicators that can help determine whether an organization is on a path to financial sustainability.

As Figure 2.2 illustrates, indicators include, but are not limited to:

■ Culture of strategic planning and performance measurement
■ Culture of stewardship and accountability
■ In-house-generated income is diverse and greater than public funding
■ Sustained high profitability (growth)
■ Sustained increase in solvency
■ Sustained increase in liquidity
■ Rainy-day fund is at least equal to the equivalent of the 1-year budget for core expenses
■ Outstanding level of staff satisfaction and commitment equal to or greater than 90%
■ Outstanding level of program efficiency equal to or greater than 90%
■ Effective and tested risk-management policy

Culture of Strategic Planning and Performance Measurement

A financially sustainable nonprofit organization should have a culture of strategic planning and performance measurement. A culture of planning and performance measurement means

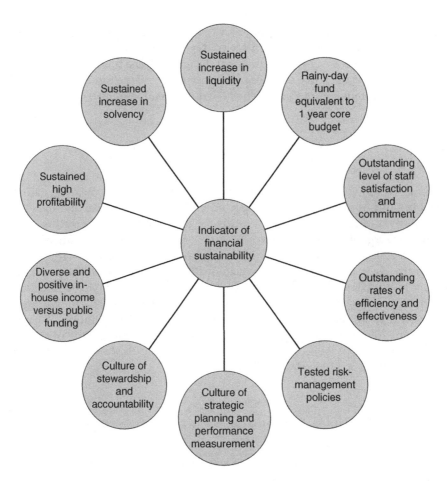

FIGURE 2.2 Indicators of financial sustainability.

that an organization reviews its goals and objectives on a regular basis and assesses the short-term, midterm, and long-term outcomes of its programs, projects, services, or activities. With a culture of strategic planning and performance measurement, an organization is always conducting a SWOT analysis to understand the strengths, weaknesses, opportunities, and threats at a given time. The findings from a SWOT analysis are used to take advantage of the strengths to compensate for the weaknesses, seek opportunities, and negate threats. With a culture of strategic planning and performance measurement, an organization is constantly reviewing the relevance of its vision and mission statements, and ensures that they inspire programs that aim to meet the needs of the target population. A culture of strategic planning and performance measurement provides evidence to donors and potential donors that the organization not only knows what it is doing, but also justifies why additional and sustained funding is needed to support its activities. A culture of strategic planning and performance is essential for an organization that is vision and mission driven.

Culture of Stewardship and Accountability

A sustainable nonprofit organization has a culture of stewardship and accountability. This means that an organization efficiently manages financial resources donated to support its vision and gives satisfactory reports on financial information and achievement to both internal and external stakeholders. An organization with a culture of stewardship makes all organizational and program performance information available in a timely manner. An organization with a culture of stewardship and accountability is proactive in encouraging internal and external stakeholders to provide feedback on published reports.

Diverse In-House-Generated Income Greater Than Public Funding

In many cases, public funding received especially through grants is restricted to specific activities. However, funds raised by an organization through fund-raising events, social enterprise, investment, or fees for services can be used for whatever program, project, or service fits the overall purpose of an organization. I call these funds "in-house-generated income," because the organization has control over them. For that reason, such funds should be diverse and greater than public funding: diverse, because this will ensure that the loss of one source does not have systemic effects greater than public funding so that the organization has enough flexibility to reallocate funds if necessary.

Sustained High Profitability (Growth)

Profitability is one indicator of organizational growth. This is not the only indicator. This is not the primary indicator for a nonprofit organization. However, this is a key factor of financial sustainability. Sustained high profitability compared to organizations of similar size will provide a nonprofit organization the latitude to be creative, expand its programs and services to more clients, and make relatively sound financial-planning decisions.

Sustained Increase in Solvency

Although debt is not necessarily the worst thing that can happen to a nonprofit organization, it is a sign that an organization may not be able to further its mission. Therefore, a sustainable nonprofit organization should strive to maintain increased solvency and rely less and less on debt. Obviously, there are healthy debts, like a mortgage or a car loan or a loan on a machine or heavy equipment, which are not necessarily a problem at all because a nonprofit can generate equity from such debts. However, any debt incurred by a nonprofit organization should be reasonable and should not affect the ability to deliver core services.

Sustained Increase in Liquidity

Nonprofit organizations usually serve people who are desperately in need and may not be able to receive help from any other entity. Therefore, the ability to pay bills on time is very critical. It is not enough for an organization to have assets. Liquidity is very important to providing daily services.

Rainy-Day Fund at Least Equal to the 1-Year Budget for Core Expenses

Recessions, which are contractions in the national economy of a country, tend to last 12 to 15 months. A recession affects the ability of companies to keep their employees or hire new ones. Therefore, some people might lose their jobs, and job seekers might not able to find work. Nonprofit organizations tend to be greatly affected by an economic recession, because some of the individual or even institutional donors might not be able to contribute as they would have otherwise. For this reason, I think that a rainy-day fund can be an effective means to help a nonprofit organization overcome the financial hardship that a recession can bring. A financially sustainable nonprofit organization should have a rainy-day fund at least equal to the equivalent of the 1-year budget for core expenses. The core expenses will vary from one organization to the other. Obviously, a rainy-day fund of that scale can be controversial. However, if the board of an organization approves such policy, it should not be a problem. In fact, it should not be controversial if the rainy-day fund is in the form of an investment that provides regular income. Further, there should be approved policies that set the objective conditions under which an organization can tap into the rainy-day funds.

Outstanding Level of Staff Satisfaction and Commitment Equal to or Greater Than 90%

No entity is organizationally or financially sustainable if the staff is not satisfied and committed to its vision and mission. An organization should know the level of satisfaction and commitment of its staff, and develop strategies to increase them or keep them greater than 90%. With that level of satisfaction and commitment, a nonprofit organization may see miracles on a daily basis. With that level of satisfaction and commitment, staff will go above and beyond their abilities to not only provide quality services, but also to attract funding that can help provide needed services over time.

Outstanding Level of Program Efficiency and Effectiveness Equal to or Greater Than 90%

Nonprofit organizations should use their resources efficiently and spend the maximum amount or percentage of funding on its programs. However, this is not always the case for reasons that can sometimes be legitimate. A nonprofit organization may provide a service that requires unavoidable administrative expenses. In that context, it is up to an organization to explain to stakeholders why the percentage of money spent on the program is low compared to other organizations. After accounting for the organizational context, a financially sustainable nonprofit organization should have program efficiency effectiveness ratios that are equal to or greater than 90%. These levels of efficiency and effectiveness are not only great for clients and beneficiaries, but also will challenge donors to continue to support the vision and mission.

Effective and Tested Risk-Management Policies

Like any agency, a nonprofit organization is not exempt from risks or liabilities that can collapse an entire enterprise. Therefore, a financially sustainable nonprofit organization should have detailed risk-management policies. One of the ways a nonprofit organization can manage its risks is to maintain a comprehensive liability policy. This policy will vary from one nonprofit organization to the next. Effective risk-management policies are the ones that successfully undergo stress tests to ensure that they can serve as an appropriate shield for an organization should an unforeseen risk incident occur. The test of a comprehensive liability policy will be the extent to which such a policy can negate any unforeseen event that could force a nonprofit organization to dissolve.

FINANCIAL SUSTAINABILITY IMPLICATIONS IN THE REAL LIFE OF A NONPROFIT ORGANIZATION

Dewan and Sack (2008) published a story about Grady Memorial Hospital in Atlanta, Georgia, which describes various facets of financial sustainability for a nonprofit organization. Grady Memorial Hospital opened in 1892 and was named after Henry W. Grady, managing editor of the *Atlanta Constitution*. Grady is a teaching hospital for at least two medical schools in Atlanta, and is among the largest public hospitals in the United States. More important, Grady provides charity and emergency care to thousands of uninsured individuals who would not be able to afford much-needed health care otherwise. Such charitable services have contributed to a multimillion dollar shortfall. As Dewan and Sack (2008, para 2) argued in their article, "Grady is operating on a business model that is no longer sustainable." The question is why they think such a business model of providing charity and emergency care is not sustainable.

Elements of responses could be found in various portions of their article. Dewan and Sack reported that Grady did not generate enough revenues to cover all their expenses: "only 8 percent of inpatients fit the privately insured category"; "over the years, the cost of caring for the uninsured has grown while taxpayer support has stagnated"; and "only short-term financial transfusions have kept it from closing its doors (2008, para 3). This explains partly why they have a multimillion dollar shortfall.

Grady was not able to take advantage of social-marketing strategies. In other words, it was not able to market its services, was outcompeted, and was left with uninsured and underinsured patients. Dewan and Sack (2008) reported that Grady has run deficits for 10 of the last 11 years, accumulating millions of dollars in debt. It became difficult for Grady to pay suppliers on time, resulting in shortages in essential supplies. Needless to say that with shortages in supplies, outdated equipment, outmoded tracking systems, stories of corruption and cronyism among managers, lawsuits from patients, stressed staff, and no ability to attract the most qualified staff, Grady has been delivering poor-quality services, ranking among the worst-performing hospitals in the United States. Dewan and Sack (2008) explained that a consultant concluded that Grady needed an organizational transformation through the creation of a new nonprofit organization that would manage the hospital. However, the consultant found that leadership was unable to make decisions needed to transform Grady. In other words, the issue of financial sustainability at Grady hospital involved not only profitability (chronic deficits), liquidity (cannot pay suppliers on time), solvency (unsustainable debt), but also problems of governance (corruption and cronyism), leadership (inability to make tough decisions), strategic planning (short-term infusion of cash to address a long-term financial problems), human resource development (stressed staff), program evaluation (poor-quality services), technology (outmoded tracking system), and other facets (social marketing, community relations, asset mapping, organizational transformation) that may seem not related to finances, but with implications for financial sustainability.

1. What is sustainability?
2. What is financial sustainability?
3. How does financial sustainability differ from financial management?
4. What are the major factors of financial sustainability identified in this chapter? How do they apply to your nonprofit organization?
5. What are the key indicators of financial sustainability? What other indicators of financial sustainability can you think of?
6. Talk with a friend about the factors related to the financial sustainability of a nonprofit organization. What factors do you think are more consequential for the financial sustainability of a nonprofit organization?

REFERENCES

Barbour, C. (2013). *Money troubles cause AMIkids to close doors.* Retrieved from http://hamptonroads .com/2013/01/money-troubles-cause-amikids-to-close-doors

Bassett, P., & Mitchell, M. (2006). *Financially sustainable schools.* Washington, DC: National Association of Independent Schools.

Bauman, V. (2013). *25-year-old Seattle housing nonprofit will close its doors.* Retrieved from http://www. bizjournals.com/seattle/blog/health-care-inc/2013/09/seattle-hivaids-housing-and-health .html

Dewan, S., & Sack, K. (2008, January 8). A safety-net hospital falls into financial crisis. *The New York Times.* Retrieved from http://www.nytimes.com/2008/01/08/us/08grady .html?pagewanted=all

Feminist Newswire. (2013). *More Texas Planned Parenthood clinics close.* Retrieved from https:// feminist.org/blog/index.php/2013/09/05/more-texas-planned-parenthood-clinics-close/

Hart, S. L., & Milstein, M. B. (2003). creating sustainable value. *Academy of Management Executive, 17*(2), 56–67.

Hulse, C. (2009, September 17). House votes to ban federal funds for Acorn. *The New York Times.* Retrieved from http://www.nytimes.com/2009/09/18/us/politics/18acorn.html?_r=0

Kingsley, A. (2012, November 7). Nonprofit agencies are closing while demand is rising. *Las Vegas City Life.* Retrieved from: http://lasvegascitylife.com/sections/news/nonprofit-agencies-are-closing-while-demand-rising.html

Nonprofit Finance Fund. (2011). *2011 state of the sector survey.* Retrieved from http://nonprofit-financefund.org/files/docs/2011/2011survey_brochure.pdf

Overturf, J. (2013). *Leon County nonprofit organization likely to close after losing funding.* Retrieved from http://www.theeagle.com/news/local/article_da466ab6-87ae-56dd-b9f6-1e3f23f69c93. html

Rovzar, C. (2013). *Damaging Brooklyn ACORN sting video ruled 'Heavily Edited,' No charges to be filed.* Retrieved from http://nymag.com/daily/intelligencer/2010/03/damaging_brooklyn_acorn_ sting.html

Thomas, M. (2013). *Did mismanagement or charity care cause Roseland Hospital's financial emergency?* Retrieved from http://www.suntimes.com/news/metro/20695030-418/did-mismanagement-or-charity-care-cause-roseland-hospitals-financial-emergency.html

Governance and Financial Sustainability

At the completion of the chapter the reader will be able to:

1. Define the concept of governance.
2. Describe the differences between governance and government.
3. Identify some common governance theories.
4. Cite the generic items in the bylaws of a nonprofit organization.
5. Explain the relationship between governance and the board of directors.
6. Cite some reasons related to the importance of boards in nonprofit organizations.
7. Describe the key governance structures and perspectives in nonprofit organizations.
8. List some key principles of nonprofit governance.
9. Explain the relationship between governance and financial sustainability of a nonprofit organization.

This chapter discusses the legal and organizational roles of the board of directors and special committees in the governance and financial sustainability of a nonprofit organization. The chapter explores conceptual and theoretical frameworks that explain governance in nonprofit organizations in the context of financial sustainability.

WHAT IS GOVERNANCE?

The word "governance" comes from the Latin, *governare*, which means "rule over, be responsible for." As Figure 3.1 indicates, governance is a process that grants *power* to a legitimate body inside a *system* (e.g., organization, institution, community, or society) to make *decisions* (e.g., strategic, managerial, administrative) through consensual *structures* (e.g., board, committee, department, unit) and principles in order to carry out the operations and activities that meet the *expectations* (e.g., goal, objectives) of *constituencies* (e.g., members, clients, communities).

As Figure 3.1 illustrates, governance does not exist without a structure in place. In the context of nonprofit organizations, the *structures* tend to be the assembly of members, the board of directors, or committees. *Power* is granted to such a structure on behalf of the collective. There are *expectations* that such a structure will exert the granted power in the best interests of the organization. The exercise of power occurs mainly in the form of *decisions* that can positively or negatively affect a group of people who are basically the *constituents* of an organization. The constituents can be internal, in the case of members of an organization. The constituents can be external, in the case of clients or potential beneficiaries of a nonprofit organization.

It is important to differentiate between governance and government. A government is a body that exerts power and authority over a geopolitical unit (e.g., town, municipality, state, country, or nation-state). On the other hand, governance is the process through which power is granted, authority is exercised, decisions are made, and performance is monitored and sanctioned; for example, the governance of a country with respect to its adequacy (good governance) will include:

■ Electoral systems, structures, and process to select representatives, so that they may govern legitimately
■ The rules, regulations, or principles that are in place for the effective and efficient management of social and economic resources for the well-being of all constituencies
■ The ability of government entities to formulate fair policies that guarantee equal rights and protection for everyone
■ The ability of constituencies to hold representatives accountable and to carry out decisions sanctioning performance
■ The existence of fair and sustainable legal frameworks used to solve conflicts peacefully among individuals or groups

Governance exists in any form of organized group. However, adequate or good governance requires participation and legitimacy. In other words, the constituencies concerned with governance process and structures must be part of and accept the rules of governance.

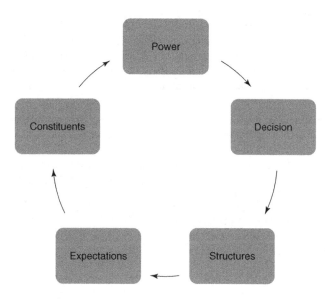

FIGURE 3.1 Governance.

CORPORATE GOVERNANCE

The governance of a corporate entity is slightly different from that of a geopolitical entity. For example, instead of a government, governance is carried out by a board of directors. In this context, governance involves rules and principles, processes, customs, policies, and laws that influence the interactions among internal and external stakeholders as well as the administration and control of a corporation. Various definitions have been provided about the term "governance." Box 3.1 provides a sample of definitions as illustration.

To sum up, the concept of corporate governance is used to signify the reality that various actors are involved in the administration and control of a corporate entity. Corporate governance explains the rights and responsibilities of stakeholders, as well as procedures for making decisions. The corporate entity can be for profit or nonprofit. This chapter focuses mainly on nonprofit corporate governance.

BOX 3.1 SAMPLE DEFINITIONS OF CORPORATE GOVERNANCE

Definition	Source
Corporate governance is the process carried out by the board of directors, and its related committees, on behalf of and for the benefit of the company's stakeholders, to provide direction, authority, and oversights to management.	Sobel, P. J. (2007). *Auditor's risk management guide: Integrating auditing and ERM*. Chicago, IL: CCH.
Corporate governance involves a set of relationships among a company's management, its board, its shareholders and other stakeholders. Corporate governance also provides the structure through which the objectives of the company are set, and the means of attaining those objectives and monitoring performance are determined.	Organization for Economic Co-Operation and Development. (2004). *OECD principles of corporate governance*. Paris: Author.
A system of law and sound approaches by which corporations are directed and controlled focusing on the internal and external corporate structures with the intention of monitoring the actions of management and directors and thereby mitigating agency risks that may stem from the misdeeds of corporate officers.	Sifuna, A. P. (2012). Disclose or abstain: The prohibition of iTrading on trial. *Journal of International Banking Law and Regulation, 27*(9), 340–353.
Corporate governance is the system by which companies are directed and managed. It influences how the objectives of the company are set and achieved, how risk is monitored and assessed, and how performance is optimized. Good corporate governance structures encourage companies to create value (through entrepreneurism, innovation, development, and exploration) and provide accountability and control systems commensurate with the risks involved.	ASX Corporate Governance Council. (2003). *ASX principles of good corporate governance and best practices recommendations*. Sydney, Australia: Author.

GOVERNANCE THEORIES

Corporate governance is often analyzed around major theoretical frameworks. The most common are agency theories, stewardship theories, resource-dependence theories, and stakeholder theories.

Agency Theories

Agency theories arise from the distinction between the owners (shareholders) of a company or an organization designated as "the principals" and the executives hired to manage the organization called "the agent." Agency theory argues that the goal of the agent is different from that of the principals, and they are conflicting (Johnson, Daily, & Ellstrand, 1996). The assumption is that the principals suffer an agency loss, which is a lesser return on investment because they do not directly manage the company. Part of the return that they could have had if they were managing the company directly goes to the agent. Consequently, agency theories suggest financial rewards that can help incentivize executives to maximize the profit of owners (Eisenhardt, 1989). Further, a board developed from the perspective of the agency theory tends to exercise strict control, supervision, and monitoring of the performance of the agent in order to protect the interests of the principals (Hillman & Dalziel, 2003). In other words, the board is actively involved in most of the managerial decision-making processes, and is accountable to the shareholders. A nonprofit board that operates through the lens of agency theories will show a hands-on management approach on behalf of the stakeholders.

Stewardship Theories

Stewardship theories argue that the managers or executives of a company are stewards of the owners, and both groups share common goals (Davis, Schoorman, & Donaldson, 1997). Therefore, the board should not be too controlling, as agency theories would suggest. The board should play a supportive role by empowering executives and, in turn, increase the potential for higher performance (Hendry, 2002; Shen, 2003). Stewardship theories argue for relationships between board and executives that involve training, mentoring, and shared decision making (Shen, 2003; Sundaramurthy & Lewis, 2003).

Resource-Dependence Theories

Resource-dependence theories argue that a board exists as a provider of resources to executives in order to help them achieve organizational goals (Hillman, Cannella, & Paetzold, 2000; Hillman & Daziel, 2003). Resource-dependence theories recommend interventions by the board while advocating for strong financial, human, and intangible supports to the executives. For example, board members who are professionals can use their expertise to train and mentor executives in a way that improves organizational performance. Board members can also tap into their networks of support to attract resources to the organization. Resource-dependence theories recommend that most of the decisions be made by executives with some approval of the board.

Stakeholder Theories

Stakeholder theories are based on the assumption that shareholders are not the only group with a stake in a company or a corporation. Stakeholder theories argue that clients or customers, suppliers, and the surrounding communities also have a stake in a corporation. They can be affected by the success or failure of a company. Therefore, managers have special obligations to ensure that all stakeholders (not just the shareholders) receive a fair return from their stake in the company (Donaldson & Preston, 1995). Stakeholder theories advocate for some form of corporate social responsibility, which is a duty to operate in ethical ways, even if that means a reduction of long-term profit for a company (Jones, Freeman, & Wicks, 2002). In that context, the board has a responsibility to be the guardian of the interests of all stakeholders by ensuring that corporate or organizational practices take into account the principles of sustainability for surrounding communities.

NONPROFIT GOVERNANCE

In the context of a nonprofit organization, governance is exercised primarily through an organizational structure called the board of directors. As such, the board of directors of a nonprofit organization ensures that management of activities and operations are consistent, effective, and efficient. As indicated in the first chapter, a nonprofit organization starts at the local or state level through a group of community members who want to create a structure that can address social, economic, cultural, religious, or environmental issues. They translate their intention into Articles of Incorporation as the first step to providing legitimacy to their community or social project, namely, a nonprofit organization. Therefore, the governance of this entity must involve all individuals who have developed a consensus on a set of community problems or issues. The consensus on issues should be accompanied by a consensus on the processes to address them. However, one must understand that people in organizations differ in their level of expertise, commitment, and availability. Therefore, not everybody may have the same level of responsibility. For this reason, nonprofit organizations have a board of directors to act on behalf of the constituencies. This is a delegation of responsibility, which signifies that the trustees (board members) are expected to exercise their best judgment, use their power with caution, and strive to fulfill the vision and mission of the nonprofit entity. As Stone and Ostrower (2007, p. 416) concluded, "In the nonprofit literature, governance has primarily been defined as the operation of boards of directors."

NONPROFIT GOVERNANCE AND BYLAWS

The purpose, roles, and the manner in which the board has to operate are defined primarily in the nonprofit bylaws. The bylaws are the constitution of a nonprofit organization. They are the foundational document on which all procedures and guidelines must be based. Generically, as indicated in Box 3.2, the bylaws describe

■ The names and purposes of a nonprofit organization
■ The profile of members, their rights, and obligations
■ The authority and duties of directors
■ The authority and duties of officers

■ The nature of indemnification
■ The roles of advisory boards and committees, if any
■ The administration of organizational finances
■ The procedures for books and records
■ The conditions under which the bylaws can be amended

Nonprofit bylaws will differ based on the nature of an organization, its purpose, and the backgrounds of the members, but the bylaws will include most all of the elements outlined above.

BOX 3.2 SAMPLE OF NONPROFIT BYLAWS

Bylaws of Hope and Dream, Inc.

ARTICLE I

NAME AND PURPOSES

Section 1.01. Name. The name of the organization is HOPE AND DREAM, INC.

Section 1.02. Objectives. Hope and Dream, Inc. has been organized exclusively for charitable purposes, including but not limited to:

1 Enrich the lives of children, families, and communities by promoting an awareness of cultural diversity, implementing programs for health, education, and economic opportunities, and preventing child abuse and neglect and domestic violence.
2 Perform all the duties and obligations of the organization.
3 Collect membership dues, receive donations in cash and all monies from any lawful means; and pay all expenses incidental to the conduct of the business of the organization.
4 Acquire by gift, purchase, or otherwise own, hold, and maintain, sell, transfer, dedicate to public use, or otherwise dispose of personal property in connection with the affairs of the organization.
5 Have and exercise any and all powers, rights, and privileges that a nonprofit corporation organized under Chapter 617 of the Florida Statutes by law may now or hereafter have or exercise.

Section 1.03. Purpose. The purposes for which this corporation is organized are mainly charitable, cultural, and educational within the meaning of Section 501(c)(3) of the Internal Revenue Code of 1986 or the corresponding provision of any future United States Internal Revenue Law and Chapter 617 of Florida Statutes. Notwithstanding any other provision of these articles, this corporation shall not, except to an insubstantial degree, engage in any activities or exercise any powers that are not in furtherance of the purposes of this corporation, and the corporation shall not carry on any other activities not permitted to be carried on

    (a) by a corporation exempt from federal income tax under Section 1(c)(3) of the Internal Revenue Code of 1986 or the corresponding provision of any future United States Internal Revenue Law,

---

(continued)

BOX 3.2 SAMPLE OF NONPROFIT BYLAWS   *(continued)*

(b) or by a corporation, contributions to which are deductible under Section 170(c)(2) of the Internal Revenue Code of 1986 or the corresponding provision of any future United States Internal Revenue Law.

(c) No substantial part of the activities of this corporation shall consist of carrying on propaganda, or otherwise attempting to influence legislation, except as provided in Section 501(h) of the Internal Revenue Code of 1986, and this corporation shall not participate in or intervene in (including publishing or distributing statements) any political campaign on behalf of any candidate for public office except as otherwise provided in Section 501(h) of the Internal Revenue Code of 1986.

(d) The property of this corporation is irrevocably dedicated to charitable purposes.

(e) No part of the net earnings of this corporation shall inure to the benefit of its directors, trustees, officers, private shareholders or members, or to any individual.

(f) On the winding up and dissolution of this corporation, after paying or adequately providing for the debts and obligations of the corporation, the remaining assets of this corporation shall be distributed to an organization (or organizations) organized and operated exclusively for charitable purposes and that is tax exempt under Section 501(c)(3) of the Internal Revenue Code of 1986.

(g) The period of duration of corporate existence of this corporation shall be perpetual.

(h) There shall be no personal liability of members for corporation obligations.

(i) This corporation shall have no capital stock and shall declare no dividends.

ARTICLE II

MEMBERS

Section 2.01. Classes. There shall be two classes of members: Corporate and Individual.

Section 2.02. Qualifications. Membership may be granted to any individual or corporation that supports the mission and purposes of the organization, and who pays the annual dues as set by the Board of Directors. Members shall have no voting rights.

Section 2.03. Termination of Membership. The Board of Directors, by affirmative vote of twothirds of all of the members of the Board, may suspend or expel a member, and may, by a majority vote or those present at any regularly constituted meeting, terminate the membership of any member who becomes ineligible for membership, or suspend or expel any member who shall be in default in the payment of dues.

Section 2.04. Resignation. Any member may resign by filing a written resignation with the Secretary; however, such resignation shall not relieve the member so resigning of the obligation to pay any dues or other charges theretofore accrued and unpaid.

Section 2.05. Dues. The Board of Directors shall establish dues for members.

Section 2.06. Meetings. The annual membership meeting shall be held in MONTH each year. A minimum of 10% of the members present in person or by proxy shall constitute a quorum for transaction of business at a membership meeting. Meetings may be called by the Chairperson or at the request of at least 10% of the members by notice mailed, telephone, or telegraphed to each member not less than thirty (30) days before such meeting.

(continued)

BOX 3.2 SAMPLE OF NONPROFIT BYLAWS *(continued)*

ARTICLE III

AUTHORITY AND DUTIES OF DIRECTORS

Section 3.01. Authority of Directors. The Board of Directors is the policy-making body and may exercise all the powers and authority granted to the Corporation by law.

Section 3.02. Number, Selection, and Tenure. The Board shall consist of not less than three (3) directors. Each director shall hold office for a term of three (3) years. Vacancies existing by reason of resignation, death, incapacity, or removal before the expiration of his/her term shall be filled by a majority vote of the remaining directors. In the event of a tie vote, the President shall choose the succeeding director. Directors will elect their successors. A director elected to fill a vacancy shall be elected for the unexpired term of that director's predecessor in office.

Section 3.03. Resignation. Resignations are effective on receipt by the Secretary of the Corporation of written notification.

Section 3.04. Regular Meetings. The Board of Directors shall hold at least two (2) regular meetings per calendar year. Meetings shall be at such dates, times, and places as the Board shall determine.

Section 3.05. Special Meetings. Meetings shall be at such dates, times and places, as the Board shall determine.

Section 3.06. Notice. Meetings may be called by the Chairperson or at the request of any two (2) directors by notice e-mailed, mailed, telephoned, or telegraphed to each member of the Board not less than forty-eight (48) hours before such meeting.

Section 3.07. Quorum. A quorum shall consist of a majority of the Board attending in person or through teleconferencing. All decisions will be by majority vote of those present at a meeting at which a quorum is present. If less than a majority of the directors is present at said meeting, a majority of the directors present may adjourn the meeting on occasion without further notice.

Section 3.08. Action Without a Meeting. Any action required or permitted to be taken at a meeting of the Board of Directors (including amendment of these bylaws) or of any committee may be taken without a meeting if all the members of the Board or committee consent in writing to taking the action without a meeting and to approving the specific action. Such consents shall have the same force and effect as a unanimous vote of the Board or of the committee, as the case may be.

Section 3.09. Participation in Meeting by Conference Telephone. Members of the Board may participate in a meeting through use of conference telephone or similar communications equipment, so long as members participating in such meeting can hear one another.

Section 3.10. Committees. The Board of Directors may, by resolution adopted by a majority of the Directors in office, establish committees of the Board composed of at least two (2) persons, which, except for an Executive Committee, may include non-Board members. The Board may make such provisions for appointment of the chair of such committees, establish such procedures to govern their activities, and delegate thereto such authority as

(continued)

BOX 3.2 SAMPLE OF NONPROFIT BYLAWS *(continued)*

may be necessary or desirable for the efficient management of the property, affairs, business, activities of the Corporation.

Section 3.11. Nominating Committee. There shall be a Nominating Committee, composed of the President and at least two (2) other members of the Board of Directors. Each member of the committee shall have one (1) vote, and decision shall be made by the majority.

Section 3.12. Reimbursement. Directors shall serve without compensation with the exception that expenses incurred in the furtherance of the Corporation's business are allowed to be reimbursed with documentation and prior approval. In addition, Directors serving the organization in any other capacity, such as employees, are allowed to receive compensation therefore.

ARTICLE IV

AUTHORITY AND DUTIES OF OFFICERS

Section 4.01. Officers. The officers of the Corporation shall be a President, a Vice-President, a Secretary/Treasurer, and such other officers as the Board of Directors may designate. Any two (2) or more offices may be held by the same person, except the offices of President and Secretary/Treasurer.

Section 4.02. Appointment of Officers; Terms of Office. The officers of the Corporation shall be elected by the Board of Directors at regular meetings of the Board, or, in the case of vacancies, as soon thereafter as convenient. New offices may be created and filled at any meeting of the Board of Directors.

Terms of office may be established by the Board of Directors, but shall not exceed three (3) years. Officers shall hold office until a successor is duly elected and qualified. Officers shall be eligible for reappointment.

Section 4.03. Resignation. Resignations are effective on receipt by the Secretary of the Board of a written notification.

Section 4.04. Removal. An officer may be removed by the Board of Directors at a meeting, or by action in writing pursuant to Section 3.08, whenever in the Board's judgment the best interests of the Corporation will be served thereby. Any such removal shall be without prejudice to the contract rights, if any, of the person so removed.

Section 4.05. President. The President shall be a director of the Corporation and will preside at all meetings of the Board of Directors. The President shall perform all duties attendant to that office, subject, however, to the control of the Board of Directors, and shall perform such other duties as on occasion shall be assigned by the Board of Directors. The President is responsible for ensuring that the Board of Directors and its members:

- are aware of and fulfill their governance responsibilities
- comply with applicable laws and bylaws
- conduct board business effectively and efficiently
- are accountable for their performance

(continued)

BOX 3.2 SAMPLE OF NONPROFIT BYLAWS *(continued)*

In order to fulfill these responsibilities, and subject to the organization's bylaws, the President presides over meetings, proposes policies and practices, sits on various committees, monitors the performance of Directors and Officers, submits various reports to the board, to funders, and to other "stakeholders"; proposes the creation of committees; appoints members to such committees; and performs other duties as the need arises and/or as defined in the bylaws.

The President is accountable to the Board of Directors or Members as specified in the bylaws.

The President may delegate specific duties to the Executive Director, Board members, and/or committees as appropriate; however, the accountability for them remains with the President.

Section 4.06. Vice President. The Vice President shall be a director of the Corporation and will preside at meetings of the Board of Directors in the absence of or request of the President. The Vice President shall perform other duties as requested and assigned by the President, subject to the control of the Board of Directors.

Section 4.07. Secretary and Assistant Secretary. The Secretary shall be a director of the Corporation and shall keep the minutes of all meetings of the Board of Directors in the books proper for that purpose. The Secretary shall also report to the Board of Directors at each regular meeting on the status of the Council's finances. The Secretary shall work closely with any paid executive staff of the Corporation to ascertain that appropriate procedures are being followed in the financial affairs of the Corporation, and shall perform such other duties as occasionally may be assigned by the Board of Directors. The Assistant Secretary assists the secretary in any assignment related to such a position.

Section 4.08. Treasurer/Vice Treasurer. The Treasurer shall make a report at each board meeting. The Treasurer shall chair the finance committee, assist in the preparation of the budget, help develop fund-raising plans, and make financial information available to Board members and the public.

Section 4.09. Paid Staff. The Board of Directors may hire such paid staff as they deem proper and necessary for the operations of the Corporation. The powers and duties of the paid staff shall be as assigned or as delegated to be assigned by the Board.

ARTICLE V

INDEMNIFICATION

Every member of the Board of Directors, officer, or employee of the Corporation may be indemnified by the corporation against all expenses and liabilities, including counsel fees, reasonably incurred or imposed on such members of the Board, officer, or employee in connection with any threatened, pending, or completed action, suit, or proceeding to which she/he may become involved by reason of her/his being or having been a member of the Board, officer, or employee of the corporation, or any settlement thereof, unless adjudged therein to be liable for negligence or misconduct in the performance of her/his duties. Provided, however, that in the event of a settlement the indemnification herein shall apply only when the Board approves such settlement and reimbursement as being in the best interest of the corporation. The foregoing right of indemnification shall be in addition and not exclusive of all other rights, which such member of the Board, officer, or employee is entitled.

(continued)

BOX 3.2 SAMPLE OF NONPROFIT BYLAWS *(continued)*

ARTICLE VI

ADVISORY BOARDS AND COMMITTEES

Section 6.01. Establishment. The Board of Directors may establish one or more Advisory Boards or Committees.

Section 6.02. Size, Duration, and Responsibilities. The size, duration, and responsibilities of such boards and committees shall be established by a majority vote of the Board of Directors.

ARTICLE VII

FINANCIAL ADMINISTRATION

Section 7.01. Fiscal Year. The fiscal year of the Corporation shall be January 1– December 31 but may be changed by resolution of the Board of Directors.

Section 7.02. Checks, Drafts, Etc. All checks, orders for the payment of money, bills of lading, warehouse receipts, obligations, bills of exchange, and insurance certificates shall be signed or endorsed by such officer or officers or agent or agents of the Corporation and in such manner as shall from time to time be determined by resolution of the Board of Directors or of any committee to which such authority has been delegated by the Board.

Section 7.03. Deposits and Accounts. All funds of the Corporation, not otherwise employed, shall be deposited from time to time in general or special accounts in such banks, trust companies, or other depositories as the Board of Directors or any committee to which such authority has been delegated by the Board may select, or as may be selected by the President or by any other officer or officers or agent or agents of the Corporation, to whom such power may from time to time be delegated by the Board. For the purpose of deposit and for the purpose of collection for that account of the Corporation, checks, drafts, and other orders of the Corporation may be endorsed, assigned, and delivered on behalf of the Corporation by any officer or agent of the Corporation.

Section 7.04. Investments. The funds of the Corporation may be retained in whole or in part in cash or be invested and reinvested on occasion in such property, real, personal, or otherwise, or stock, bonds, or other securities, as the Board of Directors in its sole discretion may deem desirable, without regard to the limitations, if any, now imposed or which may hereafter be imposed by law regarding such investments, and which are permitted to organizations exempt from Federal income taxation under Section 501(c)(3) of the Internal Revenue Code.

ARTICLE VIII

BOOKS AND RECORDS

Correct books of account of the activities and transactions of the Corporation shall be kept at the office of the Corporation. These shall include a minute book, which shall contain a copy of the Certificate of Incorporation, a copy of these bylaws, and all minutes of meetings of the Board of Directors.

(continued)

> **BOX 3.2 SAMPLE OF NONPROFIT BYLAWS** *(continued)*
>
> ## ARTICLE IX
>
> ## AMENDMENT OF BYLAWS
>
> These bylaws may be amended by a majority vote of the Board of Directors, provided prior notice is given of the proposed amendment in the notice of the meeting at which such action is taken, or provided all members of the Board waive such notice, or by unanimous consent in writing without a meeting pursuant to Section 3.08.
>
> These bylaws were adopted and approved at a meeting by the board of directors on April 9, 2012.

PRINCIPLES OF NONPROFIT GOVERNANCE

Nonprofit governance is linked with several basic principles that are inherent to the nature and purpose of nonprofit organizations:

- *Independence and commitment:* Nonprofit organizations must have a committed board of directors that is independent in thinking and decision making.
- *Fairness and equity for stakeholders:* Boards of directors must ensure that all stakeholders are treated in a fair and equitable manner.
- *Accountability to the public*: Nonprofit organizations are publicly supported entities. Therefore, they are accountable to both internal (members, beneficiaries, employees, volunteers) and external stakeholders (donors, local communities, suppliers, creditors, policy makers, regulating agencies).
- *Transparency*: Nonprofit organizations must disclose information about the roles of stakeholders in their operations, the outcomes related to such operations, and the financial statements that clarify the use of financial resources received from the public (e.g., donations, grants, endowments, etc).
- *Ethical conduct*: Board members of nonprofit organizations should be community members and citizens of high ethical standards. Further, a nonprofit organization must develop and enforce a code of ethical conduct, especially with respect to financial management, service delivery, and all operations and activities performed by board members, managers, staff, or volunteers.

GOVERNANCE AND BOARD OF DIRECTORS

Governance is more about the structures and process of decision making than the decision itself. Successful organizations maintain a governance system that enables them to make informed decisions when addressing their most complex problems or issues. A sustainable governance system is more likely to foster a sustainable organization. The role of the board of directors is to ensure that a nonprofit organization is run, managed, and properly led with the ultimate aim to protect the interests of its constituencies. In other words, the board has a responsibility to hold managers and leaders accountable for their actions and their performance. The metrics for such an endeavor reside in the existence of vision and mission statements that set the purpose of a particular nonprofit organization. The vision and mission must be translated into action plans, policies, programs, projects, and services that are carried out by management and staff. Legal obligations of the board of directors (Box 3.3) include, but are not limited to:

1. **Fiduciary duty:** Board members of nonprofit organizations have a fiduciary duty to be trustworthy by acting in the best interests of their constituencies.
2. **Duty of loyalty and fair dealing:** The duty of loyalty and fair dealing requires that a board member put organizational interests ahead of his/her own personal interests. In other words, board members should not use their position to gain personal advantages or make personal profits.
3. **Duty of care:** Board members are expected to carry out the business of a nonprofit organization with the reasonable care of any prudent individual.
4. **Duty of supervision and accountability:** Directors should exercise their oversight responsibilities with a high level of effectiveness. Effective oversight starts with the adoption of policies of ethics and accountability that set standards of behaviors for board members, the executive director, and managers. Ethics and accountability policies should also include standards for disclosure, financial reporting and internal control. Further, the duty of supervision and accountability empowers the board of directors to

- Develop and approve strategic plans, including vision, mission, organizational mandates, goals and objectives, and core strategic areas
- Establish, review, and approve organizational budgets
- Approve major or significant financial transactions
- Review auditing and accounting policies and practices
- Establish benchmarks to measure organizational performance
- Set executive compensations
- Contribute to fund-raising, advocacy, and collaborations or partnerships for organizational growth and financial sustainability

---

BOX 3.3 SAMPLE OF BOARD ROLES AND RESPONSIBILITIES FORM

ROLES AND RESPONSIBILITIES

JOB DESCRIPTION: BOARD MEMBER

Position: Board member   **Supervisor:** Board of Directors

Last Name:_____ First Name:_____

Address:_____

Street number   Street Name   Apt./suite   City State   Zip Code

Tel: Home (   ) _____ - _____ Cell (   ) _____ - _____

E-mail:_____

Together, with other members of the Hope and Dream, Inc. Board of Directors, you are legally, financially, and ethically accountable for all activities of this organization. You are in a position of public trust and are a trustee of the organization. While serving on this board, it is assumed and expected that you will:

(continued)

BOX 3.3 SAMPLE OF BOARD ROLES AND RESPONSIBILITIES FORM *(continued)*

- Know and support the organization's vision, mission, core values, guiding principles, position statements, policies, goals, and programs.
- Routinely promote all of the above to your family, friends, community contacts, and professional associates.
- Treat the affairs of HOPE AND DREAM as you would your own.
- Act in ways that will not likely be perceived as a conflict of interest with the organization or as self-serving.
- Keep confidential information confidential; sign an annual pledge.
- Expand knowledge about this organization, childhood and family empowerment, and board responsibilities through orientation, "hands-on" participation, and ongoing education.
- Offer your talents, personal and financial resources, and/or expertise regularly and generously to benefit the organization.
- Have a personal and dedicated commitment to promote a better environment for children and families.
- You are expected to contribute significantly to the well-being of the organization.
- Specific expectations are that you will:

  - Attend board meetings regularly (at least four of the six full board meetings per year).
  - Attend HOPE AND DREAM annual Conference in February, and attend as many other educational events as possible.
  - Be able to contribute an average of 15 hours per month.
  - Read and understand the minutes and financial reports of and for the board meeting, as well as other information provided to you.
  - Actively serve on at least one committee, attending meetings regularly, reading minutes and reports, and actively participating in activities of the committee.
  - Hold a personally paid annual membership of three hundred dollars ($300) or more in the organization.
  - Participate directly and actively in all fund-raising efforts, personally or financially.
  - Provide and promote public relations for the organization in your community and with personal and business contacts (arrange at least one Speakers Bureau presentation).
  - Be responsible for getting five new donors or members each year (individual or organizational).
  - Share board and donor prospects and make personal visits with staff or another board member.

In addition, the HOPE AND DREAM Board of Directors' organizational responsibilities include:

GOVERNANCE AND EXECUTIVE DIRECTOR SELECTION/EVALUATION

1. **Board membership:** recruitment, orientation, education, and development of board leadership.
2. **Selection and evaluation of chief executive officer (CEO)** who, in turn, becomes the organization's manager. The chief executive makes day-to-day and standard management and marketing decisions without interference. Individual board members will support the CEO with consulting skills when asked or deemed necessary.
3. Assure that the organization meets the needs of stakeholders and customers.

(continued)

BOX 3.3 SAMPLE OF BOARD ROLES AND RESPONSIBILITIES FORM *(continued)*

Finance

1. Identify and obtain the financial resources necessary to support the mission in the short and long term.
2. Ensure financial accountability, including an annual audit by a reputable certified public accountant.
3. Play an active role in marketing services, lobbying, fund-raising, and other revenue generation. Individual board members represent one of three sectors: civic, corporate, or professional in fields related to child, family, and community services. They will support the nonprofit with their personal resources and involvement. Corporate board members will bring additional financial support (value of $1,500 or more from their employers). Civic board members will actively work to develop partnerships and collaborations with their communities.

Professional board members will work to increase direct utilization of the organization's programs and services.

4. Provide ongoing public relations to increase funding and general support opportunities. (Board members are always emissaries of the organization in the community.)

Planning

1. Set and review mission, philosophy, and strategic and/or long-term goals.
2. Create a written plan for the long-term future of the organization.

Organizational Operations

1. Assure appropriate and adequate administrative and support systems are in place.
2. Assure board operations are appropriate and adequate.
3. Assure organizational structure is appropriate and adequate.
4. Assure that board members and organization meet all applicable legal requirements.
5. Set policies for the chief executive to implement and achieve.
6. Assure that the organization has the critical capabilities needed to achieve its goals and objectives.

ACKNOWLEDGMENT

My signature indicates that I have read and understood my responsibilities as member of HOPE AND DREAM board of directors and I will do my best to contribute to the mission and vision of the organization.

_____   _____

Print Name   Signature/Date

SEEN AND APPROVED BY:

_____

President /Date

WHY ARE BOARDS IMPORTANT?

Although we recognize that the board has a key responsibility in the governance of a nonprofit organization, some people question whether the board should play a consequential role in what a nonprofit organization is doing. During the first few years of the existence of a nonprofit organization, the role of the board is perceived more favorably. However, in many well-established nonprofit organizations, some people in management tend to perceive a board as more of a liability than an asset. At least, some people believe that the board should be involved only when requested by management to support a decision or an activity. On the other hand, other people believe that board members should be involved in daily activities of a nonprofit organization and perform tasks that fit better with the responsibilities of staff. If the board is expected to take on responsibilities that should be handled by staff, the board will never be effective in the organization. Briefly, the role of the board should not be underestimated or overestimated.

NONPROFIT GOVERNANCE: AN ECLECTIC PERSPECTIVE

Governance models or approaches are considered in an eclectic perspective that combines empirical observations and literature related to nonprofit and for-profit organizations as micro societies. There are no significant differences between nonprofit and for-profit governance, except for their nonmonetary (nonprofit) and monetary (for-profit) bottom lines. Nonprofit organizations are legal corporations. As corporations, they are business entities, except that they do not aim to maximize profit for shareholders (which they do not have), but to provide the highest quality and the greatest number of units of services possible. Further, as nonprofit entities, nonprofit organizations are not only part of the overall social organization in a society, but also are micro social structures. Therefore, an eclectic view of nonprofit governance is justifiable. Consequently, such eclectic perspective borrows concepts from sociology, and considers nonprofit board governance through functionalism, structuralism, structuro-functionalism, and symbolic perspectives. This eclectic perspective is not normative, but simply descriptive.

Functionalist Perspective

Functionalism focuses primarily on the influence of roles and functions of individuals in organizations and societies. The functionalism perspective envisions a controlling board in the light of the functionalist theory. In a functionalist perspective, board members are very protective of their specific roles and responsibilities. They want to control every inch of power that they possess and do not accept that others will step into their territory without their approval. It is good for accountability in a nonprofit organization. However, at times, this can paralyze the ability of an organization to make strategic decisions in a manner that is as quick as necessary.

Structuralist Perspective

Structuralism emphasizes the role of structures in organizations and societies. The structuralist perspective is concerned with a collaborative and empowering board. From a structuralist perspective, a board may focus a lot on procedures rather than purpose, which sometimes may hinder the ability to make outside-of-the-box decisions. A board operating from a structuralist perspective has the potential to become obsessed with rules, regulations, formality, and procedures, which may not be the smartest strategy at all times.

Structuro-Functionalist Perspective

Structuro-functionalism combines aspects of functionalism and structuralism. The structuro-functionalist perspective operates in light of resource development theory, social network theory, which is a comprehensive approach that balances the function of the board as a servant for the organization. A board operating on a structuro-functionalist perspective is aware of the individual roles and responsibilities of the directors, but uses such functions as a way to help the system function properly. A structuro-functionalist board has the potential to maintain the right balance, if board members keep their eyes on the purpose of the organization.

Symbolic Perspective

The symbolic perspective refers to symbol as a mere gesture that is not meaningful beyond the gesture itself. The board plays a symbolic role. It is advisory in nature. The board is selected by the chief executive officer or in some cases the funder, and exists to approve the decisions of the funder. A symbolic board tends to exist to satisfy a legal, social, or community requirement, but does not really play a vital role in the governance of the organization.

GOVERNANCE STRUCTURES

Nonprofit organizations adopt various models of governance, depending on its size and the overall cultural, political, and economic contexts. Every nonprofit organization is unique and deals with unique circumstances. Therefore, it is not surprising that models of governance vary.

Traditional Board: The traditional model of governance in nonprofit organizations involves a board that oversees programs, projects, and services through various committees. Most nonprofit organizations will have committees on finance and on specific projects or programs. Each nonprofit board determines how many committees are necessary and what types of committees to institute. Sometimes, new nonprofit organizations try to adopt the governance model of a well-established nonprofit organization, and feel very disappointed at the end, because such models may not fit their purposes.

Micromanagement Board: The micromanagement board oversees all the activities of the organization and performs tasks that should be handled by management or staff. A micromanagement board can be very detrimental to the growth of a nonprofit organization. Management and staff can become very frustrated because they lose the ability to make even the smallest decisions.

Cooperative Board: The cooperative board works in collaboration with management and staff. The board makes decisions that are consequential for the future of the organization and provides flexibility for management to make technical decisions for which the board may not have the time or expertise.

Delegational Board: As the name indicates, the delegational board assumes its oversight responsibilities by delegating specific tasks to special committees. The committees are formed based on various strategic or programmatic areas of the organization. The board delegates management responsibilities and decisions to the executive directors between two board meetings. In other words, any decision that must be made immediately is carried out by the executive director. There may be times when the executive director has to make a decision pending board approval or refrain from making a decision until board approval.

Representational Board: The representational board uses a bottom-up approach to balance the decisions of a nonprofit organization with inputs received from various constituents. The representational board tends to lengthen its decision-making process by providing its constituents an opportunity to voice their approval or their concerns before a final deliberation.

Outcomes-Oriented Board: The outcomes-oriented board focuses primarily on the performance and results produced by management and staff with respect to strategic and programmatic goals and objectives. The outcomes-oriented board allows flexibility for the executive director and management to make policy decisions, but holds them accountable through audit and outcome-based assessments. The outcomes-oriented board tends to maintain governance through various project-based or problem-based committees.

Strategic Board: The strategic board focuses primarily on making strategic policy decisions. Examples of strategic decisions include organizational vision and mission statements, mandates, budgets, priorities, and policies that define the extent and limitations of the relationship between the board and the executive director.

Advisory Board: An advisory board is usually selected by the executive director. In most cases, an advisory board is selected to provide legitimacy to the decisions made by the executive director. In that context, the power of governance resides in the executive director, not in the board, which plays a superficial role in the operations of the organization.

GOVERNANCE IN NONPROFIT ORGANIZATIONS AND THE "FUNDER SYNDROME"

The term "funder syndrome" expresses the tendency of funding members of a nonprofit organization to treat it as a privately owned enterprise. Members who have the funder syndrome justify their attitude by the fact that they have invested their time, money, and effort to start the nonprofit entity, and thus are entitled to special rights and privileges. The funder syndrome can affect any nonprofit organization whose major funders are still serving on the board or in an executive capacity. The funder syndrome can hinder proper governance in a nonprofit organization. This is because the funder may have a case to make regarding all the troubles that he/she has overcome, or all the pains that she/he has endured before the organization reached an actual position of success. While the other board members have to acknowledge the roles and contributions of funders, they should also put more emphasis on the vision and mission of the organization. For example, an organization might adopt a policy that makes it mandatory to screen every decision in a grid that justifies in writing how the decision will further the vision or the mission of the organization. This may seem obvious, but in the heat of the moment organizations do not always think about specific links with the vision when they make strategic decisions. Keeping constant focus on vision and mission can be an effective strategy to neutralize the funder syndrome.

NONPROFIT BOARD POLICIES

Nonprofit board policies are developed to advance the vision and mission of an organization, make systematic decisions, and guide the activities and behaviors of board members, executives, managers, staff, and volunteers. The Internal Revenue Service indicates some key board policies that a nonprofit organization should maintain (Box 3.4).

THE COMMITTEES

In a nonprofit organization that is made of board members, committees are smaller units with special assignments, as determined by the bylaws and the board. The committee helps the board or the organization stay focused on specific goals, projects, or objectives. A nonprofit organization can include standing and ad hoc committees (Box 3.5). Standing committees are statutory, thus they exist as part of the bylaws adopted by an organization. On the other hand, a board can form ad hoc committees to work on special short-term assignments.

GOVERNANCE AND FINANCIAL SUSTAINABILITY

Effective governance is indispensable for an organization to maintain the financial resources necessary to continue to provide services over time. Board members have responsibilities to perform community outreach to ensure that external stakeholders buy into the vision

BOX 3.4 IRS ITEMS FOR BASIC GOVERNANCE PRACTICES FROM FORM 990	
Item	**Source**
Minutes of all board and committee meetings	Part VI, Section A, line 8
Copy of completed Form 990	Part VI, Section B, line 11
Conflict-of-interest policy	Part VI, Section B, Line 12
Written whistleblower policy	Part VI, Section B, line 13
Written document retention/destruction policy	Part VI, Section B, line 14
Compensation and benefits policy	Part VI, Section B, line 15
Gift acceptance policy	
Partnership and joint venture policy	Part VI, Section B, line 16

Source: Internal Revenue Service (2014).

BOX 3.5 EXAMPLES OF STANDING AND ADHOC COMMITTEES IN NONPROFIT ORGANIZATIONS

Standing Committees

Committee	Description
Executive	Includes the officers of the organization. In some cases, it may also encompass the committee chairs or board members at large. The executive committee acts on behalf of the board between meetings and in case of organizational emergencies that cannot wait for a board meeting. Independent actions of the executive committees are usually reviewed and ratified by the board.
Finance	This committee reviews budget proposals and is responsible for planning, monitoring, and overseeing the organization's use of its financial resources. The finance committee develops financial policies, and recommends them to be approved by the board. This committee also oversees long-term investment, in the absence of an investment committee. In many cases, this committee oversees and reviews the organization's independent audit or financial review. However, some organizations have a separate audit committee.
Membership and board development	This committee is responsible for the general affairs of the board. The specific roles vary from one organization to the other. Overall, this committee develops guidelines for board composition and committees, meets and recommends new board members to the board, and conducts the orientation of new board members.
Fund-raising	The fund-raising committee is responsible for working with managers and the board to develop fund-raising proposals and organize fund-raising events, as well as the submission of grant proposals and the solicitation of major gifts.
Program	The program committee contributes to the development of needs assessment reports, and strategic and implementation plans. This committee helps develop systems for quality service delivery. In the absence of a public or community relations committee, the program committee may be involved in developing relationships with community leaders and other interest groups.

Ad Hoc Committees

Committee	Description
Compensation committee	Determines and reviews the compensation of the CEO and other senior executives to ensure not only fairness, but also competitiveness with other organizations of similar size. Ensures that compensation is tied to the achievement of predetermined performance goals.
Search committee	Created with the mission to recommend guidelines and a search process to hire a new executive. Depending on the organization and the mission, a search committee may select candidates to be recommended to the board.
Special Event	Created to coordinate a particular event, such as an annual dinner.

and mission of a nonprofit organization, and turn such outreach into monetary and non-monetary contributions.

Board members have the final word in approving the strategic plan and budget of a nonprofit organization. They must work with organizational executives, managers, and staff to ensure that anticipated programs, projects, and plans are cost-effective. Board members may not have the appropriate expertise, but should educate themselves enough to assume their oversight responsibility over planning and budgeting.

Board members should ensure that (a) financial plans are consistent with strategic and implementation plans, (b) financial resources exist to implement the strategic plan, (c) financial risks and risk-management strategies are carefully planned, (d) appropriate revenue-generating activities are included in the plan in order to balance the organizational budget, and (e) the organization plans for sufficient reserves that can continue to provide services in case of financial hardship of loss of a major funder.

Effective governance is a key to good stewardship and organizational accountability. Board members have the ultimate fiduciary responsibility for the financial viability of a nonprofit organization. The board is responsible not only to help generate revenues, but also to protect organizational assets and ensure that appropriate internal control procedures are in place. This requires board members to acquire a basic understanding of financial and accounting language. They should be able to read financial statements and audit reports, which will enable them to notice red flags and distinguish minor issues from other problems that have the potential to lead to a major financial crisis for the organization.

QUESTIONS AND ACTIVITIES

1. How would you define governance in your own words? How would you differentiate governance from government?
2. How is governance related to the financial sustainability of a nonprofit organization?
3. You are hired as a consultant to develop a governance policy for a newly formed nonprofit organization. What are the key items that you would include in such a policy? Why?
4. What is your preferred theoretical perspective on governance? Why?
5. What would be your approach to address an issue of funder syndrome in a nonprofit organization?
6. You are a member of a board of a nonprofit organization. The executive director insists that the board vote on a proposition to develop a partnership with a partner who has promised a large donation. What questions will you ask before making the decision?
7. How do you think a board member can concretely increase an organization's financial capacity and sustainability?
8. Search the directory of nonprofit organizations in your state or your country. Select an organization of your choice. What is the size of the board of directors? Is there a board policy available on their website? What can you learn about governance in that organization based on the board policy, if any?
9. What do you think may contribute to an effective board? An ineffective board?
10. What factors do you think can affect changes in the governance structures of a nonprofit organization?
11. What are the issues that board members should consider when going through change?
12. What do you think a nonprofit organization should consider when recruiting new board members?

13. What does the term "funder syndrome" refer to in a nonprofit organization? How do you think funder syndrome can best be managed?

14. Imagine you are invited to serve on the board of a nonprofit organization working on issues of great interest to you. Before you agree to become a board member, (a) draft a list of questions that you would like the board to answer, (b) what are some examples of documents that you will request from them to inform your decision? (c) what other criteria will you use to make your final decision?

15. Search the Internet, and identify a nonprofit organization in your area. Ask its board for permission to attend a board meeting as an observer. Take note of everything that happens during the meeting. Ask whether you can have copy of documents distributed during that meeting. Write a detailed account of what you observed. Conclude your observations with some personal thoughts regarding (a) the effectiveness of the board and (b) the governance approach in that organization.

REFERENCES

ASX Corporate Governance Council. (2003). *ASX principles of good corporate governance and best practices recommendations.* Sydney, Australia: Author.

Davis, J., Schoorman, F. S., & Donaldson, L. (1997). The distinctiveness of agency theory and stewardship theory. *Academy of Management Review, 22*(3), 611–613.

Donaldson, T., & Preston, L. E. (1995). The stakeholder theory of the corporation: Concepts, evidence, and implications. *Academy of Management Review, 20*(1), 65–91.

Eisenhardt, K. (1989). Agency theory: An assessment and review. *Academy of Management Review, 14,* 57–74.

Hendry, J. (2002). The principal's other problems: Honest incompetence and the specification of objectives. *Academy of Management Review, 27*(1), 98–113.

Hillman, A. J., Cannella, A. A., & Paetzold, R. L. (2000). The resource dependence role of corporate directors: Strategic adaptation of board composition in response to environmental change. *Journal of Management Studies, 37,* 235–254.

Hillman, A. J., & Dalziel, T. (2003). Boards of directors and firm performance: Integrating agency and resource dependence perspectives. *Academy of Management Review, 28,* 383–396.

Internal Revenue Service. (2014). *Return of organization exempt from income tax.* Retrieved from: http://www.irs.gov/pub/irs-pdf/f990.pdf

Johnson, J., Daily, C., & Ellstrand, A. (1996). Boards of directors: A review and research agenda. *Journal of Management, 22,* 409–438.

Jones, T. M., Freeman, R. E., & Wicks, A.C. (2002). Stakeholder theory: The state of the art. In N. E. Bowie (Ed.), *The Blackwell guide to business ethics* (pp. 19–37). Oxford, UK: Blackwell.

Organization for Economic Co-Operation and Development (OCED). 2004. *OECD principles of corporate governance.* Paris, France: Author.

Shen, W. (2003). The dynamics of the CEO-board relationship. *Academy of Management Journal, 42,* 7–24.

Sifuna, A. P. (2012). Disclose or abstain: The prohibition of iTrading on trial. *Journal of International Banking Law and Regulation, 27*(9), 340–353.

Sobel, P. J. (2007). *Auditor's risk management guide: Integrating auditing and ERM.* Chicago, IL: CCH.

Stone, M. M., & Ostrower, F. (2007). Acting in the public interest? Another look at research on nonprofit governance. *Nonprofit and Voluntary Sector Quarterly, 36*(3), 416–438.

Sundaramurthy, C., & Lewis, M. (2003). Control and collaboration: Paradoxes of governance. *Academy of Management Review, 28,* 397–415.

Needs Assessment and Financial Sustainability

At the completion of the chapter the reader will be able to:

1. Explain the concept of needs assessment.
2. Explain the relationship between the individual and the community.
3. Identify the different steps involved in conducting a needs assessment.
4. Explain how needs assessment can contribute to the financial sustainability of a nonprofit organization.

This chapter emphasizes how financial sustainability is rooted in the investigation and analysis of the needs of a target community. The chapter discusses theories about the needs-assessment process, as well as action steps toward the development of a community needs-assessment report. The chapter explores facets of financial needs-assessment of a nonprofit that can help chart a course to further the vision and mission statements. The reader will learn how to use primary and secondary data to conduct a targeted needs assessment that is linked to the financial sustainability of a nonprofit organization.

WHAT IS A COMMUNITY?

There is a variety of definitions of the concept "community." According to Barker (1999), a community is "a group of individuals or families that share certain values, services, institutions, interests, or geographic proximity" (p. 89). Homan (2004) viewed the notion of community as "a number of people who share a distinct location, belief, interest, activity, or other characteristic that clearly identifies their commonality and differentiates them from those not sharing it" (p. 149). Community or at least a sense of community exists wherever there is a sense of common interest that binds a group together to defend a cause or to work toward the achievement of a common goal.

A community is a group of people having a common history, ethnicity, culture, geography, or interests. There can be a physical community, which is a group of people living within geographical boundaries ruled under a common political, economic, and social system. For example, a group of individuals living in the same neighborhood constitutes a community. They share a common geographic area and share common needs for services, such as roads and safety. Similarly, the population of an entire city, county, state, or country forms a community sharing a common geographic space. Whether they like it or not, they have common interests that are inherent to such a geographic area. For example, the residents of Madison, Wisconsin, constitute a community. They may not necessary share a common neighborhood, but they are all residents of the same city. A regulation or legislation that positively or negatively affects residents of that city will be of interest to all of them. This example is applicable to any city, county, or state in the United States. Physical communities are determined either legally or conventionally by geographical boundaries, which include a group of individuals who feel attached to a particular physical place or location. For example, people who have been living for a long time in a particular neighborhood may feel strongly attached to it, and they may become familiar with one another, which would be different for people who live outside their physical territory. Members of a physical community may share strong memories, past experiences, values, and cultural practices to which they may feel strongly attached.

Unlike physical communities, communities of interests are defined by either a major issue of interest or a major goal or vision, regardless of the physical location of the people concerned by such an interest, goal, or vision. Like members of a physical community, people who form a community of interests tend to share some common values, identities, past experiences, or cultural practices to which they are strongly attached. A community of interests may encompass individuals sharing a common vision, goal, or interest. For example, teachers or members of a union organization, or parents of children with a disability, or veterans of the U.S. military, or female victims of domestic violence in each case constitute a community. These people may have different religious beliefs, be from different ethnic groups, and have a different sexual orientation, but they have a particular common interest on an issue that links them as a community, regardless of their geographic location.

INDIVIDUAL AND COMMUNITY

A community is made of individuals who develop communications and other forms of interactions, especially through affections and activities. As Brueggemann (2002) said, "communities are natural human associations based on ties of relationship and shared experiences in which we mutually provide meaning in our lives, meet needs, and accomplish interpersonal goals" (p. 114). As Figure 4.1 indicates, the individual makes the community. The community creates organizations to better the lives of individual members. In other words, the community provides a system of support for the individual. Organization enhances this system of support.

WHAT IS A NEED?

From an individual point of view, needs are physiological, psychological, or sociological deficiencies that someone may be experiencing. One of the most common theories of needs is Maslow's hierarchy model, which explains human needs in terms of the following:

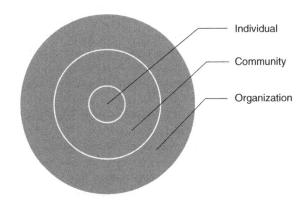

FIGURE 4.1 Individual, community, and organization.

- *Physiological*: food, water, sex, sleep, excretion, and breathing
- *Safety and security*: shelter, health, and employment
- *Belongingness, social needs, and love*: family, friendship, and love
- *Esteem*: achievement, self-esteem, and respect by others
- *Self-actualization*: creativity, spontaneity, and so forth

According to McKillip (1998), needs are judgments of values based on unsatisfied expectancies of a target group. These expectancies may be normative, felt, expressed, or comparative. Reviere, Berkowitz, Carter, and Gergusan (1996) define a need as "a gap between the real and ideal conditions that is both acknowledged by community values and potentially amenable to change" (p. 5). This definition is not different from Kaufman's (1992), who understood a need as a discrepancy between an actual and a desired situation or result. Similarly, Watkins, Leigh, and Kaufman (1998) defined a need as a gap between a current situation and a desired state of affairs.

The above definitions agree that a need is a gap, a gap between an observed situation and an expected situation. In this sense, a gap is a construct based on implicit or explicit norms about an ideal or at least an acceptable state of affairs. A need can be about one or more individuals, groups, communities, or societies. Usually, a need is identified in comparison with factors, such as natural laws, human rights, laws, resolutions, mandates, or other similar factors.

WHAT IS A NEEDS ASSESSMENT?

Needs assessment is a tool used to assess gaps in communities, activities, or services. A needs assessment can be made for an individual (client), or a small (neighborhood), medium (city, county), or larger community (state, nation). A needs assessment helps better understand the extent and intensity of a need, and advises as to appropriate actions to be taken. A needs assessment can confirm problems that people are already aware of, and provide justification for actions.

Individual needs assessment involves:

1. Assessing demographic information
2. Assessing support systems
3. Assessing physical conditions

4. Assessing diet
5. Assessing social activities
6. Assessing perceived versus real needs

According to Kaufman (1998), a needs assessment is

The formal process of identifying need as gaps between current and desired results, placing those needs in priority order based on the cost to meet each need versus the cost for ignoring it, and selecting the most important needs (problems or opportunities) for reduction or elimination. (p. 87)

Needs assessment can be performed for a society, an organization, or an individual. Kaufman (2000) argued that a needs assessment should first identify societal needs (mega level), then focus on organizational needs (macro level), and finally consider individual needs (micro level). This approach helps justify the gaps that exist in results for societal, organizational, and individual needs, and provides guidance regarding resources and activities that can fill such gaps. For example, an organization working to prevent child abuse and neglect might focus first on the cost of child abuse for the larger society, the needs of organizations to address such issues, and finally the need for a child to live in an environment free of abuse and neglect. Needs assessment is used by planners to demonstrate the potential for return on investment or the added value of a particular activity or program. In a more concrete way, the Centers for Disease Control and Prevention (CDC) estimated that the total lifetime estimated financial costs associated with just 1 year of confirmed cases of child maltreatment (physical abuse, sexual abuse, psychological abuse and neglect) is approximately $124 billion. This is a need at the societal level. A needs assessment to start a program (macro level) that can provide direct services to children at risk of abuse and neglect (micro level) in a community will be a cost-reduction strategy not only for tax payers in that community, but also for the entire country. In other words, the needs assessment provides justification for the community or the public to invest in such a program through their donations or contributions.

According to Rissel and Bracht (1999), a needs assessment is "the process of assessing and defining needs, possible barriers and opportunities, and resources involved in initiating community health action programs" (p. 59). In a broad sense, a needs assessment involves the evaluation of gaps between how a community is and how this community should be, according to the expectations of community members. The purpose of a needs assessment is to determine community discrepancies and evaluate their nature and causes, as well as potential actions that can help fill the gap. Needs assessment is a tool to assess deficiencies that hinder target groups from achieving their desired lives. When the deficiencies or gaps are identified and analyzed, they can help make decisions related to an ideal situation. United Way of America (1982) defined a needs assessment as "a systematic process of collection and analysis as inputs into resource allocation decisions with a view to discovering and identifying goods and services the community is lacking in relation to the generally accepted standards, and for which there exists some consensus as to the community's responsibility for their provision" (p. 2).

A needs assessment is not just an intellectual exercise. It is an applied social research activity to determine whether actions envisioned to fill discrepancies in a community are really needed. Therefore, a needs assessment not only identifies unmet needs with respect to what is desired, but also analyzes barriers and obstacles that may hinder these needs from being met. A needs assessment is a process and research activity used to identify the available resources of a community and the unmet needs of the people in such a community. Therefore, a needs assessment goes beyond the simple notion of data collection and analysis, but has an applied implication with respect to the utilization of the findings related to the assessment. A needs assessment can be made for an individual (client), or a small (neighborhood), medium (city, county), or larger community (state, nation).

NEEDS ASSESSMENT: AN OVERVIEW OF THE PROCESS

A needs assessment is a process using research activities to identify the available resources of a community and the unmet needs of the people in such a community. Needs assessment implies:

1. A justification or rationale
2. Identification and description of the community for which you want to clarify the unmet needs
3. A purpose for the needs assessment
4. Planning the process of information gathering
5. Setting the method that you will use to interpret the information
6. Identification and planning of the resources needed to collect the data
7. Planning the use and strategies of disseminating the findings

Justification or Rationale

Like most research activities, a needs assessment must be justified. The investigator must explain why a needs assessment is necessary. What is the target group for the needs assessment? Where is that target group located? What is the importance of that target group in a larger community or societal context? Are there previous studies that directly or indirectly support the need to collect information on that target group? Are there questions that need to be answered regarding that target group? How will the data collected be used? The justification or rationale must provide a short or brief answer for most of the preceding questions (Box 4.1). There will be situations in which not enough information is available about a target population. The justification should reflect the best attempt possible to put a needs assessment in context. The justification is very important, because this is where one can start making the case to gather support for conducting a needs assessment.

Identification and Description of the Community

The community or target population concerned by a needs assessment must be clearly defined with as much detail as possible. Where is the target community located? What is the size of the target community? What is the demographic profile of that community (e.g., race/ethnic, gender, age, occupation, education, socioeconomic status, etc), if known? What is the history of this community? Are there some cultural factors to take into consideration?

Purpose

A needs assessment can be conducted for various reasons. For example, one organization might conduct a needs assessment as a preliminary step in the development of a strategic plan. Another organization might want to have a needs-assessment report for budgeting purposes. Another organization might want to use a needs assessment primarily as a strategy for advocacy regarding a particular public policy issue. Although the findings from a needs assessment might serve multiple purposes in the future, it is important to specify

BOX 4.1 A SAMPLE NEEDS-ASSESSMENT RATIONALE

People have come to the United States for a variety of economic and political reasons, which are explained by the push–pull theory. However, the economic challenge, especially for people from developing countries, is considered the dominant push–pull factor. For example, several ethnographic studies indicate that immigration to the United States is an act of investment for many immigrant families, who expect better educational and economic opportunities in return (Gibson & Bhachu, 1991; Suarez-Orozco & Suarez-Orozco, 1995; Zhou & Bankston, 1998). Consequently, some theorists argue that immigration is a serious problem for the United States, because the immigrants produce congestion, pollution, and depend on welfare (Bouvier, 1992; Huddle, 1996b).

Unlike the push–pull approach and other purely economic theories of immigration that reduce immigrants to self-interested and rational "economic" beings or a burden for American-born citizens (Bouvier, 1992; Huddle, 1996), many dynamic approaches have strongly documented the economic contributions of immigrants to the United States. According to the National Center for Policy Analysis, in 1997, federal, state, and local governments received an estimated $133 billion in direct taxes from immigrant households. Also, in a lifetime, an average immigrant paid $80,000 more in taxes than benefits received from local, state, and federal governments (National Research Council, 1997).

The economic contribution of immigrants in the United States may be seen as an indicator of social and economic integration. However, studies show that many immigrant families feel a sort of instability as they perceive themselves as newcomers in a new country (Caplan et al., 1991). In fact, the issue of concern is real, considering their limited knowledge of English—or no knowledge at all—and their lack of knowledge and awareness about the American society and social services (Stevens, 1994).

Like any immigrants in Florida, especially in Hillsborough County, Haitians are affected by the challenge of social and economic integration in their new communities. As a matter of fact, conversations with Haitian Americans in Hillsborough County tend to indicate that their needs are not satisfactorily addressed by existing social services. In response to that, the Haitian-American Organization for Population Activities and Education (HOPE) plans to conduct a survey among Haitian leaders in Hillsborough County, Florida. The purpose of this survey is to better understand how Haitian leaders perceive the needs of the Haitian American community living in Hillsborough County and to formulate recommendations to better address gaps in services and improve the quality of life of children, youth, women, families, and individuals in our community.

the primary purpose at the planning phase (Box 4.2). What are the specific objectives of the needs assessment? What will the results or findings help accomplish? Are there specific objectives?

Planning the Process of Information Gathering

The process of data gathering will depend on which approach of needs assessment is selected by the investigators. For example, a needs assessment that aims to understand the perceptions of a community about particular issues may involve direct

---

BOX 4.2 A SAMPLE NEEDS-ASSESSMENT PURPOSE

The decision to conduct a needs assessment of the Haitian American community in Hillsborough County was made to provide a quasiscientific or a research foundation to our future intervention in this community. More specifically, the needs assessment aimed to:

■ Identify the priorities in the needs of the Haitian American community in Hillsborough county.
■ Ensure that the organization's goals match with the expectations of this community.
■ Create a database of information that can help make systemic and effective interventions within this community.
■ Use the findings to develop a strategic plan and action plans that meet the real expectations of the people in the community.

---

data collection from members of a community. Therefore, the process of information gathering will be similar to the planning of a community survey (e.g., brief literature review on archival information and possible previous studies, identification and location of potential participants, strategies to contact the participants, resources needed, and timeline). In another context, a needs assessment might prioritize social indicator analyses. In that case, the process of information gathering might focus more on collecting data from libraries, the Internet, and academic and specialized databases and sources.

Methodology

The methodology will outline the data-collection approaches to be used. Will determine who will be contacted (if surveys, interviews, or focus groups are involved). Will determine what instrument of data collection will be used (e.g., interview guides, questionnaires, focus group guides). Will indicate what sample of the population the data-collection activities will involve. Will indicate what sampling strategies will be used. And will indicate how the data-collected will be analyzed. See Box 4.3 for a sample of needs-assessment methodology.

Identification and Planning of the Resources Needed to Collect the Data

Obviously, conducting a needs assessment requires time and energy (in any case) and money (in some cases). This requires a systematic and detailed action plan. The action plan is a document that describes all the resources needed. If there are expenses to be made, a budget of expenses must be developed. The budget should include a line item justification. The plan of action should outline a timeline of activities, the resources needed to perform the tasks in such activities, the person in charge, and a completion date. All elements of planning, implementation of the data-collection process, and data analysis and reporting should be included in this action plan.

BOX 4.3 SAMPLE NEEDS-ASSESSMENT METHODOLOGY

There is no particular hypothesis for this needs assessment. Some research questions will guide the development of the data-collection instrument. For example,

■ How do Haitian American leaders in Hillsborough County perceive the needs of Haitian children, youth, and families?
■ What have they identified as barriers and obstacles that may hinder satisfying these needs?
■ What do they suggest to overcome the barriers and obstacles and to satisfy the perceived needs?

This needs assessment will collect data that are qualitative in nature. Qualitative data-collection tools primarily will include key informant interviews, focus groups, town hall meetings, and open-ended survey questions. A survey questionnaire will be developed. Individual face-to-face interviews will be conducted with 200 people. The interviews will last between 15 and 20 minutes. For validation purposes, the questionnaire will be pilot-tested on a sample of five people with profiles similar to those of the target population. The questionnaire will be revised for clarity. The sample is restricted to people in positions of leadership in groups of different sizes (e.g., small-business owners, community leaders, and religious leaders). The questionnaires will be administered in May, June, and July 20xx. Participants will be contacted via flyers, in local churches, community meetings, public markets, and through other similar strategies. In addition, there will be three (3) focus groups of six (6) to ten (10) participants. The focus groups will last 45–60 minutes. A group of 10 volunteer graduate students will help conduct the interviews and the focus groups. The survey questionnaire will serve as guide for the focus group. The data will be analyzed to identify frequencies and trends regarding the perceptions of the target population on social services available in their community. The analysis will also analyze patterns of suggestions of services or service improvement made by participants. Such information will help develop a strategic plan that accounts for the perceived and real needs expressed by participants.

Planning the Use and Strategies of Disseminating the Findings

As indicated earlier, the findings from a needs assessment can be used for various purposes. After the needs assessment is completed, the first step is to write the needs-assessment report. The needs-assessment report is similar to a survey report. Once the report is published, the investigators should make every effort to promote the findings by writing short summaries, key highlights, and presenting or distributing them to people who are involved in the decision-making process of an organization. In addition to strategic planning, a needs-assessment report can provide information to write grant proposals, justify fund-raising campaigns, and other activities that can help generate income for a nonprofit organization.

WHY IS A NEEDS ASSESSMENT NECESSARY?

What is a community needs assessment? The goal of a needs assessment is to identify the needs of a community and determine potential concerns the community faces. A straightforward way to estimate the needs of a community is to simply ask residents their opinions

BOX 4.4 SAMPLE PARAGRAPH CITING FINDINGS FROM A NEEDS ASSESSMENT

Significant numbers of Hispanic children under the age of 3 in Dekalb County have shown developmental delays (DeKalb County, 2009). This is often related to minority language status and low maternal education, as explained by Zill and West (2000). In September 2009, the Hispanic Coalition conducted a needs assessment on the needs of the Hispanic community in Dekalb County. The needs assessment revealed that many children in the Hispanic community are at risk of abuse and neglect. Their parents are not willing to participate in prevention programs that involve the state for a variety of reasons encompassing their nondocumented immigration status, the fear that the state will take away their kids, their language barriers, and their national cultural backgrounds. They prefer interacting with people who speak their language and know their culture. However, when their kids are involved in declared abuse and neglect, the costs of such abuse or neglect are carried by U. S. taxpayers. As a matter of fact, a recent study concluded that child abuse costs the United States about $94 billion annually (Prevent Child Abuse America, 2001). The same study explains that for every dollar spent on child-abuse prevention, at least $2 are saved, which could have been spent on other child welfare services (Prevent Child Abuse America, 2001). It is worth it to invest in child-abuse prevention, especially because of other costs, such as academic underachievement, violence, substance abuse, low productivity as adults, teen pregnancy, juvenile delinquency, and adult criminality, which any society cannot neglect to address by any reasonable means.

about the development of services within the community, their satisfaction with services, and what particular services are needed. A needs assessment helps better understand the extent and intensity of a need, and advise as to the appropriate actions to be taken. A needs assessment can confirm problems that people are already aware of, and provide justification for actions.

NEEDS ASSESSMENT AND FINANCIAL SUSTAINABILITY

Needs assessment informs organizational decision making, including decisions related to strategies for financial sustainability. Needs assessment helps determine gaps, as well as strategies to fill the gaps, and provides guidance for prioritization and resource allocation. Prioritization is a key strategy in allocating resources for activities that fulfill the mission of a nonprofit organization, but also provides evidence of long-term commitment, which can help mobilize additional resources needed for financial sustainability or engage an organization on a path to financial sustainability.

Needs assessment provides fact-based information about needs of the target population that are linked to an organizational mission and society at large. This serves as a basis for financial planning, a justification for the added value of programs and services, and a potential tool to attract funding that can contribute to financial sustainability. With new funding linked to a needs assessment, an organization not only provides services that are needed, but also can make long-term financial planning based on projected trends. Obviously, such financial planning would take into account the external social, political, and economic factors that influence the financial sustainability of nonprofit organizations.

Let us consider a fictitious nonprofit organization called Dayton Association for Special Needs (DASN). The DASN is an organization that provides various health and educational interventions and services to help individuals with special needs achieve their full potential. DASN includes a team of teachers, speech and language therapists, occupational therapists, and educational psychologists working together to provide vital assistance to 140 special-needs individuals in Dayton, Ohio. Over the years, DASN has received strong financial support from the community through fund-raising activities. However, for the past 3 years, DASN has not been able to meet its budgeted needs, and has been operating on a chronic deficit. In addition, despite growing demands to provide more services, the organization had to separate itself from key service personnel due to the financial stress. Running on a 3-year deficit and downsizing personnel despite growing demands are clear indications of an organization that is not financially sustainable. The board was planning additional downsizing in personnel and even considering transferring their clients to a different nonprofit organization so that DASN could be dissolved. Given the difficulty of finding a partner organization to take over DASN's clients, a board member suggested conducting a needs assessment that might help address the financial stress of DASN.

The board created an ad hoc committee to develop a needs-assessment proposal and implement it until a final report, including recommendations for action, could be written. During the literature review stage, the ad hoc committee found that about 20% of Americans self-reported a disability. Part of the findings from the needs assessment revealed that more than 3,000 individuals with disabilities live in the areas near the DASN facility. More than 60% of caregivers for individuals with special needs identified were paying out of pocket for services. About 70% of these 60% were not aware of funding opportunities that exist through Social Security disability income, Medicare, Medicaid, and Social Security income. The remaining 30% knew vaguely about the services, but they were not sure whether they qualified or how to apply for such assistance. The ad hoc committee recommended that DASN target these potential clients through community education and outreach strategies. The organization implemented the recommendations of the ad hoc committee. The number of clients increased from 140 to 430 individuals with special needs in just 1 year. DASN rehired most of the personnel laid off and hired new staff. DASN opened a reserve account and closed the fiscal year with a profit.

DASN linked the findings of their needs assessment with the fact that about 20% of Americans self-reported a disability (mega level). They articulated a justification about the need for the organization to address such community needs (macro level). They implemented an outreach program to educate potential clients about financial assistance that could relieve them from some financial pressures due to caring for individuals with special needs (micro level). As a result, DASN tripled its number of clients in just 1 year. These clients used government funding to pay for services they receive from DASN. These clients used relatively reliable funding from which the DASN could make financial plans. Consequently, not only did DASN expand its services and hire new staff, but it also opened a new reserve account that could be used in case of financial hardship in the future. The needs assessment has clearly contributed to the financial health of DASN, and in turn to its path toward financial sustainability.

QUESTIONS AND ACTIVITIES

1. What is a needs assessment?
2. Why do you think it is important to justify why a needs assessment is necessary?
3. Identify a target population in your city. Then, go to the websites of the Census Bureau and your local city. Use additional formal and informal sources. Use information collected to answer questions, such as

(a) What is the size of the target population?
(b) What are the demographic characteristics?
(c) What are the geographic boundaries where such a target population can be located?
(d) Who are the formal and informal leaders of that target population?
(e) Are there physical or cultural barriers to access the target population?
(f) What are the values, attitudes, and traditions related to the history of the target population?

4. In your opinion, what are some ways in which a needs assessment can be used to contribute to the financial sustainability of a nonprofit organization?

5. Read the following case study and answer the questions.

CASE STUDY: ABC COMMUNITY CENTER

ABC Community Center is a social service agency located in Boston, Massachusetts. The mission of the center is to empower single women so they can achieve economic self-sufficiency. ABC uses a case management approach, which enables its case workers to be very efficient. ABC provides the following services to clients:

- Parenting education
- Employment readiness training
- Job placement
- Day care assistance
- Legal assistance
- Small-business loans
- Continuing education scholarship
- Counseling

ABC plans to open an office in a nearby suburb. Before opening the program, the director of the center wants to conduct a needs assessment. The chair of the Center's board of directors argues that there is no need to waste money in conducting a needs assessment because they already know that the needs exist. He indicates that they just need to install the new office and start providing services. Assuming that you are the executive director:

(a) Write a rationale to justify why a needs assessment is necessary.
(b) Write one or more objectives for the needs assessment.
(c) Assuming that you want to organize a survey and a focus group:

   1. Write a questionnaire that will provide you with adequate information for the implementation of your new program.
   2. Write a list of questions that you will ask the participants of your focus group.

(d) Identify the line items of expenses that are needed to organize the survey and focus group.
(e) How do you plan to disseminate the findings of your needs assessment?

6. Read the following case study and answer the questions.

CASE STUDY: OSHKOSH AREA UNITED WAY (OAUW)

The Oshkosh Area United Way (OAUW), a local nonprofit organization, was established in 1962 as a result of a citizens committee created to discover the benefits of an organized campaign. The chamber of commerce, organized labor, and other community leaders came together to create the organization. Four decades later, the OAUW continues to hold a single, community-wide, annual campaign to help fund local health and human service programs. The Oshkosh Area United Way focuses its funding in four investment areas:

1. Nurturing children and strengthening families
2. Building self-sufficiency
3. Promoting health and wellness
4. Caring for people in crisis

A board of directors governs the organization. Volunteers also provide leadership to a number of committees, including the Investment Management/Fund Development Committee, Allocation & Community Investment Committee, Technology Committee, Board Governance Committee, and more. The United Way has continued to expand its role in the community to include providing leadership for various projects. This year, Oshkosh Area United Way would like to know:

■ What are the perceptions of Oshkosh residents about health, education, and family services provided by human service agencies in Oshkosh, Wisconsin?
■ What are the health, education, and family services they think they are most in need of?

You are hired as a group of consultants to draft a needs-assessment plan.

(a) Where do you think you can find preliminary information about human service agencies in Oshkosh? Provide a specific list of sources and places (e.g., websites, organizations, reports, etc.).
(b) Whom do you plan to interview to obtain information that will enable you to address the above questions? For each individual or group of individuals, explain why you think you should interview them.
(c) What strategies will you use to reach the people whom you plan to interview?
(d) Draft some examples of questions that you will ask them during an interview and explain what information each question will potentially provide to you.

REFERENCES

Barker, R. L. (Ed.). (1999). *The social work dictionary* (4th ed.). Washington, DC: NASW Press.

Bouvier, L. (1992). *Peaceful invasions: Immigration and changing America*. Lanham, MD: University Press of America.

Brueggemann, W. (2002). *The land: Place as gift, promise, and challenge in biblical faith*. Minneapolis, MI: Fortress Press.

The DeKalb County Community Mental Health Board. (2009). *The DeKalb county mental health needs assessment 2009*. Retrieved from http://www.dekalbcounty.org/MentalHealth/pdfs/needs_assess.pdf

Gibson, M. A., & Bhachu, P. K. (1991). The dynamics of educational decision making: A comparative study of Sikhs in Britain and the United States. In M.A. Gibson & J. U. Ogbu. (Eds.), *Minority status and schooling: A comparative study of immigrant and involuntary minorities* (pp. 63–96). New York, NY: Garland.

Homan, M. (2004). *Rules of the game: Lessons from the field of community change*. Pacific Grove, CA: Brooks/Cole.

Huddle, D. (1996). *Net national cost of immigration*. Washington, DC: Carrying Capacity Network.

Kaufman, R. (1992). *Strategic planning plus: An organizational guide* (rev. ed.). Newbury Park, CA: Sage.

Kaufman, R. (1998). *Strategic thinking: A guide to identifying and solving problems* (rev. ed). Arlington, VA: International Society for Performance.

Kaufman, R. (2000). *Mega planning: Practical tools for organizational success*. Thousand Oaks, CA. Sage.

McKillip, J. (1998). Need Analysis. In L. Bickman & D. J. Rog (Eds.), *Handbook of applied social research methods* (pp. 261–284). Thousand Oaks, CA: Sage.

National Research Council. (1997). *The new Americans: Economic, demographic, and fiscal effects of immigration*. Washington, DC: National Academy Press.

Prevent Child Abuse America. (2001). *Total estimated cost of child abuse and neglect in the United States: Statistical evidence*. Chicago, IL: Author.

Reviere, R., Berkowitz, S., Carter, C.C., Gergusan, & C.G. (Eds.). (1996). *Needs assessment: A creative and practical guide for social scientists*. Washington, DC: Taylor and Francis.

Rissel C., & Bracht N. (1999). Assessing community needs, resources, and readiness: Building on strengths. In N. Bracht (Ed.), *Health promotion at the community level* (2nd ed., pp. 59–71). Thousand Oaks, CA: Sage.

Roehlkepartain, E. C. (2005). Asset mapping. In C. B. Fisher & R. M. Lerner (Eds.), *Encyclopedia of applied developmental science* (Vol. 1, pp. 119–122). Thousand Oaks, CA: Sage.

Stevens, G. (1994). Immigration, emigration, language acquisition, and the English proficiency of immigrants in the United States. In B. Edmonston & J. S. Passel (Eds.), *Immigration and ethnicity: The integration of America's newest immigrants*. Washington, DC: The Urban Institute Press.

Suarez-Orozco, C., & Suarez-Orozco, M. M. (1995). *Transformations: Immigration, family life, and achievement motivation among Latino adolescents*. Stanford: CA: Stanford University Press.

United Way of America. (1982). *Needs assessment—The state of the art— A guide for planners, managers, and funders of health and human services*. Alexandria, VA: Author.

Watkins, R., Leigh, D., & Kaufman, R. (1998). Needs Assessment: A digest, review, and comparison of needs assessment literature. *Performance Improvement, 37*(7), 40–53.

Zhou, M., & Bankston, C. L. (1998). *Growing up American: How Vietnamese children adapt to life in the United States*. New York, NY: Russell Sage Foundation.

Zill, N., & West, J. (2000). *Entering kindergarten: A portrait of American children when they begin school. Findings from the condition of education, 2000* (ERIC Document Reproduction Service No. ED448899).

Asset Mapping and Financial Sustainability

At the completion of the chapter the reader will be able to:

1. Reflect on the asset-based approach to community development.
2. Define the term "asset mapping."
3. Identify the different types of assets that create opportunities for a nonprofit organization.
4. Describe the asset-mapping process.
5. Explain the relationship between asset mapping and financial sustainability.

The purpose of this chapter is to introduce the theories, concepts, and approaches of asset mapping as a strategy to help nonprofit organizations identify obvious and hidden assets within their communities, and mobilize them to connect issues and needs with assets, and foster the financial sustainability of a nonprofit organization. The chapter examines the community context of nonprofit organizations in relation to community groups, neighborhoods, and larger social systems that influence quality of life. The chapter includes the concept and theory of community capacity, models of asset-based development for building community capacity, empowering individuals and groups, generating funding from new sources, and creating additional paths toward financial sustainability.

ASSET-BASED MODEL

The premise of an asset-based conceptual model is that individual strength and opportunities must be acknowledged and the individual must feel that such strength and opportunities are contributions to a process for change or overcoming a challenge (Buckingham & Clifton, 2001). The asset-based conceptual model is an alternative approach to the traditional deficit-based model that focuses on needs, problems, deficits, as opposed to the opportunities, capacities, talents or skills of the individual (Cramer & Wasiak, 2006).

The asset-based conceptual model has been used in business as a strategy to foster growth and increase performance (Ross & Bramley, 2003). It has also been used in the community-development movement as an alternative path focusing on the individual, associational, institutional, and natural resources of a community as opposed to their problems or deficits, thus using such resources as a holistic catalyst for community action or change (McKnight & Kretzmann, 1996). Mapping individual and organizational assets and capacities is considered the first step toward community regeneration. Kretzmann and McKnight (1993) categorized these assets into four categories: (1) individual capacities (personal income, gifts of labeled people, individual local businesses, and home-based enterprises); (2) associational and organizational assets (citizen associations, associations of business, financial institutions, cultural organizations, communication organizations, and religious organizations); (3) community-based assets controlled by outsiders (postsecondary institutions, public institutions and services, public schools, police, fire department, libraries, parks, vacant land and commercial structures and housing, and energy and waste resources); and (4) non–community-based assets controlled by outsiders (public capital improvement expenditures, and public information). Buckingham and Clifton (2001) asserted that two assumptions constitute the foundations for building an asset-based organization: (1) "each person's talents are enduring and unique" (p. 7), and (2) "each person's greatest room for growth is in the areas of his or her greatest strength" (p. 7).

Chapin (1995) suggested that social work interventions and social policy development models should focus on the strength of individuals and their environment, rather than the problems and pathologies, in order to empower individuals and communities to overcome challenges they may face and to create sustainable changes. Saleebey (2000) advised social workers to learn from people who were able to survive and overcome demoralization, abuse, illness, or oppression. He believed that such natural survivors accumulated a great deal of learning experience, which is an asset that can be useful in other situations, including attaining an academic goal. Benson (1997) introduced 40 developmental assets (e.g., family support, clear and consistent boundaries and expectations, intergenerational relationship, and participation in community activities) that are considered critical for raising healthy adults for communities and society. Seligman (1991) has conducted long-term human and animal research, and found that even helpless and depressed people can use their pessimism as an asset for an optimistic worldview by learning how not to take everything personally, focusing on problem-solving actions, viewing setbacks as temporary, and recognizing that beliefs are not facts, and can thus be challenged. Katz (1997) argued that past adversities and stressful experiences or even experience of failure can be transformed into assets that an individual can use to validate pain, celebrate resilience, and build future success. In that sense, failure to complete high school and alternatively earning a general equivalency diploma (GED) can transform a past experience of failure into success, which can be used to sustain future academic persistence or attainment of an education goal. This corroborates Saleebey's assertion that an inventory of individual assets (talent, capacities, knowledge, survival skills, personal virtues) and environmental assets (healing rituals and coping skills) can serve as resources for helping a person adapt to stressful situations and overcome challenges (Saleebey, 2001). In fact, Paek (2008) found that asset-based instructions contribute to positive self-efficacy and increase performance of school children in Boston public schools.

ASSET MAPPING

Simply put, asset mapping consists of documenting tangible and intangible resources that are available in a community (Kretzman & McKnight, 1993). Asset mapping is a simple but powerful activity for a nonprofit organization. Kerka (2003) explained that in asset mapping, a community is perceived as a place that includes strengths and resources, rather than through deficits that require intervention. Recognizing the assets available in a community is a powerful statement that can inspire community collaboration or even commitment to the vision and mission of a nonprofit organization.

TYPES OF ASSETS

Assets can be individuals (e.g., skills, talents, gifts, and capacities), associations (e.g., churches, local organizations, groups, and clubs), and institutions (e.g., government agencies, human service agencies, educational institutions, hospitals, credit unions, banks, community foundations, businesses, corporate foundations, and community centers) that are potential sources of in-kind and/or financial contributions for a nonprofit organization (Figure 5.1).

Individual Assets

Individual assets are individuals in the immediate environment of your organization who possess knowledge, information, ideas, leadership, money, gifts, skills, networks, talents, and capacities that they can make available to benefit your organization. An active or retired bank executive, a retired police officer, military service member, school principal, school teacher, college professor, or accountant constitute examples of individual assets.

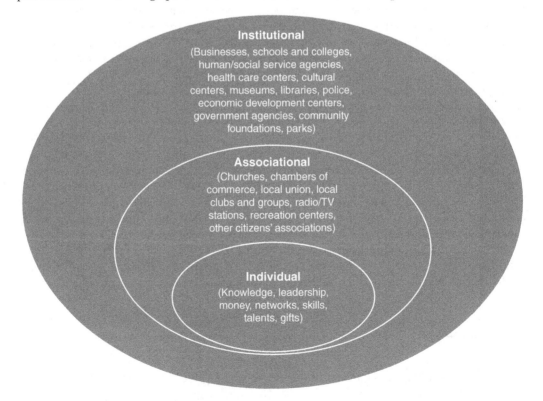

FIGURE 5.1   Types of assets.

All these individuals have one thing in common: experiences, skills, knowledge, information, networks, or even money that they can contribute to a nonprofit organization.

Associational Assets

Associational assets are citizens' associations, groups, clubs, churches, mosques, synagogues, temples, local radio and TV stations, local newspapers, and other local gatherings that exist in the neighborhood of your organization that can potentially be used in support of your programs or activities.

Institutional Assets

Institutional assets are well-established organizations or institutions (e.g., government agencies, human service agencies, offices of elected officials, educational institutions, hospitals, credit unions, banks, libraries, museums, theaters, community foundations, businesses, corporate foundations, and community centers) that conduct business in the local community of a nonprofit organization, which carry opportunities (e.g., facilities, equipment, following, revenue, and experts) that serve as potential sources of in-kind and/or financial contributions.

ASSET-MAPPING PROCESS

The asset-mapping process includes identification, location, verification, documentation, and compilation (Figure 5.2).

Identification

Community asset mapping starts with the identification of potential assets (Box 5.1). As indicated in previous paragraphs, the term *asset* refers to people, associations, and institutions within a community that can potentially contribute money, knowledge, time, ideas, information, facilities, and any other resources that can further the vision and mission of a

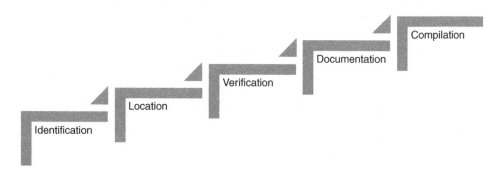

FIGURE 5.2 Asset-mapping process.

BOX 5.1 IDENTIFICATION OF ASSETS			
Identification of Assets			
	Individual	Associational	Institutional
Asset 1			
Asset 2			
Asset 3			
Asset 4			

nonprofit organization. The identification of assets should be guided by an organizational needs assessment. This will ensure that community resources can be tailored to help primarily meet the needs of local individuals or families.

Location

Identification of community assets can be specific or generic. Given the possibility of identifying assets that are generic in nature, it is important that identified assets be specifically located through any means available to ensure the full extent of their potential. Location of assets can be done by performing a map search over the Internet using web-based search engines. Then, a member of the organization can verify in person or through other credible means.

This step is very important, because it will prevent an organization from mapping fictitious community assets, which would be a loss of precious time. For example, in brainstorming during an asset-mapping activity, members of a nonprofit organization may think that a Small Business Development Center (SBDC) exists in their community, only to find out that the closest one is located miles away, in a different city. This does not mean that such a SBDC cannot be considered as an asset for this nonprofit organization. It may well be that this SBDC has jurisdictions that extend over several nearby cities, including the city of the nonprofit organization. However, it would not be wise to consider it as a local asset until further research is done, through "verification."

Verification

As the word implies, verification is performed to ensure that identified and located assets are as reliable as the nonprofit organization anticipated. Verification will help find out whether the asset is available, and to what extent a nonprofit organization can tap into opportunities offered by a particular asset (Box 5.2).

BOX 5.2 ASSET VERIFICATION			
Asset	Verified by	Findings	Date

BOX 5.3 DOCUMENTATION OF ASSET			
Asset	Potential	Contact Information	Comments

Documentation

Documentation consists of recording all relevant information related to an asset that has been identified, located, and verified (Box 5.3). The documentation should inform about the nature of an asset, the gap that such asset can help fill, and the name(s) and information of key contact person/people related to such asset.

Compilation

Compilation is necessary to mapping assets into an organized framework based on their potential to generate in-kind and/or financial contributions. Compilation involves categorizing and cataloging the community assets that are documented. There is no one way to categorize and catalog documented assets. The needs assessment that preceded an asset mapping, however, may dictate the best way to categorize and catalog. For example, assets can be categorized under broad themes, such as individual, associational, or institutional. Further, an asset mapping that is performed as a strategy for financial sustainability might categorize assets as monetary based and nonmonetary based. Monetary-based assets are individuals, associations, or institutions who can make cash contributions or cash-convertible contributions to a nonprofit organization. Outcomes of monetary-based assets will include any donation that can be listed as a short- or long-term asset in the balance sheet of a nonprofit organization. For example, although a computer is not cash, it is cash convertible. Volunteer time is not cash, but it is cash convertible. Its monetary worth can be estimated. Estimation and computation of monetary worth of donations will help assess the extent of the contribution of asset mapping to the financial sustainability of a nonprofit organization. Non-monetary-based assets consist of individuals, associations, or institutions who can contribute ideas, information, influence, and other resources that are intangible, but contribute to further the mission of an organization.

COMMUNITY ASSET MAPPING AND FINANCIAL SUSTAINABILITY

Community asset mapping creates a framework and provides a tool to target the local residents and influence them to get involved in the present and future of a nonprofit organization. By having the community involved in what the future of an organization will look like, such an organization automatically makes an investment in its sustainability, including its financial sustainability. A nonprofit organization is in essence a community-based organization. The community should view a nonprofit organization through that lens. But this view is not automatic. It is the responsibility of the organization to build and create such perception by integrating the community in the planning, implementation, and continuing quality improvement of the activities and programs offered. Community asset mapping is one among several strategies that can help to that end. Community asset mapping can be used as a strategy to identity resources available in a community and transform such resources into opportunities for financial sustainability. This will in turn create greater community commitment to the vision and mission of the organization. It is evident that a community that financially invests in an organization will pay more attention to how the organization is doing and how to best sustain it.

Noticing a significant increase in the number of unemployed or underemployed individuals in its community, a local community member, Fred Olson, organized a meeting with three other friends and started Denver Community Empowerment. The Denver Empowerment Organization (DEO) is a community-based, nonprofit organization that works to ensure that individuals and families in Denver, Colorado, can build social, political, and economic power in their communities and beyond. DEO envisions a community where all people—regardless of race, color, national origin, sexual orientation, or socioeconomic status—live and work with dignity and justice.

DEO provides a comprehensive range of educational, employment, and empowerment services, which include academic advising, financial counseling, workforce readiness (resumé writing, interviewing, and placement), GED preparation, referrals, and comprehensive supportive services to women and nontraditional students, including displaced homemakers, access to computers and office resources, financial/life skills outreach, workshops, scholarship/federal student aid resources, women-in-transition, single parents/student parents, and others to assist them in realizing their potential and capabilities. DEO also offers child abuse and neglect prevention activities, parenting classes for responsible fatherhood and motherhood (e.g., anger management, raising children, parenting roles), and after-school tutoring and mentoring.

Olson and his wife died in a terrible car accident while on vacation in Orlando, Florida. He was the primary funder of DEO through his business. The board wanted to continue his legacy, but they did not have enough funding to support all the activities. Most of the DEO's computers were very old and nonoperational. They estimated that it would cost them $30,000 to repair them, and they would still not be able to support up-to-date software. The best solution would be to replace them for an estimate of $65,000. Some board members wanted to seek grant funding, but lacked the necessary grant-writing skills. The organization did not have the financial means to hire a consultant grant writer. The organization was on the verge of dissolution although the board had not entertained that option yet. However, once a nonprofit organization does not have the ability to pay its bills, it is no longer financially sustainable. It is just a matter of time before it closes its doors, if financial support is not received.

The board created an ad hoc committee to plan and develop a community asset-mapping activity. The committee made phone calls, searched the Internet, organized brainstorming meetings, and conducted individual interviews to collect information about individual, associational, and institutional resources that were available in the immediate external environment of the organization. The committee also explored strategies to leverage local community resources in order to access opportunities at the state and the federal level.

Using the asset-mapping compilation, the board contacted (through letters, e-mails, phone calls, meetings) targeted individuals, local businesses, community colleges, and universities to receive computers and other technology equipment and supplies. DEO received computer, printer, and copier donations worth $200,000.

After a meeting with the president of a local community college, DEO received scholarships in the form of training workshops for board members and volunteers in grant writing and social enterprise worth $15,000. The community college allowed them to use their facilities at no cost to organize fund-raising events. DEO used the facilities of the local community college to organize a gala dinner with the help of local radio and TV stations, and raised $95,000 to start a day care center, a social enterprise that can help sustain the activities of the organization.

The board contacted the faculty of a nonprofit management program at a local university for assistance. Two professors volunteered to help them write a proposal to apply for a contract with the Department of Workforce Development. The bid was successful, and DEO received a contract for $800,000 over 5 years, to provide year-round programs (for both eligible in-school and out-of-school youth) that offer innovative strategies for improving and enhancing immediate and future educational and employment prospects. The programs should also integrate academics and career planning with related training in life skills, work readiness, and work experience for meeting the Colorado Common Measure goals.

The board wrote a business plan to start a day care center that would serve as a social enterprise activity to generate income in support of the mission of the organization. DEO received day care equipment and donations of supplies worth of $20,000. The day care center is anticipated to break even in 2 years. Profit from the day care center alone is expected to take over a potential mortgage and all utilities expenses. The board arranged a meeting with the director of a local credit union. The members made a case to use their business plan, the new contract secured with the Department of Workforce Development, and the money from their fund-raising as leverage. The board successfully obtained a new mortgage from the credit union, and bought a small building that can fit all the services and programs of DEO.

Later, DEO received a grant of $75,000 from the Department of Housing and Urban Development (HUD), to renovate the building and add approximately 2,000 square feet of space to the facility, which contains additional offices and classrooms. DEO negotiated with the City of Denver and obtained $50,000 of funding to offer a special financial literacy program for clients in government services in order to provide them with the skills they need to achieve long-term financial stability. Clients learn how to develop a personal budget and saving plan, pay bills on time, establish a bank account with low- or no-fee services, avoid predatory loans, and other similar skills.

The fictitious example of the Denver Empowerment Organization illustrates that individuals, local associations, and institutions doing business in a local community often possess valuable knowledge, networks, revenue, information, ideas, equipment, facilities, and other resources that nonprofit organizations can mobilize to obtain monetary and nonmonetary contributions that can contribute to their financial sustainability. Asset mapping contributed to the financial sustainability of DEO. The organization has significantly increased its assets by using the resources available in the community. DEO has used individual, associational, and institutional assets as a strategy for financial sustainability. DEO has secured funding and maintains a social enterprise that will help the organization continue to provide much-needed services. The involvement of the community in the life of the organization is an indication that the community believes in the mission and vision promoted by DEO. Such community support can help sustain DEO both organizationally and financially.

COMMUNITY ASSET MAPPING FOR FINANCIAL SUSTAINABILITY

Using community asset mapping for financial sustainability cannot be a fictitious or vague exercise. It has to be concrete in monetary or monetarily convertible terms.

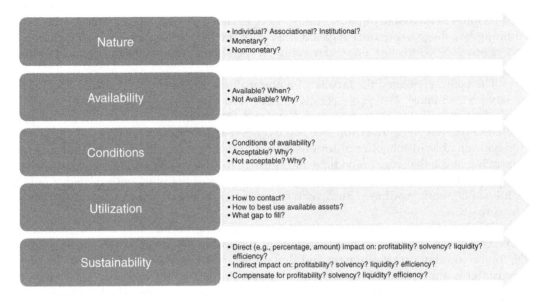

FIGURE 5.3   Community asset mapping for financial sustainability.

As Figure 5.3 illustrates, community asset mapping for financial sustainability should take into account factors such as

- *Nature* of the asset: What type of asset? Monetary? Monetary convertible?
- *Availability*: Is it available to my organization? Now? Later? When? If not, why?
- *Conditions* of availability: If available, under what conditions? Terms of references? Criteria? Process? Timeline?
- *Relevance* of its use: How to best use it? What gap to fill? Is it to increase assets? Increase human resource return on investment, etc.?
- *Contact:* How to contact?
- *Outcomes:* Worth of monetary or nonmonetary donation? Time? How many hours? What would be the cost of training? Equipment? What is the market value?
- *Sustainability:* Sustainable, use for sustainability, compensate for sustainability.

QUESTIONS AND ACTIVITIES

1. What is asset mapping?
2. How do you compare the asset-based approach to a deficit model?
3. Think about your local community and an organization that you are associated with. Identify a list of individual, associational, and institutional assets, and explain how your organization can benefit from each of them!
4. How can asset mapping contribute to the financial sustainability of a nonprofit organization?

5. Asset-mapping exercise:
   a. Make a list of the personal skills and knowledge you bring to this class. Each of you contributes certain things, such as skills in different languages, knowledge of how to motivate people, marketing expertise, group membership, and so on.
   b. Create a list that represents all of the capacities you have represented in your group.
   c. Draw the following diagram on a flip chart:

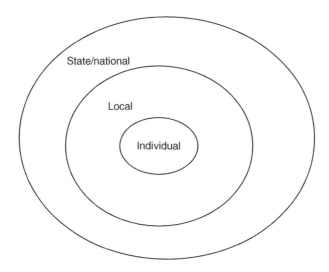

   d. In the inside circle, write all the individual skills your group has. Use the list you have just created.
   e. In the outside circle, add all of the local associations or groups that you collectively represent—for example, women's groups, religious groups, churches, schools, non-profit organizations, for-profit agencies, small business, clubs, self-help groups, neighborhood associations, and so on.
   f. In the last space around the edges, list all of the state or national institutions you all represent or with whom you have links through another organization or agency.

REFERENCES

Benson, P. L. (1997). *All kids are our kids: What communities must do to raise caring and responsible children and adolescents*. San Francisco, CA: Jossey-Bass.

Buckingham, M., & Clifton, D. O. (2001). Now, discover your strengths. New York, NY: Free Press.

Chapin, R. K. (1995). Social policy development: The strengths perspective. *Social Work, 40*(4), 506–514.

Cramer, K. D., & Wasiak, H. (2006). *Change the way you see everything: Through asset based thinking*. Philadelphia, PA: Running Press.

Katz, M. (1997). *On playing a poor hand well: Insights from the lives of those who have overcome childhood risks and adversities*. New York, NY: W. W. Norton.

Kerka, S. (2003). Community asset mapping. *Trends and Issues Alert, 47*. Retrieved from http://www.calpro-online.org/eric/docs/tia00115.pdf

Kretzmann, J., & McKnight, J. P. (1993). *Building communities from the inside out: A path towards finding and mobilizing a community's assets*. Evanston, IL: Northwestern University, Center for Urban Affairs and Policy Research.

McKnight, J., & Kretzman, J. (1996). *Mapping community capacity. The asset-based community develop-ment institute*. Retrieved http://www.racialequitytools.org/resourcefiles/mcknight.pdf

Paek, P. L. (2008, January). Asset-based instruction: Boston public schools. Case study from *Practices worthy of attention: Local innovations in strengthening secondary mathematics*. Austin, TX: Charles A. Dana Center at the University of Texas at Austin.

Ross, C. E. H., & Bramley, A. D. (2003). Has the asset-based organizational model outlived its useful-ness? *World Energy, 6*(3), 54–59.

Saleebey, D. (2000). Power in the people: Strengths and hope. *Advances in Social Work, 1*(2), 127–136.

Saleebey, D. (2001). The diagnostic strengths manual? *Social Work, 46*(2), 183–187.

Seligman, M. E. P. (1991). *Learned optimism*. New York, NY: A. A. Knopf.

Strategic Planning and Financial Sustainability

At the completion of the chapter the reader will be able to:

1. Define the terms "strategic planning" and "SWOT analysis" (strengths, weaknesses, opportunities, threats).
2. Cite some models of strategic planning.
3. Describe the key phases of the strategic-planning process.
4. Develop strategic goals and objectives.
5. Discuss the relationship between strategic planning and financial sustainability.

This chapter focuses on the principles, approaches, and processes of long-term strategic planning, the relationship of strategic management and program effectiveness, and the interrelationships between strategic planning and financial sustainability. The chapter introduces various approaches to effective strategic planning geared to the financial sustainability of a nonprofit organization.

WHAT IS STRATEGIC PLANNING?

Strategic planning is probably as old as human civilization. Almost all known human civilizations have developed practices that aim to shape the future in a relatively predictable manner. However, contemporary strategic planning in organizations may be traced from the scientific management principles developed during the Industrial Revolution. Simply put, strategic planning is the process of assessing the current situation of an organization or institution, developing incremental objectives, and designing plans and strategies, in order to achieve strategic goals that are mission focused and vision driven. Strategic planning is a systematic process that leads to basic decisions, goals, and actions to position an organization for future success. A strategic plan states what an organization will become, what goals it will attain, and what it will do to accomplish them.

IMPORTANCE OF STRATEGIC PLANNING

Why is strategic planning important for a nonprofit organization? The strategic-planning process or the development of a strategic plan responds to a need to shape the future of an organization or institution. A sustainable organization must be able to shape its future as much as possible. It is very difficult to ask people to support an organization if the organization does not have a clear vision for the future. People who support an organization need the basic assurance that the members of a particular nonprofit organization know where they want to be and have outlined a plan to get there. A strategic plan provides opportunities to clarify organizational vision. An organization with a clear vision is likely to perform better than an organization that does not. In that sense, a strategic plan can contribute to organizational performance. The strategic planning helps ensure that there is potential for efficient use of resources. There is no guarantee, of course, that an organization with a strategic plan will use its resources well. However, organizations that use their resources efficiently always have a strategic plan, which includes a long-term vision that the organization is implementing gradually. Further, the fact that members of an organization were able to sit down together and develop a strategic plan means that there was a relative consensus regarding the future of the organization. Therefore, the strategic goals set in a strategic plan can be easily interpreted as the strategic priorities of a nonprofit organization. It is an ongoing and inclusive process. It is a framework that can be broken down into parts or annual plans. The plan should be looked at—at least annually—because change happens and modifications may be needed. Each part may deal with a major issue facing the organization. For example, the program plan is about what an organization is doing and plans to do. The human resources plan outlines ways of dealing with important issues related to personnel. The financial plan deals with generation of income and expenditures to make.

STRATEGIC-PLANNING APPROACHES AND PROCESSES

There are various strategic-planning approaches, depending on the size, the age, or the culture of an organization or institution. Kriemadis and Theakou (2007) identified five models of strategic planning used by nonprofit organizations. Some benefits of strategic planning for nonprofit organizations are listed in Box 6.1.

BOX 6.1 BENEFITS OF STRATEGIC PLANNING

- Determines the changes needed for an organization to better fulfill its mission
- Establishes and sustains effective programs
- Ensures organization is aligned with its environment
- Helps meet community needs
- Enables the uses of resources in the most effective manner possible
- Helps improve public communications
- Helps gather social, political, and financial support
- Clarifies direction for effective decision making
- Shows how the organization will build on its strengths
- Helps identify and target opportunities
- Uncovers and overcomes internal weakness and external threats
- Predicts the future and positions of the organization

1. Basic strategic planning: The first model uses a basic top-down process that includes:

- Identification of purpose through definition or revision of the mission statement
- Selection of strategic goals that an organization needs to accomplish in the process of furthering its mission
- Identification of specific strategies and approaches that will enable it to reach each goal
- Identification of specific action plans to implement each approach or strategic program
- Monitoring and updating the strategic plan to ensure that activities that are being implemented reflect the strategic vision of the organization

2. Issue-based strategic planning: The second model is referred to by Kriemadis and Theakou (2007) as issue-based (or goal-based) planning, and consists of the following steps:

- Conduct a SWOT analysis to identify the strengths, weaknesses, opportunities, and threats related to the future of an organization.
- Identify and prioritize major issues or goals through strategic analysis.
- Design strategic or key programmatic areas.
- Define or update the vision, mission, and values statements.
- Design action plans that include objectives, resources needed, roles, and responsibilities.
- Record and attach documents developed during the strategic-planning process into the strategic plan document.
- Develop annual operating plan documents throughout the life span of the strategic plan, which can be 3, 5, 7, or even 10 years.
- Develop and authorize the yearly budget.
- Conduct first year of operation.
- Monitor, review, evaluate, and update the strategic plan.

3. Alignment model: The third model is called the alignment model, and is mainly a fine-tuned strategic-planning approach. It encompasses:

- Creating a planning group to define or revise the organizational mission, programs, resources, and support
- Identifying what works and what needs improvement
- Developing strategies to make possible adjustments
- Including the strategies in the strategic plan

4. Scenario planning: The fourth model is labeled scenario planning. Kriemadis and Theakou (2007) argue that this approach is more of a supplemental framework to use in conjunction with other strategic-planning models. The scenario-planning approach involves:

- Identifying forces and trends that may affect the future of an organization
- For each force or trend, identifying at least three scenarios (best, acceptable, and worst) that may have implications for the organization
- Anticipating actions that can be taken in relation to each scenario
- Anticipating strategies to respond to possible changes
- Deliberating on external factors with the most potential to affect the organization

5. Organic planning: The fifth and last model identified by Kriemadis and Theakou (2007) is called organic or self-organizing planning. This method departs from the previous linear approaches. The organic approach is a continuing and self-reflecting process of clarifying and articulating the value system that guides the actions of an organization. The process includes strategies such as story-boarding techniques and dialogues.

THE STRATEGIC-PLANNING PROCESS

A generic strategic-planning process includes three key phases of assessing, visioning, and strategizing in order to further the mission and vision of an organization (Figure 6.1).

Assessing

The first phase in a strategic-planning process is for an organization to assess its internal and external environments, and learn about its current situations. Sometimes leaders of a nonprofit organization may have preconceived ideas in terms of what they think is the real situation of their organization. This is a perceived situation that may be different from the real situation revealed by situational assessments. A thorough situational assessment is fundamental to an effective strategic-planning process. The situational assessment can include information from needs assessment, asset mapping, SWOT analysis, and financial analysis. It is almost impossible for a nonprofit organization to determine where it wants to be without an unequivocal understanding of where it is at the time it is going through the strategic-planning process.

Visioning

Visioning consists of anticipating what the future should look like for the organization from a programmatic viewpoint. Visioning makes it possible to clarify organizational mandates, vision, mission, and values. The visioning of an organization is rooted in its situational assessment.

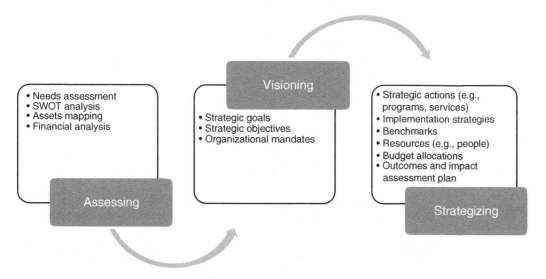

FIGURE 6.1   Strategic-planning process.

Strategizing

Strategizing involves the development and adoption of strategic goals, objectives, strategies, and action plans that will help an organization further its purpose. The essence of strategic planning is strategizing, allocating resources, and setting benchmarks or targets in relations to specific outcomes that an organization wishes to obtain, and the impact that it plans to make.

SWOT ANALYSIS

The acronym SWOT stands for *strengths, weaknesses, opportunities,* and *threats.* SWOT analysis is an assessment approach used to scan the internal and external environment of an organization or institution. As Figure 6.2 illustrates, strengths and weaknesses are internal to an organization. Therefore, an organization can influence or modify its strengths and weaknesses. Opportunities and threats are external. They are beyond the direct control of an organization. However, awareness can help an organization take proactive actions through advocacy, collaboration, or strategizing. SWOT analysis can help:

■ Identify the internal and external factors that are favorable and unfavorable to the achievement of organizational or institutional vision, mission, goals and objectives.
■ Provide information about matching an organization or institution's resources and capabilities to the competitive environment in which it operates.
■ Guide in strategy formulation and selection.

Conducting a SWOT Analysis

Conducting a SWOT analysis is a collaborative process that should include as many internal and external stakeholders as possible. The process of conducting a SWOT analysis involves:

■ Scheduling a SWOT analysis meeting
■ Setting specific outcomes for the meeting (e.g., list of areas of strengths, weaknesses, opportunities, and threats)

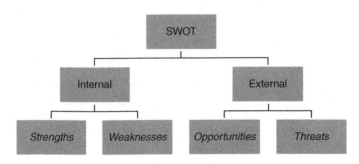

FIGURE 6.2   SWOT analysis flow chart.

BOX 6.2 SWOT MATRIX/STRATEGIES

Strategies	Opportunities	Threats
Weaknesses	W–O *(Overcome weaknesses to pursue opportunities)*	W–T *(Plan to prevent the weaknesses that increase vulnerability to external threats)*
Strengths	S–O *(Pursue opportunities that match strengths)*	S–T *(Use strengths to reduce vulnerability to external threats)*

- Inviting stakeholders (internal/external)
- Preparing materials (SWOT worksheets)
- Allowing enough time for work in groups and discussions
- Establishing group norms
- Conducting and managing meetings/ensuring outcomes
- Discussing follow-up process and timeline

After conducting a SWOT analysis, a nonprofit organization should identify and develop strategies to use strengths in order to pursue matching opportunities in place while overcoming weaknesses that may hinder the ability of the organization to pursue existing opportunities. Similarly, there should be plans or strategies to use strengths to reduce vulnerability to external threats, and address the weaknesses that increase vulnerability to potential threats (Box 6.2).

ORGANIZATIONAL MANDATES

Nonprofit organizations exist as publicly funded entities regulated by state, federal, and sometimes local laws. As a result, there are expectations about what nonprofit organizations can and cannot do. Some laws, regulations, and ordinances evolve or change. A nonprofit organization is expected to comply with them. The members, partners, and clients of a nonprofit organization have expectations about its operations and activities. The community at large has expectations about a nonprofit organization. These expectations related to the programs and services offered by an organization are called the "organizational mandate." For example, an organizational mandate of a nonprofit organization is inherent to the fact that such entities

- Have an obligation to maintain and update their legal status based on existing and new laws, ordinances, and regulations
- Maintain and update documents related to their governance (e.g., article of incorporation, bylaws, policies)
- Provide services within the realm for which the organizations were created, based on the needs of its target population, and the expectations of its internal and external stakeholders.

BOX 6.3 ORGANIZATIONAL MANDATE

1. Keep our legal status current with all applicable laws at the local, state, and federal levels.
2. Develop and maintain a secure and stable operating budget for the next 5 years.
3. Create and maintain a database of information and research on topics of interest to our target population.
4. Provide refugees and immigrants in need of social services referrals to appropriate agencies.
5. Develop and maintain a network of volunteers to offer community support to individuals, families, enterprises, organizations, and communities.

The organizational mandate constitutes the foundation of what an organization must accomplish as a means to remain connected with the fulfillment of the vision and mission statements (Box 6.3).

DEFINE OR REVISE MISSION, VISION, AND STATEMENTS

The vision, mission, and values statements constitute the core identity of a nonprofit organization (see Boxes 6.4. 6.5, and 6.6). In other words, a nonprofit organization justifies its social or community relevance through its vision, mission, and values, and the extent to which they are reflected in governance and program implementation. During the strategic-planning process, a nonprofit organization should

- Make an inventory of internal and external stakeholders.
- Develop its vision, mission, and values statements.
- Review, revise, or clarify its vision, mission, and values statements, if necessary.

BOX 6.4 SAMPLE VISION STATEMENT

To be recognized by our clients, private, and public agencies as an organization leader that provides professional and culturally competent programs, products, services, and models of community empowerment and human development that positively impact the cultural, social, and economic lives of children, families, professionals, enterprises, organizations, and communities.

BOX 6.5 SAMPLE MISSION STATEMENT

Make positive and durable change in the lives of children, families, and communities by promoting an awareness of cultural diversity, implementing health, community education, and economic opportunities and technical assistance programs, and preventing child abuse and neglect and domestic violence.

BOX 6.6 SAMPLE STATEMENT OF VALUES

RESPONSIVENESS AND ACCOUNTABILITY

The HOPE will strive to understand and meet the changing requirements of its clients by treating them as valuable partners, listening to them, responding fairly, and living up to our commitments. We must comply with all applicable laws and regulations at all government levels, and will address social, cultural, and economic issues responsibly. Therefore, we ought to provide superior performance and are accountable for our actions and results.

CONTINUOUS QUALITY IMPROVEMENT

Continuous quality improvement is both a strategy and a value through which the HOPE will achieve its vision to be an organizational leader. The ongoing quality improvement of our programs is our first priority in achieving client satisfaction. Empowerment, process, outcomes, and impact evaluation play a key role in all products, programs, and services that we provide. We believe that continuous quality improvement can help us learn from experience, embrace change, and achieve the full involvement of staff members in our quest for excellence.

SUSTAINABILITY

We believe that an organization must be financially viable in order to fulfill its mission. Therefore, we must evaluate the sustainability of our projects and programs to ensure their durability before any implementation. We are committed to manage with prudence the financial resources entrusted to us by:

- Applying fiduciary responsibility to all expenditures to assure that full value is obtained for money we spend
- Setting financial management objectives that can help implementing our strategic plan
- Providing continuing quality services
- Making all possible effort to ensure the endowment of our programs

RISK AND INNOVATION

We strongly believe that well-calculated risks and innovation are the principal drivers of organizational growth. Based on this assumption, we experiment with alternative models of programs, products, and services in order to challenge the status quo. We recognize that change and risk are the challenge of innovation. Therefore, we reward successful risk taking and do not penalize an innovative idea that failed. We foster an environment of creativity, innovation, and personal ownership.

INTEGRITY

Honesty and fairness are the basis of our code of ethics. We will strive to conduct relationships with clients and partners in a fair, open, and ethical manner. We will keep our promises to anyone. Equal opportunity for advancement will be provided to every member of the organization in an atmosphere of open communication, trust, respect, and support.

(continued)

BOX 6.6 SAMPLE STATEMENT OF VALUES *(continued)*

We will remain an organization of dedicated and competent individuals of high integrity and credibility who are in strict compliance with applicable laws, rules, and regulations that govern the communities where we are working. In accordance with the value we place on responsiveness and accountability, we will always live up to our responsibilities, meet our obligations, and fulfill our commitments.

DIVERSITY

We value cultural competency and will work to leverage the creative potential of individual differences. We are committed to considering the background and abilities of everyone and to promote a greater diversity in positions of influence, regardless of race, gender, sexual orientation, and beliefs. However, we understand diversity within the meaning of universal human rights. We believe that differing points of view must be sought and understood in a perspective of cultural diversity.

COOPERATION

We value partnership, collaboration, and teamwork, both externally and internally. We will always explore opportunities for partnership and collaboration to achieve common goals. We encourage collective problem-solving and decision-making processes and promote open and supportive frameworks for new approaches or ideas.

STRATEGIC PRIORITIES AND CHOICES

A nonprofit organization cannot solve all the problems experienced by its target population. This is simply impossible. There will always be limitations in the financial resources of a nonprofit organization to provide all the services and programs that would be helpful. Further, an organization must focus on specific activities to be effective and efficient. Therefore, nonprofit organizations must make strategic choices regarding the key areas where they want to make a significant contribution and have a long-lasting impact. The determination of strategic priorities is based on various factors, such as:

- The vision, mission, and values statements
- A prior needs assessment and asset mapping
- A SWOT analysis
- A consensus among the internal and external stakeholders

A list of programmatic areas must be developed in relation to vision and mission statements of an organization. The programmatic priorities must be defined, discussed, and adopted by the majority, based on objective criteria. For example, an organization may decide that the key programmatic areas for the next year will be:

- Early childhood education
- Economic opportunities
- Health

The decision does not stop there. Each programmatic area must be defined in a way that is operationalizable. In other words, the definition must provide implicit outcomes to evaluate. For example, does early childhood education mean starting an early childhood education center that provides direct services or a center that will conduct research on early childhood education? Or does that mean providing support to help low-income children have access to early childhood education programs?

SETTING STRATEGIC GOALS AND OBJECTIVES

Strategic goals are long-term statements that describe programmatic conditions that an organization or institution wants to accomplish within a certain period of time, usually in 3, 5, 7, or 10 years. Objectives are statements of specific activities or projects that must be accomplished toward the achievement of strategic goals. In other words, objectives are:

■ Statements of actions that will enable achieving a goal
■ Specific, quantifiable, measurable
■ Simple and easy to understand
■ Realistic and attainable

For each strategic goal in a strategic plan, there should be at least two or three objectives, whose attainment would accumulate to the achievement of the goal. Box 6.7 outlines some differences between goals and objectives. Box 6.8 provides some examples of strategic goals and objectives.

BOX 6.7 GOALS AND OBJECTIVES

Goals	Objectives
Short statement reflecting a long-term vision	Longer descriptive statement of action
Involves a broad scope	Involves a narrow scope
Directly relates to the vision and statements	Indirectly relates to the vision and mission statements
Covers long time period (such as 3, 5, 7, or 10 years)	Covers short time period (such as a 1-year budget cycle)

BOX 6.8 EXAMPLES OF STRATEGIC GOALS AND OBJECTIVES

Goals	Objectives
Goal 1 Provide technical assistance to individuals in order to assist in their social, cultural, and economic integration into American society.	*Objective 1*: Provide refugees and immigrants of all ethnic backgrounds the consultation, information and referral, translation, and other related technical assistance when needed. *Objective 2*: Provide individuals in need with employment-related services. These services include job placement, pre-employment training, employment planning, employment counseling, and other related job-readiness assistance.

(continued)

BOX 6.8 EXAMPLES OF STRATEGIC GOALS AND OBJECTIVES   (continued)

Goals	Objectives
	Objective 3: Refer and accompany individuals in need of support and social services to the appropriate agencies.
	Objective 4: Provide volunteer interpreters for refugees and immigrants who speak languages other than English, so that they can have access to social services when they first arrive in the United States.
	Objective 5: Provide, to the degree possible, financial humanitarian assistance to low-income individuals and families as well as emergency relief assistance following natural disasters.
	Objective 6: Partner with other organizations to help abused and neglected children.
Goal 2 Assist low-income individuals and entrepreneurs to increase their incomes, create jobs for themselves and their neighbors, raise their living standards, and promote economic growth.	*Objective 1:* Help individuals or groups develop successful businesses. *Objective 2:* Provide ongoing technical assistance, training, peer support, and loan assistance to existing small businesses that lack adequate access to business financing. *Objective 3:* Assist low-income individuals in finding alternative grants and loans for vocational training.
Goal 3 Offer management assistance to not-for-profit organizations in order to improve their effectiveness.	*Objective 1:* Provide ongoing consulting services to not-for-profit organizations in fund-raising, board development, accounting, marketing, strategic planning, program evaluation, staff development, organizational development, coalition building, etc. *Objective 2:* Organize workshops and seminars for the staff of not-for-profit organizations. *Objective 3:* Assist not-for-profits in website development and maintenance and management of information systems. *Objective 4:* Develop guides and communication materials for not-for-profit organizations.
Goal 4 Empower refugees and immigrants with the skills needed to achieve their highest potential and participate productively and actively in American society.	*Objective 1:* Provide students with individualized tutoring in all required subjects to strengthen the academic areas in which they are deficient. *Objective 2:* Develop after-school programs to help students at risk of leaving the school system early to remain in school, improve their performance, and embark on positive careers. *Objective 3:* Implement holistic delinquency-prevention programs for target preadolescents at-risk of teenage pregnancy and juvenile delinquency. *Objective 4:* Offer parenting education sessions to help parents participate successfully in the behavioral, emotional, social, and cognitive development of their children.

(continued)

BOX 6.8 EXAMPLES OF STRATEGIC GOALS AND OBJECTIVES *(continued)*

Goals	Objectives
	Objective 5: Provide literacy classes, computer-literacy classes, computer training, English for speakers of other language (ESOL), English as second language (ESL), general education development (GED), and other test-preparation tutoring to individuals in need.
	Objective 6: Organize cultural events to promote cultural identity and cultural competency.
Goal 5 Deliver a prevention continuum of health programs to improve the quality of life of underserved children, families, and communities.	*Objective 1:* Increase parental understanding of, access to, and information about the child-care delivery system, affordable child-care options, and available financial assistance.
	Objective 2: Provide information and referral services on reproductive health, HIV/AIDS, sexually transmitted diseases (STDs), health awareness, etc.
	Objective 3: Organize workshops on the causes and prevention of HIV/AIDS infection for HOPE clients as well as through community outreach to adult education classes, parent associations, senior citizen centers, and shelters.
	Objective 4: Train volunteers to do street outreach by distributing materials about HIV/AIDS and how to prevent infection to beauty and hair salons, businesses, and other community organizations.
	Objective 5: Provide social/recreational activities, emergency assistance, and support group and counseling services to individuals living with HIV/AIDS and their families.
	Objective 6: Publish an HIV/AIDS quarterly report based on official surveillance data made available to the public.
	Objective 7: Conduct, in partnership with other organizations, free tuberculosis education and screening for HOPE programs and clients as well as outreach services through churches, community organizations, and schools.
	Objective 8: Develop networks both regionally and nationally to address priority areas of health promotion and disease prevention, including driving under the influence (DUI), substance and alcohol abuse, women's health, smoking prevention, and others.
Goal 6 Provide services that are cost-effective, timely, and responsive to the changing needs of children, families, enterprises, organizations, and communities.	*Objective 1:* Acquire grants and other private sources of funding to maintain a stable annual operating budget that supports the implementation of this strategic plan.
	Objective 2: Seek in-kind donations, such as printing, materials and equipment, volunteers, and training, to help support our services and reduce program costs.
	Objective 3: Consider alternative approaches for providing services whenever an alternative offers quality services at the levels needed in a more cost-effective manner.

(continued)

BOX 6.8 EXAMPLES OF STRATEGIC GOALS AND OBJECTIVES *(continued)*	
Goals	**Objectives**
	Objective 4: Establish program evaluation and performance measurement standards for our programs to ensure that we meet the needs of our constituencies and provide programs of highest quality.
	Objective 5: Develop, implement, and adapt a guideline and portfolio for investment, financing, and asset-management decisions.
	Objective 6: Provide our stakeholders with required financial reports, budget comparisons, cash flow projections, audit, and other useful financial information for decision making throughout the organization.
Goal 7 By 2024, HOPE will be recognized as an organizational leader in enhancing overall organizational effectiveness through documentation of stakeholder satisfaction, high productivity, communication, and collaboration with private and public agencies and communities.	*Objective 1:* Develop and integrate data reports that identify service quality and delivery time measures and best practices for internal operations.
	Objective 2: Develop a manual of policies and administrative procedures.
	Objective 3: Organize applied and quasi experimental research that can create innovative approaches for community programs and social services.
	Objective 4: Develop a cultural competency board that is well trained and informed to assist the organization in marketing, fund-raising, legal matters, public relations, and evaluation.
	Objective 5: Offer a competitive benefits package to staff and establish a formalized ongoing training program for staff and volunteers.
	Objective 6: Develop a communication and collaboration plan to increase community involvement and coordination with private and public agencies and communities.

STRATEGIC PLANNING AND STRATEGIC MANAGEMENT

Strategic management is the process of implementing the strategic plan adopted by an organization or institution. The implementation plan uses a project management approach through the development of specific programs, projects, and activities that will contribute to help achieve specific objectives and goals in the strategic plan. For example, the implementation can include yearly, quarterly, and monthly action plans, including key personnel, tasks, policies, procedures, training, timelines, evaluation strategies, and operational budget.

STRATEGIC PLANNING AND FINANCIAL SUSTAINABILITY

The strategic plan is the primary document that inspires the financial targets set in an organizational budget. Therefore, strategic planning is directly linked to the long-term financial prospects of a nonprofit organization because the identification of strategic priorities is an integral part of financial planning and financial sustainability. The key strategic or pro-grammatic areas that will be described in the program expenditures section of a budget come from the strategic plan. Some of the approaches or strategies to generate income are usually identified during the strategic-planning process, oftentimes during the SWOT analysis. In fact, the SWOT analysis, as part of the strategic-planning process, can be used as a contribution to the financial sustainability of a nonprofit organization. For example, the strengths can be used to take advantage of opportunities that exist for an organiza-tion. If an organization shows evidence of strengths in a particular programmatic area, this organization might use these strengths to

- Seek grant income from identified funding opportunities.
- Customize fund-raising strategies to retain existing donors and attract new donors.
- Seek contracts that can expand the stream of revenue of the organization.
- Develop social enterprise initiatives to leverage internal assets as a means to generate unrestricted funds.
- Develop collaborations with stronger or bigger organizations to transfer some of the potential risks to them and use some of their assets.

Strengths can also be used to neutralize some threats or avoid facing them. For example, an organization may:

- Use the talents and expertise of its board, staff, and volunteers to adopt new policies and procedures that would make potential changes in legislation inconsequential to the activities of such organization.
- Streamline poor-performing programs or projects so that a change in governmental rep-resentatives no longer makes the organization a target for unwanted scrutiny.
- Organize special events targeting a base of loyal donors to raise alternative financial resources for a key program that may lose funding if a change occurs in legislation or politics.

In other words, strategic planning provides a framework for identifying and forecasting sources of income, and for decisions about allocating resources. An effective strategic-planning process can lay the groundwork for organizational effectiveness and efficiency, which in turn may positively influence the financial sustainability of a nonprofit organi-zation. Effectiveness means that a nonprofit organization achieves the best possible out-comes through its resources. Efficiency implies that a nonprofit organization makes the best use possible of its resources to obtain critical outcomes.

QUESTIONS AND ACTIVITIES

1. What is strategic planning?
2. What is a SWOT analysis?
3. What are the benefits of strategic planning for a nonprofit organization?
4. What are the key steps in developing a strategic plan?
5. To what extent can strategic planning contribute to the financial sustainability of a non-profit organization?

CASE STUDY: SWOT ANALYSIS

Loving Hands is a nonprofit organization headquartered in Brooklyn, New York, that focuses on raising funds in the United States to support orphaned and abandoned children in Africa. The organization started in 1992. Loving Hands currently helps over 3,600 children living at Loving Homes. These homes are in Egypt, Kenya, Uganda, Malawi, Liberia, and Senegal. It is the mission of Loving Hands to support these homes and transform the lives of orphaned, abandoned, and disadvantaged children. With about 50 staff members and hundreds of volunteers, they strive to achieve measurable goals in the form of monthly and annual financial commitments to Loving Homes. Loving Hands also receives funds through other independently run organizations similar to Loving Hands located in various countries around the world. Loving Hands hired a consultant to conduct an internal assessment. The following paragraphs were extracted from that report.

DIVERSE STAFF

Different ages, professional backgrounds, and linguistic and ethnic backgrounds combine to make a diverse staff that has the potential to learn from each other and develop innovative fund-raising and operational strategies. The diversity of staff offers more perspectives in staff meetings and strategic planning, helping Loving Hands to identify more possibilities to achieve its goals.

INCONSISTENT MARKETING STRATEGY

Internal marketing has been minimal and inconsistent. Materials are often inconsistently used in different regions, and an effort to develop a nationally recognized brand has been slow in developing. In numerous phone calls I received while working at Loving Hands, dozens of donors have been confused by materials discussing the merger, and are unsure whether their local office still exists.

COMPETITION

One of the biggest issues for Loving Hands is the increasing number of similar charities. Similar charities also offer donor trips to meet sponsored children, and several of these organizations are better funded. Perhaps the largest is Compassion International. They have a similar concept of child sponsorship, but a much more donor-accessible website that allows donors to choose a child. Their website also offers creative ways to give, such as via catalog shopping or through microfinance. Loving Hands needs to position itself with identifying qualities that appeal to donors.

LOSS OF INTEREST

Due to violence in Mali and Kenya, many people are losing interest. It is important for Loving Hands to acknowledge and reach out to these donors to keep them connected. The stories featured in the media about child poverty were compelling, but since then have moved focus onto newer tragedies.

(continued)

CASE STUDY: SWOT ANALYSIS (continued)

STAFF COMMITMENT

Although turnover is high, the entire staff is strongly devoted to the mission. The awareness of the needs of orphaned and abandoned children throughout Africa is a powerful incentive for staff to remain even when the internal culture is volatile. Many are child sponsors, and most have visited at least one Loving Hands home. Former employees continue to support Loving Hands vocally and financially. Consistent communication with active donors, Loving Hands staff, and the children help to keep the staff mission focused.

PAST VOLUNTEERS

Former Loving Hands volunteers who have spent long periods of time living at Loving Hands homes possess an amazing potential for increased awareness and fund-raising. Reaching out to these volunteers could help solidify the volunteer's closeness to Loving Hands.

STAFF TURNOVER

Loving Hands has had a high staff turnover rate since 2008. According to a recent survey, the turnover rate among surveyed nonprofits averaged 16% in 2010. Loving Hands saw a roughly 25% to 30% turnover rate in 2012. The large turnover costs the organization in knowledge sharing, and negatively affects potentially valuable donation opportunities, because new employees may need more time to become familiar with the potential for a major donation. Finally, many community relationships are affected with constant changes in field staff.

POSITIVE SPONSOR EXPERIENCE

The chance to sponsor a child at a Loving home through Loving Hands provides a tax-deductible opportunity for donors to connect in a meaningful way with where their donations are going. Correspondence to and from the child and sponsor provides an opportunity for sponsors to develop a relationship with a child. Sponsors are encouraged to visit their child on Loving Hands–organized donor trips, or on their own individual travels. Many sponsors were able to visit their sponsored child. This helps solidify the long-term connection between the donors and their child, as well as Loving Hands in general. Sponsors are generally very satisfied with their sponsorship experience.

AGING DONORS

The age of the donor base is starting to become a major issue. Most of the donors have been with the organization for 30 to 40 years. The administrative assistant reported that she received several calls from donors who asked to be removed from the list because they were moving to retirement homes, and two of the

(continued)

Midwest region's biggest supporters passed away between 2010 and 2011. The need to bring in younger donors is urgent.

PARTNERSHIP POTENTIAL

There is much potential for partnership that can contribute to the growth of the organization. Loving Hands started out of a mission trip. Although Loving Hands is not a religious entity, it can tap into its missionary genesis to develop new relationships with local churches. Loving Hands has the potential to increase its network of church partners through careful planning and well-executed strategy.

POLITICAL ISSUES

Political turmoil in the countries where Loving Hands operates poses a continual problem to the success of Loving Hands' mission. Recently, in Egypt, newly elected officials wanted to eliminate orphanages because of their negative connotations, and were trying to force Loving Hands to send children back to relatives who had already given their children up for various health and socioeconomic reasons. International pressures and changes in government had helped Loving Hands retain its orphanage operation because of its strong positive reputation. Loving Hands needs to be prepared for national crises that can emerge unexpectedly.

DONOR COMMITMENT

Loving Hands maintains a passionate base of donors who have developed long-lasting relationships with children at the Loving Homes. The reliance on a large number of individual donors had sustained Loving Hands' activities during financial crises. The large pool of small donors had protected Loving Hands from being affected by dramatic donation decline. Loving Hands can count on its loyal donors to maintain a consistent level of support.

SLOW COMMUNICATION

Correspondence between a child and a sponsor tends to be slow because of the mail systems in foreign countries. Loving Hands has little control over the speed or reliability of the foreign mail services. Alternative strategies must be developed to streamline its own operations and offset some of the delay in communications.

RESTRICTING DONATIONS

Oftentimes, donors make special donations for specific projects that are not part of Loving Hands' approved budget for the year. Restricted gifts can put immense pressure on the general operating funds budget when too many donations are specified elsewhere. Donors prefer to make donations that would go directly to the Loving Homes.

(continued)

CASE STUDY: SWOT ANALYSIS (*continued*)

ECONOMY

Although the problem is certainly not exclusive to Loving Hands, the volatile economy is threatening the organization's ability to achieve its goals. Children at Loving Homes have had to make sacrifices, and staff at Loving Hands have lost benefits and taken a 10% cut in pay for over a year. Although the impact of the economy has been buffered by the wide base of individual donors, the economy still threatens individual gifts, grants, and child sponsorships. It also poses the threat of increased need in the Loving Homes, as more children may be given up when families cannot afford to take care of them. The poor economy not only threatens individual gifts and grants, but also has severely reduced investment income that Loving Hands accounts for in its budget.

BOARD POTENTIAL

Board members of Loving Hands are often wealthy and connected. They possess great potential in their networks. There is potential for individual donations, corporate sponsorships, and skilled volunteer services provided by contacts of the board members.

Answer the following questions based on the above paragraphs!

a. What are the strengths of Loving Hands?
b. What are the weaknesses of Loving Hands?
c. What are the opportunities that exist for Loving Hands?
d. What are the potential threats for Loving Hands?
e. What will be your specific recommendations to Loving Hands' board based on the SWOT analysis?

REFERENCE

Kriemadis, T., & Theakou, E. (2007). Strategic planning models in public and non-profit sport organizations. *Sport Management International Journal, 3*(2), 27–37.

Budget and Financial Sustainability

At the completion of the chapter the reader will be able to:

1. Define the term "budget."
2. Explain the importance of the budget for a nonprofit organization.
3. Describe the different types of budgets.
4. Identify the most common budget approaches.
5. Describe the process of developing a budget in a nonprofit organization.
6. Explain the relationship between the budget and financial sustainability in nonprofit organizations.

Budget techniques are central to the successful operation of all organizations. This chapter introduces the budget and the budgeting process as key components of a financially sustainable nonprofit organization. A budget enables organizations to allocate scarce resources, control operations, and manage performance. A budget is the translation of an organization's plans and priorities. Readers will learn the basic concepts and practices of budgeting in nonprofit organizations. The chapter also explains the essential role played by budget approaches and techniques in the successful and sustainable operations of a nonprofit organization.

WHAT IS A BUDGET?

A budget is a plan that describes in monetary terms the income or revenue expected by an organization for a financial cycle and the allocation of expenses or expenditures, in order to achieve organizational goals and objectives, and consequently to fulfill the organizational vision and mission (Figure 7.1).

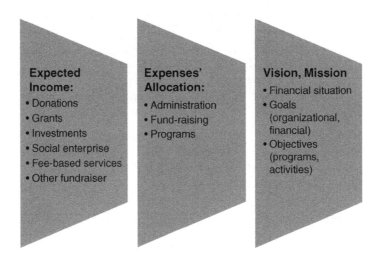

FIGURE 7.1 A nonprofit budget.

WHY A BUDGET?

A budget is one of the most critical documents that a nonprofit organization must have. A budget is the most accurate translation of the vision and mission statements of a nonprofit organization. The strategic plan makes statements about what an organization is striving to achieve. The budget provides substance and sets the means to get there. A budget anticipates income and expenditures over a period of time and facilitates effective planning. Without a budget, an organization can descend into chaos and simply dissolve. A budget provides benchmarks to establish efficiency in use of resources. With a budget an organization can easily monitor cash flow and identify departures from plans. A budget helps maintain a focus and discipline in financial decisions.

TYPES OF BUDGETS

The financial operation of a nonprofit organization involves several types of budgets compiled into a master budget. The most common types of budgets are an operating budget, an auxiliary budget, and a capital budget (Figure 7.2).

Master Budget

The master budget incorporates all the budgets of an organization. The master budget includes everything that an organization will be doing for an upcoming fiscal year. The master budget is also called the comprehensive budget, because it clarifies the other specific budgets in a more holistic context.

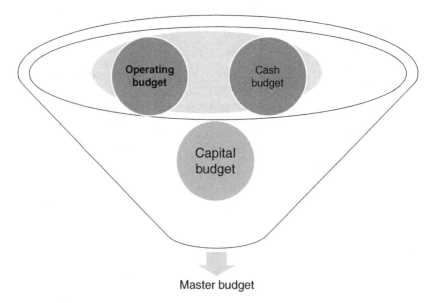

FIGURE 7.2   Common types of budgets.

Operating Budget

The operating budget is a monetary plan that describes the expected income and expenditures of an organization. Organizations tend to develop their operating budget in two stages, which include a budget of revenues and a budget of expenses. The budget of revenues is a prediction of all income that a nonprofit organization anticipates to receive. The budget of expenses is based on the past budget, and current and future trends. There should be a detailed explanation and documentation for each line item of anticipated revenue. The same applies to the budget of expenses. A justification must be provided for each line item of expenditure. At the end of the process, the budgeted expenses are subtracted from the budgeted revenues to determine whether there will be a surplus or a deficit during the upcoming fiscal year.

Cash Budget

The cash budget is a forecast for cash receipts and disbursements or payments to make on a quarterly or monthly basis. The cash budget is generally presented in the following format:

Generic Cash Budget Illustration

Beginning cash + ($10,000.00)
+ Cash receipt ($5,000.00)
Subtotal: Available cash ($15,000.00)
– Cash payment ($6,000.00)
Subtotal ($9,000.00)
+ Borrowing or – investments ($2,000.00 [borrowing])
Ending cash balance ($11,000.00)

CAPITAL BUDGET

The capital budget is developed for spending activities related to large construction, major equipment, or other infrastructures (e.g., technology) that have an impact beyond 1 fiscal year of operations. Therefore, such spending activities cannot fit into an operating budget. The capital budget is an expression of commitment to the future or sustainability of an organization through investments that may take several years to complete, but will serve as an added value.

PREREQUISITES TO DEVELOPING A BUDGET

As indicated in Figure 7.3, the development of a budget is subject to prerequisites, such as strategic and action plans (goals, objectives, programs, activities), a finance committee, a timetable, guidelines (manual, procedures, and forms), assumptions (expected or presumed income and expenses), and assessment and documentation (e.g., evaluation of past budget, financial statements, financial reports, contracts, grant documents, investment reports).

Budget Timeline

The budget timeline is the process of developing organizational budgets from start to finish. The length of the timeline will vary from one organization to another. Table 7.1 illustrates the format of a budget timeline.

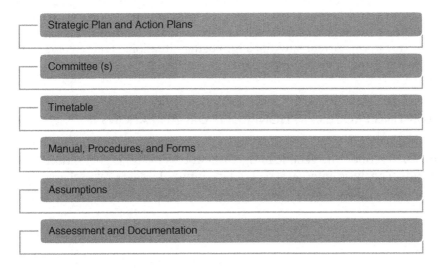

FIGURE 7.3 Budget prerequisites.

TABLE 7.1 Sample Budget Timeline

Activity	Responsibility	Outcomes	Deadline
Appointment of budget committee	Executive director	Minutes of meeting or appointment letter	August 1
First meeting of budget committee	Committee chair	Minutes of the meeting	September 1
Development of budget assumptions and guidelines	Committee	Budget assumptions and guidelines distributed	December 1
Unit/department budgets developed	Unit/department coordinator or managers	Unit/department budget submitted to committee	February 1
Development of cash and operating budget	Chief financial officer (CFO)	Budget document distributed	March 1
Negotiation and revision	All coordinators/ managers and CFO	Revised version of budget distributed	April 1
Development of master budget	CFO and budget committee	Budget proposal distributed	May 1
Vote and approval of budget	Board of directors	Adopted budget	June 1
Implementation of budget	All managers	Unit budgets are distributed	July 1

BUDGET AND STRATEGIC PLAN

A budget describes the financial situation of an organization, the sources of revenues, the expenditures and related activities that will help achieve the goals and objectives set in an organization strategic plan. Budgeting is a decision-making process that goes along with strategic planning and is connected to the past, present, and future of the organization. The past and current financial situations are used to make decisions that can help sustain, improve, or transform current situations into better situations. Frameworks to budgeting tend to be rational, incremental, or partially rational.

THE BUDGETING PROCESS IN NONPROFIT ORGANIZATIONS

As Figure 7.4 describes, the generic budgeting process includes goal setting, data gathering, past budget analysis, internal stakeholders' inputs, budget proposal, review of budget proposal, budget approval, communication and implementation, and monitoring.

Goal Setting

The goal-setting stage is the first step in developing a budget. The goal setting is inspired by the strategic and implementation plans of a nonprofit organization. As a result, a budget should clearly indicate the goals and objectives that it will help to achieve. Usually,

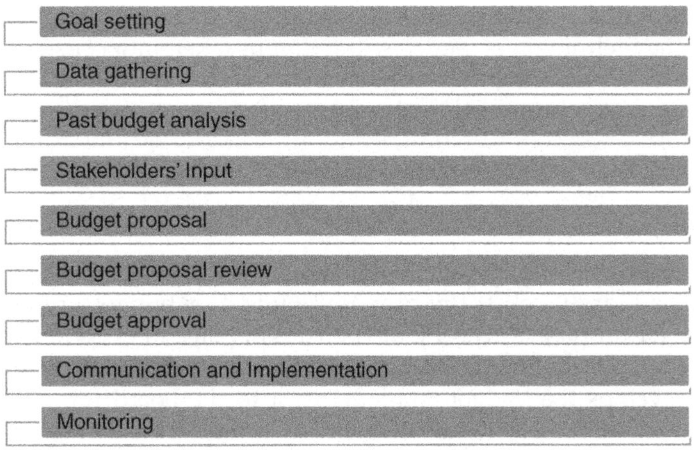

| Goal setting |
| Data gathering |
| Past budget analysis |
| Stakeholders' Input |
| Budget proposal |
| Budget proposal review |
| Budget approval |
| Communication and Implementation |
| Monitoring |

FIGURE 7.4 The budgeting process.

such goals and objectives are linked to specific programs, projects, or activities that either will generate revenue or involve expenses. The goal setting includes assumptions that may serve as guidelines for projected fund allocations to programs.

Data Gathering

A budget should be based on data that can be objectively examined. The data-gathering stage helps collect information that will justify line items and sections in a budget. For example, data on specific revenue should be based on trends, facts, and authentic documents. Similarly, data on anticipated revenue should be based on forecasting and facts. If anticipated revenues and expenses are not fact based, the budget will be useless.

Past Budget Analysis

Except for a newly formed nonprofit organization, past budget analysis should be conducted when developing a budget for the next fiscal year. Past budget analysis helps participants learn from possible under- or overbudgeting, and avoid repeating the same mistakes.

Internal Stakeholder Inputs

Internal stakeholders should contribute to the development of a new budget based on their position in the organization and their level of expertise. Some stakeholders can only make vague suggestions because of their limited influence or knowledge of budget development. Other stakeholders may be more involved because they are better positioned to provide specific information. Regardless of the level of involvement, internal stakeholders should see the budget development process as a team project, not because someone said so, but because they felt involved and saw their input taken into consideration. This can help create a sense of belonging to the organization, and may affect internal stakeholder commitment to the vision promoted by the organization.

Budget Proposal

A budget starts as a draft, called the proposed budget or budget proposal. The development of a budget proposal varies by the policies in place in every organization. Some organizations develop their budget proposal through a top-down approach. In that case, the leadership develops the budget and submits it to the board for approval. If a top-down culture exists, the board will simply approve the budget. Other organizations adopt a bottom-up approach. The leadership invites all units to develop their specific budgets, especially budgets of expenses. The unit budgets may be organized into categories according to the organizational design. The process of harmonizing the unit budgets continues until a master budget proposal is developed.

Budget Proposal Review

A budget proposal undergoes the scrutiny of various internal stakeholders, such as managers, program directors, the chief financial officer, the chief executive officer, and the finance committee. The order can be different in any given organization. What is consistent is that almost every stakeholder will make some changes, minor modifications, or suggestions.

Budget Approval

Typically, the chief executive director and the finance committee find common ground on the budget proposal, and submit it to the board of directors. In most cases, the board will make changes to ensure that the budget reflects the strategic plan and strategic priorities of the organization. The presentation of the budget is made in one meeting. The proposed budget is more likely to be approved in a subsequent meeting. The board of directors votes on the modified version of the budget proposal.

Communication and Implementation

Once the budget proposal is voted by the board of directors, it becomes the approved budget. The executive director has the responsibility to communicate the adopted budget to the rest of the organization and oversee its accurate implementation. The implementation is done through allocation of the funds to various programs, projects, and activities. Sometimes, the allocation reflects the inputs provided by the internal stakeholders. Other times, the staff gets frustrated because budgetary allocation does not reflect their needs.

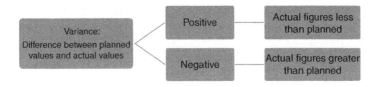

FIGURE 7.5 Budget-variance analysis.

Monitoring

Financial managers have the responsibility to provide weekly, monthly, quarterly, or annual financial reports regarding revenues and expenses in the light of the adopted budget. The monitoring is done through the variance report. The variance report compares the adopted revenues and expenses with the actual ones (Figure 7.5). The variance report helps monitor ongoing progress in the implementation of the budget. In addition to the variance report, financial managers of nonprofit organizations must develop cash flow management reports and performance reports. The cash flow management report informs one about the liquidity of an organization or the availability of cash for ongoing operations. The performance report tells how much is spent on each unit of service and per client. The performance report describes the efficiency of the budget in relation to services provided. Finally, the executive director and the board of directors must continuously review the budget to ensure that the implementation is being successful, and take corrective measures, if necessary.

BUDGET FORMATS

Budget documents are presented in two main formats:
1. Line-item format
2. Program format

Line-Item Budget

The line-item budget focuses on specific goods and services to be purchased as objects-of-expenditure (Table 7.2). The line-item format helps appropriate funds for items related to personnel, equipment, supplies, utilities, and other needed items that are associated with specific accounts, and makes it easier to compare budgeted amounts to specific spending.

Program Budget

The program budget format plans funding for specific programs. Once the budget is approved, appropriation is made to specific items. The focus is on programs rather than on specific items within a program. Table 7.3 provides an example of a program budget format.

TABLE 7.2   Oshkosh Community Foundation—Line-Items Budget

Oshkosh Community Foundation, Inc.	
Budget Federal Year 2007–2008	
Income	Total in U.S. dollars
Contracts	630,000
Fund-raising	121,000
Grant	60,000
Total income	811,000
Expenses	
Program expenses	340,000
Total program expenses	*340,000*
Administrative expenses	
Salaries	140,000
Health insurance	85,000
Dental insurance	14,000
Rent	26,000
Janitor	16,000
Liability Insurance	15,000
Supplies	36,000
Utilities	21,000
Education allowances	16,000
Total administrative expenses	*369,000*
Total expenses	709,000
Surplus (Deficit)	102,000

BUDGET APPROACHES

A budgeting approach is the method or procedure used to develop a budget. The most common approaches are incremental, zero based, performance based, and project based. Regardless of the approach, the development of a budget is based on assumptions that will determine amounts of revenue and expenses in line items.

Incremental Budgeting

The incremental budget is developed from the past-year budget template or framework. In most cases, an incremental budget maintains core line items of past budgets. However, marginal changes or adjustments to current budgeted allowances are made based on certain assumptions. Let us consider the example of the Oshkosh Community Foundation in Table 7.3. The OCF runs programs in health, education, and housing. The budget for the last fiscal year is attached. The board hired you as a consultant to develop a budget proposal for the next fiscal year based on the following assumptions:

TABLE 7.3 Program Budget Format for Oshkosh Community Foundation—Federal Year 2009–2010

Revenue	Health	Education	Housing	Administration	Total in U.S. Dollars
Grants	100,000.00	50,000.00	45,000.00	0.00	195,000.00
Contracts	75,000.00	175,000.00	155,000.00	0.00	405,000.00
United Way	85,000.00	15,000.00	35,000.00	0.00	135,000.00
Individuals	10,000.00	5,000.00	0.00	0.00	15,000.00
Fees for services	150,000.00	10,000.00	165,000.00	0.00	325,000.00
Fund-raisers and events	200,000.00	50,000.00	0.00	0.00	250,000.00
Endowment	300,000.00	100,000.00	125,000.00	0.00	525,000.00
Interest income	30,000.00	10,000.00	12,000.00	0.00	52,000.00
Total cash revenue	**950,000.00**	**415,000.00**	**537,000.00**	**0.00**	**1,902,000.00**
Expenses	**Health**	**Education**	**Housing**	**Administration**	**Total**
Staff salary	200,000.00	100,000.00	100,000.00	50,000.00	450,000.00
Benefits (25%)	50,000.00	25,000.00	25,000.00	12,500.00	112,500.00
Occupancy (rent and utilities)	6,000.00	6,000.00	3,000.00	3,000.00	18,000.00
After-school tutoring	0.00	200,000.00	0.00	0.00	200,000.00
First-time home buyer		0.00	350,000.00	0.00	350,000.00
Health prevention	400,000.00	0.00	0.00	0.00	400,000.00
Insurance	1,200.00	1,200.00	2,400.00	1,200.00	6,000.00
Legal, accounting	6,000.00	3,000.00	3,000.00	3,000.00	15,000.00
Equipment	75,000.00	10,000.00	10,000.00	15,000.00	110,000.00
Supplies	50,000.00	20,000.00	9,000.00	10,000.00	89,000.00
Printing and copying	6,000.00	5,000.00	5,000.00	5,000.00	21,000.00
Telecommunications	6,000.00	3,000.00	1,500.00	3,000.00	13,500.00
Travel and meetings	30,000.00	5,000.00	5,000.00	5,000.00	45,000.00
Marketing and advertising	10,000.00	5,000.00	5,000.00	5,000.00	25,000.00
Staff training/ development	15,000.00	10,000.00	12,000.00	5,000.00	42,000.00
Total expenses	*855,200.00*	*393,200.00*	*530,900.00*	*117,700.00*	*1,897,000.00*
Surplus (deficit)	94,800.00	21,800.00	6,100.00	(-117,700.00)	5,000.00

1. The housing contracts will not be renewed. Therefore, the agency cannot budget on these revenues.
2. The board decided to reduce the first-time home buyer program by 40%.
3. United Way stated that they will not be funding the health program next year due to changes in their strategies of community involvement.

4. The board decided to reduce all administrative costs by 10%, except salary and benefits.
5. The board plans to increase the fund-raising revenues of the agency by 20%.

Based on the above assumptions, the proposed budget for the next fiscal year will become the following (Table 7.4):

TABLE 7.4 Oshkosh Community Foundation—Proposal Budget, Fiscal Year 2010–2011

Oshkosh Community Foundation					
Proposal Budget FY 2010–2011					
Revenue	Health	Education	Housing	Administration	Total in U.S. dollars
Grants	100,000	50,000	45,000	0	195,000
Contracts	75,000	175,000	0	0	250,000
United Way	0	15,000	35,000	0	50,000
Individuals	10,000	5,000	0	0	15,000
Fees for services	150,000	10,000	165,000	0	325,000
Fund-raisers and events	240,000	60,000	0	0	300,000
Endowment	300,000	100,000	125,000	0	525,000
Interest income	30,000	10,000	12,000	0	52,000
Total cash revenue	905,000	425,000	382,000	0	1,712,000
Expenses	Health	Education	Housing	Administration	Total
Staff salary and benefits	200,000	100,000	100,000	50,000	450,000
Benefits (25%)	50,000	25,000	25,000	12,500	112,500
Occupancy (rent and utilities)	6,000	6,000	3,000	2,700	17,700
After-school tutoring	0	200,000	0	0	200,000
First-time home buyer		0	210,000	0	210,000
Health prevention	400,000	0	0	0	400,000
Insurance	1,200	1,200	2,400	1,080	5,880
Legal, accounting	6,000	3,000	3,000	2,700	14,700
Equipment	75,000	10,000	10,000	13,500	108,500
Supplies	50,000	20,000	9,000	9,000	88,000
Printing and copying	6,000	5,000	5,000	4,500	20,500
Telecommunications	6,000	3,000	1,500	2,700	13,200
Travel and meetings	30,000	5,000	5,000	4,500	44,500
Marketing and advertising	10,000	5,000	5,000	4,500	24,500
Staff training/ development	15,000	10,000	12,000	4,500	41,500
Total expenses	855,200	393,200	390,900	112,180	1,751,480
Revenue over expenses	49,800	31,800	-8,900	-112,180	-39,480

Zero-Based Budgeting

Zero-based budgeting is mostly for newly formed organizations that are starting from scratch. A zero-based budget is based on the priorities set from the strategic plan of an organization. The budget is based on assumptions set in the goal-setting stage. The zero-based budget is articulated around a justification for each line item. Let us consider the case of The Appleton Cancer Awareness Foundation (ACAF), which is a newly created not-for-profit organization that aims to increase awareness on breast cancer in Appleton. To this end, ACAF plans to organize outreach activities and community training, and conduct community-based participatory research on breast cancer in Appleton. Mr. Smith, a benefactor in Appleton, commits to donate $500,000 for the start-up. The board of directors includes community and business leaders who will pay their annual membership dues totaling $100,000. As chair of the planning committee, you are asked to develop the start-up budget based on the following assumptions:

1. ACAF will hire: (a) an executive director (salary = $60,000 per year), (b) an administrator (salary = $40,000 per year), (c) a development coordinator (salary = $35,000 per year), (d) an administrative assistant (salary = $25,000 per year), (e) and a janitor (salary = $20,000 per year).
2. ACAF requests that you add 20% of total employee salaries for fringe benefits.
3. With respect to "Facilities, equipment, and supplies," ACAF anticipates the following expenses:
   ■ $2,000 per month for rent
   ■ $1,000 per month for utilities
   ■ $500 per month for repair
   ■ $500 per month for copy rental
   ■ $3,000 per year for postage
   ■ $100 per month for telephone
   ■ $300 per month for office supplies
   ■ $500 per month for liability insurance
4. For program expenses, ACAF will spend
   ■ $12,000 per year for travel
   ■ $36,000 per year for outreach activities
   ■ $60,000 per year for training
   ■ $120,000 for research
5. Finally, ACAF will organize fund-raising activities, which will involve the following expenses:
   ■ $2,400 per year for special events
   ■ $1,200 per year for social networking
   ■ $2,400 per year for publication and literature

Considering the above assumptions, the budget will be something like the following (Table 7.5):

TABLE 7.5 Budget for Appleton Cancer Awareness Foundation

Appleton Cancer Awareness Foundation Budget Fiscal Year 2012–2013	
Revenue	Total in U.S. dollars
Membership	100,000.00
Donation	500,000.00
Total revenue	**600,000.00**

TABLE 7.5 Budget for Appleton Cancer Awareness Foundation (*continued*)

Appleton Cancer Awareness Foundation Budget Fiscal Year 2012–2013	
Expenditures	
Administrative expenses	
Salaries	
Executive director	60,000.00
Administrator	40,000.00
Development coordinator	35,000.00
Administrative assistant	25,000.00
Janitor	20,000.00
Fringe benefits	36,000.00
Total salaries	*216,000.00*
Facilities, equipment, supplies	
Rent	24,000.00
Utilities	12,000.00
Repair	6,000.00
Copy rental	6,000.00
Postage	3,000.00
Telephone	1,200.00
Office supplies	3,600.00
Liability insurance	6,000.00
Total facilities, equipment, and supplies	*61,800.00*
Program expenses	
Travel	12,000.00
Outreach	36,000.00
Training	60,000.00
Research	120,000.00
Total program expenses	*228,000.00*
Fund-raising	
Special events	2,400.00
Social networking	1,200.00
Publication/literature	2,400.00
Total fund-raising	*6,000.00*
Total expenditures	**511,800.00**
Surplus (deficit)	**88,200.00**

Performance-Based Budgeting

The performance budget is informed by performance reports developed by financial managers. The performance budget links performance goals and cost of goal attainment. Efficiency and productivity (cost per activity) constitute the baseline of performance goal costs.

Priority-Based Budgeting

Priority-based budgeting focuses on organizational priorities (goals and objectives). This budgeting approach starts with a review of existing services and ranks them based on whether a service is essential, highly desirable, or beneficial. Criteria and scale will vary from one organization to the next, and are usually adopted by the board of directors.

BUDGET AND FINANCIAL SUSTAINABILITY

The budgeting process and practices in a nonprofit organization play a key role in future financial sustainability. For example, many organizations intentionally include long-term projections into the annual budget. They update the projections each year, by taking into account the key social and economic factors affecting long-term projections (e.g., fiscal trends on national output, prices, and interest rates), and with the assumptions that the baselines for such projections will not change significantly. Further, nonprofit organizations can develop 5-year budgets, adjusting for key fiscal assumptions that underline long-term projections. Then, they would revise each upcoming fiscal year budget based on current realities. This will enable them not only to assess the accuracy of long-term projections used, but also to provide a preview regarding whether the budgetary process is an effective contributor to drive the organization on a path for financial sustainability.

QUESTIONS AND ACTIVITIES

1. What is a budget?
2. How can you describe the most common types of budget?
3. Why do you think a budget is important for the financial sustainability of a nonprofit organization?
4. What is the main difference between zero-based and incremental budgets?
5. What is the process of developing a budget for a nonprofit organization?

CASE STUDY: ROCHESTER COMMUNITY ASSOCIATION

The Rochester Community Association, Inc. is a 501(c) not-for-profit organization located in Rochester, New York, which provides health care and education services to parents and families in Rochester. You are hired as the new assistant executive director. The director is busy with other administrative tasks. She asks you to use the budget for the last fiscal year to develop the budget for the next fiscal year (2015–2016) based on the following assumptions:

1. The board anticipates that the current education grant will not be renewed and income from contracts will be reduced by 10% for the health program and 5% for the education program, for the next fiscal year.
2. The board decided to increase fund-raising revenues by 50%.

(continued)

3. The board decided to reduce education allowances for the education program by 20%.
4. The board decided to reduce salaries by 10%.
5. There will be an increase in administrative expenses by 5%, except for salaries and education allowances.

Develop a new budget based on the above assumptions!

Rochester Community Association, Inc.			
Budget Federal Year 2014–2015			
Income	Health program	Education program	In U.S. dollars
Contracts	630,000	500,000	1,130,000
Fund-raising	121,000	120,000	241,000
Grant	60,000	95,000	155,000
Total income	811,000	715,000	1,526,000
Expenses			
Program expenses	340,000	245,000	585,000
Total program expenses	340,000	245,000	585,000
Administrative expenses			
Salaries	140,000	130,000	270,000
Health insurance	85,000	80,000	165,000
Dental insurance	14,000	15,000	29,000
Rent	26,000	20,000	46,000
Janitor	16,000	15,000	31,000
Liability insurance	15,000	15,000	30,000
Supplies	36,000	40,000	76,000
Utilities	21,000	24,000	45,000
Education allowances	16,000	24,000	40,000
Total administrative expenses	369,000	363,000	732,000
Total expenses	709,000	608,000	1,317,000
Surplus (deficit)	102,000	107,000	209,000

Financial Management

At the completion of the chapter, the reader will be able to:

1. Define the concept of financial management.
2. Establish the relationship between financial management and nonprofit financial managers.
3. Discuss the various facets of nonprofit corporate finance and accounting.
4. List the most common funding sources of nonprofit organizations.
5. Describe a financial management system.
6. Explain the relationship between financial management and the financial sustainability of nonprofit organizations.

This chapter examines the financial and accounting principles and procedures related to the management of a nonprofit organization. The chapter addresses basic accounting principles that leaders of a nonprofit organization should be aware of, and the conditions surrounding the financial situation of a nonprofit organization. The chapter includes various frameworks to help understand facets of financial management in nonprofit organizations.

WHAT IS FINANCIAL MANAGEMENT?

Simply put, financial management is the efficient and effective planning of investment, financing, and asset management decisions through goal setting and identification and management of risks in order to ensure a positive cash flow and/or maximize the wealth of the organization. The ability of a nonprofit organization to deliver services to the maximum number of clients possible depends on its financial resources. The more financial resources generated by a nonprofit organization, the greater is the potential to offer more services. In times of financial and economic crisis, a nonprofit organization may find it difficult to sustain existing services and even be forced to terminate some. In fact, one of the ways to understand the level of financial sustainability of a nonprofit organization is the extent to which such an organization was able to keep providing existing services despite financial hardship. A vulnerable organization will reduce its services as soon as an external financial crisis hits. Consequently, people who rely solely on the services provided by an organization may see the overall conditions related to their survival deteriorating

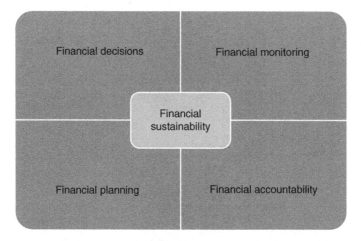

FIGURE 8.1 A nonprofit perspective of financial management.

significantly. One must understand that an organization is as good as its ability to meet the needs of its target population. Efficient and effective financial management is one of the most important tools that help an organization achieve its goals and objectives.

As Figure 8.1 illustrates, a nonprofit perspective on financial management includes financial planning, financial monitoring, financial decisions, and financial accountability in order to ensure that an organization can sustain its financial resources to fulfill its vision and mission through the achievement of organizational goals and objectives.

Financial Planning

Financial planning is a systematic process used to determine the strategic financial goals and objectives of an organization, as well as its activities and resources (human, material, and financial), and the timeline needed to achieve them. Financial planning starts with an organizational analysis, the development of a budget that accounts for the costs related to resources that are necessary to implement specific activities, and the identification of anticipated risks and strategies for risk management. Organizations use techniques, such as forecasting and analytics, to perform financial planning. Forecasting is the use of data on past performances to predict future performance for a similar period. For example, if revenues were down during the second quarter of the past 5 years, forecasting will predict that income will decrease by the second quarter of next year. The budgeting process will take such information into account. On the other hand, analytics use statistical analysis of data to predict future trends or behaviors. For example, analytics might predict that people will be more inclined to donate during the Christmas season or during the tax-filing period. Therefore, fund-raising strategy should increase efforts during such periods to increase revenue.

Financial Decisions

Financial decisions are deliberative choices made by an organization with respect to investment priorities, funding allocation, and working capital needed to conduct organizational

FIGURE 8.2 Key factors influencing financial decisions in nonprofit organizations.

operations. Figure 8.2 presents various factors that can affect financial decisions in a nonprofit organization:

- Funding opportunities
- Financial analysis
- Organizational challenges
- Organizational mandates
- Organizational leadership
- Multifaceted decision path

Funding opportunities: Funding opportunities exist to the extent that a nonprofit can adapt to the priorities set by funding sources. The funding priorities of individual, corporate, and other institutional entities influence the decision of a nonprofit organization to seek a particular funding or not. In other words, seeking funding requires a match between the priorities of a nonprofit organization and those of a grant-maker agency.

Financial analysis: The analysis of financial statements is another key factor that influences financial decisions in a nonprofit organization. The financial statements include the statement of activities (describes revenues generated and how they are spent), the statement of financial position (describes the assets and liabilities), and the statement of cash flow (describes the inflow and outflow of cash). The analysis of these financial statements can dictate decisions regarding the budget for the upcoming fiscal year, fund-raising activities, spending behaviors, and other similar financial decisions.

Organizational challenges: Nonprofit organizations exist because they want to tackle community or social challenges. These challenges are explored more systematically through the assessment of the clients' needs. In that context, needs assessment and SWOT (*strengths, weaknesses, opportunities,* and *threat*) analysis can help uncover what should be the key organizational priorities, and influence how to best use financial resources in order to be up to the challenges faced by the organization.

Organizational mandates: Effective nonprofit organizations develop strategic plans every 3, 5, 7, or 10 years to adopt strategic goals in the light of their vision and mission statements. Part of setting strategic priorities is to align with organizational mandates, which are key elements to guide the implementation of a strategic plan. Therefore, organizational mandates influence decisions about line items to be included, as well as what to increase or decrease in annual budgets.

Organizational leadership: A nonprofit organization is only as effective as its leaders. The vision of the leaders of a nonprofit organization influences not only the governance culture, but also how an organization sets strategic priorities. The leaders influence the financial decisions regarding ranking of priorities, approval of budgets, and allocation of financial resources to programs.

Multifaceted decision path: There is no one single factor that influences the financial decisions in a nonprofit organization. Funding opportunities, financial statement analysis, organizational challenges, organizational mandates, and organizational leadership combine in various forms to influence financial decisions in nonprofit organizations. Therefore, the use of multiple criteria offers a multifaceted decision path for financial decisions in nonprofit organizations.

Financial Monitoring

Financial monitoring involves a system that controls the accounting of methods and procedures, the reliability of financial reporting, and the ability of an organization to obtain feedback that can help achieve strategic and operational goals and objectives. Financial monitoring helps nonprofit organizations collect information about revenues, expenses, costs, and performance. Financial monitoring is a prerequisite for financial accountability. Without financial monitoring, it is impossible to ensure that strategic plans, annual plans, and budgets are being implemented properly. The financial monitoring in a nonprofit organization involves the board of directors, the executives, the managers, the funders, and the public in different capacities. For example, as part of its fiduciary responsibilities the board monitors financial oversight. The executives monitor the obligations of financial accountability to internal and external stakeholders. The managers monitor partly in reaction to the expectations of accountability from their supervisors. The funders monitor to ensure that their contributions are being spent properly. The public monitors to ensure that publicly supported organizations deserve the support they receive.

Financial Accountability

Nonprofit organizations have the responsibility of using their resources as promised to the constituencies or donors (e.g., individuals, groups, institutions). Donors make their contributions based on the vision that an organization shared with them and the purpose for which their contributions will be used. This creates an obligation for a nonprofit organization to use the donations for such specified purposes and to explain to the public how the organization has delivered on its commitment to use financial resources as promised. Financial accountability implies that an organization maintains a sound system for internal control, develops and adopts conflict-of-interest policies, prepares and publishes ongoing financial reports that are available to all internal and external stakeholders, and conducts internal and external audits by qualified professionals. Auditing is a key element of financial accountability because it involves the opinions of an independent third party, the CPA (certified public accountant).

The following items refer to the three levels of an organization's financial record, which are compilation, review, and audit:

1. *Compilation* is the lowest level of the record, which involves little more than gathering various financial records into a readable format. In compilation, the accountant does not express his or her opinions and does not confirm the authenticity of material presented.
2. *Review* is the middle level. For a review, the accountant compiles information into standardized forms and analyzes such information to reflect consistency. The accountant does not express her or his opinions, but performs quick analyses for the sake of consistency. This simply provides additional comfort knowing that another set of eyes has reviewed materials for inconsistencies or gaps.
3. Finally, the *audit* is the highest level of analysis of financial records. The audit is the most intensive of the three levels. This is the deepest, most intense examination of financial information. The audit tests management's representations in many ways based on pre-established protocols. This provides greater opportunity to spot errors and omissions, and make suggestions for improvement. The levels of auditing offer a different mix of complexity of the analysis. It takes more time to complete, but provides stronger assurance to external stakeholders. Independent audits are a natural means to assure the public's trust in a nonprofit organization. Yearly financial audits are becoming a necessary part of nonprofit financial management. In fact, nonprofit organizations (e.g., universities, hospitals, government entities, and public charities) receiving federal funding have specific auditing requirements that they have to meet, in order to continue to receive their funding.

Further, the Sarbanes–Oxley law, passed in response to the increase in accounting scandals and questionable financial practices, requires that boards of publicly held companies take responsibility for the relationship with the auditor. Although the Sarbanes–Oxley requirements did not specifically target nonprofit organizations, they put financial managers of nonprofit organizations on notice regarding the financial accountability of publicly supported agencies.

FINANCIAL MANAGERS

Financial managers are board members and staff who participate in making strategic financial planning, implementation, monitoring, and reporting decisions for an organization. Therefore, members of the board of directors, the chief executive officer (CEO) or executive director, the chief financial officer (CFO), program or project managers who participate in the budgeting and budget-implementation process are all financial managers. In other words, the board of directors is as responsible as the CFO and the CEO for the financial management of a nonprofit organization.

FINANCIAL MANAGEMENT AND NONPROFIT FINANCIAL MANAGERS

In most key aspects of financial planning, financial decision making, monitoring, and accountability, there are no significant differences between the financial management of a nonprofit organization and that of a for-profit corporation. However, as indicated in Chapter 1, nonprofit organizations and for-profit corporations manage their profit differently. For example, contrary to for-profit corporations, which distribute part of their profit to shareholders in the form of dividends, nonprofit organizations use their profit to maximize services to clients or communities. Further, nonprofit organizations have different standards of flexibility to make financial reallocation decisions. Donors may make donations to a nonprofit organization either for general use (unrestricted fund) or a specific purpose (restricted fund). As a result, the nonprofit manager must be a good steward of all donations received, especially restricted funds. The nonprofit manager must ensure that the organization maintains an accounting system that allows for effective management, monitoring, and reporting about restricted and unrestricted funds.

Financial management of not-for-profits is similar to financial management in the commercial sector in many respects; however, certain key differences shift the focus of a not-for-profit financial manager. A for-profit enterprise focuses on profitability and maximizing shareholder value. A not-for-profit organization's primary goal is not to increase shareholder value; rather it is to provide for some socially desirable need on an ongoing basis. A not-for-profit generally lacks the financial flexibility of a commercial enterprise because it depends on resource providers that are not engaging in an exchange transaction. The resources provided are directed toward providing goods or services to a client other than the actual resource provider. Thus the not-for-profit must demonstrate its stewardship of donated resources—money donated for a specific purpose must be used for that purpose. That purpose is either specified by the donor or implied in the not-for-profit's stated mission. The management and reporting activities of a not-for-profit must emphasize stewardship for these donated resources. The staff must be able to demonstrate that the dollars were used as directed by the donor. The shift to an emphasis on external financial reports about donor restrictions has made the use of fund accounting systems even more critical.

Budgeting and cash management are two areas of financial management that are extremely important exercises for not-for-profit organizations. The organization must pay close attention to whether it has enough cash reserves to continue to provide services to its clientele. Cash flow can be extremely challenging to predict because an organization relies on revenue from resource providers that do not expect to receive the service provided. In fact, an increase in demand for a not-for-profit's services can lead to a management crisis. It is difficult to forecast contribution revenue in a reliable manner from year to year. For that reason, the control of expenses is an area of increased emphasis. Budgeting therefore becomes a critical activity for a not-for-profit organization.

OVERVIEW OF NONPROFIT CORPORATE FINANCE

Nonprofit corporate finance deals with the funding sources, the fund-raising strategies, the capitalization structures of a nonprofit organization, and the tools or procedures used to make financial resource allocation decisions. The goal of nonprofit corporate finance should be to ensure that an organization is on a path for financial sustainability.

Fiscal Year

A fiscal year is a period that sets the beginning and the end of the annual budget and financial statements of an organization or a company. A fiscal year is different from a calendar year. A calendar year typically starts on January 1 and ends on December 31. However, a fiscal year is a corporation's or organization's annual period within which starts and ends a cycle of accounting transactions. Fiscal years will vary according to the constitution or bylaws of an organization. For example, an organization may decide to run a fiscal year based on the calendar year, thus having a fiscal year that starts on January 1 and ends on December 31. Another organization may decide to start its fiscal year on July 1 and end it on June 30. The board of another organization may adopt October 1 to September 30 or April 1 to March 31 as the fiscal year of their organization. Various factors may influence the adoption of a fiscal year by an organization. For example, an organization may adopt the fiscal year of its first or major funder. Another organization may adopt its country's or nation-state's fiscal year in order to facilitate accounting activities. In most cases, organizations adopt either the calendar or the fiscal year of a country. Table 8.1 presents a sample of fiscal years for selected countries.

TABLE 8.1   Sample of Fiscal Years for Selected Countries

Country	Start Date	End Date
Australia	July 1	June 30
Canada	April 1	March 31
China	January 1	December 31
France	January 1	December 31
Haiti	October 1	September 30
Hong Kong	April 1	March 31
India	April 1	March 31
Japan	April 1	March 31
Russia	January 1	December 31
South Africa	April 1	March 31
United Arab Emirates	January 1	December 31
United Kingdom	April 1	March 31
United States	July 1	June 30

Sources: Australia (http://www.indexmundi.com/australia/fiscal_year.html)
Canada (http://www.fin.gc.ca/purl/afr-eng.asp)
China (http://www.indexmundi.com/china/fiscal_year.html)
France (http://www.indexmundi.com/france/fiscal_year.html)
Haiti (http://www.indexmundi.com/haiti/fiscal_year.html)
Hong Kong (http://www.indexmundi.com/hong_kong/fiscal_year.html)
India (http://www.charteredclub.com/what-is-financial-year-fiscal-year-assessment-year-in-india/)
Japan (http://www.indexmundi.com/japan/fiscal_year.htmlapan)
Russia (http://www.indexmundi.com/russia/fiscal_year.html)
South Africa (http://www.indexmundi.com/south_africa/fiscal_year.html)
United Arab Emirates (http://www.indexmundi.com/united_arab_emirates/fiscal_year.html)
United Kingdom (http://www.indexmundi.com/united_arab_emirates/fiscal_year.html)
United States (http://www.conservapedia.com/Fiscal_year)

Generally Accepted Accounting Principles

Generally accepted accounting principles (GAAP) are the standards of accounting practices related to the conventions and rules that accountants must follow when recording financial information and preparing financial statements.

The GAAP are set through various documents by

- The Financial Accounting Standard Board (FASB)
- The Governmental Accounting Standard Board (GASB)
- The Public Company Accounting Oversight Board (PCAOB)

More specifically, the GAAP include the basic accounting principles and guidelines, the detailed rules and standards issued by FASB and its predecessor the Accounting Principles Board (APB), and the generally accepted industry practices. The Securities and Exchange Commission (SEC) has made a decision to merge the GAAP principles with the International Financial Reporting Standards (IFRS). The IFRS include standards and rules for financial accounting that can be used and understood across national boundaries. The

TABLE 8.2 Summary of Accounting Assumptions, Principles, and Constraints Related to GAAP

Assumptions	Summary
Entity principle	Revenues and expenses should be kept separate from personal expenses, because a company or an organization is a separate entity from the owners.
Going concern	A business is assumed to be in operation indefinitely. It will be a red flag worth noting, if there are concerns that an organization may not survive beyond 12 months.
Consistency	A stable currency is going to be the unit of record.
Time period	The economic activities of an enterprise can be divided into artificial time periods.
Principles	**Summary**
Cost	Companies must account and report based on acquisition costs rather than fair market value for most assets and liabilities.
Realization	Companies may record revenue only when it is realized and earned.
Matching	Expenses are recognized only when the service or the product actually makes its contribution to revenue.
Disclosure	The amount and kinds of information disclosed should be enough to make a judgment.
Constraints	**Summary**
Objectivity	Financial statements provided by accountants should be based on objective evidence.
Materiality	Accountants should focus on transactions that really matter, the ones that can affect the decisions of a reasonable individual.
Consistency	Companies must use the same accounting principles and methods from period to period.
Conservatism	When choosing between two solutions, accountants must select the choice with the least favorable outcome.

Source: Wagner (2007).

IFRS are set by the International Accounting Standards Board (IASB), which is an independent accounting foundation based in London, England. Table 8.2 presents a summary of accounting assumptions, principles, and constraints related to GAAP.

Nonprofit Accounting

As previously explained, nonprofit organizations differ from for-profit entities in terms of ownership, taxation, sources of revenues, and use of profit. Given these factors, there are some differences between nonprofit and for-profit accounting about how to account for contributions, capitalizing and depreciating assets, cash use, and functional expense allocation.

Contributions: Contributions are unique to nonprofit organizations. Consequently, special procedures are established to account for contributions, such as pledges, donated materials, membership dues, revenues from special events, and restricted and unrestricted funds.

Capitalizing and depreciating assets: Depreciation for long-lasting assets (e.g., buildings, cars, and computers) of a nonprofit organization must be recorded as in for-profit accounting, except for historical buildings, zoo animals, library books, museum collections, and other similar items.

Cash use: Most nonprofit organizations record their revenues and expenses using cash-basis or modified cash-basis accounting. In other words, revenue is recorded only when the cash is received, and expense is recorded only when payment is made. Finally, nonprofit organizations are required to report program expenses and support expenses (e.g., management, and fund-raising).

Functional expense allocation: Nonprofit organizations are required to report program expenses (spent directly on programs) and support expenses (e.g., management, fund-raising).

FUNDING SOURCES

Nonprofit organizations do not have shareholders. Therefore, they raise capital through fund-raising activities. Funding sources of nonprofit organizations include individual and corporate donations, grants from private and government funders, fees for services, and investment.

Gifts and Donations

Gifts and donations come from individuals, companies, charitable trusts and foundations. Usually, they are considered private funding that nonprofit organizations can use for whatever purpose related to their vision and mission. Gifts and donations are tax deductible. Some examples of gifts and donations include, but are not limited to:

Bequests: This is a donation made on the donor's death, not affected by estate tax. Bequests are like donations, but differ in the sense that they happen only when the donor passes away; then the value of the donation is removed from the donor's taxable estate.

Charitable remainder trust (CRT): The asset being donated is removed from the donor's estate and placed in a trust, thus removing the asset from the donor's taxable estate. Once the trust beneficiaries get up to 20 years' worth of income, the amount left over goes to the charity. There are two types of CRTs. There can be a charitable remainder annuity trust (CRAT), which helps ensure that the beneficiaries receive a fixed amount of income each year. The donor sets up a certain amount that the trust will pay the beneficiary each year, but must have a minimum payout of 5%. The payments are fixed. If the interest amount is not enough to cover the payment, the CRT can be a charitable remainder unitrust (CRU). In that case, the donor gives the same percentage of the trust each year to the beneficiaries. This amount can change based on the current value of the assets.

Grant Funding

Grants are money that a nonprofit organization receives from private foundations, public agencies, or other grant makers, which does not have to be repaid. However, the grant money received is tied to specific goals, objectives, and outcomes. Grants always come with the conditions under which the money can be spent.

Borrowing

Nonprofit organizations can borrow money to start income-generation activities, such as a social enterprise. Borrowing can take the form of debt finance that must be paid back. Some nonprofit organizations take advantage of the opportunity for equity finance, in which an investor takes a risk by making money available to a business with the expectation that the reward will be shared. Usually, it is very difficult for nonprofit organizations to borrow money because of their very not-for-profit nature. However, some financial institutions are open to consider borrowing requests from nonprofit organizations.

Trading

Nonprofit organizations can sell goods and services to members, or even to the public, in order to generate income for their activities. For example, a nonprofit organization can organize an event and sell tickets, or produce a publication to sell, or provide consulting services.

Donor-Advised Fund

A donor-advised fund is a charitable instrument through which a nonprofit organization administers charitable donations on behalf of an individual, a family, or an organization. The advised-donor fund provides relief to the individual, family, or organization by not having to incur the administrative expenses of creating a private foundation. Donor-advised funds are new and allow the donors to have tax advantages while directing the use of their donation.

Fee for Service

Some nonprofit organizations provide services for a small fee. This is the agreed-on money paid for services provided. There do not have to be contracts or expectations of future services, and the cost for services can be driven by market trends and/or competitors or similar organizations.

Investment

Nonprofit organizations invest in for-profit-like activities in order to generate additional income to support their activities. Investment can be made in pension funds, self-insurance funds, or endowment funds.

CAPITALIZATION STRUCTURES

Capitalization structures determine how a nonprofit organization generates capital and carries long-term debt and net assets while implementing programs and providing services to its clients or target population. Nonprofit organizations generate capital through profits and borrowing. Further, capitalization structures dictate whether an organization will buy or lease a machine or equipment. A decision to buy or lease has implications for financial sustainability or services. In most cases, leasing may be a more cost-effective option in the short term, but ownership of an asset is less expensive in the long term.

FINANCIAL ALLOCATION

Nonprofit organizations make allocation decisions based on projects and programs prioritized by the board of directors. Financial allocation or appropriation occurs after a budget has been approved. However, the real allocation or appropriation takes place during the budgeting process.

FINANCIAL MANAGEMENT SYSTEMS

A financial management system (FMS) in a nonprofit organization is a systematic process supported by software technology and internal control policies and procedures used by internal stakeholders of such organization to manage income, expenses, assets, and liabilities in a way that is effective, efficient, and accountable to the public. As Figure 8.3 illustrates, a nonprofit financial management system includes four major elements:

1. Purpose
2. Policies and procedures
3. Technology
4. Internal stakeholders' roles

Purpose

Nonprofit organizations are publicly supported entities. They receive money from the public through individual and corporate donations, as well as from foundation and government grants. The public is entitled to know whether its donations or contributions are used in a way that helps fulfill the vision and mission communicated by a given nonprofit organization. Consequently, nonprofit organizations are exposed to greater public scrutiny and expectations to show that income, expenses, assets, and liabilities are managed

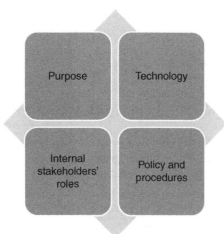

FIGURE 8.3 Major elements of a nonprofit financial management system.

efficiently. In other words, nonprofit organizations have to satisfy public expectations of accountability and stewardship. The purpose of a financial management system is to enable a nonprofit organization to maintain internal control, monitoring, and reporting procedures that help meet such expectations. To this end, a financial management system helps perform tasks and practical functions such as:

- Streamlining invoicing and billing (e.g., pledges, service fees)
- Reducing the risk for record-keeping errors and redundancy
- Complying with tax regulations, accounting principles, and financial reporting
- Managing accounting changes
- Monitoring and adjusting organizational budgets
- Ensuring transparency in management of revenues and expenses
- Keeping track of depreciation schedules and liabilities
- Coordinating accounts and financial statements
- Ensuring the integrity and security of financial operations in a way that fosters accountability and greater opportunities for stewardship
- Contributing to environmental sustainability by reducing the use of paperwork

Policies and Procedures

A financial management system is based on written policies and procedures that guide the internal financial control of an organization. Elements of policies and procedures include, but are not limited to:

- Accounting policy manuals
- Whistleblower policies
- Document destruction and retention policies,
- Codes of ethics, including conflict-of-interest policies
- Information technology (IT) control policies (e.g., user access, system, application, and data security)
- Policies for cash management, payroll, and accounts payable

The policies and procedures explain the roles and responsibilities of various internal stakeholders in internal financial control decisions, as well as procedures and principles that apply when

■ Developing or adjusting budgets
■ Recording financial transactions
■ Capitalizing on depreciating assets
■ Making deposits, monitoring petty cash and reimbursement, and reconciling bank statements
■ Managing accounts payable and receivable and accounting for bad debts
■ Preparing and reviewing financial statements
■ Conducting an internal audit of financial statements
■ Managing payrolls

Technology

Nonprofit organizations use accounting and fund-raising software to ensure a systematic functioning of their internal control system. Technology makes it possible to create systems for data input and data management that facilitate data analysis and financial decisions to improve effectiveness and efficiency.

Stakeholders' Accountability

A financial management system includes written job descriptions that define the roles and responsibilities for directors, officers, executives, managers, staff, consultants, and volunteers in the financial operations of a nonprofit organization. Table 8.3 provides a selected list of financial stakeholders' roles in financial management systems.

FINANCIAL MANAGEMENT AND FINANCIAL SUSTAINABILITY

Financial management is essential to the ability of an organization to sustain financial resources in order to continue to provide key services to clients over time, regardless of external financial circumstances. Financial management is the management of financial resources in order to achieve the goals and objectives of a business or an organization. As indicated

TABLE 8.3   Sample of Financial Stakeholders' Roles in Financial Management Systems

Stakeholder	Roles
Board director	Responsible for the overall acquisition and management of funds in an organization.
Chief executive officer	Serves as chief administrator of all operations based on delegation of authority received from the board.
Chief financial officer	Oversees the overall financial management of an organization.
Chief operating officer (COO)	Oversees the daily operations of an organization.
Treasurer	Serves as steward for an organization's financial assets.

earlier, financial management requires adequate financial planning, which includes the forecasting of cash flow (inflows and outflows of cash in monthly or quarterly periods), short-term (revenues, costs, and expenses for 1 year or less) and long-term (revenues, costs, and expenses for a period of 5 or 10 years) financial needs. Forecasting allows an organization to anticipate financial resources that are necessary for the organization to continue to provide services over time. Nonprofit organizations should ensure that they have the best possible forecasting at their disposal. Failure to do so can put an organization at risk of unforeseen dissolution. This would be unfortunate, because the clients would be the people to be most severely affected. Forecasting not only helps anticipate the future financial needs of a nonprofit organization, but also provides the support to generate funding from potential donors. It is better to make a case when you know what the needs are. And donors like donating to an organization that knows what it is doing and that is going to be around for some time.

In addition to forecasting, financial planning involves the development of operating budgets (allocation of funds to costs and expenses), capital budgets (purchase of property, buildings, and equipment), cash budgets (monthly or quarterly cash balance), and a master budget (all the organizational budgets). A budget is a translation of the organization's goals and objectives into financial terms. The execution of a budget should signify that an organization is serious about the words in its vision and mission statements. Being serious about the vision and mission statements also means that the organization has truly set a higher purpose, whose sustainability is critical. That sustainability will depend in large part on key aspects of financial management, such as forecasting and budgeting.

It is not enough to forecast financial needs and develop budgets. The appropriate execution of the budget is as important, probably even the most important function of financial management that can help an organization ensure that adequate financial resources will be available over time to continue to provide services to clients. The budget is implemented through the management of daily business operations, accounts receivable, obtaining of funding and financing, and other financial decisions. Financial control helps monitor and compare actual revenues, costs, and expenses with the projected ones to ensure that the financial planning is being executed properly. Financial control provides opportunities to uncover warning signs and take corrective actions in time. Adequate financial control is not only critical for effective management, but it also makes a statement to donors that an organization is being a good steward of its financial resources. An organization that is accountable to its stakeholders through sound financial management practices is more likely to retain existing donors and attract new ones. The opportunity to attract new funding over time is essential to continue to provide services over time.

QUESTIONS AND ACTIVITIES

1. What is financial management? What is the goal of financial management?
2. Why is financial management important for nonprofit organizations?
3. What are the characteristics of an effective financial management system?
4. What do you consider the key elements of a nonprofit corporate system to be? Why?
5. How does accounting in nonprofit organizations differ from that of for-profit corporations?

REFERENCE

Wagner, D. A. (2007). *Accounting assumptions, principles, and constraints: A short review*. Retrieved from http://mbafaq.blogspot.com/2007/08/accounting-assumptions-principles-and.html

Financial Statements

At the completion of the chapter the reader will be able to:

1. Define the concept of the financial statement.
2. Describe and develop an income statement.
3. Describe and develop a balance sheet.
4. Describe and develop a statement of cash flow.
5. Establish the differences between an income statement and balance sheet.
6. Identify the sections of Internal Revenue Service (IRS) Form 990 related to the income statement and the balance sheet.

This chapter introduces the generic structures or formats of three main financial statements: the income statement, the balance sheet, and the statement of cash flow. This chapter explores the principles and procedures used to develop various financial statements and links them to the legal financial reporting requirements for a nonprofit organization. The reader will gain experience with the basic terminology and tools to read nonprofit and public financial statements.

WHAT IS A FINANCIAL STATEMENT?

Nonprofit organizations receive their contributions from the public through various forms, which encompass, but are not limited to, individual donations, corporate donations, grants from private and/or public institutions, bequests, and trusts. Unlike in the for-profit sector, when individuals, groups, or institutions contribute to a nonprofit organization, they do not expect dividends or a return on investment directly to them. However, they expect that nonprofit organizations that receive their contributions or donations are accountable to them. One of the ways that nonprofit organizations can document their accountability is by developing and publishing financial statements that are available for public consultation.

A financial statement is a monthly, quarterly, or yearly written report that describes the financial situation or condition of a for-profit or nonprofit entity. For example, financial statements provide information about the revenues generated and expenses incurred by a nonprofit organization, as well as the assets and liabilities. These concepts will be defined further in this chapter. In the case of nonprofit organizations, financial statements are essential to the development of a financial management system, the preparation of the IRS (Internal Revenue Service) Form 990, the maintenance of a culture of accountability to the public, and to conduct effective fund-raising activities. The most common financial statements are the income statement, the balance sheet, and the statement of cash flow.

INCOME STATEMENT

Nonprofit organizations exist to provide one or several community services to individuals who may not have been able to afford such services if they had to receive them from a for-profit entity. In other words, services provided by nonprofit organizations incur costs that are for the most part supported by the generous contributions of donors or funding agencies. Therefore, nonprofit organizations generate revenues or income, which enable them to make expenses for activities that support the fulfillment of their vision and mission. The revenues or income generated and the expenses or expenditures made in implementing their activities are reported to various stakeholders, through the income statement or the statement of activities. The income statement shows an organization's financial health or net worth over time. The income statement includes three major sections:

1. The income or revenues
2. The expenses or expenditures
3. The balance or summary

Income or Revenues

Income or revenues generated by a nonprofit organization will vary, based on the fund-raising strategies adopted by any given nonprofit entity. Some of the most common sources of income or revenues include, but are not limited to, membership dues, special gifts, individual donations, corporate donations, government grants, private grants, sales, and other revenues.

Membership

Membership revenues are generated through board member contributions and/or the annual contributions of members. Some nonprofit organizations have only a board and do not have other members. Therefore, they have only one type of membership revenue.

Special Gifts

In addition to annual or regular contributions from members, some nonprofit organizations receive special gifts from either members or nonmembers who want to support the mission and vision of an entity in a very specific way. A special gift tends to be a one-time amount or an asset that is cash convertible.

Individual Donations

Individual donations come from random individuals who want to support the cause of a nonprofit organization. Individual donations can be a one-time donation or a regular monthly, quarterly, or annual donation.

Corporate Donations

Many for-profit corporations adopt the principle of corporate social responsibility, which is the contribution of a fraction of their net profit to the community in which they conduct business. Corporate donations can be solicited or unsolicited. A nonprofit organization may solicit a monetary request from a for-profit business entity for the support of a particular initiative. The request can be successful or unsuccessful. On the other hand, some for-profit corporations make their donations through a grant process managed by their own foundation (corporate foundation).

Government Grants

Government grants are grant funding received from a government entity at the local (city, county), state (state agency), or federal (federal agency) level.

Private Grants

Private grants are grants received from private foundations or other nonprofit entities. Sometimes, large nonprofit organizations receive large grants, which they have to manage in the form of subawards to smaller nonprofit organizations.

Sales

Some nonprofit organizations maintain a social enterprise or provide fee-based services that are managed like a for-profit entity; the profit then goes to support the programs or activities of the nonprofit organization.

Investments

Some nonprofit organizations have financial instruments (e.g., stocks, bonds, or other financial instruments) that produce additional income.

Other Revenues

Uncategorized or irregular contributions received by a nonprofit entity are often listed under the "other revenues" section.

Expenses or Expenditures

Expenses or expenditures report all the expenses made by a nonprofit entity in support of its vision and mission. Categories of expenses will vary by organization. Generic categories of expenses include, but are not limited to, administrative expenses, fund-raising, liabilities and insurance, and programs.

Administrative Expenses

Administrative expenses include all the expenditures incurred for the management and administration of a nonprofit entity, such as salaries, benefits, travel, transportation, facilities, equipment, supplies, utilities, and similar items.

Fund-raising

Fund-raising expenses are related to the costs to generate revenues that make it possible to provide services or conduct activities that support the vision and mission of an organization. In order to raise funds, nonprofit organizations must incur some expenses in advance (e.g., printing, mailing, transportation, rent for special events, liability insurance for fund-raising events, etc.).

Liabilities and Insurance

Liabilities and insurance expenses are made for risk-management purposes, including the sustainability of the assets of a nonprofit entity.

Programs

Program expenses are the expenditures made in direct support of a particular program. The number of program expense categories will vary with the number of programs maintained by a nonprofit entity.

Balance

The balance is the difference between revenues or income and expenses. If the balance is positive, there is a profit. If the balance is negative, there is a loss. Consider the case of the Sarah Cupcake Foundation (SCF), which was founded by a 12-year-old girl named Sarah whose mother died from breast cancer. She wanted to raise money to increase awareness about breast cancer screening and early detection. She baked cupcakes and sold them to the members of a local church. Sarah died 1 year later as a result of a car accident involving a drunk driver. Some people started the foundation to continue her legacy. For the year 2009, SCF raised $50,000 from memberships. SCF sold cupcakes for $100,000. The total cost incurred for selling the cupcakes was $15,000. SCF received a $150,000 grant from the American Cancer Society. Also, SCF received corporate gifts, which amounted to $40,000. Individual donors gave $60,000 to SCF. Furthermore, SCF paid $24,000 for rent, $12,000 for utilities and insurance, $180,000 for salaries and benefits, $6,000 for office supplies and telephone, $18,000 for educational materials, and $16,000 for printing promotional materials. Let us list all items that one would consider as income (or revenue) for SCF and its corresponding monetary value. Then, let us calculate the "total revenue." Further, we will list all items that one would consider as expenditures (or expenses) for SCF and its corresponding monetary value. Let us then calculate the total expenditures. Calculate the difference (subtract) between total revenue and total expenditures. With the information obtained from the previous operations, we can prepare a simple income statement.

The income statement developed should look like the sample in Box 9.1.

BOX 9.1 SAMPLE INCOME STATEMENT

Sarah Cupcake Foundation

Income Statement for Federal Year Ended December 31, 2009

Revenues (income)

Membership	$ 50,000
Sales	$ 100,000
Grant	$ 150,000
Corporate gifts	$ 40,000
Individual donors	$ 60,000
Total revenue	**$400,000**

Expenditures (expenses)

Cost of sales	$ 15,000
Salaries and benefits	$ 180,000
Rent	$ 24,000
Office supplies/telephone	$ 6,000
Printing promotion	$ 16,000
Educational materials	$ 18,000
Utilities and insurance	$ 12,000
Total expenditures	$ 271,000
Excess (or deficit) of revenues	$ 129,000

INCOME STATEMENT AND FORM 990

Form 990 is an annual reporting return that especially 501(c)(3) and 501(c)(4) federally tax-exempt organizations must file with the Internal Revenue Service. The most current version of the Form 990 provides information on the filing organization's mission, programs, and finances. Information from the income statement of nonprofit organizations are linked with

- Part I, summary (activities and governance, revenue, and expenses [Box 9.2])
- Part VIII, statement of revenue (contributions, gifts, grants, and other similar amounts; program service revenue; other revenue, and total revenue, categorized in total revenue, related or exempt function revenue, and revenue excluded from tax under sections 512–514 [Box 9.3])
- Part IX, statement of functional expenses (total expenses, program service expenses, management and general expenses, and fund-raising expenses [Box 9.4])

BALANCE SHEET

The balance sheet is a snapshot of the financial position of an organization at a specific point in time, generally at the close of an accounting period. The balance sheet shows an organization's financial health or net worth at a given time. The balance sheet of a nonprofit organization includes three main sections:

1. Assets
2. Liabilities
3. Fund balance

BOX 9.2 PART I SUMMARY, FORM 990

Part I	Summary				
	1	Briefly describe the organization's mission or most significant activities:			
	2	Check this box ▶ ☐ if the organization discontinued its operations or disposed of more than 25% of its net assets.			
	3	Number of voting members of the governing body (Part VI, line 1a)	3		
	4	Number of independent voting members of the governing body (Part VI, line 1b)	4		
	5	Total number of individuals employed in calendar year 2013 (Part V, line 2a)	5		
	6	Total number of volunteers (estimate if necessary)	6		
	7a	Total unrelated business revenue from Part VIII, column (C), line 12	7a		
	b	Net unrelated business taxable income from Form 990-T, line 34	7b		
				Prior Year	Current Year
	8	Contributions and grants (Part VIII, line 1h)			
	9	Program service revenue (Part VIII, line 2g)			
	10	Investment income (Part VIII, column (A), lines 3, 4, and 7d)			
	11	Other revenue (Part VIII, column (A), lines 5, 6d, 8c, 9c, 10c, and 11e) . . .			
	12	Total revenue—add lines 8 through 11 (must equal Part VIII, column (A), line 12)			
	13	Grants and similar amounts paid (Part IX, column (A), lines 1–3)			
	14	Benefits paid to or for members (Part IX, column (A), line 4)			
	15	Salaries, other compensation, employee benefits (Part IX, column (A), lines 5–10)			
	16a	Professional fundraising fees (Part IX, column (A), line 11e)			
	b	Total fundraising expenses (Part IX, column (D), line 25) ▶			
	17	Other expenses (Part IX, column (A), lines 11a–11d, 11f–24e)			
	18	Total expenses. Add lines 13–17 (must equal Part IX, column (A), line 25) .			
	19	Revenue less expenses. Subtract line 18 from line 12			

BOX 9.3 PART VIII, STATEMENT OF REVENUE, FORM 990

Form 990 (2013)   Page 9

Part VIII   **Statement of Revenue**

Check if Schedule O contains a response or note to any line in this Part VIII . . . . ☐

				(A) Total revenue	(B) Related or exempt function revenue	(C) Unrelated business revenue	(D) Revenue excluded from tax under sections 512-514
Contributions, Gifts, Grants and Other Similar Amounts	1a	Federated campaigns . . .	1a				
	b	Membership dues	1b				
	c	Fundraising events	1c				
	d	Related organizations . . .	1d				
	e	Government grants (contributions)	1e				
	f	All other contributions, gifts, grants, and similar amounts not included above	1f				
	g	Noncash contributions included in lines 1a-1f: $					
	h	**Total.** Add lines 1a–1f . . . . ▶					
Program Service Revenue			Business Code				
	2a						
	b						
	c						
	d						
	e						
	f	All other program service revenue .					
	g	**Total.** Add lines 2a–2f . . . . ▶					
	3	Investment income (including dividends, interest, and other similar amounts) . . . . ▶					

BOX 9.4 PART IX, STATEMENT OF FUNCTIONAL EXPENSES, FORM 990

Form 990 (2013)   Page 10

Part IX   **Statement of Functional Expenses**

Section 501(c)(3) and 501(c)(4) organizations must complete all columns. All other organizations must complete column (A).

Check if Schedule O contains a response or note to any line in this Part IX . . . . ☐

Do not include amounts reported on lines 6b, 7b, 8b, 9b, and 10b of Part VIII.	(A) Total expenses	(B) Program service expenses	(C) Management and general expenses	(D) Fundraising expenses
1 Grants and other assistance to governments and organizations in the United States. See Part IV, line 21				
2 Grants and other assistance to individuals in the United States. See Part IV, line 22 . . .				
3 Grants and other assistance to governments, organizations, and individuals outside the United States. See Part IV, lines 15 and 16 . .				
4 Benefits paid to or for members				
5 Compensation of current officers, directors, trustees, and key employees				
6 Compensation not included above, to disqualified persons (as defined under section 4958(f)(1)) and persons described in section 4958(c)(3)(B) . .				
7 Other salaries and wages				
8 Pension plan accruals and contributions (include section 401(k) and 403(b) employer contributions)				
9 Other employee benefits				
10 Payroll taxes				
11 Fees for services (non-employees):				

Assets

Assets include anything of value that belongs to an organization. Organizations have current assets and noncurrent or long-term assets.

Current assets: These are assets that can be turned into cash on short notice or consumed within a year.

■ **Cash (Non interest bearing):** This refers to cash on hand and money in checkbook after it has been fully reconciled. It is better for nonprofit organization to have just the necessary amount of cash and not more, because it earns no interest.
■ **Savings and temporary cash investments:** Money held in an interest-bearing account for the short term (e.g., certificates of deposit or CDs, money market funds, and U.S. Treasury bills).
■ **Accounts receivable:** This is mainly for nonprofit organizations that have fee-based service programs and bill their clients for services rendered. It can be money to be paid either by the client or a third party on behalf of the client. Accounts receivable is money that an organization expects to receive based on an invoice, but has not been collected yet.
■ **Allowance for doubtful accounts:** All receivables may not be collected. However, it can be difficult at time to collect some debts from clients, and the account remains unpaid. Unpaid accounts are called bad debts.
■ **Pledges receivable:** Similar to accounts receivable, these are the promises by donors to make a donation to a nonprofit organization, but which have not yet been paid.
■ **Grants receivable:** Pledges made by individuals, and grants by foundations, corporations, and government agencies.

Uncommon items: These include:

■ **Receivables due from current and former officers:** This refers to the very occasional practice of lending money to officers and directors.
■ **Receivables due from other disqualified persons:** Loans to organization insiders who are not current or former officers.
■ **Other notes and loans receivable:** Loans to outsiders, some of which may turn out to be doubtful accounts.
■ **Inventories:** Inventories are the accumulation of materials and supplies, which are waiting to be used in delivering services or making a product.
■ **Prepaid expenses and deferred charges:** Benefits or expenses that have been paid in advance; generally the value of paid annual insurance that crosses fiscal years.

Noncurrent assets or long-term assets: These are assets that are more difficult to turn into cash on short notice, and tend to be more long-standing.

■ **Investments:** Securities or stocks that provide interest income and can be sold to raise cash. These are noncurrent because an organization would not want to sell a security if the market is down. In fact, because of market fluctuations, the same stock that is down today may generate a gain in the upcoming months.
■ **Other investments:** Investment in for-profit entities.
■ **Land, buildings, and equipment:** These are the holdings used for the purpose of operating the nonprofit organization.
■ **Intangible assets:** Nonphysical assets, such as intellectual property and patents (generally, an asset that does not fit into any other category).

Liabilities

Liabilities are any debt or obligation that an organization owes to a third party and must be paid. Organizations have current liabilities and noncurrent or long-term liabilities.

Current liabilities: These are obligations the corporation owes within the next year.

- *Accounts payable:* These are unpaid bills of an organization. Such accounts should be paid within 30 days.
- *Accrued salary expenses:* Salary owed to staff at the end of an accounting period, possibly because a pay period may not have coincided with an accounting period.
- *Grants payable:* This item exists mainly for grant-maker agencies and represents grant awards made to grant-seeker agencies that have not been disbursed yet.
- *Deferred revenue:* This is revenue received for a transaction that is not yet complete. For example, an organization may provide consulting services, and have received money for prepaid expenses in relation to a service that has not been rendered yet. The item is listed as a liability until the service is rendered. After this time, the money is no longer a liability, but becomes revenue.

Noncurrent liabilities: Noncurrent liabilities are obligations, such as mortgages, leases, or long-term debts, that constitute less pressing claims against assets. Noncurrent liabilities are unlikely to be paid off in a year.

- *Tax-exempt bond liabilities*: Tax-exempt bonds or other obligations issued by an organization on behalf of a state or local governmental unit, or by a state or local governmental unit on behalf of an organization, and for which such an organization has a direct or indirect liability.
- *Escrow account liability*: A financial instrument (e.g., securities, funds) held by a third party (e.g., escrow service) in a transaction between an organization and another party, until the terms of such transaction are completed.
- *Loans from officers and directors*: Loans that a nonprofit organization receives from one or more officers or directors.
- *Mortgages and other notes payable*: Mortgages or lines of credit owed to a financial institution.

Fund Balance or Net Assets or Net Worth

The fund balance is the difference between an organization's assets and liabilities. The fund balance represents assets that are owned exclusively by an organization. In for-profit organizations, the fund balance is called "equity" or "owner equity" or "profit." Net assets can be unrestricted, temporarily restricted, or permanently restricted.

- *Unrestricted net assets:* Money received without restrictions on how to spend it.
- *Temporarily restricted funds:* Money received for a special purpose that cannot be spent until a specific time. At that time, the money is transferred to an unrestricted account.
- *Permanently restricted net assets:* Assets donated not to be spent, but to invest in long-term stocks, bonds, or other financial instruments. The principal cannot be spent until the donor gives consent. However, interest income, dividends, and investment income can be spent as the donor wishes.

To illustrate, let us consider the case of Tampa Community Foundation, a nonprofit organization based in Tampa, Florida. As of December 31, 2011, the foundation has $8,500 in its

BOX 9.5 SAMPLE BALANCE SHEET

Tampa Community Foundation (TCF), Statement of Financial Position or
Balance Sheet as of December 31, 2011

Assets		Liabilities and Fund Balance	
Cash	$8,500	Accounts payable	$5,000
Accounts receivable	$5,500	Mortgages	$18,000
Land, buildings, equipment	$19,000	Other liabilities	$2,000
		Net assets	$8,000
Total assets	$33,000	Total liabilities and fund balance	$33,000

checking account, accounts receivables of $5,500, land, building, and equipment that are worth $19,000. Further, TCF has accounts payable of $5,000, owns an $18,000 mortgage, and other liabilities totaling $2,000. TCF reported net assets of $8,000. Using the above data, you can prepare a simple balance sheet, illustrated in Box 9.5.

BALANCE SHEET AND IRS FORM 990

The balance sheet provides information that can help complete Part X of Form 990. Part X requests information on Assets, Liabilities, and Net Assets or Fund Balances, categorized as beginning of year and end of year (Box 9.6).

BOX 9.6 PART X, BALANCE SHEET, FORM 990

Form 990 (2013)   Page **11**

Part X **Balance Sheet**

Check if Schedule O contains a response or note to any line in this Part X . . . . ☐

			(A) Beginning of year		(B) End of year
	1	Cash – non-interest-bearing		1	
	2	Savings and temporary cash investments		2	
	3	Pledges and grants receivable, net		3	
	4	Accounts receivable, net		4	
	5	Loans and other receivables from current and former officers, directors, trustees, key employees, and highest compensated employees. Complete Part II of Schedule L		5	
Assets	6	Loans and other receivables from other disqualified persons (as defined under section 4958(f)(1)), persons described in section 4958(c)(3)(B), and contributing employers and sponsoring organizations of section 501(c)(9) voluntary employees' beneficiary organizations (see instructions). Complete Part II of Schedule L.		6	
	7	Notes and loans receivable, net		7	
	8	Inventories for sale or use		8	
	9	Prepaid expenses and deferred charges		9	
	10a	Land, buildings, and equipment: cost or other basis. Complete Part VI of Schedule D **10a**			
	b	Less: accumulated depreciation **10b**		10c	
	11	Investments – publicly traded securities		11	
	12	Investments – other securities. See Part IV, line 11		12	
	13	Investments – program-related. See Part IV, line 11		13	

INCOME STATEMENT AND BALANCE SHEET

As you may have noticed, the income statement and the balance sheet are different in purpose and format. The income statement or statement of activities shows the income generated and the expenses incurred by an organization over a period of time. The balance sheet or statement of financial position is a snapshot of the financial position of an organization at a specific point in time, generally at the close of an accounting period. The major items of the income statement are revenue or income, expenses or expenditures, and the balance or summary. On the other hand, the three major sections of the balance sheet are assets, liabilities, and fund balance. Box 9.7 illustrates the main differences between income statement and balance sheet.

STATEMENT OF CASH FLOW

The statement of cash flow describes the inflows (sources of cash) and outflows (use of cash or expenses) of a nonprofit entity for a given period. Usually, a statement of cash flow includes four main sections:

1. *The operating activities*: Cash received from various revenue sources (e.g., grants, contracts, contributions, special events, investment income) and expense sources (e.g., salaries; payments to suppliers; and payments for utilities, travel, and telephone).
2. *The investing activities*: Cash that is related to investing activities (e.g., equipment, investments, sale of investments).
3. *Financing activities*: Cash regarding financing activities related to repayment of debt.
4. *Change in cash*: Net increase or decrease in cash.

Overall, a statement of cash flow reflects either an increase or a decrease in cash. Box 9.8 is an illustration of a statement of cash flow.

BOX 9.7 INCOME STATEMENT AND BALANCE SHEET		
	Balance Sheet	**Income Statement**
Definition	Snapshot of the financial position of an organization at a specific time.	Financial statement that shows the income generated and the expenses incurred by an organization over a period of time.
Purpose	Shows organization financial health or net worth at a given time.	• Shows the organization's financial health or net worth over time • Reveals sources of income
Major Items	• Assets • Liabilities • Fund balance or owner's equity	• Revenue or income • Expenditures or expenses • Excess (or deficit) of revenues

BOX 9.8 SAMPLE STATEMENT OF CASH FLOW	
Federal Year 2013 Statement of Cash Flow, Oshkosh Community Foundation, Inc.	
Operating activities	**Federal year 2013**
Cash received from grants	$200,000
Cash received from contracts	350,000
Cash received from contributions	100,000
Cash received from special events	150,000
Cash received from investment income	50,000
Cash paid to employees	−550,000
Cash paid to suppliers	−150,000
Cash paid to utilities, travel, phone	−60,000
Subtotal operating activities	90,000
Investing activities	
Purchase of equipment	−1200
Purchase of investments	−20,000
Proceeds from sale of investments	1000
Subtotal investing activities	−20,100
Financing activities	
Investing in endowment	−20,000
Payment on mortgage	−6,000
Subtotal financing activities	−26,000
Net increase or decrease in cash	43,900
Cash at the beginning of the year	6,100
Cash at the end of the year	$50,000

STATEMENT OF CASH FLOW AND IRS FORM 990

The statement of cash flow provides information that can help provide financial information in Form 990, Part XI, Reconciliation of Net Assets (Box 9.9).

QUESTIONS AND ACTIVITIES

1. What is a financial statement?
2. How does a balance sheet differ from an income statement?
3. What is the difference between long-term assets and short-term assets?
4. What is the difference between long-term liabilities and short-term liabilities?
5. How would you describe a statement of cash flow?

BOX 9.9 RECONCILIATION OF NET ASSETSETS

Form 990 (2013)   Page **12**

Part XI   **Reconciliation of Net Assets**

Check if Schedule O contains a response or note to any line in this Part XI . . . . ☐

1	Total revenue (must equal Part VIII, column (A), line 12)	1	
2	Total expenses (must equal Part IX, column (A), line 25)	2	
3	Revenue less expenses. Subtract line 2 from line 1	3	
4	Net assets or fund balances at beginning of year (must equal Part X, line 33, column (A)) . . .	4	
5	Net unrealized gains (losses) on investments	5	
6	Donated services and use of facilities	6	
7	Investment expenses	7	
8	Prior period adjustments	8	
9	Other changes in net assets or fund balances (explain in Schedule O)	9	
10	Net assets or fund balances at end of year. Combine lines 3 through 9 (must equal Part X, line 33, column (B))	10	

Part XII   **Financial Statements and Reporting**

Check if Schedule O contains a response or note to any line in this Part XII . . . . ☐

		Yes	No
1	Accounting method used to prepare the Form 990: ☐ Cash ☐ Accrual ☐ Other _____ If the organization changed its method of accounting from a prior year or checked "Other," explain in Schedule O.		
2a	Were the organization's financial statements compiled or reviewed by an independent accountant? . . . If "Yes," check a box below to indicate whether the financial statements for the year were compiled or reviewed on a separate basis, consolidated basis, or both:	2a	

☐ Separate basis   ☐ Consolidated basis   ☐ Both consolidated and separate basis

CASE STUDY: JOHN AND ALLISON FOUNDATION

John and Allison Foundation (JAF) is a 501(c)(3) nonprofit organization based in Atlanta, Georgia. JAF collects used books and resells them as a strategy to generate income to support its activities. The balance on JAF accounts on June 1, 2010, were as follows:

Cash $20,000
Supplies $10,000
Equipment $5,000
Accounts payable $20,000
Accounts receivable $5,000

The transactions during the month of June appear below:
Bought additional equipment on account for $20,000
Received donation from individuals for $30,000
Received donation from Corrina Corporation for $50,000
On June 30, 2010, JAF has a total balance fund of $100,000.
Prepare a balance sheet for the period ending June 30, 2010.

CASE STUDY: LOVING HEART, INC.

The balance on Loving Heart, Inc. accounts on December 1, 2011, of the current year were as follows:

Cash $15,000
Supplies $3,000
Equipment $1,000
Accounts payable $5,000
Accounts receivable $20, 000

The transactions during the month of December appear below:
Bought additional equipment with cash for $6,000
Received donation from individuals for $30,000
Received donation from Corrina Corporation for $50,000
Paid consulting fees $10,000
On December 31, 2011, Loving Heart has a total balance fund of $96,000.
Prepare a balance sheet for the period ending December 31, 2011.

CASE STUDY: MARY KATE FOUNDATION

Mary Kate Foundation (MKF) is based in Brooklyn, New York. For the year 2003, MKF provided services for $50,000. They raised $60,000 from friends. They received a $75,000 grant from the Community Foundation of New York. They spent $5,000 for marketing, $70,000 for salaries and benefits, $12,000 for rent, $6,000 for utilities, and $3,000 for telephone. MKF paid $10,000 for office supplies, $2,000 for legal and accounting, and $1,000 for printing promotion. Prepare an income statement based on the information provided.

Financial Sustainability Analysis

At the completion of the chapter the reader will be able to:

1. Define the concepts of profitability, liquidity, solvency, efficiency, and effectiveness.
2. Use formulas to analyze the financial statements of a nonprofit organization.
3. Explain whether an organization is financially sustainable or on a path for financial sustainability.
4. Make recommendations to improve the profitability, liquidity, solvency, efficiency, and effectiveness of a nonprofit organization.

As previously explained, sustainability is the ability of an organization or a project to fulfill its vision and mission, meet its goals, and serve its clients over time, regardless of changing funding conditions. In that context, sustainability can be assessed in terms of the organization itself, the services provided, and its finances. Further, I have already argued that financial sustainability is the ability of a project, a program, or an organization to maintain broader sources of funding in order to provide standard services to its clients over time. Financial sustainability is a process, not an end. It can be evaluated through profitability, liquidity, solvency, efficiency, and effectiveness. The purpose of this chapter is to introduce the concept of financial sustainability in relation to the use of financial statements. The chapter introduces selected financial ratios to assess the profitability, liquidity, solvency, efficiency, and effectiveness of a nonprofit organization.

PROFITABILITY

Profitability is the surplus of revenue over expenses. Profitability used to be a forbidden word in the nonprofit world. Today, this is no longer the case. Scholars and practitioners in nonprofit organizations and nonprofit management have come to the realization that nonprofit entities cannot spend all the money that they receive every year. They must save some of their funding for future use. The lack of profit is now considered a "going concern" for a nonprofit organization. Profit margin and return on assets are two examples of measure of profitability.

Profit margin: The **profit margin** helps measure how a company uses its revenues and controls its expenses to generate an acceptable rate of return. The profit margin is calculated by dividing the net profit by the net sales. The profit margin calculates the percentage of net profit that a company generates for every dollar in sales.

$$\text{Profit margin} = \text{Net profit}/\text{Net sales}$$

Example:

The following information was found on the Annie Foundation income statement for the year ending December 31, 2009:

Net profit: $70,000   Sales: $90,000

Calculate the profit margin!

Solution:

$$\text{Profit margin} = \$70,000/\$90,000 \qquad \text{Profit margin} = 0.777$$

Interpretation:

The profit margin of Annie Foundation is 77.7%. This profit margin must be compared with the industry average profit margin to determine whether it is lower or higher.

Return on assets (ROA): The return on assets is a measure of the return on the total investment of an organization.

$$\text{ROA} = \text{Net profit}/\text{Total assets}$$

Example:

The following information was found on the HOPE Association income statement and balance sheet.

Net profit: $100,000   Total assets: $800,000

Calculate the return on assets!

Solution:

$$\text{ROA} = \$100,000/\$800,000 \qquad \text{ROA} = 0.125 \text{ or } 12.5\%$$

Interpretation:

For every $100 of assets, HOPE Association has a return of $12.50.

LIQUIDITY

Liquidity is the ability to meet cash requirements (e.g., pay bills). Many nonprofit organizations are faced with the challenge of undercapitalization and do not have enough cash or liquidity to pay their regular bills. As a result, they have to cut core programs and sometimes dissolve. It is important for nonprofit organizations to assess their liquidity, anticipate potential for undercapitalization, and develop strategies to address such an issue. The liquidity of an organization can be measured by the current ratio, the net working capital, and the acid test or quick ratio or liquidity ratio.

1. Current Ratio

The *current ratio* helps measure the ability to pay the bills on time. It is calculated by dividing the total current assets by the total current liabilities. In other words, the current ratio calculates how many dollars in assets are likely to be converted to cash within a period of 1 year to enable a company to pay its debts during that same year. Most companies consider 1.5:1 or 2:1as an acceptable ratio.

$$\text{Current ratio} = \text{Total current assets}/\text{Total current liabilities}$$

Example:

The following information was found on the Annie Foundation income statement and balance sheet, December 31, 2008.

Current assets: *$200,000*
Current liabilities: *$100,000*

Calculate the current ratio!

Solution:

Current ratio = total current assets/ total current liabilities

Current ratio = $200,000/ $100,000

Current ratio = 2.00 times

Interpretation:

Annie Foundation's current assets are two times the value of its current liabilities.

2. Net Working Capital

Net working capital (NWC) measures the ability of an organization to face unforeseen expenses. It is calculated by subtracting the current liabilities from the current assets.

$$\text{NWC} = \text{Current assets} - \text{Current liabilities}$$

Example:

The balance sheet of Corrie foundation provides the following information for June 30, 2008:

Current assets: $24,000
Current liabilities: $20,000
Calculate the working capital!

Solution:

$$NWC = \text{Current assets} - \text{Current liabilities}$$

$$NWC = \$24,000 - \$\$20,000 \quad NWC = \$4,000$$

Interpretation:

The current assets of Corrie foundation exceeded its current liabilities by $4,000 in June 30, 2008. In other words, Corrie foundation has a positive net working capital to weather an unforeseen financial crisis.

The net working capital and the current ratio (CR) serve the same purpose. The difference is that the NWC refers to an amount of cash or near-cash asset, whereas the CR is a ratio.

3. Quick (Acid-Test) Ratio

The **acid-test** or **quick ratio** or **liquid ratio** measures the ability of an organization to use its *near cash* or quick assets to immediately pay its current liabilities. A quick ratio of over 1:1 will enable an organization to pay back its current liabilities; whereas a company with quick assets lower than 1:1 cannot currently pay back its current liabilities.

Note that inventory is excluded from the sum of financial assets. Ratios are a financially viable option for business entities but the liquidity of the liabilities shows financial stability.

The higher the ratio, the greater the company's liquidity (i.e., the better able the company is to meet current obligations using liquid assets).

$$QR = (\text{Current assets} - \text{inventory})/\text{Current liabilities}$$

Example:

The following information was found on Annie Foundation's balance sheet, December 31, 2007:

Current assets: $200,000
Inventory: $80,000
Current liabilities: $100,000
Calculate the quick ratio!

Solution:

$$\text{Quick ratio} = (\$200,000 - \$80,000)/\$100,000$$

$$QR = \$120,000/\$100,000 \ QR = \$1.2$$

Interpretation:

Annie Foundation has $1.2 of quick cash for every dollar it owes. Ideally, the quick ratio should be 1:1. A quick ratio higher than 1:1 indicates that the business can meet its current financial obligations with the available quick funds on hand. A quick ratio lower than 1:1 may indicate that the company relies too much on inventory or other assets to pay its short-term liabilities. Many lenders are interested in this ratio because it does not include inventory, which may or may not be easily converted into cash.

SOLVENCY

Solvency or leverage is the ability to pay all debts if the business were sold tomorrow. Solvency is different from liquidity because it deals with the long-term ability of an organization to continue to exist and expand. The debt ratio and the debt-to-equity ratio are two common measures of organizational solvency.

1. Debt Ratio

The *debt ratio* is used to measure the ability to pay all debts if the organization was sold tomorrow. It is calculated by dividing the total liabilities by the total assets. The debt ratio calculates the long-term solvency of a company. The total debt ratio should be 1.0 or less. A company with a high debt ratio is in danger of becoming insolvent, and risks going bankrupt.

$$\text{Debt ratio} = \text{Total liabilities}/\text{Total assets}$$

Example:

The following information was found on the Christine Center balance sheet, December 31, 2008.

Liabilities: $100,000
Assets: $200,000

Calculate the debt ratio!

Solution:

$$\text{Debt ratio} = \$100,000/\$200,000 = 0.50 \text{ or } 50\%$$

Interpretation:

Fifty percent of Christine Center assets have been financed by debt.

2. Debt-to-Equity (Fund Balance) Ratio

The *debt-to-equity ratio (DER)* measures the proportion of long-term debt to common equity or fund balance.

$$DER = \frac{\text{Long-term debt}}{\text{Equity or fund balance}}$$

Example:

The following information was found on the B-Mart Foundation balance sheet, December 31, 2006.

Liabilities: $250,000
Fund balance or equity: $100,000

Calculate the debt-to-equity (fund balance) ratio.

Solution:

$$DER = \$250,000/\$100,000$$

$$DER = 2.5 \text{ or } 250\%$$

Interpretation:

B-Mart Foundation has $2.50 cents of debt and only $1.00 in equity to meet this obligation.
Or
for every dollar of equity financing, B-Mart Foundation uses $2.50 of long-term debt
or
B-Mart Foundation owes $2.50 for every dollar it owns.

EFFICIENCY

Efficiency is the ability of an organization to deliver the maximum service possible with the lowest amount of human, material, and financial resources. The asset turnover ratio is an example of efficiency measure. Other nonconventional measures, such as the percentage of change, the growth ratio, the common size ratios, and the fund mix ratio can provide valuable information to analyze trends and the efficiency of an organization.

Asset Turnover Ratio

The asset turnover ratio (ATR) measures the productivity of an organization, which is how much income or revenue was generated from assets employed. The formula used to calculate asset turnover is the total revenue divided by average total assets. The amount of average total assets is calculated by adding the values of total assets in the beginning of the year to the values of total assets at the end of the fiscal period, then dividing the number obtained by 2.

$$ATR = \text{Total revenues}/\text{Average total assets}$$

Example:

Consider the following information from the balance sheet and income statement of the ABC community foundation.

Total revenue: $4,000,000
Total assets, beginning of fiscal year: $3,000,000
Total assets, end of fiscal year: $2,000,000

Step 1:

Average total assets = ($3,000,000 + $2,000,000)/2
Average total assets = $2,500,000

Step 2:

Asset turnover ratio = $4,000,000/$2,500,000
Asset turnover ratio = $1.6

Interpretation:

For every $1 of assets employed, ABC community foundation generates $1.6 of revenue. The asset turnover ratio is compared to ratios of other organizations of similar size.
Percentage change: Percentage change is the calculation of the percentage of change from 1 year to another in line items of financial statements (balance sheet, income statement, statement of cash flow).

RULES TO CALCULATE PERCENTAGE CHANGE

1. Calculate the difference between the number for period "A" (most recent period) and the number for period "B" (preceding period).
2. Divide the difference by the number for period "B."
3. Multiply the result by 100.

Example:

The balance sheet of B-Mart Foundation for 2009 and 2010 reflect the following cash information:

	2009	2010
Cash	$50,000	$40,000

What is the percentage change from 2009 to 2010?

Solution:

1. Calculate the difference between the number for period "A" and the number for period "B."

$$\text{"A"} - \text{"B"} = \$50,000 - \$40,000 = \$10,000$$

Divide the difference by the number for period "A."

$$\$10,000/\$40,000 = 0.25$$

Multiply the result by 100.

$$0.25 \times 100 = 25\%$$

Interpretation:

From 2009 to 2010, B-Mart Foundation has recorded a 25% increase in cash.

Growth ratio (GR): The growth ratio measures the percentage of change in the fund balance of a nonprofit organization. The growth ratio indicates the financial growth of a nonprofit organization over time.

Common size ratios (CSR): Common size ratios are used to compare trends in financial statements of an organization over time or to compare the financial situations of various organizations with similar profiles. The common size ratio for a line item is calculated by dividing the item of interest by the reference item.

For assets: Common size = Asset of interest / Total assets

Example:

Cash : $4,135   Total assets: $18,056

Calculate the common size ratio for cash!

Solution:

Common size cash = $4,135/$18,056 = 0.23
Multiplied by 100

Common size cash = $4,135/$18,056 = 23%

For liabilities: Common size = Liabilities of interest/Total liabilities and fund balance

Example:

Accounts payable: $1,553
Total liabilities and fund balance: $18,056

Calculate common size ratio for accounts payable!

Solution:

Common size ratio for accounts payable = $1,553/$18,056 =0.09
Multiplied by 100

Common size accounts payable = 9%

For income or revenue: Common size = Income of interest/Total income or revenue

Example:

Cost of goods sold: $2,000
Operating expenses: $100
Total revenue: $2,400

Calculate common size ratio for cost of goods sold, then for operating expenses!

Solution:

Common size cost of goods sold = $2,000/$2,400 =0.833
Multiplied by 100
Common size cost of goods sold = 83.3%
Common size operating expenses = $100/$2,400 = 0.042
Multiplied by 100

Common size operating expenses = 4.2%

TABLE 10.1   Sample Comparative Balance Sheet and Comparative Common Size
Balance Sheet

Assets	2002 (in U.S. Dollars)	Percentage (%)	2003 (in U.S. Dollars)	Percentage (%)
Current assets				
Cash	4,135	23	5,347	29
Accounts receivable	1,661	9	1,188	6
Inventory	2,546	14	2,674	14
Grants receivable	1,950	11	1,114	6
Total current assets	10, 292	57	10,323	56
Long-term assets				
Land building and equipment	6,283	35	7,074	38
Vehicle	1,481	8	1,170	6
Total long-term assets	7,764	43	8,244	44
Total assets	**18,056**	100	**18,567**	100
Liabilities and fund balance				
Current liabilities				
Accounts payable	1,553	9	2,432	13
Notes payable	1,228	7	1,318	7
Acquisition contracts	11,935	66	6,202	33
Total current liabilities	14,716	82	9,952	54
Long-term liabilities				
Notes payable	5,543	31	1,504	8
Deferred credits	36	0	0	
Total long-term liabilities	5,579	31	1,504	8
Total liabilities	20,295	112	11,456	62
Fund balance	−2,239	-12	7,111	38
Total liabilities and fund balance	**18,056**	100	**18,567**	100

TABLE 10.2 Sample Comparative Income Statement and Comparative Common-Size Income Statement

	2008 (in U.S. Dollars)	Percentage (%)	2007 (in U.S. Dollars)	Percentage (%)
Net sales	2 400	100.0	1800	100.0
Cost of goods sold	2 000	83.3	1400	77.8
Gross margin on sales	400	16.7	400	22.2
Operating expenses	100	4.2	80	4.4
Net income	**300**	**12.5**	**320**	**17.8**

Fund Mix Ratio

Nonprofit organizations use different types of funds, which include, but are not limited to:

■ *Current unrestricted funds or undesignated funds:* All funds that can be spent at the discretion of the administration and the board of the organization.
■ *Current restricted funds or designated funds:* Funds that must be spent only for the specific purpose designated by a donor (individual, corporation, or government). These funds cannot be reallocated for nondesignated purposes regardless of the financial needs within an organization.

The FMR measures the level of flexibility that an organization has to make fund reallocation decisions. The FMR is calculated by dividing the amount of unrestricted funds by the total assets.

$$\text{FMR} = \text{Unrestricted funds/Total assets}$$

Example:

The United Way of Oshkosh balance sheet provides the following information for December 31, 1999:

Total assets: $800,000
Unrestricted funds: $100,000
Calculate the fund mix ratio!

Solution:

FMR = Unrestricted funds/Total assets
FMR = $100,000/$800,000
FMR = 0.125
Multiplied by 100
FMR = 12.5%

Interpretation:

Only 12.5% of United Way of Oshkosh funds are available for reallocation. This ratio indicates a very small level of flexibility, depending on the size of an organization and the standard in comparison to other organizations of the same size.

EFFECTIVENESS

Effectiveness is the ability to manage the resources and programs to fulfill the mission and vision of an organization. Effectiveness can be measured through the program emphasis ratio.

Program emphasis ratio (PER): The program emphasis ratio measures the proportion of its income or revenue that a nonprofit organization spent on program support. It is calculated by dividing the cumulating of expenditures on management and fund-raising by the total income or revenue. There is a common agreement among stakeholders of non-profit organizations, that NPOs should spend at least 65% of their resources on program support expenditures.

$$PER = 100\% - [(\text{Management} + \text{Fund-raising})/\text{Total income}]$$

Example:

Oshkosh Historical Foundation (OHF) income statement for the year ended December 31, 2004:

Total management: $75,000
Fund-raising: $15,000
Total income: $450,000
Calculate the program emphasis ratio!
PER = 100% − [(Management + Fund-raising)/Total income]
PER = 100% − [($75,000 + $15,000) / $450,000]
PER = 0.80
Multiplied by 100
PER = 80%

Interpretation:

OHF spent 80% of its income on program support expenditures.

QUESTIONS AND ACTIVITIES

What formula(s) will you use to answer each of the following questions? Explain!

1. Does the management of ABC Foundation revenue reflect its mission statement? Explain!
2. Do the financial statements of ABC Foundation provide indicators of organizational growth? Explain!
3. How much flexibility does the management of ABC Foundation have to make financial decisions? Explain!
4. Do you think the ABC Foundation has the ability to pay its bills on time? Explain!
5. Do you think that ABC Foundation has become more solvent or less solvent? Explain!

6. What factors account for an increase or decrease in ABC Foundation solvency?
7. How efficient is ABC Foundation?
8. How well is ABC Foundation doing compared to other nonprofit organizations of its size?
9. Do you think that ABC Foundation is on a path for financial sustainability? Explain!

CASE STUDY: MANITOWOC HUMANE SOCIETY

The mission of the Corporation is to ensure the humane and compassionate treatment of all animals entrusted to its care; reunite lost animals with their owners; and provide for all adoptable animals to be placed in responsible, permanent homes; euthanize animals when necessary; and extend humane education to the public. The Manitowoc Humane Society (MHS) has partnered with several local veterinary clinics in an effort to help low-income pet guardians who cannot afford the full cost of spaying or neutering their pets.

The standard ratios for other nonprofit organizations the size of MHS are the following:

- Current ratio: 2.1
- Quick ratio: 1.1
- Working capital: $52,000
- Return on assets: 44%
- Fund mix ratio: 61%
- Program emphasis ratio: 55%

Questions

You are a member of an ad hoc committee that must answer the following questions using the information from the balance sheet and income statement, which follow:

1. Does the management of MHS revenues reflect its mission statement? Explain!
2. Do the financial statements of MHS provide indicators of organizational growth? Explain!
3. How much flexibility does the management have to make financial decisions? Explain!
4. Do you think the foundation has the ability to pay its bills on time? Explain!
5. Do you think that MHS has become more solvent or less solvent? Explain!
6. What factors account for increase or decrease in MHS solvency?
7. How efficient is MHS?
8. How well is MHS doing comparing to other nonprofit organizations of its size?
9. Do you think that MHS is on a path for financial sustainability? Explain!
10. What would be your financial management recommendations to the MHS board for the next fiscal year?

MHS Balance Sheet

Balance sheet	2008	2007
Assets		
Current assets		
Cash	$195,000.00	$185,000.00
Accounts receivable	$150,000.00	$180,000.00
Grants receivable	$250,000.00	$200,000.00
Inventory	$450,000.00	$425,000.00
Prepaid expenses	$130,000.00	$135,000.00
Total current assets	**$1,175,000.00**	**$1,125,000.00**
Fixed assets		
Investments	$200,000.00	$175,000.00
Land, buildings, & equipment	$320,000.00	$310,000.00
Vehicles	$175,000.00	$155,000.00
Less: Accumulated depreciation	($100,000.00)	($85,000.00)
Net equipment	$150,000.00	$140,000.00
Total fixed assets	**$745,000.00**	**$695,000.00**
Total assets	**$1,920,000.00**	**$1,820,000.00**
Liabilities and fund balance		
Current liabilities		
Accounts payable	$180,000.00	$160,000.00
Grants	$290,000.00	$185,000.00
Acquisitions contracts	$225,000.00	$180,000.00
Total current liabilities	**$695,000.00**	**$525,000.00**
Long-term liabilities		
Notes payable	$245,000.00	$215,000.00
Total long-term liabilities	**$235,000.00**	**$205,000.00**
Total liabilities	**$930,000.00**	**$730,000.00**
Fund balances		
Current, unrestricted	$470,000.00	$420,000.00
Current, restricted	$520,000.00	$670,000.00
Total fund balance	**$990,000.00**	**$1,090,000.00**
Total liabilities and fund balance	**$1,920,000.00**	**$1,820,000.00**

MHS Income Statement

Income statement	2007	2008
Revenues		
Endowment	$120,000.00	$170,000.00
Membership	$60,000.00	$50,000.00
Corporate gifts	$40,000.00	$50,000.00
Individual donations	$30,000.00	$40,000.00
Government grants	$150,000.00	$100,000.00
Foundation grants	$80,000.00	$60,000.00
Total revenues	**$480,000.00**	**$470,000.00**
Expenditures		
Salaries and benefits	$110,000.00	$100,000.00
Fund-raising	$60,000.00	$75,000.00
Shelter	$25,000.00	$20,000.00
Salaries and benefits	$20,000.00	$15,000.00
Neuter assistance	$30,000.00	$20,000.00
Health care	$20,000.00	$40,000.00
Utilities and insurance	$24,000.00	$18,000.00
Educational materials	$10,000.00	$8,000.00
Total expenditures	**$299,000.00**	**$296,000.00**
Net income	**$181,000.00**	**$174,000.00**

CASE STUDY: HOUSING COMMUNITY COALITION

The Housing Community Coalition (HCC) was formed by a partnership between Greater Fox Cities Area Habitat for Humanity and Goodwill Industries of North Central Wisconsin. Program coordinators provide real case management services to families by helping people qualify for and retain ownership of their Habitat homes and help struggling families become applicants in the Habitat program. HCC addresses the needs of prospective homeowners whose Habitat applications have been denied because of a lack of sufficient employment or financial instability and assists existing Habitat homeowners who are struggling to make their monthly mortgage payments. This program can be seen as a stepping stone in the housing continuum as well as a safeguard to keep families moving in the right direction on that continuum.

The standard ratios for other nonprofit organizations the size of HCC are the following:

■ Current ratio: 1.0
■ Quick ratio: 1.1
■ Working capital: $40,000
■ Return on assets: 15%
■ Fund mix: 45%
■ Program ratio: 75%

(continued)

CASE STUDY: HOUSING COMMUNITY COALITION   *(continued)*

Questions

You are a member of an ad hoc committee that must answer the following questions, using the information from the balance sheet and income statement, which follow:

1. Does the management of HCC revenues reflect its mission statement? Explain!
2. Do the financial statements of HCC provide indicators of organizational growth? Explain!
3. How much flexibility does the management have to make financial decisions? Explain!
4. Do you think the foundation has the ability to pay its bills on time? Explain!
5. Do you think that HCC has become more solvent or less solvent? Explain!
6. What factors account for an increase or decrease in HCC solvency?
7. How well is HCC doing compared to other non profit organizations of its size?
8. Do you think that HCC is on a path for financial sustainability? Explain!
9. What would be your financial management recommendations to the HCC board for the next fiscal year?

HCC Balance Sheet

Balance Sheet	2009	2008
Assets		
Current assets		
Cash	$75,000.00	$85,000.00
Accounts receivable	$30,000.00	$50,000.00
Grants receivable	$120,000.00	$80,000.00
Inventory	$330,000.00	$305,000.00
Prepaid expenses	$30,000.00	$35,000.00
Total current assets	**$585,000.00**	**$555,000.00**
Fixed assets		
Investments	$80,000.00	$55,000.00
Land, buildings, & equipment	$100,000.00	$90,000.00
Vehicles	$55,000.00	$35,000.00
Less: Accumulated depreciation	($10,000.00)	($15,000.00)
Net equipment	$30,000.00	$40,000.00
Total fixed assets	**$255,000.00**	**$205,000.00**
Total assets	$840,000.00	$760,000.00

(continued)

HCC Balance Sheet (*continued*)

Liabilities and fund balance		
Current liabilities		
Accounts payable	$80,000.00	$70,000.00
Grants	$70,000.00	$75,000.00
Acquisitions contracts	$105,000.00	$80,000.00
Total current liabilities	**$255,000.00**	**$225,000.00**
Long-term liabilities		
Notes payable	$125,000.00	$105,000.00
Total long-term liabilities	**$125,000.00**	**$105,000.00**
Total liabilities	**$380,000.00**	**$330,000.00**
Fund balances		
Current, unrestricted	$280,000.00	$100,000.00
Current, restricted	$180,000.00	$330,000.00
Total fund balance	**$460,000.00**	**$430,000.00**
Total liabilities and fund balance	**$840,000.00**	**$760,000.00**

HCC Income Statement

Income statement	2009	2008
Revenues		
Endowment	$120,000.00	$170,000.00
Membership	$60,000.00	$50,000.00
Corporate gifts	$40,000.00	$50,000.00
Individual donations	$30,000.00	$40,000.00
Government grants	$150,000.00	$100,000.00
Foundation grants	$80,000.00	$60,000.00
Total revenues	**$480,000.00**	**$470,000.00**
Expenditures		
Salaries and benefits	$210,000.00	$190,000.00
Fund-raising	$60,000.00	$75,000.00
Financial education	$25,000.00	$20,000.00
Debt assistance	$20,000.00	$15,000.00
Career development	$30,000.00	$20,000.00
Housing	$20,000.00	$40,000.00
Utilities and insurance	$24,000.00	$18,000.00
Educational materials	$12,000.00	$8,000.00
Total expenditures	**$401,000.00**	**$386,000.00**
Net income	**$79,000.00**	**$84,000.00**

CASE STUDY: HARRY AND ROY COMMUNITY CENTER

The Harry and Roy Community Center (HRCC) is based in Appleton, Wisconsin. The mission of HRCC is to provide educational, recreational, and career development programs and services that assist low-income individuals in Appleton to become economically self-sufficient and more responsible citizens. Prior to the annual board of directors meeting, the following financial statements (balance sheet and income statement) were distributed to all members.

The standard ratios for other nonprofit organizations the size of HRCC are the following:

- Current ratio: 2.1
- Quick ratio: 1.4
- Working capital: $70,000
- Return on assets: 30%
- Fund mix ratio: 50%
- Program emphasis ratio: 70%

Questions

You are a member of an ad hoc committee that must answer the following questions, using the information from the balance sheet and income statement, which follow:

1. Does the management of HRCC revenues reflect its mission statement? Explain!
2. Do the financial statements of HRCC provide indicators of organizational growth? Explain!
3. How much flexibility does the management have to make financial decisions? Explain!
4. Do you think the foundation has the ability to pay its bills on time? Explain!
5. Do you think that HRCC has become more solvent or less solvent? Explain!
6. What factors account for the increase or decrease in HRCC solvency?
7. What can you say about the efficiency and effectiveness of HRCC?
8. How well is HRCC doing compared to other nonprofit organizations of its size?
9. Do you think that HRCC is on a path for financial sustainability? Explain!
10. What would be your financial management recommendations to the HRCC board for the next fiscal year?

HRCC Balance Sheet

Balance sheet	2011	2010
Assets		
Current assets		
Cash	$ 95,000.00	$ 85,000.00
Account receivable	$ 50,000.00	$ 80,000.00
Grants receivable	$ 150,000.00	$100,000.00
Inventory	$ 350,000.00	$325,000.00

(continued)

HRCC Balance Sheet (*continued*)

Prepaid expenses	$ 30,000.00	$ 35,000.00
Total current assets	**$ 675,000.00**	**$625,000.00**
Fixed assets		
Investments	$ 100,000.00	$ 75,000.00
Land, buildings, & equipment	$ 120,000.00	$110,000.00
Vehicles	$ 75,000.00	$ 55,000.00
Less: Accumulated depreciation	$ (20,000.00)	$ (15,000.00)
Net equipment	$ 50,000.00	$ 40,000.00
Total fixed assets	**$ 325,000.00**	**$265,000.00**
Total assets	**$ 1,000,000.00**	**$890,000.00**
Liabilities and fund balance		
Current liabilities		
Accounts payable	$ 80,000.00	$ 70,000.00
Grants	$ 90,000.00	$ 95,000.00
Acquisition contracts	$ 125,000.00	$100,000.00
Total current liabilities	**$ 295,000.00**	**$265,000.00**
Long-term liabilities		
Notes payable	$ 135,000.00	$125,000.00
Total long-term liabilities	**$ 135,000.00**	**$125,000.00**
Total liabilities	**$ 430,000.00**	**$390,000.00**
Fund balances		
Current, unrestricted	$ 350,000.00	$120,000.00
Current, restricted	$ 220,000.00	$480,000.00
Total fund balance	**$ 570,000.00**	**$600,000.00**
Total liabilities and fund balance	**$ 1,000,000.00**	**$890,000.00**

HRCC Income Statement

Income statement	2011	2010
Revenues		
Endowment	$150,000.00	$200,000.00
Membership	$ 60,000.00	$ 50,000.00
Corporate gifts	$ 40,000.00	$ 50,000.00
Individual donations	$ 30,000.00	$ 40,000.00
Government grants	$150,000.00	$100,000.00
Foundation grants	$ 70,000.00	$ 30,000.00
Total revenues	**$500,000.00**	**$470,000.00**

(*continued*)

HRCC Income Statement (*continued*)

Expenditures		
Salaries and benefits	$230,000.00	$200,000.00
Fund-raising	$ 20,000.00	$ 15,000.00
Financial education	$ 25,000.00	$ 20,000.00
Recreation	$ 20,000.00	$ 15,000.00
Career development	$ 30,000.00	$ 20,000.00
Health education	$ 20,000.00	$ 40,000.00
Utilities and insurance	$ 24,000.00	$ 18,000.00
Educational materials	$ 12,000.00	$ 8,000.00
Total expenditures	**$381,000.00**	**$336,000.00**
Net income	**$119,000.00**	**$134,000.00**

CASE STUDY: APPLETON CHILDREN ASSOCIATION

The Appleton Children Association (ACF) was created through an endowment from the late Jenna Herzig. The mission of ACF is to provide educational programs and services that contribute to creating a safe and nurturing environment for the children living in Appleton. Prior to the annual board of directors meeting, the following financial statements (balance sheet and income statement) were distributed to all members.

The standard ratios for other nonprofit organizations the size of ACF are as follows:

■ Current ratio: 2.1
■ Quick ratio: 1.2
■ Working capital: $40,000
■ Return on assets: 25%
■ Fund mix: 55%
■ Program ratio: 60%

Questions

You are a member of an ad hoc committee that must answer the following questions using the information from the balance sheet and income statement, which follow:

1. Does the management of ACF revenues reflect its mission statement? Explain!
2. Do the financial statements of ACF provide indicators of organizational growth? Explain!
3. How much flexibility does the management have to make financial decisions? Explain!
4. Do you think the foundation has the ability to pay its bills on time? Explain!
5. Do you think that ACF has become more solvent or less solvent? Explain!
6. What factors account for the increase or decrease in ACF solvency?
7. How well is ACF doing comparing to other non-profit organizations of its size?
8. Do you think that ACF is on a path for financial sustainability? Explain!
9. What would be your financial management recommendations to the ACF board for the next fiscal year?

(*continued*)

ACF Balance Sheet

Assets		
Current assets		
Cash		$30,000
Accounts receivable	$72,000	
Less allowance for bad debts	($3,000)	$69,000
Inventory (at cost)		$93,000
Total current assets		$192,000
Fixed assets		
Land, buildings, & equipment	$66,000	
Vehicles	$60,000	$126,000
Less: Accumulated depreciation		($6,000)
Total fixed assets		$120,000
Total assets		**$312,000**
Liabilities and fund balance		
Current liabilities		
Accounts payable	$54,000	
Notes payable (due within 1 year)	$24,000	
Accrued liabilities	$6,000	
Total current liabilities		$84,000
Long-term liabilities		
Notes payable (due after 1 year)		
Total long-term liabilities		$24,000
Total liabilities		$108,000
Fund balances		
Current, unrestricted		$6,000
Current, restricted		$198,000
Total fund balance		$204,000
Total liabilities and fund balance		**$312,000**

ACF Income Statement

Revenues	
Endowments	$100,000
Membership	$50,000
Grants	$100,000
Individual donations	$50,000

(continued)

ACF Income Statement (*continued*)

Total revenue	**$300,000**
Expenses	
Management and operating	$246,000
Fund-raising	$25,000
Recreation programs	$5,000
Parenting education	$4,000
Total expenses	**$280,000**
Net income	**$20,000**

Financial Sustainability Plan

At the completion of the chapter, the reader will be able to:

1. Describe a financial sustainability plan.
2. Explain the importance of a financial sustainability plan for nonprofit organizations.
3. List and discuss the elements of a financial sustainability plan.
4. Develop an outline of a financial sustainability plan.

Many nonprofit organizations are faced with a constant challenge to match financial sustainability with their vision and mission statements. Some of the challenge may have to do with how much money they can successfully raise. This aspect can be manipulated by greater fund-raising efficiency and effectiveness. However, the other part is more challenging because it has to do with the nature of a nonprofit organization whose bottom line is value based, and not money based. This chapter will suggest approaches and best practices in developing a financial sustainability plan (FSP) for a nonprofit organization. The chapter will include a step-by-step process to use to develop a financial sustainability plan.

WHAT IS A FINANCIAL SUSTAINABILITY PLAN?

The financial sustainability plan is a document that outlines long-term financial goals, strategies, and action plans that will enable it to sustain unforeseen times of financial hardship. Some may wonder, "Why is a financial sustainability plan needed?" This is a fair question, especially when an organization may already have a strategic plan. However, you need to remember that a strategic plan aims to set the strategic orientation of an organization and tends to focus primarily on programmatic priorities. It is common practice to find some aspects of financial or fund-raising goals in a strategic plan, but this is not its primary purpose. Therefore, a plan that focuses essentially on financial sustainability is very important. The lack thereof is also a statement about the level of emphasis put on financial sustainability in a particular nonprofit organization. A financial sustainability plan forces an organization to engage in systematic analysis about its financial ability to continue to provide services over time. It helps an organization understand whether there will be long-term financial resources to continue to fulfill its vision and mission. A financial sustainability plan focuses on priorities and on how sustainable some priorities may be. Further, with a financial sustainability plan, a nonprofit organization has to make a concrete commitment by allocating budgetary resources to implement an action plan that can engage in or sustain a path for financial sustainability.

ELEMENTS OF A FINANCIAL SUSTAINABILITY PLAN

A financial sustainability plan should include an executive summary, financial sustainability analysis, financial ratios analysis, strategic goals and objectives, action plan, benchmark and outcomes, continuing quality improvement strategies, and budget (Figure 11.1).

EXECUTIVE SUMMARY

The executive summary is a synthesis of the overall financial sustainability plan. It is a single page summarizing the justification for the plan, the main findings from the financial sustainability and financial ratios analyses, the strategic goals and objectives, the key benchmarks and outcomes, the strategies for continuing quality improvement, and the total costs.

FIGURE 11.1 Financial sustainability plan.

JUSTIFICATION

The justification of a financial sustainability plan must take into account the short- and long-term needs of the target population, the challenges and/or obstacles to overcome, the strategies and action steps needed to generate or mobilize needed resources and overcome anticipated challenges, and the key partners that can make a significant positive contribution to the process.

As indicated in Figure 11.2, the justification of a financial sustainability plan should include information on the critical needs of the client or the target population, the challenges for the future, the contextualization of what I refer to as an expression of criticality, a call to action, and an overall purpose.

Client needs: Nonprofit organizations are created primarily because of needs in communities or target populations. Obviously, some of the needs are "real need" or serious issues that constitute threats one way or another to individuals or groups in a community. Other needs are simply "perceived needs" or what people may want or desire, although they do not pose a threat to their health or security. Clients can live with their perceived needs, but may not be able to without having their real needs met. It is up to an organization to develop appropriate analytical tools to distinguish between real and perceived needs. A justification of a plan for financial sustainability must provide evidence related to the literature that the needs targeted by such a plan are real needs, and not perceived needs. This is important for accountability and stewardship. The description of client needs must provide background information about the target population to set the overall context of the plan. Information can be found in various sources, such as national censuses, electronic databases, survey reports, scholarly publications, internal data collected from programs, and any other credible source.

Challenges: The justification must describe current trends, issues, or challenges in the target population, and explain the likelihood of such challenges to be part of the reality of the target population. Projections from credible sources should be provided. In the absence of such a projection, there should be an effort to develop projections based on current trends, taking into account internal and external factors that can affect the target population.

Criticality: Organizations are likely to be confronted with challenges, especially financial constraints that can jeopardize their ability to continue to remain in operation. These

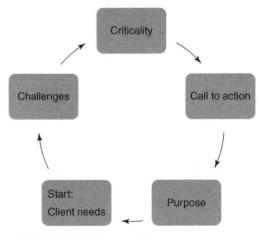

FIGURE 11.2 Justification statement.

constraints must be anticipated to the best of the ability of leaders and managers of non-profit organizations, and I label that fact "criticality." *Criticality* refers to a point at which there is a need to acknowledge a sense of urgency. Criticality is a sense of alertness in relation to an organization's ability to secure enough financial resources to continue to provide quality services to clients over time, even in the event of changes in funding sources or a financial or economic crisis.

What If ...	Probability			Severity			Consequences	
	Low	Medium	High	Low	Medium	High	Least likely	Most likely

For example, the matrix could contain information like, "What if a major grant is not renewed next year?" Based on the situation of an organization, the probability can be low, medium, or high. The severity of the probability can be low, medium, or high. Consequences from the "What if ..." probability and severity can be least likely or most likely. The criticality describes past and current options to address the clients' needs and overcome challenges, the limitations of the options, and the meaning of inaction.

Call to action: The call to action is basically one or two paragraphs that summarize the rationale for an organization to develop a plan for financial sustainability based on client needs, challenges, and criticality.

Purpose: The purpose is one or more sentences or possibly a paragraph that sets the overall purpose of a plan for financial sustainability. The purpose focuses on (a) what the future financial position of the organization will look like if the plan is successful, (b) what change will look like for the target population when their real needs are met irreversibly.

FINANCIAL SUSTAINABILITY ANALYSIS

There are three major factors related to the financial sustainability of a nonprofit organization (Box 1.1):

1. Inherent factors
2. Collateral factors
3. Environmental factors

Inherent Factors

The inherent factors are directly linked to financial sustainability. They determine whether an organization is financially sustainable or not. Inherent factors of financial sustainability include, but are not limited to, financial management, budget, financial statement analysis, a financial sustainability plan, social enterprise, fund-raising, grant seeking, investment, and risk management.

Collateral Factors

Collateral factors are indirectly related to financial sustainability and include governance, leadership, strategic planning, human resources, needs assessment, asset mapping, community relations, services delivery, technology, program evaluation, social marketing, and organizational transformation.

Environmental Factors

The environmental factors are social, economic, and political (SEP) issues that may affect funding, support, operations, or even the survival of a nonprofit organization.

BOX 11.1 FINANCIAL SUSTAINABILITY ANALYSIS

INHERENT FACTORS

- Financial management
- Budget
- Financial statement analysis
- Financial sustainability plan
- Social enterprise
- Fund-raising
- Grant seeking
- Investment
- Risk management

COLLATERAL FACTORS

- Governance
- Leadership
- Strategic planning
- Human resources
- Needs assessment
- Asset mapping
- Community relations
- Services delivery
- Technology
- Program evaluation
- Social marketing
- Organizational transformation

ENVIRONMENTAL FACTORS

- Social
- Economic
- Political

Overall, financial sustainability analysis involves a thorough assessment of the internal strengths and capacity building of an organization, its ability to develop community relations that include strategic partnership, and its potential to overcome challenges from its internal and external environment and adapt to changing conditions.

FINANCIAL RATIOS ANALYSIS

Financial ratios analysis is based on the analysis of the financial statement. The financial statement analysis focuses primarily, but not exclusively, on profitability and growth, liquidity, solvency, and efficiency and effectiveness.

- *Profitability* is the surplus of revenue over the expenses. The gross profit margin, the net profit margin, return on assets, and return on equity are examples of tools used to measure the profitability of a nonprofit organization.
- *Financial growth* is the measure of the percentage of increase in the financial operations of an organization in comparison to previous periods.
- *Liquidity* is the ability to meet cash requirements. Simply put, it is the ability to pay the bills. The current ratio, acid test, acid test ratio, inventory turnover, and average collection period are example of instruments used to measure liquidity.
- *Solvency* is the ability to pay off all debts if the organization were dissolved tomorrow. Debt ratio and debt-to-equity ratio are examples of tools used to measure solvency.
- *Efficiency* is the ability of an organization to deliver the maximum service possible with the lowest amount of human, material, and financial resources.
- *Effectiveness* measures the extent to which an organization uses its resources adequately to fulfill its mission and vision.

STRATEGIC GOALS AND OBJECTIVES

The strategic goals and objectives constitute the translation of the purpose of a financial sustainability plan in terms that are measurable. Strategic goals are long-term-oriented and are linked to strategic outcomes, such as profitability, liquidity, solvency, efficiency, or effectiveness rates, over a period of time in the future. Strategic objectives are midterm and short-term oriented, and are linked to shorter outcomes to be obtained in order to reach a long-term goal. The definition of strategic goals and objectives can be inspired from the indicators of financial sustainability listed in Box 11.2. Examples of goals and objectives for a financial sustainability plan are provided in Box 11.3.

BOX 11.2: INDICATORS OF FINANCIAL SUSTAINABILITY

- Culture of strategic planning and performance measurement
- Culture of stewardship and accountability
- In-house-generated income is diverse and greater than public funding.
- Sustained high profitability (growth)
- Sustained increase in solvency
- Sustained increase in liquidity
- Rainy-day fund is at least equal to the equivalent of a 1-year budget for core expenses.
- Level of staff satisfaction and commitment are equal to or greater than 90%.
- Level of program efficiency is equal to or greater than 90%.
- Effective risk management policy

BOX 11.3 EXAMPLES OF GOALS AND OBJECTIVES

Goal: Increase ratios of profitability, solvency, liquidity, efficiency, effectiveness, and employee satisfaction and commitment by 50% within the next 10 years.
Examples of objectives could be:

- Develop a framework for diversifying the funding sources of the organization, and outline financial resource allocation strategies that ensure the ability to provide quality activities, projects, programs, or services over time.
- Develop a framework for financial resource allocation strategies that support the strategic goals and objectives of the organization.
- Open a contingency fund representing 1% of the total organizational budget that will enable the organization to overcome unforeseen times of financial hardship.
- Develop action steps to gradually and significantly reduce the dependency of core programmatic activities on grant funding.
- Develop and implement action plans to diversify the funding portfolio of the organization by shifting the focus on fund-raising though earned-income strategies.
- Implement continuing quality improvement strategies regarding the financial sustainability of the organization.

For example, if a nonprofit organization set a goal to increase revenue from fund-raising by 50% over the next 5 years, the objectives could be to (a) organize fund-raising events that will account for an increase of 20% in revenue by year 2, (b) organize a capital campaign to upgrade corporate donations that will account for an increase of 30% in revenue by year 3, and other specific short-term targets. The attainment of all the objectives will help achieve the goal.

ACTION PLAN

An action plan is a document that outlines strategic initiatives and concrete actions that must be taken to materialize the initiatives. The strategic initiatives are usually formulated using the format of key themes or topics or initiatives linked to the achievement of strategic objectives. The actions are concrete tasks that must be performed within a specific timeline. The implementation of the actions gives concrete form to the key initiatives. For example, if a strategic initiative is to "strengthen the long-term fiscal position of an organization," some of the actions in relation to such an initiative might be to (a) review the fiscal policies of the organization and develop new directions, principles, priorities, and tools to address fiscal issues in an expedited manner; (b) develop more targeted and accurate fiscal projections that underlie the budget; (c) make long-term investments that are fully guaranteed; and (d) develop a financial-risk policy for asset and liabilities management. The action should be based on a thematic design, which includes activities and strategies related to organizational sustainability, strategic partnership, fund-raising, social enterprise, and investment portfolio (Figure 11.3).

Strategy and Action Plan: Organizational Sustainability

Organizational sustainability is as important as financial sustainability. In fact, an organization cannot be financial sustainable without being a sustainable entity in itself. Therefore,

FIGURE 11.3 Financial sustainability action plan design.

the action plan should include strategic initiatives and actions related to organizational sustainability, such as:

- Refining vision and mission statements
- Refining strategic goals and objectives
- Strengthening governance and accountability systems
- Developing staff and talent
- Documenting and disseminating outcomes and impacts of programs, services, and activities.

Strategy and Action Plan: Fund-raising Plan

As indicated in previous chapters, fund-raising is essential to the financial sustainability of a nonprofit organization. Based on the spirit of the law for charitable entities, fund-raising is the primary source of revenue for a nonprofit organization. As a result, a financial sustainability action plan must include strategic initiatives and actions related to fund-raising. Some examples of initiatives and activities might be:

1. Diversification of fund-raising sources of revenue through:

   - Membership development
   - Strategic donor fund-raising
   - Bequests
   - Charitable remainder trust
   - Fund-raising events

2. Adoption of a donor management system to

   - Create a base of loyal donors who upgrade their donations
   - Reach out to new categories of donors through social media platforms
   - Organize ongoing hangout events with donors

Strategy and Action Plan: Social Enterprise and Investment Portfolio

Social enterprises and investments represent various options used to raise funds for non-profit organizations. They require different policies, procedures, and practices. They can also help generate flexible and sustainable income. Therefore, they deserve special considerations in an action for financial sustainability. Key strategies and actions might be:

- Development of fee-based services programs
- Development and implementation of business plans for social enterprises
- Development of marketing plans for activities to generate earned income
- Contracting with an investment manager to handle short-term and long-term investments

Strategy and Action Plan: Strategic Partnerships

The financial sustainability of a nonprofit organization depends partly on its internal strengths, capacity-building priorities, and adaptability to changing conditions. The other part is based on the ability of an organization to build community support and develop strategic partnerships. Consequently, a financial sustainability action plan must include strategic initiatives and actions for strategic partnerships through the development of strategic collaborations or alliances with public agencies, private corporations, other nonprofit organizations, community groups, financial entities, grant-maker agencies, and other similar entities.

Implementation Strategies

The development of a financial sustainability plan is a great statement that an organization is confident of its ability to continue to provide quality services to clients regardless of changes in funding sources or economic or financial crises. However, the implementation of the plan is as critical as the plan itself. The implementation of a financial sustainability plan requires an organization to make more concrete decisions, such as:

- Development of a detailed budget for each activity in the financial sustainability plan
- Development and funding of a main budget that incorporates all the project-specific budgets
- Development and implementation of a comprehensive financial sustainability management system
- Develop and implementation of a monitoring and evaluation system

The implementation plan must include a timeline that connects strategic goals, objectives, initiatives, actions, benchmarks and outcomes, responsibilities (person responsible), and period (dates). The implementation plan should answer the classic questions: "Who does what?" "When?" "How?" and "Why?"

BENCHMARKING AND OUTCOMES

The financial sustainability plan must describe specific benchmarks and outcomes that will be used to monitor progress. Benchmarking is the process of measuring various dimensions of quality, efficiency, and effectiveness about an organization in order to compare performances with similar organizations. An outcome is a concrete result obtained from the achievement of a goal or an objective. A goal or an objective express an intention to achieve a result in the future, after certain actions have taken place. The result obtained if the goal or objective is achieved is called an outcome. Benchmarking is an ongoing process that can help ensure that specific financial sustainability outcomes are obtained.

CONTINUING QUALITY IMPROVEMENT

As indicated in a Chapter 2, sustainability is more of a process than an end in itself, given the nature of a nonprofit organization to prioritize the fulfillment of its vision and mission over anything else. Consequently, a financial sustainability plan for a nonprofit organization cannot be a static document. It has to be a plan available for constant revision, especially when forecasting and the internal and external environments of the organization change. Therefore, there must be ongoing assessment and evaluation of the plan and revision strategies for continuing quality improvement.

BUDGET

A financial sustainability plan is not a list of ideas and activities. It is a systematic plan based on sound fact-based analyses. As a result, it requires expenses that must be justified in a budget. A budget developed within the framework of a financial sustainability plan is essential for an organization to follow a path toward financial sustainability.

QUESTIONS AND ACTIVITIES

1. What is a financial sustainability plan?
2. Why do you think a nonprofit organization should have a financial sustainability plan?
3. What are the key elements of a financial sustainability plan?
4. How would you differentiate an organization's strategic goal, strategic objective, and strategic initiative?

Fund-Raising and Financial Sustainability

CHAPTER

12

At the completion of the chapter, the reader will be able to:

1. Define "fund-raising."
2. Discuss why people donate to nonprofit organizations.
3. Identify some common effective fund-raising strategies used by nonprofit organizations in the United States.
4. Describe the items in a fund-raising proposal.

This chapter provides conceptual frameworks and approaches to organize fund-raising activities that can generate alternative funding for financial sustainability. The chapter includes an overview of various types of fund-raising strategies, existing sources of funding for nonprofit organizations, and the planning of fund-raising activities.

DEFINE "FUND-RAISING"

The term "fund-raising" can be used for any activity whose primary purpose is to raise money to support the activity of a nonprofit organization. The meaning of the term "fund-raising" can change based on approaches used by a particular nonprofit organization. For example, an organization might use telemarketing as its main source of fund-raising, whereas another organization may rely solely on board members, staff, and volunteers to operate its fund-raising activities. For some other organizations, grant seeking might be a facet of fund-raising strategy. Investment and social enterprise might be considered as fund-raising strategies for another organization. Organizations in arts and culture–related activities may build their fund-raising approach around performances and sale of artistic merchandise. There is no right or wrong approach if the strategy is to raise money in a lawful manner to further the vision and mission of an organization.

Increased competition and declining funding sources in the nonprofit sector have put the pressure for efficiency and effectiveness on nonprofit organizations in the United States, and made fund-raising an important alternative to generate additional and flexible revenue. According to the 2013 *Charitable Giving Report*, nonprofit organizations received donations representing $12.5 billion in fund-raising from government, corporate, foundation, and individual sources (MacLaughlin, 2014).

WHY DO PEOPLE DONATE TO NONPROFIT ORGANIZATIONS?

People donate to nonprofit organizations for a variety of reasons. I do not intend to list all of them. However, based on the literature, I select the following reasons as an illustration to argue that motivation for charitable giving is diverse. The literature suggests that people donate to nonprofit organizations based on compassion, altruism, values, tax deductibility, corporate social responsibility, stewardship, and solicitation.

Compassion

The word "compassion" means a feeling of pity or great concern toward the suffering of others. On January 12, 2010, a devastating earthquake hit the country of Haiti. The stories that were reported through international media were heartbreaking. Very little persuasion was required to convince people that there was a need. Out of that evidence of a need, people donated with compassion. They wanted to help. They wanted to make a difference. They wanted to contribute by alleviating the human suffering that they were witnessing. The same is true for what happened after Hurricane Katrina in New Orleans, after the tsunami in Southeast Asia, after the recent earthquake in Japan, after the tornado in Joplin, Missouri, and after Hurricane Sandy in New York and New Jersey. The list is too long to cite all the examples of natural disasters that awoke compassion in the hearts of individuals, organizations, and institutions, and influenced them to donate. Cheung and Chan (2000) found that the awareness of a need has a positive effect on donations to international relief organizations. Similarly, Lee and Farrell (2003) conducted a study on donations to panhandlers, and found a positive correlation between perceived need and donations. Weerts and Ronca (2007) conducted a study on alumni contributions to academic institutions, which revealed that perceived need influenced alumni contributions to their alma matter. It is fair to infer that the ability of a nonprofit organization to increase the awareness of potential donors of a need may contribute to an increase in donations.

Altruism

Altruism refers to doing good without an expectation of rewards, because doing good makes sense. However, economists have studied motivations behind altruistic giving and found that selfish implicit factors might influence people who claim to donate out of altruism.

   Various studies have found that social concerns tend to be at the root of altruistic donations, when controlling for social distance (Bohnet and Frey, 1999) or communications among donors (Andreoni & Rao, 2011; Xiao & Houser, 2005). Andreoni and Bernheim (2009) argue that some claim they donate for altruistic reasons while seeking to be perceived as generous, thus trying to cultivate their social image. Some economists argue that altruistic contributions tend to decrease when people become aware of the existence of other contributions that are designated to social concerns that they would financially support (Kingma, 1989). However, subsequent studies found no objective evidence of that occurrence (Kropf & Knack, 2003; Marcuello & Salas, 2001).

Values

Some people donate because of their social, cultural, political, religious, or family values (Bennett & Savani, 2003). For example, for some people, charitable giving is doing God's will. Their donation is a spiritual devotion. For others, donation to charitable organizations is their way to give back to the community that contributed directly or indirectly to their success (Weerts & Ronca, 2007). For others, donation may be part of a family tradition. Some studies found that some individuals are motivated to donate because they want to contribute to make the world a better place to live (Schuyt, Smit, & Bekkers, 2004).

Tax Deductibility

As Box 12.1 illustrates, charitable donations are tax deductible. This encourages people to donate to nonprofit organizations to claim their tax deductions.

BOX 12.1 DEDUCTIBILITY OF CHARITABLE CONTRIBUTIONS

You may deduct a charitable contribution made to, or for the use of, any of the following organizations that otherwise are qualified under section 170(c) of the Internal Revenue Code:

1. A state or U.S. possession (or political subdivision thereof), or the United States or the District of Columbia, if made exclusively for public purposes
2. A community chest, corporation, trust, fund, or foundation, organized or created in the United States or its possessions, or under the laws of the United States, any state, the District of Columbia or any possession of the United States, and organized and operated exclusively for charitable, religious, educational, scientific, or literary purposes, or for the prevention of cruelty to children or animals
3. A church, synagogue, or other religious organization
4. A war veterans' organization or its post, auxiliary, trust, or foundation organized in the United States or its possessions
5. A nonprofit volunteer fire company
6. A civil defense organization created under federal, state, or local law (this includes unreimbursed expenses of civil defense volunteers that are directly connected with and solely attributable to their volunteer services)
7. A domestic fraternal society, operating under the lodge system, but only if the contribution is to be used exclusively for charitable purposes
8. A nonprofit cemetery company if the funds are irrevocably dedicated to the perpetual care of the cemetery as a whole and not a particular lot or mausoleum crypt

(continued)

BOX 12.1 DEDUCTIBILITY OF CHARITABLE CONTRIBUTIONS *(continued)*

TIMING OF CONTRIBUTIONS

Contributions must actually be paid in cash or other property before the close of your tax year to be deductible, whether you use the cash or accrual method.

DEDUCTIBLE AMOUNTS

If you donate property other than cash to a qualified organization, you may generally deduct the fair market value of the property. If the property has appreciated in value, however, some adjustments may have to be made.

The rules relating to how to determine fair market value are discussed in Publication 561, *Determining the Value of Donated Property*.

LIMITATIONS ON DEDUCTIONS

In general, contributions to charitable organizations may be deducted up to 50% of adjusted gross income computed without regard to net operating loss carrybacks. Contributions to certain private foundations, veterans organizations, fraternal societies, and cemetery organizations are limited to 30% of adjusted gross income (computed without regard to net operating loss carrybacks), however. *Exempt Organizations Select Check* uses deductibility status codes to indicate these limitations.

The 50% limitation applies to (1) all public charities (code PC), (2) all private operating foundations (code POF), (3) certain private foundations that distribute the contributions they receive to public charities and private operating foundations within 2½ months following the year of receipt, and (4) certain private foundations the contributions to which are pooled in a common fund and the income and corpus of which are paid to public charities.

The 30% limitation applies to private foundations (code PF), other than those previously mentioned that qualify for a 50% limitation, and to other organizations described in section 170(c) that do not qualify for the 50% limitation, such as domestic fraternal societies (code LODGE).

A special limitation applies to certain gifts of long-term capital gain property. A discussion of that special limitation may be found in Publication 526, *Income Tax Deduction for Contributions*.

FOREIGN ORGANIZATIONS

The organizations listed in this publication with foreign addresses are generally not *foreign organizations* but are domestically formed organizations carrying on activities in foreign countries. These organizations are treated the same as any other domestic organization with regard to deductibility limitations.

Certain organizations with Canadian addresses listed may be *foreign organizations* to which contributions are deductible only because of a tax treaty. For these organizations, in addition to the limitations on the amount of the deduction allowed by section 170 of the Code, the deduction may not exceed the amount allowed as a deduction under Canadian law computed as though the taxable income (in the case of a corporation) or adjusted gross income (in the case of an individual) from sources in Canada is the aggregate income. A deduction for a contribution to a Canadian organization listed in this publication is unallowable if the contributor reports no taxable income from Canadian sources on the U.S. income tax return.

Except as indicated above, contributions to a foreign organization are not deductible.

(continued)

> ### BOX 12.1 DEDUCTIBILITY OF CHARITABLE CONTRIBUTIONS (*continued*)
>
> RELIANCE ON EXEMPT ORGANIZATIONS SELECT CHECK
>
> Revenue Procedure 2011-33, 2011-25 I.R.B. 887 describes the extent to which grantors and contributors may rely on the listing of an organization in electronic Publication 78 and the IRS Business Master File extract in determining the deductibility of contributions to such an organization. Grantors and contributors may continue to rely on the Publication 78 data contained in Exempt Organizations Select Check to the same extent provided for in Revenue Procedure 2011-33.
>
> Similar reliance provisions apply to an organization's foundation classification as it appears in the list. See also Revenue Procedure 89-23.

Source: Internal Revenue Service (2013).

Corporate Social Responsibility

Some businesses donate because doing "good" is good business within the spirit of corporate social responsibility. The term "corporate social responsibility" refers to the good will of corporations to conduct business in a manner that is consistent with the law and ethical standards, and to contribute to social good in communities where they do business. According to the Committee Encouraging Corporate Philanthropy (Phillips, 2013), total corporate donations have increased from $3.67 billion 30 years ago to more than $18 billion in 2012. Some employers or corporations encourage their employees to donate and they match their contributions. However, Stern (2013) argues that on a dollar-for-dollar basis, companies donate less than they used to when adjusting for inflation.

Stewardship

Stewardship is a significant driver of charitable donations. Some people like to donate to organizations that will be good stewards of their money. They want to make donations that contribute to reverse negative social outcomes in their communities (Duncan, 2004; Smith & McSweeney, 2007). People who condition their donation with stewardship like to have evidence that their contributions will be used for a designated purpose. These are the types of donors who will attempt to hold leaders and managers of nonprofit organizations accountable in relation to fund-raising or contributions received. Usually, such contributors donate based on their level of trust in the efficiency and effectiveness of a nonprofit organization. Various surveys have found that donors do not like their contributions to be spent on fund-raising strategies, but on program expenditures (Bennett & Savani, 2003; Sargent & Woodliffe, 2007). The willingness of such donors to contribute increases with their trust in the leadership and management of a nonprofit organization (Sargeant & Lee, 2004). Some people are not sold on the message, or the vision and mission of a nonprofit organization, but on the extent to which the organization is efficient, effective, accountable, and shows evidence of good stewardship of its resources.

Solicitation

Some people donate because someone asked for a contribution. Solicitation to these people can take various forms, such as a personal request, fund-raising letter, or e-mail. Individuals who are sensitive to solicitation tend to act relatively quickly on nonprofit organizations requests (Bekkers, 2010). The advantage of solicitation has unflattering implications as well. Given the efficacy of personal solicitation, potential donors may receive more requests than necessary, and may have no other choice than to turn some of them down. Therefore, solicitation may be effective for some nonprofit organizations, and not so effective for others.

FUND-RAISING SOURCES

Fund-raising sources are diverse and encompass (a) donations from individual and organizational donors; (b) contributions from proposals or specific requests, annual campaigns, corporate and business support; and (c) in-kind contributions and partnerships. The purpose of fund-raising is to acquire new donors, retain current donors, upgrade current donors, or build new relationships with potential donors. As you may notice, fund-raising should focus on donors rather than on donations. The emphasis on donation may produce a one-time contribution. The focus on donors may translate into ongoing donations and multiplication of new donors through a current base of loyal donors.

FUND-RAISING PROPOSAL

An effective fund-raising proposal requires effective planning. The planning of fund-raising activities should start with a fund-raising proposal that sets clear justification, goals, objectives, and overall approaches and strategies (Box 12.2).

Introduction

A fund-raising proposal should start with an introduction that explains why a systematic fund-raising plan is necessary as opposed to a shopping list of fund-raising activities that may be disconnected with one another. The introduction will then set the overall purpose of the fund-raising proposal, based on its overall impact in helping further

---

BOX 12.2 FUND-RAISING PRINCIPLES

- Focus on the mission
- Build relationships
- Use effective strategies
- Planning
- Solicit diverse sources
- Have fun!

the mission, vision, strategic goals, and programmatic objectives of the organizations. Examples of impact may be to:

- Develop a systematic and coherent fund-raising process with the organization.
- Maximize individual and institutional giving.
- Increase donor commitment and loyalty.
- Improve fund-raising efficiency and effectiveness.
- Contribute to the financial sustainability of the organization.

Profile of the Organization of the Agency

A fund-raising proposal should not take it for granted that people already know about the organization, and therefore there is no need for presentation. The profile of the organization should be outlined by presenting key information to contextualize the fund-raising proposal. Some of the key information includes, but is not limited to:

- Name and location of the agency or organization
- Mission and vision statements
- Governing bodies
- Services/programs/projects
- Beneficiaries (provide statistics)

Box 12.3 provides an example of some basic information included in the profile of an organization.

Case Statement

The case statement (Box 12.4) is a concise document that makes the case about

1. What needs an organization helps meet
2. How the organization has managed to help meet the needs so far
3. What the challenges are to satisfy the needs more effectively or efficiently
4. What additional resources are needed to overcome the challenges

Goals and Objectives

The goals are the broad intents of the fund-raising proposal. The goals should be expressed in monetary terms and should constitute targets related to specific activities.

BOX 12.3 PROFILE OF OSHKOSH AGAINST CANCER

- Oshkosh Against Cancer
- Mission: *Provide support to eliminating cancer as a major health problem by preventing cancer, saving lives, and diminishing suffering from cancer, through research, education, advocacy, and service.*
- Governing bodies: A board of 12 members
- Services: Health education, cancer prevention, and breast cancer screening
- Beneficiaries: 4,000 women per year

BOX 12.4 CASE STATEMENT

- *Need:* Fifty percent of women in our target areas are at high risk of breast cancer.
- *Service:* About 3,000 low-income women received free mammograms from our centers.
- *Challenges:*
  - A mammogram costs $100.00
  - Forty percent of our clients cannot afford the cost of a mammogram.
  - Federal grant is not available at the end of this fiscal year.

- *Additional resources:* Funds needed to support mammogram cost for more than 1,000 women.

The objectives are the specific intermediary targets that the plan will help accomplish. Each goal should incorporate at least two objectives. The attainment of the objectives will concur to help achieve the goal (see Box 12.5).

Activities

For each objective, indicate one or more activities that will make it possible to achieve the objective and achieve a revenue target. Provide a description of each activity! Activities can focus on capital campaign and major gifts, annual giving, planned giving, and special events.

Capital campaign and major gifts: The capital campaign is a time-limited event organized to encourage existing donors and potential new donors to make a major contribution in support of a specific project or initiative, such as a new building or to open an endowment fund. In the case of an endowment fund, a capital campaign would serve as a strategy to help secure long-term funding for a nonprofit organization. Traditional tactics like direct mail or personal solicitation are often used when organizing a capital campaign. A nonprofit organization can create an ad hoc committee that is focused exclusively on planning and implementing a capital campaign. A capital campaign must be systematically designed in order to be successful. Strategies, such as setting gradual and monitored money targets, developing a list of prospects, ongoing appeals, and communications with donors, have contributed to successful capital campaigns for many nonprofit organizations.

Annual giving: Annual giving is an annual solicitation for contributions made by a nonprofit to individual and business donors. Solicitation can target both existing and new donors. Annual gifts tend to be unrestricted, and can be used for whatever purpose that can best help further the mission of an organization.

BOX 12.5 SAMPLE GOAL AND OBJECTIVES

Goal: Raise $ 35,000 from special events.

Objectives:

1. Organize a fund-raising dinner for the friends of ABC foundation by March 2014.
2. Organize three bake sales by December 2014.

Planned giving: Planned giving occurs when donors agree to name a nonprofit organization in their wills or estates. Some donors will do this in the form of a trust. Others may specify an amount to donate to the organization. Nonprofit organizations can be proactive in seeking planned-giving opportunities as part of their overall fund-raising strategies.

Special events: Special events are events planned by an ad hoc committee for the purpose of raising funds for the activities of a nonprofit organization. A special event can be anything from a dinner, a banquet, a marathon, a dance contest, a concert with a popular artist, a sporting event, or other similar activities. See Box 12. 6 for a sample of activities, descriptions, and revenue targets.

BOX 12.6 SAMPLE OF ACTIVITIES, DESCRIPTIONS, AND REVENUE TARGETS

Activities	Description	Revenue Target
New Year's Eve Dinner/Dance	The YWCA will be having a New Year's Eve dinner and a dance on December 31, 2012. The YWCA will charge $30.00 a person and $50.00 a couple. The YWCA hopes to mobilize approximately 200 attendees. We anticipate that 50 single guest tickets will be purchased.	$10,000.00
5K Run/Walk-A-Thon (×2)	The YWCA plans to host a fall and spring 5K Run/Walk-A-Thon to increase awareness about domestic violence within the Marathon County area. The first race will be on September 21, 2013, and the second one on May 25, 2014. The YWCA plans to charge $30.00 a person to those who sign up a week before the date of the race and $35.00 on the day of the race. Based on past events, the YWCA expects to have 1,000 participants in the race. The YWCA anticipates that 172 people per race will sign up on the day of the race.	$60,040.00
Host 17 Woodchucks Games	The YWCA plans to host 17 games out of the 34 home games of the Woodchucks baseball season. The YWCA will collect all food sales proceeds on the night they are hosted.	$45,500.00
Dinner and a Silent Auction	The YWCA will organize a dinner accompanied by a silent auction on October 19, 2013. The YWCA will charge $40.00 a person and $70.00 a couple. The YWCA expects approximately 300 attendees. The YWCA plans to sell 63 single tickets.	$21,020.00
Domestic Violence Awareness Concert Headlining Taylor Swift	The YWCA will organize a Domestic Violence Awareness Concert headlining popular singer Taylor Swift. The concert will be held on July 27, 2013. The YWCA expects about 2,500 attendees paying $30 a ticket.	$74,000.00

BOX 12.7 SAMPLE CALENDAR OF IMPLEMENTATION		
Period	**Activity**	**Person Responsible (Position)**
December 1, 2013	Submit a grant for a food drive	Executive director
January 9, 2014	Organize the dinner at Players Pizza and Pub	Event coordinator
March 15, 2014	Recruit volunteers for food drive and 5K run	Event coordinator
May15, 2014	Organize 5K run	Event coordinator

Calendar of Implementation

For each activity, indicate the completion period as well as the person responsible. Use the position as opposed to an actual individual name. For example, instead of putting Jean Usher as the person responsible, indicate "event coordinator," or "project coordinator" or whatever the title of the person who will be held accountable for the completion of a specific task. See Box 12.7 for a sample calendar of implementation.

Budget and Budget Justification

The budget should indicate the line items of expenses, the justification for each line item, and the total per line item. A fund-raiser is organized to make a profit. There are costs involved. In other words, there will be some expenses to account for in the budget. The total expenses must be less than the total revenue generated by a fund-raising event. Every fund-raising event must be profitable. The forecasting of income for a fund-raising event must be based on realistic trends and should use a conservative estimate. A conservative estimate implies that you anticipate the least amount likely, given the scale of the event and the expenses involved. If the budget cannot predict a profit for a fund-raising event, the event should not be part of a fund-raising proposal. See Box 12.8 for an example of a simple budget.

FUND-RAISING AND TECHNOLOGY

Progress in technology provides additional options for nonprofit organizations to conduct their fund-raising activities. An effective fund-raising campaign should make use of fund-raising management software. Fund-raising management software will help with efficiency and effectiveness. Such software will increase the efficiency of fund-raising strategies, maintain better communications with donors, and develop quick and accurate reports to strengthen the culture of stewardship and accountability. Fund-raising management software helps better plan and monitor fund-raising activities. Box 12.9 provides some examples of fund-raising management software that nonprofit organizations have used.

BOX 12.8 EXAMPLE OF A SIMPLE BUDGET

Item	Description	Total
Income		
Ticket sales	400 tickets × $50.00	$20,000.00
Sponsorship	20 sponsors × $ 500.00	$10,000.00
Total income		$30,000.00
Expenses		
Event manager	40 hours × $20.00/hour	$800.00
Food/drink & catering	$ 10.00 × 210 people	$2,100.00
Fliers	1,000 fliers × $.10	$100.00
Rental (ballroom)	$200.00/hour × 4 hours	$800.00
Total expenses		$3,800.00
Total fund-raising profit		$26,200.00

BOX 12.9 SELECTED FUND-RAISING MANAGEMENT SOFTWARE

NEON CRM
DEVELOPED BY Z2 SYSTEMS INC.

This software was designed to increase donations and services by donors while saving time and money for the organization. It does this by automatically inputting and completing many of the parts of the fund-raising process so the user can use her or his time for the bigger parts of the fund-raising process. Some of the key features of this software are online donation forms that make tracking donors, donations, and donor history easy and less time-consuming. There is a payment-processing function that is used when donations are sent using credit cards. This software has the ability to send out custom e-mails and tax receipts to large numbers of people. It can track where funds are coming from and put them in the correct program folder and sends a thank you letter to the donor. This software will track grants, manage letters of inquiry, and remind the user of due dates. In order to attain more donors it will keep track and organize all contact with each person. The pricing of this software is determined by how many constituent records will be saved in the software.
URL: http://www.z2systems.com/neoncrm/features/fund-raising-donations?pid=capterra &fund-raising

ALLEGIANCE FUND-RAISING
DEVELOPED BY ALLEGIANCE SOFTWARE INC.

This software is specifically designed for nonprofit organizations. It will allow you to divide more than 400 files in order to treat each separately and minimize risk of mistake and/or deletion. It will automatically process donation renewals of credit card information. It will organize amounts and percentages of donations in order to see each individual donor level of donations.
URL: http://www.allegiancesoftware.com/fund-raising-software.html

(continued)

BOX 12.9 SELECTED FUND-RAISING MANAGEMENT SOFTWARE *(continued)*

EXCEED! PREMIER
DEVELOPED BY TELOSA SOFTWARE

This software manages contacts and e-mails while being able to move them back and forth when you need to use them. It manages/organizes donation amounts, when the donation occurred, and records the donor and all of his or her contacts in order to better analyze donation history. This software developer stresses the need to spend more time at the beginning to convert all your data so you will not have more problems later. The developer offers classes in web and phone training for this software.
URL: http://www.telosa.com/software-nonprofits/exceed-premier/

DONORSNAP
DEVELOPED BY DONORSNAP

DONORSNAP allows you to manage and organize all contacts and donations and stay organized. It allows you to attach and send donation statements to every e-mail in one click. This software will process recurring payments by setting them up on a monthly or annual basis. You can create custom forms for online registration for fund-raising events. The software also has the ability to print a large amount of mail-merge letters, thank-you letters, or any other type of fund-raising letters. You can create online forms, such as change-of-address and volunteer and contact-update forms. This software makes it easy to transfer from Excel or other types of spreadsheets.
URL: http://www.donorsnap.com/fund-raising-software/features/index.php

BLACKBAUD CRM
DEVELOPED BY BLACKBAUD

This software will manage contacts from a variety of sources, including online communication and social media, and all the information will be organized and stored in one place. This software will make it easier to plan and complete fund-raisers and/or marketing strategies.
URL: https://www.blackbaud.com/fund-raising-crm/blackbaud-nonprofit-crm

FUNDRAISER SOFTWARE
DEVELOPED BY FUNDRAISER

This software is designed to expand outreach to potential donors, increase money, and create better relationships with donors. It will store and manage donor records, and will alert other staff members to new information with "sticky notes." It will organize donations and automatically create thank you letters for the donors. It has a built-in ability to create reports, including membership reports, correspondence reports, and solicitation and appeals reports.
URL: http://www.fund-raisersoftware.com/

CHARITYMASTER
DEVELOPED BY CHARITYMASTER

This software manages donor contact and history, along with tracking membership and volunteering. It will help organize events. This software includes 1 year of e-mail support. It works well with all Microsoft Office software. The system requirements for this software are

(continued)

BOX 12.9 SELECTED FUND-RAISING MANAGEMENT SOFTWARE *(continued)*

Windows XP or a newer version, Microsoft 2003 or later, and minimum screen resolution of 1024 × 768.
URL: http://charitymaster.com/index.html

GIFTWORKS
DEVELOPED BY GIFTWORKS

This software has many of the same features as the other fund-raising software. It stores and organizes contact information, while storing and managing donations and history, as well as processing recurring donations. It has built-in mail-merge software. It has the ability to custom create many types of reports from the data that you store. This software will easily transfer information from QuikBooks.
URL: http://www.giftworksconnect.com/

STAYCLASSY
DEVELOPED BY STAYCLASSY

This software is designed to increase a nonprofit organization's online presence and increase online donations. It will help create fund-raising campaigns and make the process faster and more efficient. Some of the features include an unlimited number of fund-raising campaigns, the ability to create e-mail receipts for donations, manage donations and donor contacts along with processing recurring donations, and also provides technical support by phone, e-mail, or in person.
URL: http://www.stayclassy.org/

TRAILBLAZER NONPROFIT MANAGER
DEVELOPED BY TRAIL BLAZER CAMPAIGN MEDIA INC.

This software is much like the previous ones. Some of the main features include donor and donation tracking, processing recurring donations, and mail merge. It will help you set up events easily and more efficiently, and produce multiple e-mails quickly. One special aspect of this software is that it also works on a Mac so it will work on your iPad or other Macintosh devices.
URL: http://www.trailblz.com/Nonprofit-Donor-Management-Software/Features.aspx

FUND-RAISING AND FINANCIAL SUSTAINABILITY

Nonprofit organizations received grants from government agencies and private and corporate foundations to support their activities. However, individual giving represents the largest share of the revenue raised by nonprofit organizations to implement their programs, projects, and services. Grants are restricted funds, because they are awarded based on submission of proposals that outline what the money received will be used for. Once that purpose is set, it is difficult or even impossible for nonprofit organizations to reallocate these funds to other activities that may turn out to be more important. This is not to say that nonprofit organizations should be able to reallocate their funding whenever they want. This could lead to all kinds of issues of accountability and stewardship for grant makers who want their money to be used as they promised to their constituents. Grant money is restricted, and cannot be used for investments that may secure long-term funding for a nonprofit organization. Therefore, there are limitations in terms of how grants can contribute to the financial sustainability of nonprofit organizations. This is where fund-raising income becomes significant for the financial sustainability of a nonprofit organization.

Fund-raising income is unrestricted most of the time. Being unrestricted, fund-raising funds do not have to be spent right away if there is another source of income that can provide funding for current activities. For example, while an organization is within a grant cycle, fund-raising money can be saved or invested, and can be used to continue to provide services when grant money is no longer available. It is important to underline that fund-raising can generate restricted funds as well. However, such restricted funds would generate ongoing income, which makes the restriction different from that of a grant. Further, fund-raising is an ongoing endeavor for every nonprofit organization. The public at large expects to receive solicitations from nonprofit organizations. Some people will donate. Others will not. However, as long as an organization exists, it can continue to generate funding through fund-raising. This makes fund-raising one of the most, if not the most sustainable income-generation strategy for nonprofit organizations. Fund-raising may also be, by far, the most important contributing factor to the financial sustainability of a nonprofit organization.

QUESTIONS AND ACTIVITIES

1. What is fund-raising?
2. Why do people donate to nonprofit organizations?
3. How would you describe a fund-raising proposal?
4. How does fund-raising contribute to the financial sustainability of nonprofit organizations?

CASE STUDY: REDEEM

Redeem is a nonprofit organization that assists children who are victims of abuse and women who are victims of domestic violence. Redeem services include emergency shelter, advocacy services, outreach, and education programs for battered women and their children. The Redeem Shelter and Advocacy Program is often the only opportunity for women and children to achieve productive and violence-free lives. Redeem Programs and Services, located at three sites, are designed to complement each other and provide clients with comprehensive care. For the past 2 years, Redeem has been forced to let some of its key staff go because of serious budget cuts. Consequently, Redeem is struggling to help some of its clients. The next fiscal year will be worse if the organization cannot generate additional income. The board is asking for your support to indicate strategies that can help raise at least $100,000.00 of additional funds.

(continued)

CASE STUDY: REDEEM *(continued)*

Questions

1. What are some of the questions that you will plan to ask the board members?
2. What are some generic ideas that you think may help them generate additional funds to support their activities?
3. State at least one fund-raising goal.
4. State at least three fund-raising objectives.
5. Indicate at least one activity that will help you achieve each objective.
6. Draft a budget of income and expenses for your fund-raising activities.

REFERENCES

Andreoni, J., & Bernheim, B. (2009). Social image and the 50/50 norm: A theoretical and experimental analysis of audience effects. *Econometrica, 77*(5), 1607–1636.

Andreoni, J., & Rao, J. M. (2011). The power of the ask: How communication affects selfishness, empathy and altruism. *Journal of Public Economics, 95*, 513–520.

Bekkers, R. (2010). Who gives what and when? A scenario study of intentions to give time and money. *Social Science Research, 39*, 369–381.

Bennett, R., & Savani, S. (2003). Predicting the accuracy of public perceptions of charity performance. *Journal of Targeting, Measurement and Analysis for Marketing, 11*(4), 326–342.

Bohnet, I., & Frey, B. (1999). The sound of silence in prisoner's dilemma and dictator games. *Journal of Economic Behavior and Organization, 38*(1), 43–57.

Cheung, C. K., & Chan, C. M. (2000). Social-cognitive factors of donating money to charity, with special attention to an international relief organization. *Evaluation and Program Planning, 23*, 241–253.

Duncan, B. (2004). A theory of impact philosophy. *Journal of Public Economics, 88*, 2159–2180.

Internal Revenue Service. (2013). *Charitable contribution deductions.* Retrieved from http://www.irs.gov/Charities-&-Non-Profits/Charitable-Organizations/Charitable-Contribution-Deductions.

Kingma, B. R. (1989). An accurate measurement of the crowd-out effect, income effect, and price effect for charitable contributions. *Journal of Political Economy, 97*, 1197–1207.

Kropf, M., & Knack, S. (2003). Viewers like you: Community norms and contributions to public broadcasting. *Political Research Quarterly, 56*, 187–197.

Lee, B. A., & Farrell, C. R. (2003). Buddy, can you spare a dime? Homelessness, panhandling, and the public. *Urban Affairs Review, 38*, 299–324.

MacLaughlin, S. (2014). *Charitable giving report: How nonprofit fund-raising performed in 2013.* Retrieved from https://www.blackbaud.com/nonprofit-resources/charitablegiving?utm_source=npengage&utm_medium=blog&utm_campaign=CGR2014

Marcuello, C., & Salas, V. (2001). Nonprofit organizations, monopolistic competition, and private donations: Evidence from Spain. *Public Finance Review, 29*(3), 183–207.

Phillips, E. (2013). *Philanthropy as corporate R&D.* Retrieved from http://curtisgroupconsultants.com/index.php/blog/archive/2013/10/

Sargeant, A., & Lee, S. (2004). Donor trust and relationship commitment in the U.K. charity sector: The impact on behavior. *Nonprofit and Voluntary Sector Quarterly, 33*(2), 185–202.

Sargeant, A., & Woodliffe, L. (2007). Building donor loyalty: The antecedents and role of commitment in the context of charity giving. *Journal of Nonprofit and Public Sector Marketing, 18*(2), 47–68.

Schuyt, T. N. M., Smit, J., & Bekkers, R. (2004, November). *Constructing a philanthropy scale: Social responsibility and philanthropy.* Paper presented at the 33d Arnova Conference, Los Angeles.

Smith, J. R., & McSweeney, A. (2007). Charitable giving: The effectiveness of a revised theory of planned behaviour model in predicting donating intentions and behaviour. *Journal of Community and Applied Social Psychology, 17*, 363–386. doi:10.1002/casp.906

Stern, S. (2013). *Why don't corporations give to charity? Their profits soar, yet they only get stingier.* Retrieved from http://www.slate.com/articles/business/moneybox/2013/08/corporations_don_t_give_to_charity_why_the_most_profitable_companies_are.html

Weerts, D. J., & Ronca, J. M. (2007). Profiles of supportive alumni: Donors, volunteers, and those who "Do It All." *International Journal of Educational Advancement, 7*, 20–34.

Xiao, E., & Houser, D. (2005). Emotion expression in human punishment behavior. *Proceedings of the National Academy of Sciences, 102*(20), 7398–7401.

Social Enterprise and Financial Sustainability

OBJECTIVES

At the completion of this chapter, the reader will be able to:

1. Define the concept of social enterprise.
2. Explain the term "social entrepreneurship."
3. Identify the steps needed to develop a social enterprise.
4. Describe the key components of a business plan.
5. Explain the relationship between social enterprise and financial sustainability.

This chapter emphasizes social entrepreneurship as a mission-driven enterprise and a strategy for financial sustainability in nonprofit organizations. The chapter provides introductory information on the field of social entrepreneurship, social entrepreneurship models, and frameworks to develop a business plan for a social enterprise, as well as management strategies.

DEFINE "SOCIAL ENTERPRISE"

Simply put, the term "social enterprise" refers to a business activity intended to generate profit to finance a social, educational, cultural, religious, or charitable cause. A social enterprise is a for-profit business whose primary purpose is to reinvest its profits in not-for-profit activities. In other words, a social enterprise engages in trading activities or formal business trade practices for the benefit of the community.

Figure 13.1 is a classic illustration of what a social enterprise stands for: a business activity that must generate profits and returns to invest in social activities that will benefit the clients of a nonprofit organization. A social enterprise can be a formal business entity owned by a nonprofit organization for a social purpose or an earned-income business to generate revenue that can support a social cause.

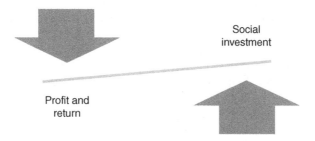

FIGURE 13.1 Social enterprise as a business.

SOCIAL ENTREPRENEURSHIP

The concept of social enterprise has been on the rise all over the world. Many social problems have increased in intensity and complexity, therefore, they require entrepreneurial approaches that are most likely to create social value with limited resources. Societies worldwide seek innovative approaches to address persistent social, educational, health, and environmental problems that affect their communities and that are yet to be tackled by business or public agencies. Many nonprofit organizations are faced with the challenges of confronting these social problems and attempting to bring sustainable solutions to such issues. Financial pressures on most nonprofit organizations have increased in recent years due to the financial crisis and are unlikely to lessen. Costs have been rising faster than inflation. Societies strive to find better ways to provide socially important goods and services, and take advantage of opportunities by testing new approaches and organizational models to achieve social goals. Social entrepreneurship has proven to be one of the best options available to nonprofit organizations to reach that end, because it includes the social purpose for nonprofit organizations and the potential benefits of entrepreneurship in terms of innovation, efficiency, high performance, and economic sustainability. A social entrepreneurship approach has the advantage of generating resources to enhance the effectiveness of nonprofit activities and make significant and sustainable contributions that change the lives of disadvantaged people. Social entrepreneurship is rooted in the broader field of entrepreneurship and has drawn on the definition of entrepreneurship as the pursuit of opportunities to further a social purpose. In other words, entrepreneurial organizations focus on opportunities, not resources. Social entrepreneurship is an innovative, social-value-creating activity that can help diversify the revenue stream of the nonprofit organizations in ways that fund-raising or grant seeking cannot.

CHARACTERISTICS OF SOCIAL ENTERPRISE

A social enterprise is a hybrid organization mixing nonprofit and for-profit elements. The profit element meets all the characteristics of a for-profit business. As such, a social enterprise must exist as a legal entity and satisfy all the requirements necessary to start a new business. A social enterprise requires a business that outlines its development, including projections of when it will start making a profit. As a business, profit is essential for a social enterprise. Without profit there is no social enterprise. The reason that a social enterprise exists is to support the other side of the coin, which is its nonprofit nature. There must be profit to support the social purpose of a social enterprise. In that sense, a social enterprise needs the appropriate business discipline in the conduct of its operations, including, but not limited to, the quality of products or services, the satisfaction of its clients or customers, and of the maintenance of sound accounting and financial management principles. However, it must be stated clearly to everyone that a social enterprise is not a charitable entity. Clients or customers should not expect to walk into a social enterprise and obtain products or services for free. There can be bargaining. There can be special donations to individuals desperately in need. However, a social enterprise must cultivate a strong base of clients or customers who have the ability to pay for products or services. Lastly, a social enterprise is accountable to its founding nonprofit organization, the service users, employees, and the public in general. The assets of a social enterprise belong to the community.

TYPES OF SOCIAL ENTERPRISE

Social enterprises exist within the spirit of social and community impact, creative thinking, decisiveness, innovation, resilience and fortitude, and persistence. Therefore, there can be various types of social enterprises. Some of the most common types are:

Small-business entities: An independently owned entity with limited investment that engages in trade activities primarily with local clients or customers. Examples would include a grocery store, a coffee or sandwich shop, a retail store that sells used items, or a repair shop.

Co-operative: Organization created through voluntary and open membership and managed by members to achieve a social or community purpose (e.g., fair trade).

Social firm: Business created to help disadvantaged people in the labor market find employment.

Credit union: Helps members save and borrow money.

Trading arm to charity: Engages in trading activities to raise money for a charity (e.g., charity shop, thrift stores, catalogues, training & consultancy).

Public sector spin-outs: Delivers services that were once provided by public sector organizations.

SOCIAL ENTERPRISE DEVELOPMENT FRAMEWORK

The development of a social enterprise should include the following generic steps outlined in Figure 13.2: need statement, purpose statement, organizational readiness, identity and legality, business plan, start-up and implementation, management, and evaluation and growth.

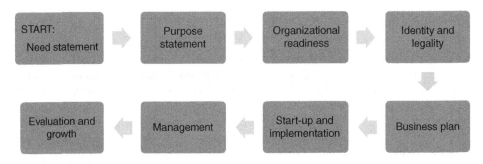

FIGURE 13.2   Social enterprise development framework.

Need Statement

The need statement describes the vision, mission, and the target population of a nonprofit organization, as well as the needs that the organization is meeting through its current activities. Further, the needs statement describes the limitations of the current stream of funding to continue to support current activities in a sustainable manner. The need statement also outlines several funding approaches and their limitations or reliability, and justifies why the starting of a social enterprise is an effective option to generate income to support organizational programs and services.

Purpose Statement

The purpose statement describes the earned income business activity or strategy that the organization will implement in order to have specific social impact. For example, it can be something like, "Start a local green restaurant in order to generate income that can help homeless youth in Boston achieve economic self-sufficiency."

Organizational Readiness

A social enterprise is not a nonprofit activity. It is not a traditional business activity either. It is a combination of the two. Therefore, it requires different attitudes and dispositions from a nonprofit organization. There should be an assessment of the organizational understanding of the nature of a social enterprise, its ability (i.e., governance, management, financial), readiness, willingness, and commitment to invest in such new endeavors. The readiness assessment should also include elements of a SWOT (strengths, weaknesses, opportunities, threats) analysis in relation to the creation of a social enterprise.

Identity and Legal Issues

Identity refers to the type of social enterprise that will be created, and the necessary legal requirements it must satisfy. For example, as a business, a social enterprise will apply for local and state business licenses, and will be required to pay sales taxes.

Business Plan

As indicated earlier, a social enterprise is a business. Like any new business, it requires the development of a business plan. A business plan is a written document that describes the nature, goals and objectives, and operations of a new business. Generically, a business plan includes:

■ Cover sheet
■ Table of contents
■ Business identification

- Executive summary
- Vision–mission–goals–objectives
- Description or profile of the business
- Description of product(s)/service(s)
- Market analysis
- Competitive situation
- Marketing and sales strategies
- Operations management
- Action plan
- Financial framework
- Appendices

Cover sheet: The cover sheet includes the following information:

- The name of the business
- The label "BUSINESS PLAN"
- The date
- The contact person (name, title, address, telephone, fax, e-mail)

Table of contents: The table of contents presents the chapters, sections, or subsections of the business plan, and the page numbers used to find them.

Business identification: The business identification section presents:

- The name of the business
- The business EIN (Employer Identification Number)
- The business address, telephone and fax numbers
- Owners of the business and contact addresses
- Possibly other people involved in the business (accountant, attorney, insurance ...) and their addresses

Executive summary: The executive summary is an overview of the business plan and synthesizes the vision and the mission of the business, the goal(s) and objectives, the strategies and capitalization needed to achieve the goals and objectives, and the potential capability of the business to make a profit. The executive summary should be no more than one page.

Vision–Mission–Goals–Objectives: The vision statement describes what the business aspires to become. The mission statement describes the purpose, client, and the products or services that the business will offer. The goals describe the main targets or benchmarks related to products and services that the business will offer. The objectives describe short-term targets that will accumulate to achieve the goals, which are long-term targets.

Description or profile of the business: The description or profile of the business describes:

- The precise nature of the business
- Whether this is a new business or the purchase of an existing business, or a franchise, or other
- Whether it is a seasonal or year-round business
- Whether there is any contract or agreement or not
- The vendors, suppliers, outside contractors (if any)
- The operational procedures
- The local and national economic trends that influence the business, and how the organization owning the business will deal with them
- Any other relevant information that can help better understand the profile of the business

Description of product(s)/ service(s): This section explains all relevant information about products or services, describes what makes the product or service unique, the tests or approvals that they passed, and the guarantee that will be promised to customers.

Market analysis: The market analysis section describes the demographic, economic, and social profiles of the clients that are most in need of the products or services. Further, it includes the identification of all competitors, their strengths and weaknesses, and strategies to compete with them.

Competitive situation: This section identifies the local and national trends that may affect the business, and strategies to address these trends.

Marketing and sales strategies: This section is about the marketing and sales strategies that will be used to reach clients or customers.

Operations management: The operations management section describes the administration and the conduct of regular activities related to running the business. It also includes the people involved in decision making and the implementation process of production or service delivery.

Action plan: The action plan details the steps or benchmarks that will help implement the business plan.

Financial framework: The financial framework includes:

- Capital requirements
- Depreciable assets
- Sales forecast
- Pro-forma balance sheet
- Projected income statements
- Cash-flow projections and analysis
- Break-even analysis

Capital requirements: The capital requirements concern the money needed to start the business. This is basically a budget of investment. The capital requirements include all the start-up expenses and working capital.

Depreciable assets: Depreciable assets are all assets of the business that depreciate over a period of time. For example, when you purchase a copier, you have a depreciable asset that helps you run your business. There is an initial cost for the copy machine, which is the price of purchase. But, once you start using this asset, it loses some value until it becomes useless. This deterioration in value of an asset (real estate may go up in value) is called depreciation. In accounting, depreciation is considered as an expense. The most common depreciation method is called straight-line depreciation. It consists of:

- Identifying the initial cost of the asset
- Estimating how many years you think the asset will have some value for your business
- Dividing the initial cost by the number of years

In other words,

$$\text{Depreciation} = \text{Initial cost} \div \text{Estimated asset lifetime}$$

Figure 13.4 offers an example of depreciation for a $40,000.00 copier machine.

Year	Straight-Line Depreciation	
	Book Value	Annual Depreciation
Starting	$40,000	$ –
First	36,000	4,000
Second	32,000	4,000
Third	28,000	4,000
Fourth	24,000	4,000
Fifth	20,000	4,000
Sixth	16,000	4,000
Seventh	12,000	4,000
Eight	8,000	4,000
Ninth	4,000	4,000
Tenth		4,000
Eleventh		
Twelfth		
		40,000

FIGURE 13.4   Sample straight-line depreciation.

Sales forecast: Sales forecasting is the process of estimating sales volume, expenses, and projected profits for the first 5 years of a business.

Projected income statements or profit-and-loss statement: The projected income statement or profit-and-loss statement is an estimation of income and expenses of the business within a period of time, which can be 3 to 5 years. The projected income statement includes:

■ Sales: Net sales in dollars (or currency).
■ Direct cost of sales or cost of goods sold: Cost of products or services that you have sold.
■ Gross margin or gross profit: Sales less cost of goods sold.
■ Selling expenses: Sales salaries, advertising, delivery expenses, bad debt expenses, credit card fees, and other similar selling expenses.
■ Administrative expenses: Salaries, utilities, depreciation, rent, building services, insurance, phone, and other similar administrative expenses.
■ Operating expenses: Costs of goods sold plus selling and administrative expenses.
■ Profit before tax: Sales less operating costs.
■ EBITDA: Earnings before interest, tax, depreciation and amortization.
■ Net profit: Profit before taxes less taxes.

Cash-flow projections: The cash-flow projection displays inflows and outflows of cash in the business within a period of time, which can be 12 to 36 months or even more. The cash-flow projection concerns the net income of the business. In other words, it deals only with actual cash transactions. It shows the amount of cash needed to operate the business over time and when there will be positive cash flow. The cash-flow projection includes:

■ Starting cash: The amount of cash you start with.
■ Cash disbursement: Receivables from sales of products or services and possibly from other sources.

■ Cash uses: Includes costs of goods sold, operating expenses, income tax, and so forth.
■ Ending cash: This refers to the cash in hand at the end of the period. Except for the first month, the ending cash of a period is the starting cash for the following period. See Chapter 9 for an example of a statement of cash flow.

Pro-forma balance sheet: The pro-forma balance sheet is a projected balance sheet that shows the distribution of the assets, liabilities, and equity of the business at a given point in time.

■ Assets: This includes current assets (cash, accounts receivable, notes receivable, prepaid expenses, inventories, and any other item convertible in cash within 1 year in the normal course of business), fixed assets or long-term assets (land, buildings, equipments, vehicles, leasehold improvement, machinery, and any other item with estimated useful life measured in years), and other assets (deposit on a franchise, preopening expenses, etc.).
■ Liabilities and owner's equity: This includes current liabilities (debts and obligations that will be paid within 1 year, such as accounts payable, notes payable, taxes payable, salaries), long-term liabilities (debts and obligations due in more than 1 year, such as mortgages, equipment loans, bank loans, etc.), and owner's equity (initial investment, retained earnings, common stock, etc.).

Appendices: The appendices include all documents that can illustrate or help support assertions made in the body of the business plan. For example, appendices can include legal (e.g., legal registration), financial (e.g., audit, copy of 990 form, bank statements), and administrative documentation (e.g., organizational structures, letter of support, résumés of key personal).

Start-up and Implementation

Start-up and implementation are the translation into actions of all the ideas described in the business plan. The start-up includes decisions and activities to satisfy all the legal requirements for the social enterprise, secure the location of the business, purchase equipment, hire staff to run the social enterprise, design the service delivery system, and implement marketing strategies to attract customers.

Management

Management of a social enterprise includes all aspects of ongoing planning, operating, monitoring, and making managerial decisions so that the business can generate profit that can be used for the purpose for which the social enterprise was created.

Evaluation and Growth

Performance measurement is a key to the success of a social enterprise. Performance measurement should be at the center of financial and human resource management, as well as the relationship with customers. Effective performance assessment though evaluation frameworks and tools will provide data that can be used for the growth and sustainability of a social enterprise.

SOCIAL ENTERPRISE AND COSTS

The development of a social enterprise requires an investment, which implies some costs. The costs will be fixed and variable.

Fixed Costs

These are costs that must be paid on a regular basis or over a period of time regardless of the volume of activity of an organization.

Examples:

- Rent (paid monthly)
- Monthly salaries
- Yearly salaries
- Property tax

Variable Costs

These are costs that vary in proportion to the level of activity of an organization.

Examples:

- Postage and shipping
- Hourly wages

CONTRIBUTION MARGIN

Excess of total revenue or income (R) generated from a unit of product or service over the variable costs (VC) per unit. The contribution margin (CM) is calculated by subtracting the variable costs per unit from the total revenue (R) per unit.

$$CM = R - VC$$

Andrew Foundation is a nonprofit organization that is planning to provide a fee-based service counseling program. The total weekly cost for one counseling session is $25. They plan to charge $40.00 per week for one session. What is the contribution margin?

The total revenue per child is $40.00.

$$\Rightarrow R = \$40.00.$$

The total variable cost is: $25.00.

$$\Rightarrow VC = \$25.00$$

$$CM = R - VC$$

$$CM = \$40.00 - \$25.00$$

$$CM = \$15.00$$

Interpretation:

Each time a client pays $40.00 for one counseling session, the organization will have $15.00 left.

BREAK-EVEN ANALYSIS

Break-even analysis is a formula used to determine how much income or revenue or sale volume a project, program, or an activity has to generate in order to start making a profit. A break-even point indicates whether a self-generated income program will be sustainable. The break-even point is calculated by dividing the total fixed costs by the contribution margin.

Break even (BE) = Fixed costs (FC)/Contribution margin (CM)

Andrew Foundation is a nonprofit organization that is planning to provide a fee-based service counseling program. The total weekly cost for one counseling session is $25. They plan to charge $40.00 per week for one session. The total weekly fixed costs for salaries, rent, utilities and insurance is $2,000.

How many sessions does the program need to have to start making a profit? Suppose that the demographic trends in the area where the day care is located indicate that the program can expect between 120 and 150 counseling sessions per month. Will the counseling program be financially sustainable? Explain

Response 1

■ BE = FC/CM

We must calculate the contribution margin first. The contribution margin was calculated earlier. It was: $15.00

■ Total fixed costs: $1,500.00
■ BE = $1,500/$15.00 BE = 100

Interpretation:

Andrew Foundation will need to have more than 100 sessions per month to start making a profit.

Response 2

If Andrew Foundation starts the counseling program, it will be sustainable. It must have more than 100 sessions per month to start making a profit; they expect to have between 120 and 150 sessions monthly.

SOCIAL ENTERPRISE AND FINANCIAL SUSTAINABILITY

Social enterprise can contribute to the financial sustainability of nonprofit organizations in various ways. As social entrepreneurship, a social enterprise can develop products or services that change people's lives in the same way some for-profit business do. I am referring to the way Microsoft changed people's lives with personal computers, or Apple with the iPhone, or Yahoo! and Google with the Internet search engine, just to name a few examples. The same can be said about fair-trade businesses that open markets to disadvantaged farmers, or the Grameen Bank in Bangladesh that provides socioeconomic opportunities to help people lift themselves out of poverty through their own trade activities. By offering transformative products or services, a social enterprise will continue to prosper and generate income to support the activities related to its social purpose.

A social enterprise generates unrestricted income for a nonprofit organization. With unrestricted funds, nonprofit organizations can develop policies within the context of applicable local, state, and federal laws, to design options to use their income in activities that are not supported by grant money, in a contingency fund, or in investments that can bring regular income while the capital remains secure for long-term needs.

Further, starting a social enterprise requires capital investment. The capital investment may automatically contribute to increasing the total assets of a nonprofit organization. This increase in total assets will in turn positively influence the solvency of a nonprofit organization. It is important to underline that investment to start a social enterprise can be funded by a loan. In that case, there will not be the same positive effect on solvency, because the increase in assets will be relatively neutralized by an increase in total liabilities. However, the return on investment in equipment, materials, or information technology infrastructure, as well as the profitability of a social enterprise, can offset an increase in liability and provides the positive influence of solvency.

QUESTIONS AND ACTIVITIES

1. What is a social enterprise?
2. What would you say to someone who said, "A nonprofit organization should not start a for-profit business"?
3. Conduct an Internet search and create a list of social enterprise activities that you identified. For each activity that you found, write a short description about what they do, and explain what their social purpose is.
4. What would you say are the key steps to starting a social enterprise?
5. What are some ways in which you think social enterprises can contribute to the financial sustainability of nonprofit organizations?

CASE STUDY: OSHKOSH EMPOWERMENT FOUNDATION

At the end of last year fiscal year, Oshkosh Empowerment Foundation (OEF) realized that they will fall short of balancing their next year's budget. One board member proposed organizing a T-shirt fund-raiser. An ad hoc committee was created to assess the financial sustainability of the proposal. A for-profit corporation offered to sell the foundation quality T-shirts at $2.00 a piece. They board

(continued)

CASE STUDY: OSHKOSH EMPOWERMENT FOUNDATION (*continued*)

estimated that the foundation will spend $3.00/T-shirt for volunteer and over-head expenses. In addition, they will have to commit an annual $25,000 of fixed costs. Given these facts, they chose a selling price of $10.00 per T-shirt.

Questions

1. How many T-shirts do they have to sell before the fund-raiser starts making a profit?
2. The committee expects that they will be able to sell between 3,000 and 4,000 T-shirts. What should be their recommendation to the board? Explain the recommendation.
3. Given the quality of the T-shirts, a member of the committee suggested raising the selling price to $15.00. Should they suggest approval of the proposal based on that scenario? Explain your recommendation!

Investment and Financial Sustainability

At the completion of this chapter, the reader will be able to:

1. Define the concept of investment.
2. Describe the items in an investment policy statement.
3. Identify the different types of investments available for nonprofit organizations.
4. Summarize the key principles for investment management.
5. Describe the management structures involved in investment for nonprofit organizations.
6. Explain the extent to which investments can contribute to the financial sustainability of nonprofit organizations.

Nonprofit organizations rely to a certain extent on private donations to provide services to clients or targeted populations. However, this stream of revenue tends to represent a low percentage of nonprofit revenues. Nonprofit organizations use a variety of sources of income to generate revenues for their programs and activities. Investment is one of these sources of revenues. This chapter suggests selected investment options that nonprofit organizations can use to strengthen their financial sustainability.

DEFINING "INVESTMENT"

Investment is the purchase of a financial or real asset by an individual, an organization, or an institution, in order to generate a return over time, which is proportional to the risk assumed during the investment period. In other words, an investment implies a purchase to generate a return or a profit. An investment occurs for a specific period of time. An investment is made with an assumed risk of earning a return or incurring a loss. *Investment* refers to any item or asset purchased by an individual or an organization with the hope that such purchase will generate income in the future. In other words, an investment is not expected to generate income immediately, although that is possible. For example, a student who goes to school to earn a degree is making an investment that can result in securing a better employment position to earn more money than before holding the degree. The investment is expected to generate a result, mostly after graduation. The student who invests in earning a degree usually cannot expect to secure a new employment position immediately for which holding a degree is mandatory. However, that is possible in the future. As I said earlier, it is possible that a student can earn a better job while in school, which can constitute an early return on investment. The profit will be generated in the future. The meaning of the term "investment" may vary depending on whether one is in finance or economics. In finance, "investment" means purchasing an asset that can be appreciated, earn interest, or generate dividends over time. In economics, "investment" implies the accumulation of new equipment, machinery, buildings, inventories, or other physical entities that can help generate income.

TYPES OF INVESTMENTS

The are several types of investment. The most common are short-term investment vehicles and fixed-income securities.

Short-Term Investment Vehicles

Short-term investment vehicles are investments made for a maturity period of 1 year or less. Usually, short-term investment vehicles are traded in the money market. They tend to generate a lower return on investment and carry more risks than long-term investments.

Short-Term Investment Strategies

Short-term investments are investments, such as an operating reserve or a rainy-day fund, which are set aside to be used for unexpected events. They must generate market returns while being invested in an a safe and liquid investment vehicle. Nonprofit organizations use cash-flow forecasting systems to track their short-term investment decisions. Usually, the budgeting process is the venue that provides the opportunity to either make or anticipate short-term investment decisions. The idea is that the operating budget will provide indications of cash inflows and cash outflows, and indicate when is the best time to make an investment. Examples of short-term investments are commercial paper, money market mutual funds, bankers' acceptances, repurchase agreements, bank offerings, and U.S. Treasury securities.

- *Commercial paper*: Investment of $1 million or more for a period of a few days up to 270 days.
- *Money market mutual funds*: Investments of $1,000 or less in mutual funds, which can be redeemed at short notice.
- *Bankers' acceptances*: Bankers' acceptances are short-term securities through which a bank agrees to repay a loan to the holder of the vehicle in case the debtor fails to pay.
- *Repurchase agreement*: Contractual agreement to sell an investor securities while agreeing to purchase the securities at set dates and prices.
- *Certificates of deposit*: A certificate of deposit is a debt instrument that a bank issues to attest that a specific sum of money has been deposited by an account holder at the issuing institution. A certificate of deposit bears a maturity date and generates a specified interest rate.

- ■ *Bank offerings*: Interest-bearing accounts or certificates of deposit offered by banks and insured by the Federal Deposit Insurance Corporation (FDIC).
- ■ *Treasury securities*: These represent financial obligations of a government issued at a discount from the nominal value for a period of less than a year. They include securities, such as Treasury bills, Treasury notes, and Treasury bonds, which are guaranteed by the full faith and credit of the U.S. government.

LONG-TERM INVESTMENT STRATEGIES

Contrary to short-term investments, long-term investments are made with funds that are not needed for use in a period of less than a year. The long-term or fixed-income securities are based on a fixed return either for a specified period of time or indefinitely. Examples of long-term investments are pension funds, self-insurance funds, and endowment funds.

Pension Funds

Pension funds are funds that an employer establishes as a means to manage the employees' retirement funds, which encompass contributions from both the employee and the employer. As the name indicates, pension funds are used to provide pensions for employees on retirement. Pension funds are invested in various activities in order to make them generate more income. Usually, pension funds are managed by a financial institution on behalf of the employer and employees. Some companies manage their pension funds without the involvement of an intermediary party.

Self-Insurance Funds

Self-insurance funds are money that an organization or an entity sets aside to use for future insurance needs. An entity develops a self-insurance fund if a particular coverage is not available from insurance companies or is too costly compared to self-insurance. Some companies create a subsidiary entity to manage their self-insurance funds. The self-insurance funds are invested in other activities to generate more income.

Endowment Funds

Endowments started in medieval times as farmland donated to churches, which would then be rented out to farmers, and consequently generated income to support various church activities. In the United States, endowment funds include various financial instruments, such as real estate and partnerships in the forms of capital appreciation, interests, dividends, rents, and royalties. In most U.S. states, the investment of endowment funds is governed by the 1972 Uniform Management of Institutional Funds Act (UMIFA). Educational institutions (e.g., colleges and universities) call their long-term investment funds endowments. Health care organizations call them long-term operating funds.

MANAGEMENT STRUCTURES

Federal and state laws recognize the board of directors as the structure with fiduciary responsibility to ensure that the resources of a nonprofit organization are being properly managed to further the vision and mission of a nonprofit organization. When a nonprofit organization decides to make long-term investments, this implies automatically that a structure other than the board of directors will manage a part of the assets of an organization. Therefore, if the investment decision is not adequately made, the board may exert a fiduciary responsibility without any real responsibility. To prevent such a situation, nonprofit organizations establish or must establish policies and guidelines, select key qualified officers and mangers to oversee the implementation of investment decisions, and set benchmarks to evaluate outcomes that will make it possible to take appropriate corrective actions when necessary. The structures differ in various nonprofit organizations. Some organizations create a committee to manage their investment funds. Other organizations hire external professional consultants supervised by a committee or internal staff. The best strategy is for the board to explore and discuss options, and make the decision that best suits the interests of the organization in accordance with objective criteria accepted by a majority of directors.

INVESTMENT POLICY STATEMENT

An investment policy statement is a document that acknowledges and defines the terms under which the board of directors delegates its fiduciary responsibility to a third party that will manage specific assets of a nonprofit organization.

Best practices suggest that a nonprofit organization should create an investment committee, which will be responsible for developing investment policy to be approved by the board of directors. An investment policy statement is developed by a nonprofit organization to set guidelines for the investable assets.

The investment policy should specify the purpose of investments to be made by the organization and the constraints attached to investments. In most cases investments are overseen by the investment committee, and managed by the investment manager with the support of the investment consultant. The investment statement outlines the responsibilities of the investment committee, as well as the investment consultant and investment manager.

The investment committee has fiduciary responsibilities to:

- Exercise reasonable care, skill, and caution regarding the overall investment strategy, which should incorporate reasonable risks and return objectives
- Diversify the portfolio, unless there are reasons to the contrary
- Analyze and make considered decisions concerning the levels of risk appropriate to the organization's purposes
- Conform to fundamental fiduciary duties of loyalty and impartiality
- Act with prudence in deciding whether and how to delegate authority and in the selection and supervision of agents (i.e., investment consultants and/or investment managers)
- Incur only costs that are reasonable in amount and appropriate to the management of the portfolio

A statement about conflict of interest should be unequivocal concerning any person or organization involved in the oversight or management of the portfolio. In addition, the

---

> ### BOX 14.1 ITEMS FOR INVESTMENT POLICY STATEMENT
>
> - Overall investment environment of a nonprofit organization
> - Objective and strategies for asset investment
> - Roles of organizational structures involved in managing investments
> - Level of acceptable risks
> - Allocation guidelines
> - Prohibited investment vehicles
> - Selection of consultants, managers, and custodians
> - Reporting procedures
> - Methods and benchmarks for performance measurement
> - Procedures to initiate changes

---

statement of investment policy should define classes of assets, guidelines for each asset, strategic and tactical allocation strategies, procedures to monitor investment and performance, red lines for the asset manager, and review procedures (Box 14.1).

INVESTMENT ANALYSIS

Investment analysis is an analysis of an investment based on its development costs and maintenance costs in relation to revenue generated. Various formulas exist to conduct investment analysis. The most common are net present value (NVP), internal rate of return (IRR), payback period (PP), and break-even point.

The net present value is the "difference amount" between the sums of discounted cash inflows and cash outflows, when taking into account the present value of money today in comparison to the present value of money in the future, and the inflation and returns. Investment managers use the NPV to make financial decisions regarding a portfolio. The principle is that an investment should be accepted if its net present value is greater than zero and rejected if it is not.

The internal rate of return or economic rate of return (ERR) is the rate of profitability of an investment. The internal rate of return does not take into consideration the external factors that can affect an investment. The IRR is a measure of efficiency and quality. An organization should accept an investment if its internal rate of return is greater than an established minimum acceptable rate of return or cost of capital.

The payback period or break-even point is the period of time required to recover the funds expended in an investment. The payback period is often used to compare similar investments, and make a judgment about a particular investment decision to be made.

MANAGEMENT OF INVESTMENT

Short-term investments must be safe. In other words, the fund manager must be sure that the principal will be available at the end of the investment period. This is not something that can be left to probability. You may understand that any issue of not getting the principal back when anticipated can affect the liquidity of an organization, and have unintended financial and organizational consequences. A short-term investment must past the scrutiny of liquidity. In other words, the investment must be cash convertible in a short period of time, so that the money is available as soon as it is needed. The cash convertibility of the principal should not in any circumstance result in a loss. Finally, a short-term investment must generate a profit, a positive return after taking all the expenses into account. Obviously, the rate of net return will vary with the level of risks accepted by a fund manager.

Given that any investment has some level of risk involved, fund managers must assess the soundness of an investment vehicle or issuing company before making a short-term investment. The existence of Ponzi schemes is not a myth, but a reality that can affect any investor, whether it is an individual, a for-profit, or nonprofit entity. Part of assessing the level of soundness of issuing companies is to research their financial conditions, the projections for future performance of the securities, and information published by rating agencies (e.g., Standards & Poor's, Moody's, and Fitch). It is fair to say that rating agencies do not always get it right as evidenced by their failure to anticipate the recent 2008 financial crash. Despite their past mistakes, their judgment is one of the most objective supports possible that a nonprofit organization can rely on when making investment decisions. It is ironic to say this, but many nonprofit organizations may not have the appropriate resources to develop their own ratings. However, a nonprofit organization may conduct its own financial investigation and compare the findings with information provided by the rating agencies.

Further, managers of nonprofit short-term investment assets should be aware of potential market risks before making investment decisions. The investment market is subject to changes in interest rates beyond the control of the issuing agency. This should be factored in when making investment decisions to avoid surprises (e.g., premature liquidation of the investment). Obviously, there are fewer market risks in short-term investments compared to long-term investments.

INVESTMENT POLICIES AS STRATEGY FOR LONG-TERM INVESTMENTS

Long-term endowments and pension funds represent an important stream of income for many nonprofit organizations. The decision to develop such investments and their success or failure can have significant consequences on the financial sustainability of a nonprofit organization. A well-developed investment policy can make all the difference. A well-developed investment policy provides guidelines that can anticipate avoidable risks and direct investment decisions on paths with more potential for success. As indicated earlier, investment policies should set the purpose, management structures, asset allocation and rebalancing guidelines, permissible instruments, consultant, custodian, manager selection and evaluation, reporting requirements, and policy review (Box 14.2).

Members of the governing board who came of age in the private sector may tend to think of ultimate objectives in terms of net profit, return on investment, and shareowner value—all of which are measurable. In their nonprofit roles, however, they had to cope with more subjective goals. What can create confusion is that the terms employed resemble those used in business. Profit and growth certainly have relevance to the management of a nonprofit investment. Success has very different applications.

Further, it is difficult for some board members to reconcile payout policy with the social purpose of nonprofit organizations. Payout is the total amount of money distributed from the nonprofit investment fund to support current programs. Educational institutions have a significant degree of latitude in setting their own payout policies, as there are no statutory mandates that dictate minimum payout levels. However, there are certain

---

BOX 14.2 PRINCIPLES OF ENDOWMENT MANAGEMENT

Purpose: Objectives of the endowment and statement of investment policies

Responsibilities: Roles of the board members, staff, and consultants

Payout: Amount of the endowment to transfer each year to the operating budget

Asset allocation: Optimum balance of the portfolio to achieve the targeted level of return while limiting risk

Costs: Link performance with cost-effectiveness

Manager: Select the right investment manager based on portfolio diversification

Risk management: Proactively search for risks in every facet of the investment process

---

practical considerations that affect payout policies, as these institutions are generally dedicated to fulfilling their education mission in perpetuity. Foundations tend to have very special legal requirements concerning their minimum payout level, currently a minimum of 5% of the endowment value. Further, there are fairly technical requirements as to what types of spending may be counted against the 5% minimum. Health care organizations differ from endowments both in how assets are obtained and how funds are spent. Health care organizations maintain fee-based services. The fees are generated from insurance companies, government programs, and patients. Despite the data and analytic tools available to inform decisions, it is challenging to make asset allocation decisions in nonprofit organizations. This is due in part to the not-for-profit mission of nonprofit organizations.

A nonprofit investment will run unavoidable risks that may cause the investment to fail. Failures can occur in any part of the investment process, internal or external in operations, in the safekeeping and accounting of assets, in legal or regulatory issues, or in outright fraud.

Cost increases can be a critical issue in investment management. In addition to investment manager fees, sometimes organizations can be charged for other custodial, legal, accounting, consulting, or overhead fees that are excessive or even abusive. The investment policy should spell out its policy regarding cost increases to avoid being surprised.

INVESTMENT AND FINANCIAL SUSTAINABILITY

Nonprofit organizations can make strategic decisions to invest in companies that contribute to sustainability and thus contribute to their own sustainability. By making strategic decisions to contribute to the sustainability of its environment, nonprofit organizations contribute to their own sustainability.

Investment is one of the key financial sustainability strategies available to nonprofit organizations. Investment helps maintain assets and regular income that contribute to the profitability of a nonprofit organization. If an organization is not in a position to report profits, investment income will contribute to reduce loss or deficits. Investment contributes to improve the liquidity of a nonprofit organization. By providing regular income, investment makes an organization more likely to have the ability to pay its bills on time. Further, investment can help improve the solvency of a nonprofit organization through the contributions to total assets and regular income it provides. Finally, investment contributes to diversifying the revenue streams of a nonprofit organization, and makes such organizations less likely to dissolve if one source of funding disappears.

QUESTIONS AND ACTIVITIES

1. How would you define "investment"?
2. What is the difference between short-term and long-term investment?
3. What are the responsibilities of the board in investment strategies of nonprofit organizations?
4. What do you think justifies the need for nonprofit organizations to adopt investment strategies?
5. Imagine you are a board member of a nonprofit organization: What would you look for in an investment policy document?
6. How can investments contribute to the financial sustainability of a nonprofit organization?

Grant Seeking and Financial Sustainability

At the completion of this chapter, the reader will be able to:

1. Define the term "grant."
2. Cite the potential funding sources for nonprofit organizations.
3. Discuss the overall grant-seeking process.
4. Describe the items of a generic grant proposal or application.
5. Explain how grant seeking can contribute to the financial sustainability of a nonprofit organization.

This chapter focuses on how grant seeking can serve as a strategy to generate revenues that may ultimately contribute to the financial sustainability of a nonprofit (NPO) organization. The chapter discusses the grant-searching and proposal-development process, criteria for writing quality grant proposals, and management of grants and contracts to further the financial sustainability goals of a nonprofit organization.

GRANT, CALL FOR PROPOSAL, AND GRANT WRITING

A grant is a monetary fund disbursed by an institutional or organizational donor to a recipient (individual or entity), which does not have to be paid back. Agency use calls for proposals to inform grant-seeker organizations about funding opportunities. A call for proposals is a statement or announcement that indicates the availability of funding for a particular purpose and according to certain guidelines. This is the point of entry to receive a grant. You cannot apply for a grant that is not available. A call for proposals in any form confirms that funding is available. Grant seekers use grant-writing principles and strategies to apply for funding. Grant writing is simply the process of searching and completing the applications and requirements needed to apply for a grant opportunity.

FUNDING SOURCES

Founding sources for nonprofit organizations to seek grant opportunities include federal (e.g., U.S. Department of Education, National Science Foundation, Department of Health and Human Services, and other similar agencies) and state (e.g., State Department of Agriculture), and local (e.g., county agencies) agencies, private and corporate foundations, and community foundations. The grant-maker agencies maintain websites where they post funding opportunities with conditions of eligibility and deadlines for application. Further, there are agencies that publish directories and other online resources to aid the search for funding opportunities (see Box 15.1).

ABOUT THE GRANT-SEEKING PROCESS

The grant-seeking process encompasses searching, complying with requirements, and applying for grant opportunities. Searching is the first step of exploring funding opportunities through various sources (e.g., websites, directories, and databases). *Complying* means ensuring that a nonprofit organization is eligible and can meet the requirements (e.g., documentation, deadlines, matching requirements). *Applying* refers to the tasks of compiling, writing, and submitting grant application documents (Box 15.2).

Successful grant proposals stem from innovative and creative ideas, suggest new solutions to address existing gaps, result from effective communication with the funder, follow the grant proposal guidelines accurately, and adhere to all headings and format restrictions. Some of the preliminary questions to ask include, but are not limited to:

- Will the grant opportunity help further the mission and vision of my organization?
- Is the size of the award ceiling worth the time required to prepare the proposal?
- Does my organization have available expertise on board to develop the proposal?

BOX15.1 SAMPLE FUNDING SOURCES

- Federal government: www.grants.gov
- States: http://dpi.wi.gov
- Local government (county or city): www.ci.oshkosh.wi.us
- Foundations:
  - www.bmtfoundation.com
  - www.blankfoundation.org
- Corporate foundations
  - www.fordfoundation.org
  - www.bestbuy.com
  - www.walmart.com
  - www.bcbsla.com
- Local foundations
  - www.oshkoshareacf.org
  - www.oshkoshunitedway.org
- Directory of funding sources
  - www.guidestar.org
  - www.foundationcenter.org

BOX 15.2 KEY INFORMATION IN CALLS FOR PROPOSALS

■ Description of the funding opportunity (What is the purpose of the funding?)
■ Target population (Which demographic category is targeted by the funding?)
■ Eligibility (Who is eligible to apply? state, 501(c)(3), individuals, etc.)
■ Award ceiling (What is the maximum amount for your budget? Ask if not specified!)
■ Deadline (What is the deadline for submission? Is a letter of intent required?, etc.)
■ Guidelines (What are the guidelines and documents for submission?)

■ Is there conflict of interest?
■ Will there be human subjects involved?
■ Is it realistic to meet the deadline?
■ What is the page limit for the grant or per section?
■ What are the spacing, numbering, and margin requirements, if any?
■ Does my organization need letters of support for the grant application?
■ Briefly, is my organization fully eligible for this grant?

Best practices in grant writing suggest contacting the program officer prior to submission of a proposal. One of the reasons for this is that the program or project officer is the individual in most grant-maker agencies who checks on guidelines and on eligibility when nonprofit organizations submit their grant applications. Other audiences for a grant application include peer reviewers, who review and rate proposals, and the generalist panel, which votes on proposals to receive awards.

GENERIC CONTENTS OF A GRANT PROPOSAL

A grant proposal is a written document or application submitted in response to a call for proposals issued by a grant-maker agency or as a result of opportunities for funding or an invitation received by an applicant. A generic grant proposal includes a cover letter (optional), cover page, table of contents (optional), abstract, problem or needs statement, goals and objectives, project description, timeline, organizational capability, evaluation, references, budget, and appendices (optional; see Box 15.3).

COVER LETTER

The cover letter introduces the grant proposal to the project or program officer of the grant-maker agency. Sometimes the cover letter is not needed, because the grant application may have to be processed through a web-based system. When necessary, a cover letter includes standard greetings. Then, state one or two sentences that specify the purpose of the proposal and amount (e.g., Grant Middle School in Naples, Florida, is seeking a grant for the amount of $200,000 to provide after-school tutoring to help at-risk students improve their reading skills). There can be:

■ One or two sentences about the objectives
■ One or two sentences summarizing the project description
■ One or two sentences about the credibility of the applicant
■ One or two sentence about the best ways to contact the applicant

---

BOX 15.3 GENERIC CONTENTS OF A GRANT PROPOSAL

- Cover Page
- Table of contents
- Abstract
- Problem or needs statement
- Goals and objectives
- Project description or activities
- Timeline
- Organizational capability
- Evaluation
- References cited
- Budget
- Budget narrative
- Appendices

TITLE AND ABSTRACT

The title and abstract can make a high-impact first impression about a grant proposal. The title is the short summary version of a grant proposal. It should give an idea of what the proposal is about. The development of a grant proposal starts with a title that can be revised and refined throughout the writing process.

The abstract presents a brief summary of the project (Box 15.4). It must be clear and concise, and no longer than one page (usually 250–300 words, single space!). The abstract is the last section to be written. The abstract may be all some reviewers will read.

PROBLEM OR NEEDS STATEMENT

"Need" as a verb refers to what is required or desired to fill a discrepancy. The word "need" also means solutions or means to an end. A need is a gap or discrepancy between a current (what is) and a desired situation (what should be).

BOX 15.4 ABSTRACT

- One or two sentences summarizing the gap or the need for the project
- The specification of the target population
- The goal(s) and objectives of the project
- One or two sentences summarizing the activities
- One or two sentences summarizing the evaluation
- One or two sentences summarizing the organizational capability
- The amount of funding sought through the proposal

Current Situation	Need	Desired Situation
(What is...)	*(Gap)*	*(What should be...)*

A need can be formulated through a normative, expressive, comparative, or emotive approach.

Normative approach: In a normative approach, a need will be defined based on evidence of current situations that are considered below the established desired situation stated by standards, opinions, and experiences of experts and/or current research and findings. The difference between the current and desired situation is a gap or a normative need (see Box 15.5).

Expressive approach: An expressive approach is based on the gap between the desired supply required to meet the demands for an evident need and the current supply of a particular service or product as documented by facts or data (see Box 15.6).

Comparative approach: A comparative approach refers to an unfavorable situation when comparing what is available to one group with what is available to another group (Box 15.7).

BOX 15.5 ON NORMATIVE NEED

- ■ *Desired situation:* All children should have the opportunity to go to school.
- ■ *Current situation:* Suppose a significant group of children in a particular community cannot go to school for reasons that are not related to illness.
- ■ *Gap:* This would be evidence of a *normative need.*

BOX 15.6 ON EXPRESSIVE NEED

- ■ *Desired situation:* Single mothers should have a safe child-care facility to leave their children in if they have to go to work or attend school.
- ■ *Current situation:* Suppose the waiting list of the only child-care center in a small town is triple the number of children they are currently serving.
- ■ This would be evidence of an *expressive need.*

BOX 15.7 ON COMPARATIVE NEED

- ■ *Desired situation:* All children should have the same opportunity to succeed in school.
- ■ *Current situation:* Children in Zip Code 54903 have well-equipped school facilities, whereas children in Zip Code 54905 are attending crumbling schools with almost no equipment and no lunch programs.
- ■ This would be evidence of a *comparative need.*

> ## BOX 15.8 ON EMOTIVE NEED
>
> ■ *Desired situation:* Individuals with mental illness should not be allowed to buy a gun.
> ■ *Current situation:* Suppose there is evidence that there are no restrictions for people with mental illness to buy a gun, in order to respect the freedom of people to bear arms.
> ■ This would be evidence of an *emotive need.*

Emotive approach: An emotive approach is used when anecdotal or personal stories or testimonies illustrate a gap between a current situation and a more desired situation that a group or individuals see as a problem or issue to be addressed (Box 15.8).

PROBLEM STATEMENT

Grant-maker agencies award money to nonprofit organizations in order to help them address a problem or an issue or fill a gap related to a need in a community or society. The role of the problem statement is to clarify and justify the existence of such a need or problem. A compelling problem statement should:

■ Describe the problem (be as specific as you can).
■ Explain the impact of the underlying problem on the target population (provide statistics and references, if available).
■ Describe what may happen if the problem is not solved (provide statistics and references, if available).
■ Summarize the service(s) or additional service(s) that can be provided to prevent the underlying problem from happening.

Describe the problem: The formulation of a problem statement can use a normative, expressive, comparative, or emotive approach, or a combination of such approaches (Box 15.9).
Impact of the underlying problem on the target population: The problem statement should (see Box 15.10):

■ Explain the impact or effect of the problem.
■ Provide statistics and references, if available!
■ Provide illustrations.
■ Define the target population.

> ## BOX 15.9 DESCRIBE THE PROBLEM
>
> Every individual deserves a healthy life and access to quality and affordable preventive or curative care, which is unfortunately lacking in our country. Over the past 20 years, the HIV/AIDS epidemic in our country has escalated enormously. According to a World Health Organization (WHO) report, there are currently 1 million people infected with HIV living in ANONYMOUS country."

BOX 15.10 IMPACT OF THE UNDERLYING PROBLEM

Over the past 10 years, AIDS has become the main cause of mortality in ANONYMOUS country, and over the past 3 years, there have been nearly 1 million AIDS-related deaths (WHO, 2013). The WHO report estimates that there are at least 250,000 AIDS orphans in the country. An estimated 5, 000 orphans are living in each district.

BOX 15.11 WHAT HAPPENS IF THE PROBLEM IS NOT SOLVED?

We already have a sizeable AIDS orphan population in this country. Research in other developing countries has shown that, where the problem of AIDS orphans is not addressed successfully, infection rates begin to climb again when these orphans reach young adult-hood. Children growing up without parental or community support are more likely to contract the disease than those who enjoy such support.

What may happen if the problem is not solved? The problem statement should answer these questions (Box 15.11):

- Will the problem produce other consequences in the target population?
- Will the problem produce other consequences in other groups in a community or society?
- Will the problem produce other consequences that are more costly for the community or the society?
- Link the problem to a bigger picture (community, society, world).
- Provide statistics and references, if available!

Statement of anticipated services: The problem statement should summarize (Box 15.12):

BOX 15.12 STATEMENT OF ANTICIPATED SERVICES

Our country has very few facilities or services for addressing the issue of AIDS orphans. The resources that exist are in the form of institutions. These institutions provide care for very few children. Studies such as that of the UNDP mentioned above confirm that children raised in institutions are more vulnerable to HIV than those cared for in the community. Institutional care can lead to the break-up of young families, already devastated by the loss of a parent or parents. The difficult logistics of cost-effective institutional care often mean that siblings are separated and children lose their last contact with their family support system. Institutional care has also been shown to be very costly. In studies done in other developing countries, the cost of providing support to an AIDS orphan within the community has been shown to be less than a third of the cost of institutionalized care. The proposed project aims to open special care centers that can contribute to significantly reducing the incidence of HIV/AIDS in our country through community-based participatory health education and economic opportunity programs.

■ What service(s) or additional service(s) can be provided to prevent the underlying problem from happening?
■ What can fill the gap between a current situation and a preferred situation?
■ Note: Usually one or a few *(five)* sentences, up to one paragraph are all that are desired!

Briefly, a problem statement should provide the picture of a current situation versus a desired situation. The desired situation is the End. The proposal is the means to that End. The problem statement should explain how the means will help achieve the End. It is important to remember that lack of something does not necessarily justify a need for funding. A need must be justified with facts, data, stories, research findings, expert opinion, or historical information.

GOALS AND OBJECTIVES

Goals are broad statements that indicate how your project (if successful) will help meet a need, solve a problem, fill a gap, or change a situation. There is a close relationship between the problem statement and the goal set in a grant proposal (Figure 15.1).

Objectives describe specific, operational, and measurable short-term or intermediate accomplishments that will help achieve a goal. A project objective should be SMART, which is an acronym that stands for

■ *Specific* (what you are going to achieve? Use action verbs, be concrete)
■ *Measurable* (when will you know you have reached your objective? (i.e., numeric, quantity, cost))
■ *Achievable* (are your objectives achievable?)
■ *Realistic* (do you have the resources to achieve your objectives, i.e., personnel, facilities, equipment, etc.)
■ *Time limited* (when will you achieve the objectives? i.e., weekly, monthly, or annually)

A project can have outcome objectives (describe an expected result or outcome) and/or process objectives (describe a process, an activity, or a task). Box 15.13 contains some sample objectives.

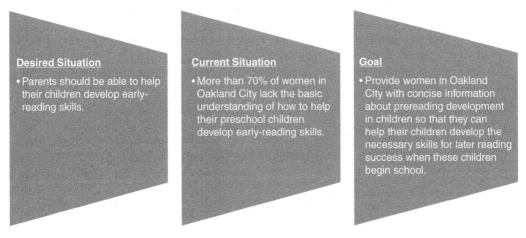

Desired Situation
• Parents should be able to help their children develop early-reading skills.

Current Situation
• More than 70% of women in Oakland City lack the basic understanding of how to help their preschool children develop early-reading skills.

Goal
• Provide women in Oakland City with concise information about prereading development in children so that they can help their children develop the necessary skills for later reading success when these children begin school.

FIGURE 15.1 Goal and problem statement.

BOX 15.13 SAMPLE OBJECTIVES

OUTCOMES OBJECTIVES

- Increase the number of students from educationally and/or economically disadvantaged backgrounds graduating from University of Wisconsin Oshkosh (UWO) by 40% during each project year.
- Decrease the rate of infant mortality in Winnebago County to at least the state average of 7.5 per 1,000 births within the first 3 years of the Outreach program.

PROCESS OBJECTIVES

- Provide financial support to 50 students per year to increase enrollment of racial and ethnic minority students from rural and underserved areas.

The objectives must be connected to the goal. More specifically, the objectives must be informed by the goals. For each goal, there should be at least two objectives. And, the goals and objectives must be designed to address need(s) identified in the problem statement. Box 15.14 lists some example of how goals and objectives can be related to needs.

PROJECT DESCRIPTION OR ACTIVITIES

I keep six honest serving men /(They taught me all I knew)/Their names are What and Why and When /And How and Where and Who.

—Rudyard Kipling (1865–1923)

BOX 15.14 SAMPLE GOALS AND OBJECTIVES RELATED TO A NEED

NEED

Desired situation: Seniors should be able to maintain independence in their own homes for as long as possible.
Current situation: More than 80% of seniors participating in our survey are living in a nursing home facility that they cannot afford because of lack of assistance in developing living skills and access to health care and service.
Gap: Assistance in developing living skills and access to health care and service is lacking.

Goal	Objectives
Assist seniors in South Side Chicago to maintain independence in their own homes for as long as possible.	■ Increase the ability of 100% of participants to perform daily living tasks. ■ Provide 240 hours of homemaker/chore services per month to 50 senior participants in our program. ■ Organize six modular independent living skills training sessions per year for 120 senior participants. ■ Provide assistance for transportation needs related to health care and services.

BOX 15.15 ABOUT THE PROJECT DESCRIPTION

WHAT?

■ What task(s) will be performed?
■ What specific service(s) will be provided?
■ What specific activity(ies) will be conducted?

HOW?

■ What is the process or method or strategy that will be used to perform this activity?
■ What will be the standards followed?
■ What are the guidelines?

WHY?

■ Why is this activity needed?
■ To what extent will this activity help solve the identified problem, reach a stated goal, or achieve a set objective (or set of objectives)?

WHO?

■ Who will receive the service(s)?
■ Who is/are the beneficiary(ies)?
■ Who will perform the activity?
■ What qualifications, skills, or experiences do they need or have?
■ Who will participate in the activity?
■ Who will provide assistance to the activity?

WHEN?

■ When will the activity start?
■ How long will the activity last?
■ A year? A month? A week?
■ What day?
■ What time?

The project description explains the activities that must be completed to solve the gap identified in the problem statement (Box 15.15). Each activity must be related to at least one goal and one objective. The project narrative should describe:

■ *What?* (What will happen?)
■ *How?* (What are the methods, strategies, techniques that will be used to make it happen?)
■ *Why?* (Why do you decide to do "what will happen?")
■ *Who?* (Who will be involved?)
■ *When?* (What is the date or the timeline?)
■ *Where?* (Where will that take place?)

Box 15.16 provides an illustration of one activity, After using the template to organize your thoughts, your project narrative paragraph would be like the following (Box 15.17):

BOX 15.16 DESCRIPTION OF ONE ACTIVITY

Component	Description
What?	After-school math and reading tutoring
	Oshkosh Community Association (OCA) will provide after-school math and reading tutoring sessions.
Why?	Only 10% of the schools in the Oshkosh district provide on-site after-school math and reading tutorial services. Their waiting list is 10 times the number of students they can service. The site where the tutorial support will be provided does not currently have a tutoring program. Therefore, our program will contribute to increasing the percentage of schools in Oshkosh that provide after-school assistance in reading and math, which is desperately needed to improve the low proficiency of the students, as indicated by the last academic yearly progress report, ranking Oshkosh next to last among the Wisconsin school districts.
How?	At the beginning of a tutoring session, each participant will receive a nutritional snack that conforms with the state nutrition standards for school-based food service. Supervised homework and one-on-one or group tutoring activities will take place after the snack. The length of time spent with any one student will vary with the student's academic situation and needs.
Who?	A total of 150 of the school's K–3 students will receive tutoring and a nutritional snack. A tutor will work with groups of 10 students. Each tutor will be required to complete successfully course training and undergo the school district's screening process. The project director will coordinate the snack menus with the school district nutritionist and the school cafeteria supervisor.
When?	After-school tutoring in reading and math will be provided for a 2-hour session three times a week, for 12 weeks, Monday, Wednesday, and Friday, from 3:00 pm to 5:00 pm.
Where?	All tutoring services will be provided at the school site. The school has a well-equipped cafeteria that can receive over 300 hundred students, two computer labs, and modern classrooms designed for 24 students.

TIMELINE

The timeline answers the questions, "What activity will be performed?" "When will the activity be completed?" "Who will be the primary responsible person?" "What will be the indicator documenting that the activity was completed?" (see Box 15.18).

ORGANIZATIONAL CAPABILITY

The organizational capability section explains the ability of an organization to manage the project for which funding is being sought. This section describes the profile of the organization (e.g., name and nonprofit nature of the organization, short history, vision, mission,

BOX 15.17 SAMPLE PROJECT DESCRIPTION PARAGRAPH

SAMPLE PROJECT DESCRIPTION PARAGRAPH

Oshkosh Community Association (OCA) will provide after-school math and reading tutoring sessions. Only 10% of the schools in the Oshkosh school district provide on-site after-school math and reading tutorial services. Their waiting list is 10 times the number of students that they can service. The site where the tutorial support will be provided does not currently have a tutoring program. Therefore, our program will contribute to increase the percentage of schools in Oshkosh that provide after-school assistance in reading and math, which is desperately needed to increase the low proficiency of the students as indicated by the last academic yearly progress report, ranking Oshkosh next to last among Wisconsin school districts. At the beginning of a tutoring session, each participant will receive a nutritional snack that conforms to the state nutrition standards for school-based food service. Supervised homework and one-on-one or group tutoring activities will take place after the snack. The length of time spent with any one student will vary with the student's academic situation and needs. A total of 150 of the school's K–3 students will receive tutoring and a nutritional snack. A tutor will work with groups of 10 students. Each tutor will be required to successfully complete course training and undergo the school district's screening process. The project director will coordinate the snack menus with the school district nutritionist and the school cafeteria supervisor. After-school tutoring in reading and math will be provided for a two-hour session three times a week, for 12 weeks, Monday, Wednesday, and Friday, from 3:00 pm to 5:00 pm. All tutoring services will be provided at the school site. The school has a well-equipped cafeteria that can receive over 300 students, 2 computer labs, and modern classrooms designed for up to 24 students.

BOX 15.18 TIMELINE

TIMELINE

Timeline	Activity	Responsible parties	Outcomes
06/2011	Complete contract negotiation process with John elementary school	Project director	Signed contract
07/2011	Create after-school registration and outreach process	■ Project director ■ Outreach coordinator	Registration form Program brochure Flyer News release Outreach calendar
09/2011	Recruit 150 students for the program	■ Project director ■ Outreach coordinator	Completed registration forms

target population, size of beneficiaries, and other similar information), its governance structures (e.g., board, committee), its service design system (e.g., What is the system in place for service delivery? Does the organization have adequate facilities and equipment?), experience (e.g., the prior project management experiences of the organization), community involvement (e.g., How is the community involved in the activities of the organization? What collaboration or partnership was sought or will be sought for the project?), and the quality of its staff (What are the credentials, qualifications, and experiences of key staff who will manage the project?).

EVALUATION

The evaluation section describes what criteria will be used to measure the success of a project and who will be involved in evaluating this work (staff, board, constituents, community, consultants). The project evaluation will be used to:

- Measure the extent of achievement of goals and objectives
- Comply with funder accountability
- Provide information to help improve the project
- Provide new insight or new information for future funding opportunities
- Provide information for communicating to a variety of stakeholders

EVALUATION AND PROJECT OBJECTIVES

The evaluation of a project is linked to its goals and objectives. The evaluation will be summative in nature for the outcomes objectives and mainly formative for the process objectives (Figure 15.2).

Outcomes/summative evaluation: Outcomes evaluation measures whether a project changes a problematic situation into a new desired situation (Box 15.19). It assesses the impact of the program on the target population. Table 15.1 outlines different types of project evaluation.

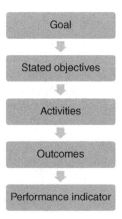

FIGURE 15.2   From the goal to performance measurement.

BOX 15.19 SAMPLE OUTCOMES EVALUATION STATEMENT

OUTCOME OBJECTIVE

■ Increase participant awareness about prereading activities that can help children develop necessary skills for later success in reading when these children begin school.

EVALUATION PLAN

■ All participants in the program will complete pre- and postknowledge-based surveys, each quarter, on the various topics that will be addressed during our seminars. The difference in scores during pre- and postsurveys will help determine whether participants' awareness has increased or not.

TABLE 15.1 Types of Evaluation

Based on...	Evaluation
Methodology	■ Quantitative ■ Qualitative

Timing	■ Preassessment
	  ● Conducted before implementing a project as part of the planning
	  ● May also be referred to as "Needs Assessment."
	■ Postassessment
	  ● Conducted after the project is completed
	  ● Helps assess sustainability of project effects, impacts
	  ● Informs about factors of project success

Evaluator status	■ Internal evaluation
	  ● Evaluation conducted by an individual or people who is/are part of the project or program
	■ External evaluation
	  ● Evaluation conducted by an individual who was not involved in implementation of the project
	  ● May be a requirement as part of contractual agreement
	  ● Guided by project staff

Purpose	Formative
	  ■ Measures whether the project is on track to meeting its goals
	  ■ Assesses whether activities are being completed as planned and scheduled
	Summative
	  ■ Measures whether a project changes a problematic situation into a new desired situation
	  ■ Assesses the impact of the program on the target population

---

BOX 15.20 SAMPLE PROCESS EVALUATION STATEMENT

PROCESS OBJECTIVE

■ Provide Monday through Friday on-site after-school tutoring in reading and math to 100 low-income K–3 students in East Oshkosh.

EVALUATION PLAN

■ An after-school program log will be developed and used to track the number of participants and the number of hours of after-school tutoring provided to participants. A monthly report will be generated to summarize the data that have been collected.

Process/formative evaluation: Measures whether the project is on track to meeting its goals. It assesses whether activities are being completed as planned and scheduled (Box 15.20).

BUDGET AND BUDGET NARRATIVE

A budget is the translation of the project plan into financial terms. Funders use budgets to:

■ Analyze whether an organization has the capability to complete a project
■ Judge whether the project is realistic

Budget and cost: Whether explicitly or implicitly indicated, a grant proposal budget includes direct and indirect costs. Direct costs are expenses directly related to the implementation of the project (Box 15.21). Examples of direct costs are salaries and wages of staff, supplies and materials, and special equipment.

Indirect costs are items that will contribute to the project, but are generally provided within the normal operation of the organization. Examples are rent, telephone, electricity, depreciation, secretary, and receptionist (Box 15.22).

BOX 15.21 SAMPLE DIRECT COST ITEMS

Budget category	Justification	Requested funding
Personnel salaries	Full-time director @ $2,000/month for 12 months = $24,000	$24,000
Employee benefits	Full-time director @ $24,000 annual salary × 26% representing the benefit rate = $6,240	$6,240
Supplies	$100 program supplies per 50 participants = $5,000	$5,000
Total direct costs		$35,240

BOX 15.22 SAMPLE INDIRECT COST ITEMS

Category	Justification	Requested funding
Facilities & communications	10% of total direct costs (10% × $35,240) = $3,524	$3,524
Total costs		$38,764

The updated budget will be ...

Budget category	Justification	Requested funding
Personnel salaries	Full-time director @ $2,000/month for 12 months = $24,000	$24,000
Employee benefits	Full-time director @ $24,000 annual salary × 26% representing the benefit rate = $6,240	$6,240
Supplies	$100 program supplies per 50 participants = $5,000	$5,000
Total direct costs		$35,240
Indirect costs	10% of total direct costs (10% × $35,240) = $3,524	$3,524
Total costs		$38,764

Budget and funds: A grant proposal budget can include different types of funds. The most common are requested and matching funds. Requested funds are money that a grant seeker requests from the grant maker (Box 15.23).
Matching funds are money that a grant seeker must contribute toward the total funds requested from a grant maker (Box 15.24). Matching funds can be:

■ *Cash:* Actual money that the grant seeker will contribute to complete the project.
■ *In-kind:* Assistance in personnel, services, materials, or equipment that would be otherwise covered either through direct or indirect costs.

BOX 15.23 SAMPLE BUDGET WITH REQUESTED FUNDING

Budget category	Justification	Requested funding
Personnel salaries	Full-time director @ $2,000/month for 12 months = $24,000	$24,000
Employee benefits	Full-time director @ $24,000 annual salary × 26% representing the benefit rate = $6,240	$6,240
Supplies	$100 program supplies per 50 participants = $5,000	$5,000
Total direct costs		$35,240

BOX 15.24 SAMPLE BUDGET WITH MATCHING FUNDING

Budget category	Justification	NPO contribution	Requested funding
Personnel salaries	Full-time director (50%) @ $2,000/month for 12 months = $24,000	$12,000	$12,000
Employee benefits	Full-time director @ $24,000 annual salary × 26% representing the benefit rate = $6,240	$6,240	0
Supplies	$100 program supplies per 50 participants = $5,000	0	$5,000
Total direct costs	$35,240	$18,240	$17,000

Budget categories: Budget categories vary per grant-maker guidelines. A standard grant proposal budget will include the following:

- Personnel salaries
- Employee benefits
- Travel and per diem
- Supplies, materials, and equipment
- Indirect costs or overhead

Computing wages for project personnel.

By percentage involvement based on annual salary	Monthly rate	Hourly rate
Example: Executive director (20%) Executive director will devote 20% of his time to the project. The salary will be $1,200, which is 20% of his $60,000 annual salary.	Example: Program coordinator: $5,000/month × 12 months = $60,000	Example: ■ Project director: 70 hours @ $20/hour ■ Project assistant: 60 hours @ $7.50/hour

Employee or fringe benefits include worker's compensation insurance, health insurance, and retirement benefits computed as a percentage of wages. The percentage is predetermined either in the grant guidelines or in the policies of an organization.

- Travel and per diem are usually for airline tickets, taxis, shuttle or lease cars, lodging, and mileage (Box 15.25).

Indirect costs are for space, communications, heat, lights, and air conditioning. Percentages of indirect costs vary per institution or organization. For example, if an organization's indirect cost policy is 22% of the total direct costs, and the total direct cost is $200,000, the indirect cost will be ($200,000 × 22%) $44,000.

BOX 15.25 TRAVEL AND PER DIEM

Travel: Project director will travel to Chicago and Boston for the annual conferences of our network. The total travel cost is $2,950. Travel costs are calculated based on past experience:

■ Airfare: 2 trips @ $500 each = $1,000
■ Lodging: 10 days @ $125 = $1,250
■ Per diem: 10 days @ $50 = $500
■ Ground transportation: 4 @ $50 = $200
■ Supplies, materials, and equipment

Example

■ $500/month (average) for paper, books, notebooks, pencils students, 4 days/week for 9 months = $4,500
■ 4 computers @ $800 = $3,200
■ $50 per person × 200 attendees

(Package includes facility, breakfast, lunch, audio) = $10,000

GRANT SEEKING AND FINANCIAL SUSTAINABILITY

Grants account for a smaller percentage of funding for nonprofit organizations as compared to individual contributions. In addition, grant funding is by its nature a restricted fund, because the income received has to be used for the purpose described in the grant proposal. Restricted funds limit the abilities of an organization to make financial reallocations that can help sustain the activities of an organization. Grant funding is guaranteed only when it is received and is time limited. A grant can be renewed in some circumstances. However, grant funding is never a reliable source for a nonprofit organization, given the environmental factors that can affect it at any time, and sometimes with short notice. Therefore, a nonprofit organization should not rely solely or primarily on grant revenue to survive. This is a recipe for disappointment that can lead to the dissolution of a nonprofit organization. In other words, overdependence on grant funding is a threat to its financial sustainability.

However, grant funding is a contributor to the financial sustainability of an organization for various reasons. Grant awards provide financial resources for short-term and midterm activities. Therefore, grant revenue enables an organization to confirm that a particular service will be available next year or within the next 2, 3, or 5 years. Grant income generates indirect costs that can help support organizational and administrative expenses, and can facilitate the ability of an organization to provide other services that are not necessarily funded by a grant. For example, the ability to hire and retain staff is useful not only for a project, but also for other activities that can help generate additional funding. The ability to maintain a facility and purchase equipment contributes to the financial sustainability of an organization. If that revenue did not come from a grant, the organization would have to use other contributions to satisfy its basic operations. Also, when an organization secures funding from a grant, unrestricted income generated from other activities, such as fund-raising, contracts, or fee-based services, can be used to create contingency and endowment funds that will enable an organization to ensure that financial resources are available for it to continue to provide services over time. In other words, a grant alone does not guarantee financial sustainability. This is in fact true for any aspect of the financing of an organization. However, a grant enables an organization to diversify its stream of revenue, which is essential for financial sustainability.

QUESTIONS AND ACTIVITIES

1. What is a grant?
2. Go online, and type: www.grants.gov. Make a list of all the federal agencies where your nonprofit organization can seek potential funding. What are the conditions of eligibility? What are the deadlines? What is the ceiling amount for each grant you identified? Which grant opportunities do you believe your organization is eligible for? Which grant opportunities do you think you are more likely to get? Why?
3. Conduct a Google search: "community foundation + your city or your county, or your state. What are the community foundations that serve the areas of the target population of your nonprofit organizations? Do they have grant opportunities that your organization is eligible for? What are the funding cycles?

CASE STUDY: PRECOLLEGE READINESS PROJECT

Goal

■ Increase college enrollment in science, technology, and math by stimulating interest of high school students.

Objectives

■ Recruit 500 high school students to participate in a tutoring program in science, technology, and math during the academic year 2011–2012.
■ Increase by 50% the number of students applying for college in science, technology, and math during the academic year 2012–2013.

Activities

■ About 500 high school students will receive tutoring services in science, technology, and math.
■ Counseling services will be provided confidentially.
■ Qualified tutors will receive appropriate training to ensure that the program addresses student needs.
■ Students will visit at least three university campuses and meet with faculty in science, technology, and math.
■ Students will receive all necessary supplies.

(continued)

CASE STUDY: PRECOLLEGE READINESS PROJECT (*continued*)

Based on the preceding information:

1. What kinds of information will you collect in order to measure whether each objective was achieved or not?
2. Where you will obtain the information?
3. How will you get the information?
4. Who will collect the information?
5. When will you collect that information?

CASE STUDY: DELTA HIGH SCHOOL

Consider the following table of frequency and percentage of high school dropouts in Marian School District for the year 2011–2012.

High School	Frequency	Percentage
Abe	28	11
Bee	15	6
Carrie	28	11
Delta	65	26
Hull	40	16
Kelly	32	13
Lee	42	17
Total	250	100

Note: National mean dropout rate is 10%.

Using the data provided in the table:

1. Write a gap statement related to Delta High School.
2. Write one goal to address that gap.
3. Write at least two objectives related to the goal.
4. Describe the activities that will help you achieve one or both objectives, using the six-questions format.
5. Draft a timeline for the activities you described.

CASE STUDY: PROJECT BUDGET

You want to organize a conference on "Current Leadership Challenges in Human Services Organizations." You plan to invite a guest speaker and organize a reception for 300 participants. You are instructed to write a grant proposal budget to solicit funding for this activity. Draft the budget with all appropriate line items. Please, justify each line item expense!

CASE STUDY: GRANT PROPOSAL BUDGET

Loving Heart Day Care Center is applying for a grant to start an after-school child-care program in Appleton, Wisconsin. The day care will have 200 children. The grant writer requests your assistance in writing the grant proposal budget, and said to you:

> I want to pay the program director $5,000 per month. In addition, I will pay 25% of her annual salary for benefits. She will work during 12 months. I will hire nine child-care substitutes, and pay them $15.00 per hour. They will work 15 hours per week, during a period of 30 weeks per year. I will pay 20% of their annual salary for benefits. I plan to spend $100.00 per year and per student for supplies and books. I plan to send my child-care substitutes to a local annual conference in early childhood education. They will not travel. Therefore, they will only receive $ 40.00 per diem. I will be responsible for paying a $100.00 registration fee for each substitute. I plan to buy a computer for $800.00 and a printer for $400.00. Please, budget 20% for indirect cost.

Please draft a budget to the best of your ability, including the following line items:

- ■ Personnel salaries
- ■ Employee benefits
- ■ Supplies and books
- ■ Equipment
- ■ Training and travel
- ■ Indirect cost
- ■ Total costs

Risk Management and Financial Sustainability

OBJECTIVES

At the completion of this chapter, the reader will be able to:

1. Define the concept of risk.
2. Discuss the mechanics of risk management.
3. Identify the common areas of risk for nonprofit organizations.
4. Identify various types of risks related to the management of a nonprofit organization.
5. Describe the nature and contents of a risk-management policy.
6. Explain the relationship between risk management and financial sustainability.

This chapter introduces the theories and practices of integrated risk management in relation to its contributions to the financial sustainability of a nonprofit organization. Topics will include, but are not limited to, analytical frameworks for risk assessment and risk-management plans.

WHAT IS A RISK?

A risk is the potential for negative, unwanted, or unpredictable consequences from an event, an activity, or a decision. A risk is some exposure to a situation that can produce a loss in comparison to a possible gain in the absence of the risk factor. From the definition, it is clear that risk exists in almost every human activity, because there is always the possibility of a negative, unwanted, or unpredictable return even with the most accurate planning. Risk exists in the practices of both for-profit and nonprofit organizations. When stockholders invest their money in a business, there is a risk that they can lose their investment. When a nonprofit organization holds a community event to help some people in need, there is a risk that one of the participants might slip and fall, and sue that nonprofit organization that was trying to help with limited resources. This is just one example. Risk in nonprofit organizations can be associated with board members and volunteers, staff, programs and events, services offered, operations, technology, and financial management. Nobody can control the risks that result from an event or an activity. However, a risk can be managed.

DEFINE "RISK MANAGEMENT"

Risk management involves making and carrying out decisions for the organization that will minimize the effects of risk. It can save money, as well as improve the quality of the organization. There are several types of insurance that can be provided. Some common insurance coverage includes workers compensation, corporate automobile, life insurance, errors and omissions, property and casualty, unemployment, surety bonds, and directors and officers insurance. Overall risk management helps organizations achieve quality services.

INTEGRATED RISK MANAGEMENT

Integrated risk management is a comprehensive assessment and management of internal and external risks that challenge a nonprofit organization. Integrated risk management enables nonprofit leaders to ensure that their objectives are met while identifying and managing both internal and external risks across the entire organization. By conducting risk assessment for both their internal and external environments, nonprofit organizations can link all of the related risks to the organization's key initiatives. Consequently, this can better and more efficiently mitigate the impact of risk in various contexts. Risk management is very important to nonprofit organizations, because it helps protect them from risks that can lead to dysfunction, ineffectiveness, or even dissolution. Nonprofit organizations' successes depend in large part on their ability to be creative, to design alternative programs or projects that may not meet all the requirements or standards that would be necessary in a for-profit business. Some of the new initiatives of a nonprofit organization may be untested. Therefore, it is difficult to anticipate with a fair level of certainty how it will turn out. In other words, that opportunity to be creative also carries certain risks. Sometimes, the greater the anticipated impact of a new or untested program, the greater the risks will be. The solution is not to stop being creative or taking risks. The solution is to continue to be cautiously creative and find ways to balance such creativity with a significant return, which can neutralize the effects of potential risks. The challenge for nonprofit organizations is the way results are measured in comparison to for-profit businesses. In business, the bottom line is the amount or rate of profit generated. Any initiatives that can generate a profit tend to be welcomed in business, except in special circumstances. It is not the same for nonprofit organizations. The bottom line is a cause, a need to be addressed. Nonprofit organizations address various social issues related to education, social justice, health, arts, the quality of life of individuals, and their overall well-being; such returns cannot be measured in monetary terms, for a short-term project.

Integrated risk management is a systematic approach that requires nonprofit organizations to measure the mission-related impact of their activities and also consider the implications of such impacts in various contexts. As indicated in previous chapters, the board of directors and staff of nonprofit organizations are supposed to work on behalf of the public, because they are publicly supported organizations. Leaders and managers of nonprofit organizations must be good stewards of resources entrusted to them through various types of contributions, awards, or grants. The management and use of these resources carry the potential for risks. The many stories of fraud and corruption in some nonprofit organizations constitute an illustration of the potential for such organizations to lose income or assets through the decisions and actions of leaders and managers. In most cases, leaders and managers have to make their own interpretations regarding what is in the best interest of the public. In this case, there is still a risk that such leaders and managers may not use their best judgment, which should be rooted in the interests of all internal and external stakeholders.

Some nonprofit leaders may be more inclined to take risks than others. The hope is that their risk preference is influenced by the vision and mission of their organizations. Obviously, there is always the possibility that nonprofit leaders will, in fact, reach out to their constituents before they make consequential decisions. However, there have been countless cases in which nonprofit leaders completely dismissed the interests of their constituents to satisfy the requests of partners who want to further their own community agendas. It is not surprising that many nonprofit leaders make decisions that are very costly for the vision and the mission of the organizations they are leading. Sometimes, they get away with it internally, and the clients pay the consequences without knowing it. Other times, the problem spills over and plays out in public. This happens mostly when the results have negative consequences for the majority of internal and external stakeholders.

INTEGRATED RISK MANAGEMENT AND GOVERNANCE

Nonprofit organizations can use their governance structures to prevent decisions of individual leaders and managers from leading an organization off the cliff. It is a responsibility of the board of directors to ensure that the decisions that are made and actions that are taken do no generate avoidable risks with potential to dissolve the organization. For example, the board can create a risk-management committee to oversee the risk-management process. The creation of a risk-management committee makes a statement that an organization does not intend to address risks in an informal manner. However, a risk-management committee can be effective only if empowered by the board to consider all aspects or facets of risks within an organization and make recommendations for actions to the board. Specific responsibilities of the risk-management committee will includ, but are not limited to,

- Preparing risk management policies and plans
- Establishing procedures for the implementation of risk-management plans
- Establishing procedures for safety inspections
- Establishing and monitoring inspection schedules
- Developing contingency plans for crisis management
- Reviewing insurance policies of the organization for their adequacy
- Developing continuing-education programs for risk awareness
- Recommending best practices for risk prevention and management
- Making recommendations to the board on all matters related to risks involving the organization

COMMON AREAS OF RISKS FOR NONPROFIT ORGANIZATIONS

Special events and other fund-raising activities tend to be the most common areas of risk for nonprofit organizations. A nonprofit can be at risk on several different levels regarding both individual fund-raising and fund-raising through special events. The potential of risk is great when a nonprofit organization gathers together a lot of people. An accident can erase any funds generated by a nonprofit organization. No matter how well planned, the event can be a disaster if anything goes wrong. To prevent this, there should be an event director, a committee, whenever possible, devoted to planning, directing, and managing every logistical detail to ensure that continuous communication is taking place.

Not all fund-raising is done through major events. In fact, most nonprofits count on individual donors for the majority of their revenue generation. Many organizations rely heavily on their volunteers to take on formal responsibilities, such as when they accept the role of board member, as well as driving many of the programs and fund-raising efforts. Understaffed and overworked nonprofits tend to accept volunteers—who may be no more than warm bodies—and put them to work on projects and programs. This can lead to incredible risk if there is no vetted process to ensure that volunteers meet a certain criteria. Insufficient internal controls, programs that continuously run at a deficit or ineffective fund-raising activities can all put the organization at risk. Costly and inefficient programs can also put the organization in a dangerous financial situation as can fund-raising activities that are not carefully managed and measured.

RISK AND ACCOUNTABILITY ISSUES

Nonprofit organizations must comply with all legally required reporting procedures. They have an obligation to use resources responsibly toward achieving the mission of the organization and to benefit the community. They have a responsibility to establish and regularly determine clear performance measurements and to share those results with the public. They have a responsibility to adhere to established industry standards that apply to particular areas of activity. However, there is a risk that fraud, corruption, or lack of internal monitoring can negatively affect the assets of a nonprofit organization.

What is fraud? According to Miriam-Webster's *Dictionary of Law*, fraud is "any act, expression, omission, or concealment calculated to deceive another to his or her disadvantage" (Figure 16.1).

Anatomy of fraud: Fraud exists if:

- A statement is materially false
- Knowledge that the statement is false when made
- A victim relies on the statement
- The victim suffers damages as a result of relying on the false statement

See Figure 16.2 for a depiction of the anatomy of fraud.

For example, during the past 3 months, Erin never worked for more than 20 hours per week, because of a change in her class schedule. In her time sheet, she reported that she worked for 40 hours per week. The administrative director found out, and fired Erin's

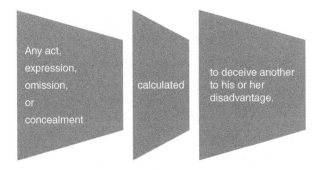

FIGURE 16.1 Definition of fraud.
Source: Merriam-Webster (1996).

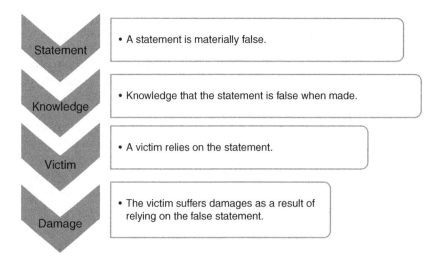

FIGURE 16.2   Anatomy of fraud.

supervisor for complicity. Would you consider that as fraud? Of course, it is. There was a materially false statement made. Erin worked for 20 hours, but stated that she worked for 40 hours. There is no doubt that such a statement is materially false. Erin knows how many hours she worked. Therefore, she had the knowledge that the statement was false when she submitted her time sheet. Erin's supervisor relied on that false statement to process payroll. Her supervisor suffered damages as a result of her false statement. This is clearly a fraud.

What is corruption? Corruption is the use of public or community trust for personal gain. Corruption can occur in the form of a bribe, reward, extortion, or conflict of interest (Figure 16.3).

RISK IDENTIFICATION

Providing services through a nonprofit organization involves risks that are no different from what a for-profit organization will encounter. The reason is because service delivery or implementation of projects or social activities requires human interactions that have the potential for pure risk or may be affected by pure and speculative risks. The term "pure risk" generically refers to unavoidable natural risks. On the other hand, speculative risks

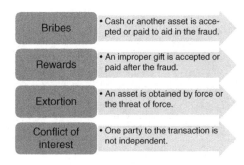

FIGURE 16.3   Types of corruption.

are voluntary and preventable risks, such as an investment in a stock. Common pure and speculative risks that can affect a nonprofit organization include, but are not limited to:

▆ *Loss of assets* due to fraud, corruption, employee theft, robbery
▆ *Damage to property* (e.g., facilities, equipment, computers, and records) as a result of natural causes, fire, negligence, or faulty equipment
▆ *Liability losses* (harassment, privacy, auto related, and disability) due to accidents or negligence of employees or volunteers
▆ *Security problems,* such as defective door locks, insecure equipment, work injuries, and lack of an information backup system
▆ *Loss of revenue or increased costs* due a financial crisis or inflation
▆ *Loss of employee productivity* due to employee illness, lack of motivation, drug and alcohol abuse, smoking, or obesity

Nonprofit organizations must be aware of these risks, and adopt policies and strategies to identify and manage them in a manner that can create a safe working environment and save money that the organization could lose if the risks are not properly managed. You can ask your consultant to help you categorize risks as being of high, moderate, or low severity and frequency. Figure 16.4 is a matrix that may be helpful when conducting risk assessment.

Based on the internal and external environments, nonprofit organizations can categorize their potential risks as being of high, moderate, or low frequency. Each organization is best positioned to define what constitutes a high-, moderate-, and low-frequency risk.

RISK MANAGEMENT AND RISK-MANAGEMENT POLICY

As indicated in other contexts, risk management is a structured approach used to assess threats, develop strategies to control the risks associated with the identified threats, and implement actions and procedures to minimize them, and possibly transform them into opportunities.

A risk-management policy is a set of guidelines and procedures adopted by an organization or an entity to identify, define, prevent, mitigate, and administer risks related to the overall functioning of the organization or entity. A risk-management policy provides specific guidelines regarding the assessment of potential risks related to the operation of a nonprofit organization, as well as a set of strategies, procedures, actions, and resources to address them (Box 16.1).

Frequency	Severity		
	High	Moderate	Low
High			
Moderate			
Low			

FIGURE 16.4   Risk frequency and severity analysis matrix.

BOX 16.1 SAMPLE RISK-MANAGEMENT POLICY ITEMS

- Confidential and proprietary information
- Conflicts of interest
- Crisis-management plan
- Donor recognition
- Fiscal management
- Employment discrimination
- Abuse prevention
- Accessibility
- Copyright law violations
- Board succession planning, recruitment, and orientation
- Bullying
- Negligence
- Child protection
- Safety in the workplace
- Sexual abuse
- Sexual harassment
- Social media, computing, and acceptable use of technology equipment
- Volunteer conduct and volunteer recruitment
- Whistle-blowing and fraud prevention
- Workplace violence and harassment prevention
- Codes of conduct
- Investment
- Privacy
- Public relations
- Services to people with disabilities

RISK-MANAGEMENT OPTIONS

Risk-management options refer to the decisions of an organization to take action or purchase insurance for the purpose of:

- Risk avoidance
- Risk reduction
- Risk retention
- Risk sharing
- Risk transference

Risk elimination or avoidance: Risk elimination is a strategy used to prohibit any activity that can lead to identified high levels of frequency and severity risks (Box 16.2). In other words, avoidance or elimination automatically prevents some risks from being a concern for an organization because they are inherent to activities that will not be conducted by such an organization. For example, a nonprofit organization working with youth may decide that their outdoor activities will not include sky diving because of the risks associated with it. In that context, the organization does not have to purchase a policy for sky diving, because the associated risk or liability is no longer an issue of concern.

BOX 16.2 SAMPLE RISK-MANAGEMENT-PREVENTION ACTIVITIES

- Safeguarding any activity that carries risks and hazards
- Establishing procedures for maintenance and safe use of vehicles, machines, and equipment
- Inspection of noncompany-owned vehicles (e.g., registration, insurance)
- Establishing standards of qualifications for drivers and users of machines and equipment
- Making prompt repairs or changes where there is risk for slips, falls, or other accidents
- Organizing safety training for employees
- Ensuring that first-aid kits and guidelines for personal protective equipment are readily available on site
- Introducing policies about assaults, physical fights, and harassments
- Obtaining formal guarantees from providers or suppliers that the products you are selling will not do harm if used properly
- Fire prevention (smoke detectors, extinguishers, and inspections)
- Maintenance of storage, electrical equipment, gas appliance, and heating equipment
- Proper storage of flammable liquids
- Proper insurance and equipment-insurance warranty
- Burglary prevention through control of access to property buildings and a surveillance system
- Robbery prevention
- Vandalism prevention
- Computer crime prevention

Risk mitigation or reduction: Risk mitigation or reduction is the decision of an organization to focus on actions and strategies that can help prevent risks or significantly reduce their effect when they occur (Box 16.3). Risk mitigation encompasses actions and strategies, such as education and training, to increase awareness of potential risks, adoption of best practices to reduce the likelihood of certain risks identified in the literature related to a field of practice, or thorough assessment of physical facilities to prevent the effect of natural disasters (e.g., hurricane).

Risk retention: A nonprofit organization may decide to accept the occurrence of a potential risk, provided that such occurrence and its severity are low. For example, a nonprofit organization may decide to no longer purchase an insurance package for a particular copier because it costs less to fix it in-house. On the other hand, an organization may decide to increase the deductibility insurance on a new set of vehicles because it has been found to be less expensive. In these two examples, there are risks associated with the decision not to purchase insurance or to purchase insurance that means a loss of money in the short term, but the organization decides that it is in its best interest to retain such risks.

BOX 16.3 SAMPLE OF ITEMS FOR RISK REDUCTION

- Identification of areas of vulnerability
- Training plans
- Communication plans
- Evacuation plans
- Emergency plans for damaged facilities
- Emergency plans to assist the injured
- Emergency plans for building shutdown

Risk sharing: Nonprofit organizations can engage in activities with some potential for risks, but do so in partnership with another organization, and decide to share the costs that may be associated with such risks. For example, a nonprofit organization might use the facilities of another agency to organize an event. There is a risk for liability that both organizations agree to share through an agreement.

Risk transference: Nonprofit organizations can reduce some risks, but will never be able to eliminate or avoid the potential for occurrence of most of them. Therefore, it is important to purchase insurance policies, and transfer these risks to another party, generally an insurance carrier agency (Box 16.4). Examples of insurance policies are:

- General liability to cover bodily injury suffered by a third person and claims in court
- Property insurance to protect a nonprofit organization from loss, theft, or damage to its property
- Health insurance to cover employee health care costs
- Life insurance for employee mortality
- Surety bonds to cover losses due to embezzlement
- Worker's compensation for employees as required by law
- Unemployment insurance to cover lost wages related to layoffs
- Employment discrimination policy to cover employment discrimination claims
- Directors' and officers' insurance to cover director and officers from personal liability due to their participation in the governance or management of a nonprofit organization
- Volunteer accidental medical insurance to cover potential volunteer injuries
- Automobile insurance for transportation-related issues

PURCHASE INSURANCE OR SELF-INSURE?

Some debate whether a nonprofit organization should purchase insurance or self-insure. The argument is that by self-insuring a nonprofit organization would protect its own capital. The more an organization relies on using someone else's capital, the more the insurance will cost. Therefore, in a cost-effective perspective, self-insurance might turn out to be a better approach compared to purchasing insurance coverage from a carrier. This sounds like a great argument at first, and can be a good idea for a large nonprofit organization. But with self-insurance, there is a risk that the organization could lose its capital if there were a serious claim. Purchasing insurance may cost more in the short term, but the organization will manage its capital with peace of mind, knowing that unforeseen events will not lead to dissolution.

BOX 16.4 TYPICAL ITEMS IN AN INSURANCE POLICY

Declaration pages: Name of the insured, policy number, risks or property covered, premium, deductible, cap, policy period

Definitions: Definitions of key policy coverage and interpretation

Insuring agreement: Claims that will be paid

Conditions: Conditions for payment by insurer

Exclusion: Conditions for coverage cancellation

Endorsement: Additional change provisions

Limits on coverage: Maximum amount of payment and occurrence of claims

Umbrella coverage: Supplement to amount of coverage

RISK STRATEGIES

To mitigate these issues, nonprofit organizations can rely on accurate budgets and financial forecasts to keep them out of trouble. Many future employees expect that a nonprofit organization will offer a more informal easygoing atmosphere than that of a typical business environment. Sometimes nothing could be further from the truth. Nonprofit organizations can be forced to do more with less, and executive directors can be stretched beyond their limits as they deploy limited resources to provide much-needed programs and services for their constituents, while in many instances they rely on sometimes undependable volunteers to fill the gaps. Instead of a warm atmosphere employees may find themselves in tense situations as they scramble to attract donors and serve the community at the same time. To address the concerns of staffing risk, nonprofit leaders need to institute the same employment practices as their for-profit counterparts.

Nonprofit organizations struggle to gain adequate funding, and in many cases are very eager for grants that can help them close the gap between revenue and costs. If the grant was awarded and the nonprofit cannot fulfill its part of the bargain, the leadership has put the entire organization at risk. Reputation risk in the nonprofit sector can bring a loss of confidence in the organization, resulting in a decline in demand for its services, diminished donor support, fewer volunteers, or even a withdrawal of strategic alliances and collaboration partners. To combat these challenges, nonprofit leaders must listen to their stakeholders, ask their board for advice, and consider all feedback as essential. Every nonprofit should provide communication channels that encourage compliments, complaints, and concerns as well as suggestions for improvement. A strong reputation is a key to attracting donors, volunteers, and constituents by building credibility, confidence, and trust. Nonprofit organizations that have an audit or finance committee, or an executive committee that assumes these functions, should be expanding their role to include not only financial reporting, but also assessing the organization for risk (see Box 16.5).

RISK MANAGEMENT AND FINANCIAL SUSTAINABILITY

Risk management is a financial sustainability strategy. Nonprofit organizations are exposed to financial risks (e.g., fraud, loss in investment, misuse of funds, loss of tax-exempt status, and fund-raising liabilities), which can be anything from reduction in value of an asset to fraud committed by an employee or a member or a burglary committed by someone outside the organization. Financial, personnel, program, and capital expenditure decisions have great potential to generate risk because they involve interactions with changing, complex, volatile, or intrinsically stochastic economic, political, and social environments. Financial risks can affect the liquidity of a nonprofit organization and even lead to its dissolution. As a set of actions, procedures, and tools put in place to prevent and manage risks and emergency situations, risk management helps prevent expenses that could affect the existence of a nonprofit organization. In other words, risk management protects a nonprofit organization against disastrous outcomes that could threaten its survival and abilities to fulfill its vision and mission. The best and most cost-effective way to manage risks is by practicing prevention. Risk management helps put safeguards in place to prevent risks and consequently protect the assets of a nonprofit organization while minimizing liabilities. In nonprofit organizations, the most likely risk is financial loss regardless of the type of risk. Financial loss damages the financial sustainability of an organization. On the other hand, prevention of financial loss can positively affect its financial sustainability.

BOX 16.5 PRACTICAL STEPS TO IMPROVE ACCOUNTABILITY AND PREVENT RELATED RISKS

1. Recognize that better accountability leads to greater credibility for the organization and wider support for it.
2. Hold discussions among executives and board members about ways in which this organization might work toward that goal.
3. Explore measurable options (e.g., internal control policies, reports).
4. Follow federal and state laws and Internal Revenue Service requirements carefully.
5. Contract with accountants to conduct financial audits annually.
6. Establish planning and control procedures for each job and each department, including the board of trustees.
7. Provide ongoing training so all board members and employees know what is expected of them.
8. Require compliance with policies regarding conflicts of interest.
9. Develop and disseminate whistle-blower policies so that employees feel free to report concerns without fear of reprisal or retaliation.
10. Have an independent board of directors.
11. Develop a culture of transparency: Have a manual of procedures in place and train board members and staff!
12. Adopt a Statement of Values and a Code of Ethics.
13. Make public your organization's Form 990.
14. Stay current with the law.

Nonprofit organization decisions are made by board members, executives, or volunteer trustees. The impacts of such decisions are felt by the clients or the community served by such nonprofit organizations, or external stakeholders who support or partner with an organization. Risk management includes prevention strategies and insurance plans related to all internal (nonprofit organization owners and employees) and external stakeholders (nonprofit organization partners, providers, clients or customers). It also encompasses preventive measures and procedures and insurance plans concerning all property owned by the nonprofit organization. Finally, it carries liability-based risk provision package insurance coverage for all potential liability claims that can affect the operation or even existence of the nonprofit organization. Therefore, risk management enables a nonprofit organization to ensure that the decisions or actions take into account factors that have the potential to harm internal and external stakeholders and future generations.

QUESTIONS AND ACTIVITIES

1. How would you define the concept of risk?
2. What do you think are the key mechanics for risk management in a nonprofit organization?
3. What are the common areas of risk for nonprofit organizations?

4. What are some types of risks related to the management of a nonprofit organization?
5. What do you expect to find in the contents of a risk-management policy?
6. What is the relationship between risk management and financial sustainability?
7. What type of risk would you consider as more harmful for the sustainability of a nonprofit organization? Why?
8. Should a nonprofit organization self-insure or purchase insurance?
9. The Red Cross disclosed how it used the record donations that came in the wake of the 9/11 terrorist attacks. Donors believed that their contributions would go to help victims and their families. The Red Cross, however, set aside more than half of the $564 million in funds raised for 9/11 for other operations and future reserves. Although this was a long-standing organizational practice, it was not well known. The donors were outraged, and the Red Cross had to issue a public apology and redirect the funds. Was that a case of fraud or not? Why?
10. Allan is the chief financial officer of Liberty Health Care Network, a statewide non-profit assisted-living agency. He noticed that one of the suppliers overcharged the organization by almost $100,000. A few days later, that supplier sent him a thank-you gift for good business, which includes a week in Las Vegas, all expenses covered. He did not return the gift.
This case is an example of_____.
   a. Extortion
   b. Bribery
   c. Reward
   d. Conflict of interest

11. The Baptist Foundation of Arizona (BFA) was established in 1948 to raise funds for Southern Baptist–related charities by selling financial services to coreligionists. It was, in effect, a faith-based mutual fund, managed by laymen and overseen by a governing board composed of prominent Southern Baptist pastors and seminary presidents. The foundation generated hundreds of millions of dollars in revenue, most of which was invested in ventures controlled by its managers—who also richly rewarded themselves with lavish salaries, loans, and other perks. Over the course of a half century, BFA contributed only $1.3 million to the church and its charities—though in 1996 it sold more than $500 million worth of securities and paid its staff more than $16 million in salaries. The foundation went bankrupt. Many people lost their financial investments.
This case is an example of_____.
   a. Fraud
   b. Conflict of interest
   c. None of the above
   d. Both A and B

REFERENCE

Merrriam-Webster. (1996). *Dictionary of law*. Springfield, MA: Author.

Human Resources, Job Satisfaction, and Financial Sustainability

OBJECTIVES

At the completion of this chapter, the reader will be able to:

1. Define the term "human resource management."
2. Describe a human resource management system.
3. Define "job satisfaction."
4. Discuss various job satisfaction approaches and theories.
5. Reflect on the role of job satisfaction in organizations.
6. Explain the relationship among human resources, job satisfaction, and financial sustainability.

This chapter explains the key roles of human resources management and job satisfaction in the financial sustainability of a nonprofit organization. Topics in this chapter include, but are not limited to, human resource management systems, job satisfaction approaches and theories, staff turnover, and staff retention, and the relationship between human resources and financial sustainability.

WHAT IS HUMAN RESOURCE MANAGEMENT?

Simply put, human resources management is the set of managerial activities involved in planning, recruiting, motivating, retaining, and developing a workforce that can contribute to the efficiency, effectiveness, overall performance, and sustainability of an organization. Systematic human resources management started primarily during the early twentieth century to address issues related to worker's compensation and safety raised by labor and union organizations (Li, 2003). Then, human resources management evolved to include issues of equal-employment opportunities, diversity, organizational management, performance management, information systems, and talent management (Li, 2003; Vosburgh, 2007).

Increases in the workforce and growth of organizations have shifted human resources management from being an employment unit inside an agency to becoming a more systemic specialization focused on the overall organization (Narsavage, 2008). Companies increasingly started to view employees or workers not just as entities to negotiate and deal with (Vosburgh, 2007), but also as "valuable organizational resources" (Kaufman, 2001, p. 509). The middle of the twentieth century saw the professionalization of human resources management, and more emphasis was put by organizations on issues of benefits, compensation, labor relations, and training and development as a vital element to the growth and sustainability of an agency (Narsavage, 2008; Scott, 2003). It is important to underscore that the pressure of grassroots movements, especially the labor and union organizations, has influenced government regulations to play a pivotal role in transforming the extent of human resources management within organizations. As Connor and Ulrich (1996) explained, changes in legislations were critical in "equal employment opportunity, occupational safety, and health and pension reform" (p. 29).

The late twentieth century saw the evolution of human resources management as a sector in which organizations started to seek for more accountability in the form of return on investment (Laabs, 2000). This led to more focus on human resources management costs, productivity, and quality, but also on the added value of employees to the bottom line of organizations (Tren, 2000). Obviously, this facilitated the emergence of initiatives and decisions about layoffs, restructuring, employee displacement, and downsizing (Mackavey, 2006; Rynes, 2004). It is important to underline that the clash between union organizations, as well as structural adjustment policies in the context of globalization of markets and workforce were significant contributors to massive organizational changes that had great implications for human resources management (Morley, Gunnigle, O'Sullivan, & Collings, 2006; Payne & Huffman, 2005).

LEGAL ASPECTS OF HUMAN RESOURCES MANAGEMENT

Managing human resources in a nonprofit organization has various legal implications inherent to equal-employment opportunity laws and regulations. The most common laws and regulations are found in Table 17.1.

TABLE 17.1 Common Employment Laws and Regulations

Laws and Legislation	Brief Description
National Labor Relations Act of 1935	Guarantees basic rights of private-sector employees to organize into trade unions, engage in collective bargaining for better terms and conditions at work, and take collective action, including strikes, if necessary.
	Created the National Labor Relations Board, which conducts elections that can require employers to engage in collective bargaining with labor unions (also known as trade unions).
Title VII of the Civil Rights Act of 1964	Prohibits discrimination by covered employers on the basis of race, color, religion, sex, or national origin.
Executive Order 11246 and 11375 of 1965 and 1967	Prohibits discrimination on the basis of sex in hiring and employment in both the United States federal workforce and on the part of government contractors.
	Employers must take affirmative action to ensure that applicants and employers are not treated differently based on sex, religion, race, color, or national origin.

(continued)

TABLE 17.1 Common Employment Laws and Regulations (*continued*)

Laws and Legislation	Brief Description
▦ Age Discrimination in Employment Act of 1967	▦ Applies to employers of 20 or more employees, and prohibits employment discrimination against anyone at least 40 years of age in the United States, as well as standards for pensions and benefits provided by employers.
▦ Executive Order 11478 of 1969	▦ Prohibits discrimination in employment on the basis of race, color, religion, sex, national origin, handicap, and age. ▦ Requires all departments and agencies to take affirmative steps to promote employment opportunities to groups affected by discrimination.
▦ Occupational Safety and Health Act of 1970	▦ Requires that employers provide employees a safe and healthy environment that is free from recognized hazards, such as exposure to toxic chemicals, excessive noise levels, mechanical dangers, heat or cold stress, or unsanitary conditions.
▦ Vocational Rehabilitation Act of 1973 and 1974	▦ Prohibits discrimination against individuals with disabilities. ▦ Requires affirmative action in the employment of handicapped people.
▦ Vietnam Era Veteran's Readjustment Act of 1974	▦ Requires equal opportunity and affirmative action to provide equal opportunity and affirmative action for veterans in the Vietnam era, disabled veterans, and any veterans who served active duty time during a war event that qualifies for a campaign badge.
▦ Pregnancy Discrimination Act of 1978	▦ Prohibits discrimination in employment on the basis of pregnancy.
▦ Immigration Reform and Control Act of 1986, revised in 1990 and 1996	▦ Prohibits employers from hiring illegal immigrants. ▦ Requires employers to attest to their employees' immigration status.
▦ Americans with Disabilities Act of 1990	▦ Prohibits discrimination against disabled people.
▦ Older Workers Benefit Protection Act of 1990	▦ Prohibits discrimination in hiring, promotions, wages, or termination of employment and layoffs of individuals 40 years old and older.
▦ Civil Rights Act of 1991	▦ Same as Title VII
▦ Family and Medical Leave Act of 1993	▦ Requires that employers provide 12 weeks of unpaid leave for family and medical emergencies.
▦ Congressional Accountability Act of 1995	▦ Requires U.S. Congress and associated agencies to apply some of the employment and workplace safety laws applied to businesses and the federal government.

HUMAN RESOURCES PLANNING

Strategic human resources management is based on the assumption that the abilities and talents of staff can contribute to the effectiveness of an organization and its ability to adapt to change. Therefore, organizations must be proactive in assessing their staff's abilities and talents, and develop appropriate strategic plans to use such resources to meet the demands of their internal and external environments. In other words, organizations should articulate strategic human resources management and planning, which is the development and implementation of goals, objectives, activities, and strategies to anticipate and manage trends, and become more effective and sustainable.

According to the U.S. Office of Personnel Management (2005), strategic human resource planning involves five key steps:

1. *Strategic direction*: Anticipate future needs and determine workforce necessary to carry out long- and short-term strategic goals and objectives adopted in an organization's strategic plan.
2. *Workforce analysis*: Analyze specific workforce needs and skills gaps between current and required workforce.
3. *Development of an action plan*: Develop strategies for recruiting, training, retraining, and restructuring of the workforce based on strategic direction and workforce analysis.
4. *Implementation of the action plan*: Secure appropriate fiscal resources and execute a human resources action plan.
5. *Monitoring, evaluation, and revision*: Monitor progress based on specific milestones, and conduct assessments for continuing quality improvement.

HUMAN RESOURCES MANAGEMENT AND HUMAN RESOURCE INFORMATION SYSTEMS

Progress in technology has provided organizations with various opportunities to manage personnel activities through human resource information systems (HRIS). HRIS is also referred to as electronic human resource management (e-HRM) or electronic human resources (e-HR). Current literature defines HRIS as a set of information technology tools used by organizations in their management of human resources in order to make strategic decisions (Chinho & Ming-Lung, 2010), gain a competitive advantage (Ball, 2001; Bondarouk & Ruel, 2009), and improve process efficiencies and overall quality (Lin, 2011; Tansley, Newell, & Williams, 2001; Zafra, 2010). According to Hendrickson (2003),

> HRIS can be briefly defined as integrated systems used to gather, store, and analyze information regarding an organization's human resources. But, as is the case with any complex organizational information system … it also includes the people, policies, procedures, and data required to manage the human resources function. (p. 381)

HRIS helps an organization follow human resources legislations and guidelines, monitor employee performance, monitor the ability to provide benefits, and ensure that payments to personnel are made accurately and in a timely manner. A generic HRIS includes components related to personnel management, time and attendance, payroll, and benefits:

1. *Personnel management*: To manage job analysis and design, employee screening, interview, recruitment, performance appraisals, succession planning, career development, and training. Effective personnel management contributes to employee productivity (Spence & Laschinger, 2008) and quality of services (Khan & Santos, 2002).
2. *Time and attendance*: To manage and monitor employee scheduling and attendance. This component can help an organization hold its staff accountable, increase productivity, and develop standardization (Caroll, 2008, Shani & Tesone, 2010).
3. *Payroll*: To manage and administer compensation plans and payroll. Effective payroll management positively affects the health and stability of an organization (Marwick, 2001).
4. *Benefits*: To keep track of employee benefits, such as health insurance plans, health claims, sick and vacation days, and administration of the Consolidated Omnibus Budget Reconciliation Act (COBRA). Proper administration of benefits contributes to staff retention, helps prevent lawsuits, and positively affects organizational stability (Townsend & Bennet, 2003).

JOB ANALYSIS

Job analysis is the systematic process of collecting data on past and current issues, forecasting human resources needs, and identify knowledge, skills, and abilities required from future employees, in order to make decisions regarding job design, recruitment, compensation plans, career development, performance evaluation, and risk management. The 1978 Uniform Guidelines on Employee Selection Procedures requires that employers conduct job analysis as part of their human resource management practices. Employers must show that requirements for recruitment, compensation and benefits, and performance evaluation are related to the job, based on valid criteria.

JOB SATISFACTION

Job satisfaction is a multidimensional concept whose meaning has evolved over time. Hoppock (1935) defined job satisfaction as "any combination of psychological, physiological, and environmental circumstances that cause a person truthfully to say, 'I am satisfied with my job'" (p. 47). After a few decades, Locke (1976) referred to job satisfaction as "a pleasurable or positive emotional state resulting from the appraisal of one's job or job experiences" (p. 1300). Later, Vroom (1982) defined job satisfaction or job attitude as "affective orientations on the part of individuals toward work roles which they are presently occupying" (p. 99). Wheeless, Barraclough, and Stewart (1983) define job satisfaction as one's affective response to aspects or facets of an employee's work environment. There is a common reference to the affective aspect of job satisfaction in the above definitions. This affective aspect is also reflected in Jayaratne's (1993) definition, which indicates that "virtually all [job satisfaction] theories subscribe to the notion that 'satisfaction' is an affective state, which is a function of an interaction between a person and his or her environment" (p. 112). Subsequent definitions seem to corroborate Jayaratne's (1993) assertion. For example, Spector (1997) later defined job satisfaction in terms of "how people feel about their jobs and different aspects of their jobs" (p. 2). Chellandurai (1999) indicated that job satisfaction is an attitude that people have about their job. In a more consistent way than previous definitions, Preziosi and Gooden (2003) said that job satisfaction is the overall perceptions and feelings of an employee about his/her work. For Smucker and Kent (2004), the concept of job satisfaction implies the feelings that workers have about their jobs or job experiences in comparison to previous experiences, expectations, or available alternatives. Overall, the above definitions emphasize that job satisfaction is more of a composite variable that includes various behavioral, affective, and environmental factors related to one's job or job experiences. Such factors are analyzed in more systematic manners by various job satisfaction theories.

JOB SATISFACTION THEORIES

Various theories have attempted to explain job satisfaction. Lawler (1994) categorized the theories of job satisfaction in four conceptual frameworks: (1) the fulfillment theory, (2) the discrepancy theory, (3) the equity theory, and (4) the two-factor theory. According to Lawler (1994), the fulfillment theory includes the approaches of Vroom (1964) and Schaffer (1953), which explain job satisfaction based on whether people's jobs have positive impacts on helping them find satisfaction of their needs. The discrepancy theory refers to differential job satisfaction and job dissatisfaction among workers (Locke, 1969). The equity theory explains the causes of job satisfaction and dissatisfaction (Adams, 1963). Finally, the two-factor theory refers to Hertzberg's motivator and hygiene factors of job satisfaction (Hertzberg Mausner, & Snyderman, 1959). This categorization has the merit of synthesizing several theories based on patterns of similarities and differences. Campbell, Dunette, Lawler, and Weik (1970) categorized job satisfaction theories into either content theories or process theories. However, the literature on job satisfaction suggests that some theories are neither content nor process, but situational (Campbell, Dunette, Lawler, & Weik, 1994). Therefore, the theories in job satisfaction will be examined with respect to content, process, and situational theories.

Content Theories

According to Campbell, Dunette, Lawler, and Weik (1994), the content theories of job satisfaction prescribe the needs and values that must be fulfilled in the job in order to have positive job satisfaction. Examples of content theories are (a) Maslow's need-hierarchy theory (Maslow, 1954; Whaba & Bridwell, 1976), the Alderfer theory of needs (Alderfer, 1972), the Mumford theory of needs (Mumford, 1976), and Herzberg's motivation–hygiene theory (Herzberg, 1966).

Maslow's Need-Hierarchy Theory

Maslow's need-hierarchy theory argues that job satisfaction implies that an individual's need in the job environment is based on a five-tier model of human needs, arranged in ascending order of importance (physiological, safety, belonging, esteem, and self-actualization).

1. *Physiological needs* (food, water, shelter, sex, and other bodily needs) refer to salary and working conditions.
2. *Safety needs* (security, protection from harm, stability) are related to job security, employment benefits, and safe working conditions.
3. *Social needs* (affection, acceptance, feelings of belonging, friendship) refer to interpersonal relationship with workers, supervisors, and subordinates.
4. *Esteem needs* (autonomy, self-respect, recognition) are related to titles, promotion, status, and rank.
5. *Self-actualization needs* (personal growth, achievement of one's potential, advancement, self-fulfillment) refer to career advancement and challenging work assignments.

According to Maslow (1954), the more basic needs must be satisfied in a gradual manner as translated into the hierarchy before the ultimate needs, especially self-actualization needs, can be fulfilled. Wahba and Bridwell (1976) conducted a review of research about Maslow's theory and found no evidence of a human hierarchy of needs.

Hertzberg's Two-Factor Theory

The two-factor theory is built on the foundations of Maslow's theory and aims to understand the factors that determine job satisfaction. According to Herztberg (1959), job satisfaction is inherent to the job itself, and is positioned in a double continuum composed of motivator and hygiene factors. The motivators are "job satisfiers" that fulfill the psychological growth of a worker, and include intrinsic factors, such as responsibility, recognition, advancement, and opportunity for growth. The hygiene factors are "job satisfiers" associated with the work environment and constitute needs that must be met to prevent dissatisfaction. Hygiene factors encompass extrinsic variables, such as wages and salaries, work conditions, supervision, organizational policies, relationships with peers, and personal life (Castillo & Cano, 2004).

Hertzberg's two-factor theory contributed to the advancement of research on job satisfaction. This theory has introduced the use of double scales (satisfaction/dissatisfaction) to measure job satisfaction. Basset-Jones and Lloyd (2005) argue that Hertzberg's theory challenges the conventional assumption that money is the principal factor of employee satisfaction. However, some argue that the motivation-hygiene theory is limited by its methodology (Solomon & Corbit, 1973), ignores situational variables (House & Wigdor, 1967), and is based on a nonevident relationship between satisfaction and productivity (House & Wigdor, 1967).

Alderfer's Existence Relatedness Growth Theory

Maslow's hierarchy of needs and the Hertzberg two-factor theory inspired the development of the existence relatedness growth theory (Alderfer, 1969). Similar to Maslow and Hertzberg, Alderfer (1969) believes that employees do have needs that must be satisfied. However, he argues that these needs must be understood through a continuum of

- *Existence needs*: Physiological and safety needs (salary, employment benefits, job security, and work conditions)
- *Relatedness needs*: Social and esteem needs (interpersonal relationships with co-workers, supervisors, subordinates, family members, friends, and other people)
- *Growth needs*: Self-actualization needs (personal development, career advancement, and fulfillment of one's potential)

Contrary to Maslow's argument that a lower-level need must be satisfied before the next-level need in the hierarchy becomes operative, Alderfer (1969) argues that employee needs can be satisfied simultaneously. Contrary to Maslow, Alderfer believes that a satisfied need can remain a motivator for other job satisfaction needs. Schmidt, Gast-Rosenberg, and Hunter (1980) found evidence that indicates the validity of Alderfer's theory. Wanous and Zwany (1977) conducted a cross-sectional study that supports the existence of growth, relatedness, and existence needs as classified by Alderfer. However, Wanous and Zwany (1977) found that Alderfer's theory is not applicable to some organizations.

PROCESS THEORIES

Process theories focus primarily on the cognitive process that determines the level of job satisfaction of an employee. These theories argue that job satisfaction can be explained through examination of variables, such as value, goal, attribution, and behavior (Hoy & Miskel, 1982). In fact, the expectancy theory (Vroom, 1982), the goal theory (Locke, 1969), the attribution theory, the behavior theory, and the equity theory (Adams, 1963) are the classical examples of process theories.

Expectancy Theory

The expectancy theory also called valence–instrumentality–expectancy (VIE) and value theory is based on the assumptions that individual decision-making processes in organizations are inspired by one's ability to think, reason, and anticipate future events. Individual behavior is influenced by the interactions between an employee's values and attitudes with the organizational climate (Vroom, 1964). The expectancy theory argues that such interaction occurs around the notions of valence, instrumentality, and expectancy. Valence refers to the perceived value that a person places on expected rewards. Instrumentality is the relationship between individual performance and the expected rewards. Expectancy implies the individual's belief that a task will be performed at a specific level of success. In short, expectancy theory argues that employee compensation is proportional to their level of performance, and therefore is a source of job satisfaction. A discrepancy will lead to dissatisfaction. Vroom (1982) suggests that an employee may decide to complete a task based on the perceived fairness of the compensation, whether such compensation is monetary or nonmonetary.

Goal Theory

Goal theory explains job satisfaction by the awareness of employees that the task being completed will help achieve a goal (Locke, 1969). The assumptions of the goal theory are that specific goals are superior to general goals, and difficult goals lead to greater performance. Locke (1970) argues that goal setting leads to job satisfaction through a series of processes that involve:

- Existents (incentives, objects, actions, outcomes)
- Evaluation (cognition, values)
- Emotions and desires
- Anticipated existents (incentives, objects, actions, outcomes)
- Judged instrumentality of anticipated action and anticipated effect
- Goal setting
- Action

SITUATIONAL THEORIES

Situational theories argue that there are situational factors that influence job satisfaction, and such factors result from the job's characteristics. The assumption is that people have similar needs, and therefore can be satisfied by the same job characteristics. Some of the situational theories follow the job characteristics model (Hackman & Oldham, 1980) and the operant approach.

The Job Characteristics Model

The job characteristics model explains that there are five core job characteristics (skill variety, task identity, task significance, autonomy, and feedback from job) that influence the outcomes of job satisfaction (high internal work motivation, high growth satisfaction, high general satisfaction, and high work effectiveness). Hackman and Oldham (1980) argue that job satisfaction outcomes are moderated through critical psychological states (experienced meaningfulness, experienced responsibility for outcomes, and knowledge of actual results) like other moderators, such as knowledge, skill, growth, and need strength.

The Situational Occurrences Theory

The situational occurrences theory argues that an individual's job satisfaction depends on a combination of situational characteristics and situational occurrences (Quarstein, McAfee, & Glassman, 1992). Situational characteristics are characteristics that an individual considers before accepting a job offer (wages, working conditions, supervision, promotion, and organizational policies). Other situations that an individual considers while in the job are called situational occurrences. The situational occurrences can be positive (for example, giving an employee an unexpected pay increase for completing a task outstandingly) or negative (e.g., coworkers are constructing roadblocks that prevent an employee from efficiently completing his or her assignment).

MEASURES OF JOB SATISFACTION

Job Satisfaction as a Criterion Variable

Job satisfaction has been investigated as a criterion variable with respect to personal (gender, age, education, and tenure) and work-related characteristics (working conditions, rewards, relationship with co-workers, and challenging work). Some researchers indicate that males are more satisfied with their work than females (Locke, Fitzpatrick, & White, 1983), whereas others suggest either the reverse (Hoppock, 1935) or found no differences on job satisfaction based on gender (Golding, Resnick, & Crosky, 1983). Hulin and Smith (1965) found that job satisfaction increases in a positive linear relationship with age. Quinn, Staines, and McCullough (1974) indicated that older workers are more satisfied with their jobs. Quinn and Baldi de Mandilovitch (1980) conducted a meta-analysis that showed a positive relationship between education level and job satisfaction. However, some studies suggest that younger workers with higher levels of formal education tend to be more dissatisfied when performing routine tasks (DeSantis & Durst, 1996). More recent studies found that older employees tend to be more satisfied with their job (Gigantesco, Picardi, Chiaia, Balbi, & Morosini 2003).

Supportive, safe, and comfortable working conditions as well as supportive and constructive relationships with colleagues are found to be criteria of job satisfaction (Bruce & Blackburn, 1992; Vroom, 1982). Other work-related characteristics that researchers claim to be criteria for job satisfaction are equitable rewards (Bruce & Blackburn, 1992) and challenging work (Vroom, 1982). Recent studies have also found a strong correlation between employee job satisfaction and their work environment (Nel et al., 2004).

Job Satisfaction as a Predictor Variable

Job satisfaction has also been studied as a predictor variable with respect to performance, organizational commitment, turnover, and absenteeism. Early research in industrial/organizational psychology suggested that performance is related to job satisfaction

(Brody, 1945; Korhauser & Sharp, 1932). The human relations movement sought to improve performance through satisfying employees' needs (Katz, Maccoby, Gurin, & Floor, 1951). Various subsequent studies found no correlation between employee job satisfaction and their performance (Brayfield & Crocket, 1955; Chapman & Chapman, 1969). Other studies revealed a weak correlation between job satisfaction and performance (Laffaldano & Muchinsky, 1985; Petty, McGee, & Cavender, 1984; Vroom, 1964). However, more recent studies found that job satisfaction is positively associated with higher productivity (Egan, Yang, & Bartlett, 2004). According to White (2000), increased employee productivity is strongly related to improved job satisfaction. Similarly, Al-Hussami (2008) found that employees who are more satisfied tend to be more productive and committed to their job. Tzeng (2002) found a positive correlation between employee satisfaction and the quality of service delivery.

Job satisfaction is considered to be a predictor of organizational commitment (Miller, 1997; Petrides & Furham, 2006; Tett & Meyer, 1993). Ajayi (1981) found significant relationships between job satisfaction and organizational commitment of college professors. Other studies claimed a positive and significant correlation between organizational commitment and variables of job satisfaction, such as satisfaction with work itself, opportunity for promotion, satisfaction with supervision, satisfaction with co-workers, pay satisfaction, and overall job satisfaction. Adeyemo (2007) found that job satisfaction is a predictor of turnover intention, but is mediated by emotional intelligence. Also, job satisfaction has been researched as a predictor of employee absenteeism and turnover (Locke, 1976; Mobely, 1982; Schwepker (2001). Mayer and Botha (2004) argue that low job satisfaction results in a lack of employee commitment to contribute to further organizational goals.

JOB RETENTION

According to a survey conducted by The Improved Group (2013), the turnover rate in U.S. nonprofit organizations was about 17% in 2013. It is always a challenge for organizations to retain their best employees if they do not give such outstanding employees a compelling reason to stay instead of looking or accepting opportunities from competitor agencies. The retention of competent and productive professionals in organizations has been and remains a major problem for employers. Norris (1982) indicates that most Americans change jobs about 15 times by age 35. Recent studies have shown also that retention has become the major concern of today's employers (Abbasi & Hollman, 2000; Kiger, 2000; Taylor, 1999). Job retention is closely related to job satisfaction, which is "an employee's affective reactions to a job based on comparing desired outcomes with actual outcomes" (Egan, Yang, & Bartlett, 2004, p. 5). Job satisfaction is associated with respectful treatment that employee receives at work (Knudsen, Johnsonn & Roman 2003; Lund, 2003). Employees who are satisfied with their job tend to be more productive and most likely to stay in their organizations (Egan et al., 2004).

Staff Turnover and Its Impacts

Employee turnover tends to have significant impact on organizational performance. When a gifted employee leaves an organization, especially a nonprofit organization, there is always a void or a disruption in continuity that can affect output capacity. Obviously, when there is a high rate of employee turnover in organizations, the void is most likely to be filled by less experienced employees who may not be able to provide the same level of productivity at a quality standard.

A preliminary study of employment trends in a small telecom company revealed that staff turnover affects a company performance. During a 3-month period, the company had a turnover of 32.5%. This was forcing the company to rely on a contractor workforce at costs averaging 35% higher than the costs for in-house staff (www.superbstaff.com). Gooden and Bailey say, "Some employers indicate that it costs between $2500 and $3000 to hire and lose an employee within the first 60 days of employment" (Gooden & Bailey, 2001). Parrry & Lacy (2000) noted that it costs six times more to hire new employees than to retain a current one. They indicated that 50% of loss of production comes from absences of a week or less and job stress and related problems costs organizations as much as $ 200 billion annually (Parry & Lacy, 2000).

Employee turnover in organizations and businesses is a critical issue that employers cannot neglect if such organizations or businesses want to attain their goals.

Factors of Turnover

Some staff turnover results from an employee's personal life decision, which is beyond employer control. Abbasi and Hollman (2000) identified lack of good hiring and screening practices, managerial styles, lack of employee recognition, noncompetitive wages, and a toxic work environment as the main employee turnover factors (Abbasi & Hollman, 2000). In fact, most of the studies on job satisfaction agree that people will not commit too long to something that cannot satisfy their needs (DuBrin, 1997; Egan et al., 2004). The question is what do employees want from their jobs? Employee turnover is a complex phenomenon that employers cannot address with a single strategy. For example, a worker can decide to leave a work environment that a supervisor finds challenging, because of good wages, job security, and promotion and growth with the company. For example, the physician and the social worker might be interested in autonomy in their work place, but the nurse might be looking for monetary compensation.

Employees quit organizations when their needs are not met. They stay in organizations when their needs are met. In other words, the same explanatory factors of employee turnover can be used as strategies of employee retention.

STAFF RETENTION PROCESS AND/OR LEVEL

The retention of an employee in organizations starts during the hiring process and continues through the orientation and integration of the employee within the organization.

Hiring

Taylor found that most employees' turnover is due to hiring mistakes that could be avoided. Some of the strategies for a hiring process that can help staff retention include:

1. Establish good relations with communities and schools to create a pool of candidates.
2. Identify the strengths and personal self-actualization goals of potential employees.

3. Create a well-skilled hiring team that matches the strengths and personal goals of candidates.
4. Provide the hiring team with the necessary tools and flexibility to conduct a good interview.
5. Do not rush the hiring process; bad hires can create disaster in a short amount of time.
6. Define clear expectations with candidates.
7. Develop an employee growth portfolio upon hiring.

Orientation

Orientation aims to ease a new hire's adjustment to an organization, providing information about work expectations, and creating the employee's strength-based self-confidence to work toward the achievement of the organization's goals. The orientation stage is very critical to retaining staff in organizations. Too often employees leave their jobs right after they have been hired because the orientation process made them think they should quit. To be successful, orientation must involve appropriate strength-based matching between the orienteer and the new hire.

Integration

The integration of an employee in an organization is a key factor for retention. Integration can foster the commitment of employees to organizations. Kiger (2000) explained that employees commit to organizations that offer opportunities to learn, valuable compensation, career growth, caring human resources management, competitive benefits package, and organizational reputation.

In addition, integration should provide the employee a work environment of trust, respect, and happiness. Howard and Gould (2000) argue that employee happiness is related to job success, achievement of career goals, being valued, opportunity for professional development, accommodation for individual difference, recognition of achievement, and personal support. This will in turn contribute to employee commitment and higher productivity (Howard & Gould, 2000). According to Schwepker (2001), turnover rates tend to be lower in organizations that offer a climate of innovation and creativity.

Integration is an ongoing organizational challenge to promote and practice strength-based promotion and self-improvement opportunities, continuing assessment of employee satisfaction/dissatisfaction, continuing education, immediate rewards and recognition, and consistency in organization philosophy and practices. Some people leave organizations because they feel rejected. They are not integrated as a part of the organizational system and structures. In a 2000 survey of the American Management Association (AMA), high-tech workers said they would stay in their job if someone had tried to keep them there (Branham, 2000).

Rewards and Benefits

The reward system is the basis of all motivation and staff-retention strategy. Behavioral scientists have attempted to design explanatory models that present reward as a predominant causal factor of motivation and behavior modification. However, the value an individual attaches to a reward may vary from one category of employee to another, and may also vary over time.

In fact, monetary compensation undoubtedly helps satisfy the most basic needs of every human being. However, to be valuable, the wages must be part of a competitive inclusive work environment through noncompensation rewards, such as:

- Promoting constructive social relationships with coworkers
- Allocating sufficient resources to perform work assignments
- Designing jobs that require adequate attention and effort
- Granting sufficient control over the job to meet personal demands
- Offering supportive leadership and management
- Enhancing dignity and satisfaction from work performed
- Enhancing physiological health, psychological well-being, and emotional maturity (Henderson, 1989)

Participation

Participation can generate commitment of employees to organizations and help employers retain productive professionals. Participation means matching strengths and personal goals of employees with their tasks/assignments. Participation means inviting employees to help solve organizational problems. This allows employees to commit to determining the basis on which their performance will be assessed and appreciated. Also, participation can increase employee commitment toward the fulfillment of an organization's mission, vision, values, and goals. Participative involvement of employees in an organization's decision making increases productivity and decreases resistance to change.

HUMAN RESOURCES, DIVERSITY, AND CULTURAL COMPETENCE

During the past two decades, cultural diversity in workplaces and organizations has become an international challenge. Much like the personality of a person that is shaped and molded by parents, relatives, and friends, the personality of an organization is molded and shaped by the founders, board members, and the experiences of each and every employee. Organizations and agencies often establish a socialization process, a pecking order in which there are those who are included and others who are excluded from the organizational social norm (Glass ceilings).

The most significant problem is not the lack of diversity in agencies and organizations but rather effective management of the diversity already there. Consequently, diversity is seldom acknowledged and understood as an asset for the organization. Organization managers—intentionally or not—tend to see or present a picture of inclusion and cultural competency at their organization as being much better than the reality. This is not surprising as we all have some blind spot that we are often unaware of but others see. Religious background, sexual orientation, gender, age, place of birth, and things as minute as individual talents and special abilities contribute to the employee's organizational microcosm, which emulates the real world. In other words, the organizational environment is a smaller version of what we all experience globally. Just as in the real world agencies and organizations are susceptible to hiring and retaining bigots, racists, and those with hubristic and elitist personal beliefs and attitudes. Therefore, nonprofit organizations have responsibilities to ensure that racism, discrimination, prejudice, and other forms of bigotry are not part of hiring and personnel management practices and the work experience of employees. This will contribute to employee dissatisfaction, high turnover, reduced morale, lack of commitment, and decrease in productivity. Organizations should develop a plan that is designed to assist in implementing a system that encourages diversity in hiring practices and prepares staff to become culturally sensitive. In other words, nonprofit organizations should strive to set the stage for understanding diversity, for the purpose of improving relationships, increasing employee morale and productivity, facilitating employee buy-in/loyalty, and influencing the consciousness of organizational goals and effectiveness. The ultimate goal is to create an environment that will institutionalize cultural competence by new knowledge and changes in policy and procedures.

ORGANIZATIONAL AMBIDEXTERITY

The term "organizational ambidexterity" was first introduced by Duncan (1976) when asserting that an "organization has to be strategically responsive in making major changes while at the same time it must be concerned with carrying out its activities in the most efficient manner" (p. 172). In other words, organizations should make changes in a way that does not cost too much. March (1991) defined organizational ambidexterity as the ability of an organization to explore and exploit simultaneously. Exploration means that an agency or company transforms itself as a learning organization (He & Wong, 2004) that is continually exploring new knowledge, ideas, and strategic initiatives for transformation (Han, 2007). Exploitation implies that an organization should seize the opportunity to make routine changes (Beck, Brüderl, & Woywode, 2008), and experiment with new processes, products, and services (Im & Rai, 2008). Several studies have found that organizational ambidexterity as a measure of exploration and exploitation contributes to organizational performance (Bierly & Daly, 2007; Cao, Gedajlovic, & Zhang, 2009; Sarkees, 2007). This principle also applies to human resources management and development, because team commitment plays a key role in organizational ambidexterity (Bolman & Deal, 2008). As Rothaermel and Alexandre (2009) suggested, organizational ambidexterity is "not simply achieved through organizational structure, but requires a shared vision, a common set of values, and a reward system that enables managers to resolve the paradox of ambidexterity and harness its benefits" (p. 776). Organizational ambidexterity is considered by some scholars as a strategy for organizational survival or sustainability (Andriopoulos & Lewis, 2009; Markman, Gianiodis, & Phan, 2009).

HUMAN RESOURCES AND FINANCIAL SUSTAINABILITY

Findings from recent studies show that staff turnover is a major problem that affects organization effectiveness (Mayer & Botha, 2004). We have seen also that monetary compensation is not the dominant factor that hinders employee retention in organizations. Likewise, there is no single strategy for staff retention. There needs to be a global, systemic strategy to retain staff in organizations and avoid the high costs of employee turnover. Staff retention starts during the hiring process, through the integration of employees in organizations. Other factors such as a strength-based approach that seeks employee commitment and participation have been shown to contribute to productivity and organization effectiveness and sustainability.

Human resources management plays an important role in fostering organizational sustainability because of the role of human capital in organizational performance (Hersey, Blanchard, & Johnson, 2008). Human resources management has various implications for financial sustainability, such as organizational ambidexterity, cost of hiring, cost of job stress, cost of high staff turnover, return on investment of staff development, saving through staff retention, higher productivity through job satisfaction and employee motivation, return on investment of cultural competency, and in-kind contribution of volunteer personnel.

For example, turnover costs are significant to organizations, including nonprofit organizations. Egan et al. (2004) argued that organizations with lower turnover rates benefit in increases in organizational performance, reduction in costs associated with organizational and job-specific knowledge, hiring, and retraining of replacement employees. This is in contrast to the potential of high turnover rates that cost organizations in the areas of severance pay, higher unemployment taxes, training costs for replacement employees, paying overtime to other staff or temporary staffing, lost productivity, reduced morale, and loss of organizational knowledge. The ability of an organization to reduce turnover results in cost savings. Turnover reduction will make money available that can be used for other activities, including activities to strengthen the financial sustainability of an organization.

Further, the financial sustainability of an organization is not a linear initiative. Financial sustainability requires an organizational environment that is committed to the higher purpose of an entity. If staff is not motivated, there will be no commitment to take actions and follow up on tasks that would engage a nonprofit organization on a path toward financial sustainability. Although the connection may not seem obvious for some, an organization cannot become financially sustainable without the belief, commitment, and the hard work of its staff.

QUESTIONS AND ACTIVITIES

1. What do human resources refer to in organizations?
2. How would you define "job satisfaction"?
3. What are some common theories of job satisfaction?
4. What would you consider are the main causes of employee turnover in your organization?
5. What are some staff retention strategies that you would recommend to the managers of a nonprofit organization?
6. How can cultural competence contribute to employee satisfaction?
7. Go to the website of your state government: What are the laws and regulations that affect hiring and human resources management in your agency?
8. How do you think human resources and job satisfaction are related to financial sustainability in nonprofit organizations?
9. Search the Internet, and write one or two paragraphs describing each of the following pieces of legislation:
   - Civil Rights Acts of 1866 and 1871
   - National Labor Relations Act of 1935
   - Title VII of the Civil Rights Act of 1964
   - Executive Order 11246 and 11375 of 1965 and 1967
   - Age Discrimination in Employment Act of 1967
   - Executive Order 11478 of 1969
   - Occupational Safety and Health Act of 1970

- Vocational Rehabilitation Act of 1973 and 1974
- Vietnam Era Veteran's Readjustment Act of 1974
- Pregnancy Discrimination Act of 1978
- Immigration Reform and Control Act of 1986, revised in 1990 and 1996
- Americans with Disabilities Act of 1990
- Older Workers Benefit Protection Act of 1990
- Civil Rights Act of 1991
- Family and Medical Leave Act of 1993
- Congressional Accountability Act of 1995

REFERENCES

Abbasi, S., & Hollman, K. (2000). Turnover: The real bottom line. *Public Personnel Management, 29,* 333–342.

Adams, J. S. (1963). Toward an understanding of inequity. *Journal of Abnormal and Social Psychology, 67*(5), 422–436.

Adeyemo, D. A. (2007). Emotional intelligence and the relationship between job satisfaction and organizational commitment of employee in public parastatals in Oyo State, Nigeria. *Pakistan Journal of Social Sciences, 4,* 324–330.

Ajayi, S. A. (1981). *Job satisfaction and commitment among Nigeria University teachers* (Unpublished doctoral dissertation), University of Ibadan, Ibadan.

Alderfer, C. P. (1972). *Existence, relatedness and growth.* New York, NY: Free Press.

Al-Hussami, M. (2008). A study of nurses' job satisfaction: The relationship to organizational commitment, perceived organizational support, transactional leadership, transformational leadership and level of education, *European Journal of Scientific Research, 22*(2), 286–285.

Ball, K. S. (2001). The use of human resource information systems: a survey. *Personnel Review, 30*(6), 667–693.

Basset-Jones, N., & Lloyd, G. F. (2005). Does Herzberg's motivation theory have staying power?" *Journal of Management Development, 24,* 929–943.

Beck, N., Brüderl, J., & Woywode, M. (2008). Momentum or deceleration? Theoretical and methodological reflections on the analysis of organizational change. *Academy of Management Journal, 51*(3), 413–435.

Bierly, P., & Daly, P. (2007). Alternative knowledge strategies, competitive environment, and organizational performance in small manufacturing firms. *Entrepreneurship: Theory and Practice, 31*(4), 493–516.

Bolman, L. G., & Deal, T. E. (2008). *Reframing organizations.* San Francisco: Jossey-Bass.

Bondarouk, T., & Ruël, H. J. M. (2009). Electronic human resource management: Challenges in the digital era. Guest-editors' introduction to a special issue. *International Journal of HRM, 20*(3), 505–514.

Branham, L. (2000). *Keeping the people who keep you in business.* New York: American Management Association.

Brayfield, A. H., & Crocket, W. H. (1955). Employee attitudes and employee performance. *Psychological Bulletin, 52,* 396-424.

Brody, M. (1945). *The relationship between efficiency and job satisfaction.* Unpublished master's thesis. New York: New York University.

Bruce, W. M., & Blackburn, J. W. (1992). *Balancing job satisfaction and performance.* Westport, CT: Quorum Books.

Campbell, J. P., Dunnette, M. D., Lawler, E. E., III, & Weick, K. E., Jr. (1970). *Managerial behavior, performance, and effectiveness.* New York. NY: McGraw-Hill.

Cao, Q., Gedajlovic, E., & Zhang, H. 2009. Unpacking ambidexterity: Dimensions, contingencies, and synergistic effects. *Organization Science, 20,* 781–796.

Carroll, A. B. (2008). A history of CSR: Concept and practices. In A. Crane, D. Matten, A. McWilliams, J. Moon, & D. Siegel (Eds.), *The Oxford handbook of corporate social responsibility:* 19–45. Oxford, UK: Oxford University Press.

Castillo, J. X., & Cano, J. (2004). Factors explaining job satisfaction among faculty. *Journal of Agricultural Education, 45*(3), 65–74.

Chapman, L. J., & Chapman, J. P. (1969). Illusory correlation as an obstacle to the use of valid psycho-diagnostic signs. *Journal of Abnormal Psychology, 74,* 271–280.

Chelladurai, P. (1999). *Management of human resources in sport and recreation.* Champaign, IL: Human Kinetics Publishers.

Chinho, L., & Ming-Lung, H. (2010). Holistic decision system for human resource. *Industrial Management and Data Systems,* 110(2), 230–248.

Conner, J., & Ulrich, D. (1996). Human resource roles: Creating value, not rhetoric. *Human Resource Planning, 19*(3), 38–49.

DeSantis, V. S., & Durst, S. L. (1996). Comparing job satisfaction among public and private sector employees. *American Review of Public Administration, 26*(3), 327–343.

Dubrin, Andrew J. (1997). *Fundamentals of organizational behavior. An applied approach.* Cincinnati, OH: Southern College Publishing.

Duncan, R.B. (1976). The ambidextrous organization: Designing dual structures for innovation. In R. Kilman & L. Pondy (Eds.), *The management of organizational design* (pp. 167–188). New York, NY: North Holland.

Egan, T. M., Yang, B., & Bartlett, K. R. (2004). The effects of organizational learning culture and job satisfaction on motivation to transfer learning and turnover intention. *Human Resource Development Quarterly, 15*(3), 279–301. doi:10.1002/hrdq.1104

Golding, J., Resnick, A., & Crosby, F. (1983). Work satisfaction as a function of gender and job status. *Psychology of Women Quarterly, 1,* 286–290.

Gooden, S., & Bailey, M. (2001). Welfare and work: Job-retention outcomes of federal workforce welfare-to-work employees. *Public Administration Review, 61,* 83–91.

Hackman, J. R., & Oldham, G. R. (1980). *Work redesign.* Reading, MA: Addison-Wesley.

Han, M. (2007). Achieving superior internationalization through strategic ambidexterity. *Journal of Enterprising Culture, 15*(1), 43–77.

He, Z.-L., Wong, P.-K. (2004). Exploration vs. exploitation: An empirical test of the ambidexterity hypothesis. *Organizational Science, 15*(4), 481–494.

Hendrikson, A. (2003). Human resougoogle.comrce information systems: Backbone technology of contemporary human resources. *Journal of Labour Research, 24*(3), 382–387.

Herzberg, F. (1966). *Work and the nature of man.* New York, NY: Thomas Y. Crowell Publishers.

Herzberg, F., Mausner, B., & Snyderman, B. B. (1959). *The motivation to work.* New York, NY: Wiley.

Hoppock, R. (1935). *Job satisfaction.* New York, NY: Harper Brothers.

Howard, B., & Gould, K. (2000). Strategic planning for employee happiness: A business goal for human services. *American Journal on Mental Retardation, 105,* 377–386.

Hoy, W. K., & Miskel, C. G. (1982). *Educational administration: Theory, research, and practice* (2nd ed.) New York, NY: Random House.

Hulin, C. L., & Smith, P. C. (1965). A linear model of job satisfaction. *Journal of Applied Psychology, 49,* 209–216.

Improved Group. (2013). *2013 Nonprofit employment trends survey.* Retrieved from http://www.nonprofithr.com/wp-content/uploads/2013/03/2013-Employment-Trends-Survey-Report.pdf

Jayaratne, S. T. (1993). The antecedents, consequences, and correlates of job satisfaction. In R. T. Golembiewski (Ed.), *Handbook of organizational behavior* (pp. 111–134). New York, NY: Marcel Dekker.

Katz, D., Maccoby, N., Gurin, G., & Floor, L. G. (1951). *Productivity supervision and morale among railroad workers.* Ann Arbor, MI: Universirt of Michigan Press.

Kaufman B. (2001). *Expanding the intellectual and normative foundations of modern industrial relations: Lessons from John R. Commons and the Wisconsin School.* Working paper, Georgia State University.

Khan, H., & Santos, M. (2002). *Contribution of ICT use to output and labour productivity growth in Canada.* Ottawa and Ontario: Bank of Canada.

Kiger, P. (2000). Retention on the brink. *Workforce, 79,* 58–65.

Knudsen, H. K., Johnson, J. A., & Roman, P. M. (2003). Retaining counseling staff at substance abuse treatment centers: Effects of management practices. *Journal of Substance Abuse Treatment, 24*(2), 129–135. doi: 10.1016/S0740-5472(02)00357-4

Laabs, J. (2000). Need peak HR performance? Consider a coach. *Workforce, 79*(10), 132–135.

Laffaldano, M. T., & Muchinsky, P. M. (1985). Job satisfaction and job performance: A meta-analysis. *Psychological Bulletin, 97,* 251–273.

Lawler, E.E., III. (1994). *Motivation in work organizations.* San Francisco, CA: Jossey-Bass.

Li, J. (2003). Strategic human resource management and MNEs' performance in China. *International Journal of Human Resource Management, 14,* 157–117.

Lin, K.-L. (2011). Human resource allocation for remote construction projects. *Journal of Construction Engineering and Management, 27*(1), 13–20.

Locke, E. A. (1969). What is job satisfaction? *Organizational Behavior and Human Performance, 4,* 309–336.

Locke, E. A. (1970). Job satisfaction and job performance: A theoretical analysis. *Organizational Behavior and Human Performance, 5,* 484–500.

Locke, E. A. (1976). The nature and causes of job satisfaction. In M. D. Dunnette (Ed.), *The handbook of industrial and organizational psychology* (pp. 1297–1349). Chicago, IL: Rand McNally.

Locke, E. A., Fitzpatrick, W., & White, F. (1983). Job satisfaction and role clarity among university and college faculty. *Review of Higher Education, 28,* 681–682.

Mackavey, M. G. (2006). Practicing ethics in HR: Where's the action? *Journal of American Academy of Business, 9*(2), 244–249.

March, J. G. (1991). Exploration and exploitation in organizational learning. *Organization Science, 2,* 71–87.

Marwick, A. (2001). Knowledge management technology. IBM Systems Journal, 40(4), 814–830.

Maslow, A. H. (1943). A theory of human motivation. *Psychological Review, 50*(4), 370–396.

Maslow, A. H. (1954). *Motivation and personality.* New York, NY: Harper & Brothers.

Mayer, M., & Botha, E. (2004). *Organizational development and transformation in South Africa* (2nd ed.). Durban, South Africa: Lexis Nexis Butterworth.

Miller, J. (1997). *Job satisfaction and organizational commitment of Ohio State University Extension agents* (Unpublished masters thesis). Columbus, OH: Ohio State University.

Mobely, W. H. (1982). *Employee turnover: Causes, consequences, and control.* Reading, MA: Addison Wesley.

Morley, M., Gunnigle, P., O'Sullivan, M., & Collings, D. (2006). New directions in the roles and responsibilities of the HRM function, *Personnel Review, 35*(6), 609–617.

Mumford, E. (1976). *Work design and job satisfaction.* Manchester, UK: Manchester Business School.

Narsavage, D. A. (2008). *A history of human resources.* Alexandria, VA: Society for Human Resource Management.

Norris, P. E. (1982). *How to find a job?* Fairhope, AL: National Job Search Training Laboratories.

Parry, T., & Lacy, P. (2000). Promoting productivity and workforce effectiveness. *Financial Executive, 16,* 51–53.

Petrides, K. V., & Furnham, A. (2006). The role of trait emotional intelligence in a gender-specific model of organizational variables. *Journal of Applied Social Psychology, 36,* 552–569.

Petty, M. M., McGee, G. W., & Cavender, J. W. (1984). A meta-analysis of the relationships between individual job satisfaction and individual performance. *Academy of Management* Review, 9, 712–721.

Preziosi, R. C., & Gooden, D. J. (2003). *A comparative analysis of faculty job satisfaction for traditional vs. online instruction in graduate business education.* Retrieved from: http://www.abe.sju.edu//.pdf

Quarstein, V. A., McAfee, R. B., & Glassman, M. (1992). The situational occurrences theory of job satisfaction. *Human Relations, 45*(8), 859–873.

Quinn, R. P., & Baldi de Mandilovitch, M. S. (1980). Education and job satisfaction. *Vocational Guidance Quarterly, 29*(2), 100–111.

Quinn, R. P., Staines, G. L., & McCullough, M. R. (1974). *Job satisfaction: Is there a real trend? Manpower Research Monograph, 30 Washington DC: Manpower Administration, U.S. Department of Labor.*

Rynes, S. (2004). Where do we go from here? Imagining new roles for human resources. *Journal of Management Inquiry, 13*(3), 203–13.

Sarkees, M. E. (2007). *Exploitation versus exploration: Getting the mix right* (Unpublished doctoral dissertation). Katz Graduate School of Business, University of Pittsburgh). Available from ProQuest Information and Learning Company (UMI Microform No. 3284620).

Schaffer, R.H. (1953). Job satisfaction as related to need satisfaction in work. *Psychological Monographs: General and Applied, 67*(14), 1–29.

Schmidt, F. L., Gast-Rosenberg, I., & Hunter, J. E. (1980). Validity generalization results for computer programmers. *Journal of Applied Psychology, 65* (6), 643–661.

Schwepker, C. H. (2001). Ethical climate's relationship to job satisfaction, organizational commitment, and turnover intention in the salesforce, *Journal of Business Research, 54*(1), 39–52. doi: 10.1016/j.bbr.2011.03.031

Scott, W.R. (2003). *Financial accounting theory.* Toronto, Ontario: Prentice Hall.

Shani, A., & Tesone, V. D. (2010). Have human resource information systems evolved into internal e-commerce? *Emerald Group Publishing Limited, 2*(1), 30–48.

Smucker, M., & Kent, A. (2004). The influence of referent selection on pay, promotion, supervision, work and co-worker satisfaction across three distinct industry segments. *International Sports Journal, 24,* 27-35.

Solomon, R. L., & Corbit, J. D. (1973). An opponent-process theory of motivation: 11. Cigarette addiction. *Journal of Abnormal Psychology,* 1973, 81, 158–171.

Spector, P. E. (1997). *Job satisfaction: Application, assessment, causes, and consequences.* Thousand Oaks, CA, Sage.

Spence-Laschinger, H. (2008). Effect of empowerment on professional practice environments, work satisfaction and patient care quality: Further testing the nursing work life model. *Journal of Nursing Care Quality, 23*(4), 322-330. doi:10.1197/01.NCQ.0000318028.67910.6b

Tannenbaum, R., & Schmidt, W. H. (1973). How to choose a leadership pattern. *Harvard Business Review, 51*(3), 162–180.

Tansley, C., Newell, S., & Williams, H. (2001). Effecting HRM-style practices through an integrated human resource information system: An e-greenfield site? *Personnel Review, 30*(3), 351–370.

Taylor, J. (1999). Avoid avoidable turnover. *Workforce, 78,* (Suppl.) 1–3.

Tett, R. P., & Meyer, J. P. (1993). Job satisfaction, organizational commitment, turnover intention and turnover: Path analyses based meta–analytic findings. *Personnel Psychology, 46*(2), 259–294.

Townsend, A. M., & Bennett, J. T. (2003a). A Perfect market: Living and bidding in an auction economy. *Communications of the ACM, 46*(12), 351–353.

U.S. Office of Personnel Management. (2005). *OPM's workforce planning model.* Retrieved from: http://www.opm.gov/policy-data-oversight/human-capital-management/reference-materials/strategic-alignment/workforceplanning.pdf

Vosburgh, R. M. (2007). The evolution of human resource: Developing human resource as an internal consulting organization. *Human Resource, 30*(3), 1–23.

Vroom, V. H. (1964). *Work and motivation.* New York, NY: Wiley.

Vroom, V. H. (1982). *Work and motivation.* New York, NY: Wiley.

Wahba, M. A., & Bridwell, L. G. (1976). Maslow reconsidered: A review of research on the need-hierarchy theory. *Organizational Behaviour and Human Performance, 15,* 212–240.

Wanous. J. P., & Zwany, A., (1977). A cross-sectional test of need-hierarchy theory. *Organizational Behavior and Human Performance, 18*(1), 78–97.

Wheeless, L. R., Barraclough, R., & Stewart, R. (1983). Compliance-gaining and power in persuasion. In R. N. Bostrom (Ed.), *Communication yearbook 7* (pp. 105–145). Beverly Hills, CA: Sage.

White, A. W. (2000). Job satisfaction and professional development of health information, administration faculty. *Journal of Allied Health, 29,* 129–137.

Zafar, J. Shaakat, M., & Mat, N. (2010). An analysis of e-human resource management practices: A case study of State Bank of Pakistan. *European Journal of Social Sciences, 15*(1), 18–21.

Service Delivery and Financial Sustainability

At the completion of this chapter, the reader will be able to:

1. Discuss the term "service delivery."
2. Describe a service delivery system in the context of a nonprofit organization.
3. Describe a customer service design.
4. Explain the relationship between service delivery and financial sustainability.

This chapter is designed to help understand how service delivery and financial sustainability are interconnected. The chapter discusses the roles of client-centeredness, decision making, scheduling, priority setting, effective and efficient flow of services or activities, quality assurance, and continuing quality improvement, and how these factors contribute in their own context to influence positively or negatively the financial sustainability of a nonprofit organization.

WHAT ARE SERVICES?

The term "services" is often used to refer to industrial activities that do not produce manufactured goods, especially when classifying activities in national statistics (John, 1999). This perspective tends to be vague, because types of services vary within specific industries or organizations. For example, Lovelock and Yip (1996) classified services based on core transformation process and distinguished among people-processing, information-processing, and possession-processing services. Lovelock (1983) has categorized services based on the orientation of the service provided, and classified services directed at people's bodies, minds, belongings, and intangible assets.

Further, the term "services" can be the process through which activities are performed for customers. For example, Mohr and Bitner (1995) define services as the "manner in which the outcome is transferred to the customer" (p. 239). In that sense, service delivery is not only a process, but an outcome. Both are important for customer satisfaction. If the process is frustrating or terrible, even when the outcome is great, clients will keep the memory of such an uncomfortable process. This will not only affect their perception about an organization, but also they will seek for alternative ways to obtain the same outcome without going through an unpleasant process. Nonprofit organizations compete for scarce resources. Therefore, the satisfaction of the clients or customers is the best ally that a nonprofit can have to attract additional funding in support of activities and services. On the other hand, if the process is bad and the outcome is awful, the customer will still have a negative experience about services offered by an organization. In fact, customers can be tempted to believe that they were misled by a process that was promising, but did not deliver the corresponding outcome. Such perception has also the potential to affect financial resources generated by an organization.

SERVITIZATION

Servitization is the process whereby an organization develops creative and innovative ways to create a product–service system that integrates value-based products and service offerings (Vandermerwe & Rada, 1988). Servitization is very popular in the manufacturing industries, especially manufacturing firms in developed economies that strive to adjust to new forms of competition on the global market. For example, Siemens is a company that mainly offers electronic and electrical products. On the other hand, Xerox offers pay-per-click scanning as well as copying and printing of documents. With servitization, they combine their products with various consulting and maintenance services, which add value to the product they are selling. Servitization uses advanced technology–enabled services to reduce costs and negate risks in a way that is beneficial to both the company and the client. This approach transforms the client into an engaged customer. Baines (2013) found that servitization promises sustained annual business growth of 5% to 10%, reduces costs by up to 25% to 30% for customers, and delivers resilience and growth to a country's national economy. Considering servitization as a comprehensive package that is value based, nonprofit organizations can learn from such an approach.

SERVICE DELIVERY AND THE STRATEGIC PLAN

The strategic plan sets or reaffirms an organization's vision and mission statements, its strategic goals and objectives, and the organizational mandates. These elements dictate the makeup of the implementation or operational plan, which includes service delivery. "Service delivery" is not just a word. It is at the core of the implementation of the strategic plan of a nonprofit organization. It can take different forms based on the programmatic areas of an organization. For some organizations, service delivery means providing direct assistance to client on a first come, first served basis (e.g., a food pantry). For other organizations, service delivery is case management for children and/or families (e.g., a foster care agency). For another organization, service delivery means organizing a community outreach program to increase awareness on a particular issue (e.g., community outreach agency). In another case, it might be the organization of training (e.g., continuing education) or a formal education program (e.g., school, college, university). Box 18.1 provides an illustration based on the priorities for service delivery set by the Delta Community Center.

BOX 18.1 SERVICE DELIVERY STRATEGIC PLAN OF DELTA COMMUNITY CENTER

PRIORITY 1

Delta Community Center will ensure that those most in need have access to basic needs, such as shelter and food, by connecting the homeless, working poor, elderly, disabled, and victims of violent crimes to core services available in our metropolitan area.

STRATEGIES

- Increase the effectiveness of existing and new programs through the implementation of innovative service delivery models with increased emphasis on accountability and performance-based assessments.
- Enhance the referral program to delivery systems of core services, including shelter, utility assistance, housing, and food to vulnerable populations.
- Enhance the coordination of emergency programs to streamline client access to services.

PRIORITY 2

Delta Community Center will empower all residents to live in safe, affordable housing and achieve economic self-sufficiency through access to social, employment, and other economic resources needed to maximize their quality of life.

STRATEGIES

- Develop community collaborations to provide at-risk populations, including the disabled, elderly, and chronically homeless, with access to supportive services leading to greater self-sufficiency.
- Develop a new service delivery system that facilitates more efficient linkages to job training and other employment and educational resources empowering low-income households to earn a living wage.
- Develop efficiency, effectiveness, and quality measures to promote effective program management and responsible fiduciary stewardship of fiscal resources.

PRIORITY 3

Delta Community Center will promote rich, diverse, and innovative networks of public and community programs, services, and facilities to maximize the potential of our target population.

(continued)

> ## BOX 18.1 SERVICE DELIVERY STRATEGIC PLAN OF DELTA COMMUNITY CENTER *(continued)*
>
> ### STRATEGIES
>
> ■ Develop new and innovative mechanisms to improve the alignment and efficiency of local social services resources to meet neighborhood needs.
> ■ Provide technical assistance to partner community-based organizations by promoting awareness of social services issues and developing their ability to actively respond to these needs.
> ■ Assist community partners in identifying resources and developing strategies to increase their capacity to provide health, education, and economic opportunity services.
> ■ Enhance and expand the formal and informal networks connecting the social services sector (nonprofits, faith community, etc.) to individuals and families in high-need neighborhoods.

IMPLEMENTATION PLAN OR OPERATIONAL PLAN

An implementation plan or operational plan is simply the breakdown of a strategic plan into short-term and midterm activities through which the strategic goals outlined in a strategic plan can be achieved. The implementation plan must be broken down into specific programs or services through program design. A program design is a document that outlines sets of principles and procedures that must be implemented for a program to achieve its goals. Designing a social services system includes at least the following elements:

■ Analysis of the social problem
■ Determination of direct program beneficiary
■ A conceptual framework
■ Specification of services
■ Required personnel
■ Specification of helping environment
■ Description of actual helping behaviors
■ Identification of emotions and responses

Analysis of the Social Problem

The analysis of a social problem considers whether there is evidence of a problem for society, a problem for individuals, and factors contributing to the problem's existence or prevalence. As a problem for society, a program design should explain the extent to which an issue is a resource cost to society, a threat to the health and safety of members of society, and a threat to societal values, such as social integration. As a problem for individuals, a program design should describe how an issue constitutes a deprivation of a minimal standard of health and decency, a threat of abuse or exploitation, or a barrier to full social participation. Finally, the program design should inform about the factors that contribute to the problem's existence or prevalence (e.g., biological/physical, political, behavioral, societal, psychological, economic, community, and historical).

Determination of Direct Program Beneficiaries

The determination of direct program beneficiaries is very important for efficient and effective service provision. It is also important for performance measurement and accountability to various stakeholders. The program design should specify whether the beneficiaries will be:

- General population (e.g., children)
- At-risk population (e.g., children at-risk of abuse)
- Target population (e.g., children from a specific community, city, county, state, country)
- Client population (number of clients in the target population the program will serve)

Conceptual Framework

The conceptual framework is a reminder of the mission of the program or services that will be provided. The conceptual framework links your service concept (e.g., *case management services*) with a social or community issue that the program aims to change or influence (e.g., *increase self-reliance and successful transition to safe and stable housing of battered women*). The conceptual framework also includes the goals and objectives, as well as outcomes.

Service Procedures

The service procedures answer the questions:

- How will client enter the program?
- What is/are the intake procedure(s)?
- What services will be provided?
- What system of follow through will be in place?
- How will the system be evaluated?

Personnel

The service design specifies the personnel who will be involved in every aspect of a service delivery system. Although teamwork is important for a system to be efficient and effective, task distribution is just as important. Every member of a team must know exactly what his or her primary role is. Then, he or she should know about his or her supporting role, which reflects the teamwork aspect. Teamwork "works" only when every member does his or her part and supports the part of another member. It is not either or. Both are essential. Therefore, a service delivery system must answer questions, such as:

- Who will manage the program?
- Who are the partners in managing the program?
- What will be the responsibility of the personnel?

Helping Environment

Service delivery in nonprofit organizations is another way of saying the organization is help-ing or providing assistance to others. The service will take place in a setting called the "help-ing environment." The helping environment can be the office of an organization (e.g., walk-in services). The helping environment can also be the home of the client (e.g., case management for children and families). The helping environment can be an outdoor setting (e.g., commu-nity event, assistance during a natural disaster). Regardless of the type of setting, the service delivery system must answer the question: Where will the service provision be taking place (e.g., agency office, client home, partner's agencies office)? The answer to this question is critical to clarify clients' expectations. If clients know that the service will be provided door to door, they will not go to an office. Inversely, if clients know that they have to walk to an office to receive a service, there is no expectation that they will receive this service at home.

Helping Behavior

People who receive assistance from nonprofit organizations are human beings. They may be in a situation in which they have lost almost everything and need help. However, there is one thing that every human deserves, and that these people who need help have not lost: dignity. Their dignity may have been compromised as a result of an accident, a catastrophe, negligence, or malfeasance. Yet, they have not lost it. The point is, they deserve the respect of the people who are helping them. I know people may say that those who need help owe respect to the people who are serving them. Yes, I agree! The other side of the coin is true as well: People who are help-ing also owe respect to their clients. Respect means that you see the good and hope in people who are in need, so that you can use any asset they have to empower them. The service delivery system should specify clear helping behaviors for staff when assisting or helping clients.

Emotions and Responses

Clients who need the assistance of a nonprofit organization are usually in a special emo-tional place because of their situation. Clients need help as a result of an event that affected their ability to assist themselves at a given time. This need never arises without some emo-tional pain. The service delivery system must anticipate possible emotional expressions. The service delivery design must answer the questions: What are the emotions most likely to be experienced by the client? What will be the staff responses? Not all scenarios will be anticipated. However, an organization should attempt to anticipate as many scenarios as possible, and learn about new scenarios during the helping process. This will positively affect the quality of service and client satisfaction.

SERVICE DELIVERY AS A SYSTEM

A system is a set of parts that are connected in order to achieve an end. In other words, a system is a set of functions, activities, and structures that interact to achieve a goal. A sys-tem has several characteristics, such as

- *Synergy*: The interconnection of the parts in a system makes the whole greater than the sum of the parts
- *Adaptive behavior*: A system develops unpredictable behaviors that are rooted in the dynamic of interactions of its parts, which is called adaptive behavior
- *Hierarchy*: There is a hierarchy among the parts of a system
- *Boundary*: A system has boundaries delimiting where the eternal environment starts and where the system ends
- *Openness*: A system maintains interactions with its environment

GENERIC CUSTOMER-CENTRIC SERVICE DESIGN

A customer-centric service design outlines guidelines that define functions, roles, responsibility, chain of decision making and approval of requests, definition of clients, conditions of eligibility, validation or verification of eligibility, exceptions in conditions of eligibility, definition of service packages, assessment of client satisfaction, and continuing quality improvement. As the term indicates, a customer-centric service design is a service delivery system that focuses on providing the best quality service possible to customers or clients or the service target, based on a service concept, a service decision path, service sustainability, and service quality. Figure 18.1 illustrates the key factors of a generic customer-centric service design.

Service Target

The service target simply refers to the clients or the customers who will be beneficiaries of a service delivery system. The service target must be clearly defined. Agents in a service delivery system should have clear guidelines that answer questions such as:

- Who is eligible for services? What are the social, geographic, psychological, or demographic characteristics?
- What are the conditions of eligibility?
- What information or documents are required to validate eligibility?
- What are the circumstances under which exceptions can be made?
- Who can approve special eligibility?

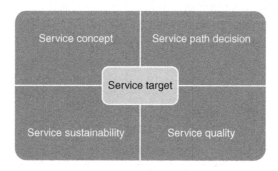

FIGURE 18.1   Service delivery system for sustainability.

Service Concept

The service concept describes the unit of service or package of services offered to customers or clients. The service concept is part of the identity of a delivery system. The service concept is the assistance that helps meet a client's needs (e.g., financial counseling, food pantry, job placement). The service concept is what an organization is known for. The service concept should be defined in a way that is comprehensible to potential clients or customers. A clear service concept can help avoid frustration. When the expectations of services are clearly defined, clients are satisfied if they received exactly what they were promised. A unit or package of service may not completely meet their needs, but they will be satisfied with the service and service delivery if the concept matches the service received.

Service Decision Path

The service decision path includes planning, coordination, and provision. An effective service decision path will answer the questions: Decision about what service? Why should the decision be made? Who will make the decision? When will the decision be made? How will the decision be made? Where will the decision be made? More specifically, the service decision path indicates who is doing what in the service delivery process. In other words, the service decision path answers questions such as (a) who is involved in service provision? (b) What is the level of competence for the people who are involved? (c) What are the levels of efficiency and effectiveness expected from the people who are involved? (d) How will their performance be measured? (e) What is the level of involvement? The levels of involvement can be:

1. Collection (information, requests)
2. Compilation (compilation, categorization)
3. Validation (ensuring that eligibility criteria are met)
4. Intermediary approval (any approval that is not final, prerequisites for further approval are met)
5. Final approval (final decision that authorizes service provision to client or customer)

Service Sustainability

The ability to continue to provide services over time is very critical for a nonprofit organization. This is called "service sustainability." A service is sustainable if it satisfies a continuous need, and is efficient and self-sufficient. Therefore, a customer-centered service delivery system should be able to collect information that documents or data that provide evidence of quality, efficiency, and self-sufficiency, and analyze the sustainable of the service concept and service decision path.

Service Quality

The main purpose of a customer-centric service design is to provide quality services to clients. Quality services involve not only the service concept, but also the service decision path. In fact, an organization may have a great service concept and deliver poor quality services if the service decision path is not competent and efficient. As a result, a service design should answer questions such as (a) What are the criteria of quality services? (b) What are the levels of quality? (c) How do clients assess service quality? (d) How can assessment of quality help streamline the service design for continuous quality improvement? The quality of service delivery influences donor and community support to contribute money to support the vision and mission of a nonprofit organization. Without donor and community support, an organization can close its doors and cease to provide key needed services.

SERVICE DELIVERY AS OPERATIONS MANAGEMENT

A service delivery system is similar to the processes of operations management in business. The main difference is the perception of the target population. Operation management develops a delivery system to meet the needs of markets, increase the pool of customers, and make more profit. For a nonprofit organization, the service delivery system is the implementation of the strategic plan designed to fulfill the overall purpose of the organization. In other words, it is the implementation of programs, projects, and activities as a strategy to make a difference in the life of the client or target population as much as possible.

Service delivery uses the necessary system technology together with other inputs, particularly staff capabilities, to meet the needs of clients. In that context, the costs profiles and profit targets are not the primary drivers. What is important is whether the service contributes to make a difference in the life of the client. What is important is whether the service can provide outcomes that help assess its fitness to help achieve program goals and objectives.

The extent to which these characteristics exist in the service delivery systems of nonprofit organizations differs from one service to another. Clients receive impressions about the purpose of a nonprofit organization through their experience of the way a service is delivered. These impressions are created both by the service itself and by the service experience that a client undergoes and that is uniquely linked to the service delivery system. A delivery system creates the intangible client experience that constitutes the service element of the benefit received, and becomes a critical element of the relationship between a nonprofit organization and the target population. The simultaneous provision and consumption of services provided by nonprofit organizations precludes the use of inventory as one way to help absorb fluctuations in demand. It also reduces the opportunities for controlling the quality of the service provision in terms of meeting the service specialization. In other words, in the heat of the moment it is very hard to make an objective assessment of the quality of service. This should be a rationale for staff involved in service delivery to be reminded constantly of the potential danger of getting caught up by random satisfaction or dissatisfaction and lose sight of the big picture, namely, a service system is complex and can be improved while being implemented.

Further, nonprofit organizations can work around the complexity of service delivery systems by developing creative ways to make the client part of the delivery system as an engaged participant in the system itself. In other words, the client becomes not just a recipient, but a partner who provides some form of contribution that can be monetary or nonmonetary or a combination of both. There is no set formula for that, except in the case of fee-based services in which the client contributes a nominal fee. The degree of customer involvement in the system affects many factors, including the provision and management of capacity, service levels, and staff training requirements and costs. Higher levels of customer participation in the delivery system make capacity management easier and reduce the cost of its provision, whereas lower levels decrease the degree of customer contact and the opportunities to personalize the service and encourage customer loyalty. Organizations need to have a clear understanding of the implications for their organizational alternative delivery systems. When companies invest in systems, they need to incorporate into that decision the trade-offs involved.

Understanding how services differ is an important prerequisite when designing the delivery systems to be used. Organizations typically design and develop a number of delivery systems to meet the services provided. The community or target population provides the external context in which the service delivery system needs to be set and where the process of design and development starts. The service encounter and the service experience are the essence of the delivery system.

Service delivery systems can include staff who deal directly with clients and staff who work in the back office that does not directly interact with clients. The key distinction between back office and front office is that in the back office activities take place without the customer being present or involved. Undertaking tasks in the back office means that the system is not required to respond to some client demands, and allows the completion of work to be planned as it best suits the system itself. Similarly, higher processing volumes and delayed completion allow the back office system to accumulate volumes and provide the opportunity to undertake tasks more efficiently, as all the work can be done at the same time. On the other hand, the front office is the point of contact or interactions with clients. The characteristics inherent in this part of the system include structural facilities. The structural facilities need to reflect the standards of the organization and meet the needs of clients as much as possible. The service delivery system must meet the service specification involved while ensuring sufficient capacity to meet the service targets concerning queues as well as the length of time it takes to deliver the service and the costs of overcapacity provisions. Front office staff roles and skills are essential to the effective functioning of delivery systems. In other words, staff in the front office must know what the generic turnaround time (TAT) is, and also be able to explain factors that can alter TAT. Staff must have enough basic knowledge to assist clients using a particular system, application, or software involved in the service provision system, if necessary. The mastery of these facets of service delivery can help avoid a lot of client frustration, which tends to have unintended consequences on the partnership or collaboration needed between a nonprofit organization and its clients. If an organization provides nonrepeat services, staff must be aware that their skills and capabilities do meet the specific needs of a client, as well as the service specification, which will be determined by any individual client. Therefore, the service specification will change throughout its delivery.

SERVICE DELIVERY COORDINATION

Nonprofit organizations are publicly funded entities that are required to show a level of accountability. They are required to show some form of report card that indicates how much money they receive and how they spend these monies. Accountability is not just about financial reports or accounting. Accountability implies effective coordination in service provision in a way that shows an acceptable level of performance. As a result, service coordination is connected to the financial management of a nonprofit organization. Administrators should ensure not only that they allocate financial resources properly, but that they also assign tasks in a manner that facilitates efficient service coordination. Ineffective task assignment is a waste of the human resources of an organization.

Consequently, a waste of human resources is a waste of financial resources, and can affect both service coordination and cost-effectiveness of services. Similarly, the adequate training of staff is important for efficient and effective service coordination. Incompetent and ill-prepared staff are costly for coordination of services. This can cost an organization its reputation and its key donors.

SERVICE DELIVERY AND COSTS

Service delivery incurs a cost. The client may not pay the cost, but the donors to a nonprofit organization pay on behalf of the client. The donors want to know what type of return on investment is documented for their donations. The donors do not seek a return on investment for themselves as in a for-profit business. They simply want to know that service performance is measured with appropriate indicators so that they know how many clients benefit from their donations or how their contributions have changed some clients' lives. Assessment of performance of service delivery in relation to its cost-effectiveness makes it necessary to collect data on unit service counts, number of beneficiaries, money spent per unit of service, the time spent on service coordination and delivery, wages and salaries of staff involved in service delivery, and the amount spent on risk/liability prevention. These data are informative regarding the areas or the types of services and clients for which financial resources are being used. If there is a discrepancy, it is easy to find out, and take corrective actions. If the cost of unit of service is too high, an organization may not be able to support a loss of funding, because clients will have been accustomed to a level of service that the organization will no longer be able to afford. If the cost of unit service is too high, an organization may not be able to save for contingencies and will be vulnerable to dissolution if funding is lost. If the cost of a unit of service is too high, there is a risk of losing community support or receiving pressure to cut services at the expense of quality. Some organizations provide services that are deemed standard rather than special. When designing delivery systems, organizations use developments in information technology (IT) to rethink approaches while others choose different ways to deliver the services they offer. It is fair to underline that IT developments have not only reduced costs and lead times within systems and procedures but have also enabled organizations to redesign many of these delivery systems. The Internet offered the capability to personalize the service to the client. Since its early days, online booking has grown rapidly. When designing the delivery system, organizations need to decide the extent to which customers will or will not participate in the creation of the service. Nonprofit organizations must recognize the key differences that exist among services, and incorporate these differences into delivery system design by taking into account factors such as volume, variety, type of client, of service provision, availability and access to support for utilization of services, and the overall proactiveness of the service delivery system design.

SERVICE DELIVERY AND FINANCIAL SUSTAINABILITY

Service delivery is closely linked to the financial sustainability of a nonprofit organization both as input and output. As input, service delivery must be of good quality in order to secure the support of clients, donors, and the public at large. As an output, service delivery must be cost-effective to provide services to the maximum number of clients possible and have a high rate of return on investment. Quality service contributes to organizational sustainability. Cost-effective services contribute to financial sustainability. Quality and cost-effective services contribute to financial sustainability in the forms of savings, donor and community support in fund-raising, profitability, solvency, income generation, liquidity, solvency, and efficiency.

QUESTIONS AND ACTIVITIES

1. What does the term "service" mean?
2. How would you define "servitization"?
3. How do you think servitization is applicable to nonprofit organizations?
4. How do service delivery systems differ in nonprofit organizations compared to for-profit business?
5. How can service delivery systems contribute to the financial sustainability of nonprofit organizations?
6. You are hired as a consultant to advise on the design of a service delivery system for a nonprofit organization working with women victims of abuse or violence.

   ■ What are some of the questions that you will ask the agency in order to gather information for the design of the service delivery system?
   ■ Outline specific strategies that you will use to include technology as part of the service delivery system?
   ■ What are some strategies that you will use to ensure that the service delivery system is cost-effective?

REFERENCES

Baines, T. (2013). *Servitization impact study: How UK based manufacturing organisations are transforming themselves to compete through advanced services.* Birmingham, UK: Aston University Press.

John, D. R. (1999). Consumer socialization of children: A retrospective look at twenty-five years of research. *Journal of Consumer Research, 26*(3), 183–213.

Lovelock, C. H. (1983). Classifying services to gain strategic marketing insights. *Journal of Marketing, 47*(3), 9–20.

Lovelock, C. H., & Yip, G. S., (1996). Developing global strategies for services businesses. *California Management Review, 38*(2), 64–86.

Mohr, L. A., & Bitner, M. J. (1995).The role of employee effort in satisfaction with service transactions. *Journal of Business Research, 32*(3), 239–252.

Vandermerwe, S., & Rada, J. (1988). Servitization of business: Adding value by adding services. *European Management Journal, 6*, 314–324.

Program Evaluation and Financial Sustainability

OBJECTIVES

At the completion of this chapter, the reader will be able to:

1. Define the concept of program evaluation.
2. Define the term "logic model."
3. Identify the items in a logic model.
4. Explain the benefits of a logic model for a nonprofit organization.
5. Describe the process used to conduct a program evaluation.
6. Explain the term "performance measurement in a nonprofit organization."
7. Explain the relationship between program evaluation and financial sustainability.

This chapter focuses on the role played by program evaluation and performance measurement in influencing the financial sustainability of a nonprofit organization. Topics in this chapter include theories, concepts, and principles of program evaluation, a logic model, performance measurement, basic research skills related to program evaluation, and development of program evaluation plans for quality assurance and continuing quality improvement.

DEFINE "PROGRAM"

Yen, Terao, and Shmidt (2009) define a program as a "set of planned and purposive activities" (p. 6). Two words are worth emphasizing: "planned" and "purposive." If I were to summarize, I would say a program is a plan with a purpose. The plan includes a set of activities. This is very close to the definition given by Royse, Thyer, and Logan (2006) who argue that a program is "an organized collection of activities designed to reach certain objectives … series of planned actions designed to solve some problem … to have some kind of an impact on the program participants" (p. 5). In both definitions, we can see that a program is a plan, a plan with a set of activities. I could even say a plan with a set of activities that are designed to achieve an objective, a goal, or a purpose.

PROGRAM EVALUATION AND THE LOGIC MODEL

A program evaluation design is a document outlining principles and procedures to assess the achievement of a program's goals. The logic model is one of the most common program design frameworks used in program evaluation. A logic model is a graphic depicting what a program will accomplish. It is a series of interconnected assumptions that can lead to a set of desired outcomes. Assumptions are beliefs about conditions expected to be met or satisfied by the program and the participants in order for the program to be successful. Assumptions are based on a problem or a gap. Assumptions are also based on goals or objectives used to fill the identified gap. Assumptions involve a form of if–then relationship between some variables related to a community or social issue to be addressed (Figure 19.1).

Let us consider the issue of child abuse and neglect in a community. Let us assume that data published by a reputable research institute found that many children are being abused or neglected by their teenage parents in Wasau, Wisconsin. With appropriate data obtained from a credible source, there will be no doubt about concluding that this is a problem to be addressed. Bear with me, this is an illustration. In the real world, this problem must be justified through a fact-based approach, using appropriate literature. For the sake of the illustration, we agree this is a problem. Great!

Now, here is my suggestion to address the problem: I want to develop a parenting skills training program. You may wonder, "Why do you suggest a parenting program when the issue that you were trying to justify was child abuse and neglect?" I would have asked the same question, because there is a sense of disconnect in that idea. You may ask, "How do you know this is the right program to address such an issue?" Great question! I don't know the answer. Maybe you think that I should suggest taking these children away from the abusive parents and placing them in foster homes. This may be the answer, but this is not what I suggest in the context of this illustration. What I do know is that I made an assumption when suggesting a parenting program in order to address an issue of child abuse and neglect. I made the assumption that parents abuse their children because they lack parenting skills. If this happens to be the case, I also assume that increased parenting skills will prevent parents from abusing their children. My objective in that case is to increase the parenting skills of parents at risk of abusing their children. This is what an assumption is about when developing a logic model. The if–then relationship is there. If parents lack parenting skills, then they will abuse their children. If parents learn parenting skills, then they will stop abusing their children. If parents stop abusing their children, then more children will be living in a safe environment at home.

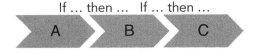

FIGURE 19.1 Assumptions.

GOAL:								
Situation: ■ Needs ■ Assets	**Priorities:** ■ Vision ■ Mission ■ Values ■ Mandates	**Inputs**	**Outputs** **Activities and strategies**	**Participation**	**Outcomes** **Short-term results in 1–3 years**	**Medium-term results in 4–6 years**	**Impact** **Long-term results in 7–10 years**	
What is the justification?		What resources are necessary?	What do we do?	Whom do we reach?	What are the short-term results? (e.g., awareness, knowledge, skills, attitudes, opinions, motivations, aspirations)	What are the medium-term results? (e.g., change in behavior, practice, decision making, policies, or social action)	What are the long-term results? (e.g., change of conditions in society, economy, environment, or civic life)	

Logic Assumptions

Evaluation Focus—Outcomes

External factors

Evaluation focus—Impact

FIGURE 19.2 Logic model.

KEY ITEMS OF A LOGIC MODEL

As Figure 19.2 illustrates, the key items of a logic model include the situation and priorities, assumptions, inputs, outputs, outcomes, external factors, and evaluation relevant to the situation.

GOAL

Nonprofit organizations implement programs, projects, or activities in order to achieve an overarching goal. Therefore, the goal and objectives are integral parts of the logic model.

SITUATION AND PRIORITIES

The situation refers to the needs of a target population that a program attempts to satisfy, as well as the vision, mission, values, and organization. The situation and priorities serve as justification to design and implement a program. The situation is anticipated to be addressed based on the mission, vision, and values of an organization, as well as its organizational capability.

INPUTS

Inputs are resources that nonprofit organizations use to implement programs, projects, or activities. In other words, inputs are monetary and nonmonetary investments made in a program in order to obtain a return called "outcomes." For example, the staff and volunteers who are involved in a program, the materials, the equipment, supplies, or energy that they use, and the money spent are all examples of inputs or resources.

OUTPUTS

Outputs include activities and strategies on the one hand and participation on the other hand. Outputs are the activities and products or services produced by the program (work accomplished, units of service provided, persons referred). Participation refers to the beneficiaries, clients, community partners, policy makers, community agencies, and other participants involved in the programs.

OUTCOMES

Outcomes are results that programs or projects produced for individuals, families, or communities. Outcomes can be short term, medium term, or long term.

The *short-term outcomes* are learning that results from participation in programs or projects. Short-term outcomes are measured based on changes in motivation, knowledge, attitudes, skills, awareness, opinion, and aspirations.

Medium-term outcomes are actions that result from learning provided by the program or project. Medium-term outcomes are measured through changes in social action, policies, behavior, and decision making.

Long-term outcomes or impact refers to conditions that change as a result of action produced by a program or project. Impact is measured through changes in health, education, economic, civic, and environmental conditions of a community or society.

EXTERNAL FACTORS

The external factors refer to the conditions related to the external environment of a program, which can affect input, output, and outcomes.

Evaluation: Refers to the collection of data on input and output to assess whether the program delivered the anticipated outcomes.

BENEFITS OF THE LOGIC MODEL

The logic model provides a common framework for better program planning and management and better understanding among program stakeholders. The inputs, outputs, and outcomes can be visualized in a graphic that clarifies differences between outputs and outcomes. The clarification provided by the logic model helps ensure consistency and coherence in a program. The logic model contributes to the creation of a sense of purpose. The existence of a logic model enables an organization to prioritize, make appropriate resource allocations, and identify key variables to measure.

PROGRAM EVALUATION

Simply put, program evaluation consists of use of social research methods and procedures to collect data and analyze the effectiveness of programs run by an organization (Box 19.1). Program evaluation is useful when examining the worth of specific programs and suggests recommendations to decision makers. Program evaluation can be conducted to assess the needs of a program, the adequacy of program design, the implementation of activity or service delivery, the outcomes, or the efficiency of the overall program or project.

Types of Program Evaluation

Program evaluation can be a needs assessment, a formative or process evaluation, a summative or outcomes evaluation, or an impact evaluation.

Needs assessment: Program evaluation can be conducted to assess a need and provide a community foundation to a future program or project. This form of evaluation occurs before starting a new program and is called a needs assessment. Needs assessments are conducted to answer questions, such as:

BOX 19.1 ABOUT THE RESEARCH PROCESS

WHAT IS SCIENTIFIC RESEARCH?

Scientific research is a systematic process of investigation about a natural or a social phenomenon or problem in order to find an explanation or a solution.

OBSERVATION

A problem is observed or identified.
   Example: "Many women are paid less than men for the same position, qualifications, and types of work."

VARIABLE

A property of people or objects that takes on two or more values.
   Must include categories that are both exhaustive and mutually exclusive. *Example: Age or income (can take values such as 1, 2, 3, 4, 5, 6, 7, etc.).*

HYPOTHESIS OR RESEARCH QUESTION

Research Question

■ A research question is a question about the relationship between at least two variables.
■ *Example: Is there a correlation between student employment status and academic performance?*

Hypothesis

■ A hypothesis is a tentative answer to a research question that must be empirically verified.
■ *Example: Students who are employed part-time have higher grade point averages (GPAs) than students who are employed full time.*
■ *Note: This suggests a relationship between employment status and academic performance (GPA).*

VERIFICATION OR EXPERIMENTATION

Data Collection

Population: The population is the total set of individuals, objects, groups, or events in which the researcher is interested.
Sample: A sample is a relatively small subset selected from a population.

(continued)

BOX 19.1 ABOUT THE RESEARCH PROCESS   (*continued*)

Data Analysis

■ Descriptive statistics: Procedures that help us organize and describe data collected from either a sample or a population.

Example: Total participants = 25; men = 12; women = 13

■ Inferential statistics: The logic and procedures concerned with making predictions or inferences about a population from observations and analyses of a sample.

Example: There is a positive correlation between academic performance and the employment status of a student. Students who work part-time have higher GPAs than students who work full-time.

Generalization

■ Predictions or inferences about a population from observations and analyses of a sample.

Example: There is a positive correlation between academic performance and the employment status of a student. Students who work part time have a higher GPA than students who work full time.

Research Process

■ Step 1: Problem statement
■ Step 2: Research plan
■ Step 3: Data collection
■ Step 4: Data analysis
■ Step 5: Presentation of findings

■ What are the characteristics, needs, and priorities of the target population?
■ What are potential barriers/facilitators?
■ What is the most appropriate response?

Formative or process evaluation: Formative or process evaluation aims to measure the outputs of a project and ensure that it is on track to meeting its goals. Formative evaluation assesses whether activities are being completed as planned and scheduled. It is designed to answer key questions, such as:

■ Who are the beneficiaries or clients?
■ What activities or services are provided to them?
■ Where are the services being provided?
■ When and how long will the services be provided?

Summative or outcome evaluation: As the name suggests, summative evaluation aims to measure the short-term and medium-term outcomes of a project. Summative or outcomes evaluation assesses whether a project changes a problematic situation into a new desired situation. Summative or outcomes evaluation helps answer questions like:

■ To what extent did the program produce the intended results or outcomes?
■ How effective was the program?
■ Did the program achieve its goals?
■ What was the level of quality of the services provided?

Impact evaluation: Impact evaluation is designed to measure the long-term outcomes or the impact of the program on the target population. Impact evaluation will attempt to answer questions such as:

■ To what extent can changes be attributed to the program?
■ What are the net effects?
■ What are final consequences?
■ Is the program worth the resources it costs?

Planning Program Evaluation

A program evaluation starts with a proposal, which describes the program to be evaluated, the purpose and scope of the evaluation, the questions that will guide the investigation, the research design, the instruments of data collection, the data-analysis procedures, an evaluation management plan, and a budget.

Description of the Program

A program evaluation plan must describe with as much detail as possible the program to be evaluated. The description introduces the justification that was set to start the program; the goals and objectives of the program; the activities and strategies used by the program; the target population; and the anticipated short-, medium-, and long-term outcomes of the program.

Purpose and Scope

The program's purpose and scope explain the justification for a program evaluation and what facets of the program will be concerned with the evaluation (Box 19.2). For example, the purpose and scope should answer questions such as

■ Will the evaluation assist in future program planning and provide information to stakeholders?
■ Will it judge the overall value, worth, and merit of the program for participants?
■ Will it determine whether program goals or objectives are being met, and to what extent, for the stakeholders?
■ Will it support, reinforce, and enhance the attainment of desired program outcomes?

BOX 19.2 SAMPLE PURPOSE AND SCOPE PARAGRAPH

The purpose of the evaluation is to support, reinforce, and enhance the attainment of the outcomes of the Parent-Connections program. Also, the evaluation aims to engage the key partners of the program in holistic thinking about best practices that can further help fulfill the vision to foster a safe, caring, and nurturing environment for children in our communities.

Evaluation Questions

The evaluation questions are the main questions that will guide the overall evaluation endeavor. What are the issues to be addressed by the evaluation? What are the specific questions to be answered by the evaluation? The evaluation question should be related to the main goals (for a large program) or the goals and objectives of the program (for a small program). The evaluation questions should not be confused with the survey questions. The survey questions are specific questions to ask individual interviewees. The evaluation questions are the broad questions about the overall purpose or worth of the program that the process of evaluation is trying to answer. A survey question is answered during an interview or once an interviewee has answered a question. An evaluation question can be answered only after the evaluation process has been completed. One effective way to ask good evaluation questions is to reformulate the goals of the program in the form of questions. For example, if the goal of a program is to "increase the academic performance of participating children," the evaluation question can be "To what extent has the program contributed to improving the academic performance of participating children?" Understand that the evaluation question focuses on assessing or measuring whether the program achieved its goal. See Box 19.3 for sample evaluation questions.

Research Design

The research design describes the form of the data in which the evaluation will be collected and the general plan of data collection and analysis. The form of data can be qualitative (interview, focus groups, program records) or quantitative methods (sampling) of data collection. The design for data collection and analysis can use one of the four common types of designs:

BOX 19.3 SAMPLE EVALUATION QUESTIONS

- To what extent did the Oshkosh Community Foundation after-school program contribute to increasing the academic performance of the participating children?
- What are the impacts of the program on the integration of the refugee families into the Appleton community?

1. *Exploratory*: Usually conducted in the beginning of a program to identify best approaches to service delivery and appropriate outcomes to measure. Exploratory design tends to a focus on situation and priorities.
2. *Descriptive*: Usually a formative evaluation used to assess whether a program is being implemented as planned. A descriptive design provides feedback that can help improve a program. A descriptive design focuses on input and output.
3. *Experimental and quasiexperimental*: Aims to find evidence of a causal or correlational relationship between the outputs and the outcomes of a program. An experimental or quasi experimental design focuses on outcomes.
4. *Mixed*: A combination of the above-mentioned designs. A mixed approach may focus on a combination of input, output, and outcomes.

See Box 19.4 for a sample research design paragraph.

Instruments of Data Collection

The evaluation plan should specify what instruments of data collection (e.g., question-naire, interview guide, program records) will be used in conducting the evaluation, as well as the type of information (activity indicator) that the instruments will help collect (Box 19.5). Instruments of data collection can be secondary data (e.g., program reports) and program records, interview questionnaires, standardized tests, a focus group guide, observation guide, photography, and other.

BOX 19.4 SAMPLE RESEARCH DESIGN PARAGRAPH

The evaluation will combine qualitative and quantitative methods of data collection and analysis, including teacher and staff interviews, student pre tests/post-tests, and parent surveys, in order to assess the perceptions of participants about the programs, the benefits for the target population, and the attainment of short-term and mid term outcomes described in the program proposal.

BOX 19.5 SAMPLE INSTRUMENTS OF DATA COLLECTION

Data will be collected through:

- An English proficiency test to assess the participant's progress in learning basic English.
- A participant satisfaction questionnaire to assess the perception of the participants about their experience in the program.
- Use of level-of-functioning scales before, during, and after each client is involved in the program.

BOX 19.6 SAMPLE PARAGRAPH OF DATA ANALYSIS

Descriptive statistics and paired sample t-tests for pre- and post-test variables will indicate the level of change in students' science knowledge due to program participation. The program coordinator will be comparing data from 2012–2013 with information collected in 2011–2012 to explore whether the program has improved.

Data Analysis

Data analysis explains how the data will be analyzed and the criteria that will be used to perform the analysis. For example, do you plan to analyze the outputs, the outcomes, or both? Will you use statistical analysis? See Box 19.6 for a sample paragraph of data analysis.

Evaluation Management Plan

The evaluation management plan provides an overall plan for conducting the evaluation (Box 19.7). It describes a work plan detailing the evaluation questions, the indicators, and the data-collection procedures used (source, method, sample, timing, and the person responsible).

Program Evaluation Report

A program evaluation report is a document that summarizes the findings from a program evaluation (Box 19.8). An evaluation report includes most of the items included in an evaluation plan, plus the plan's findings and recommendations. It is important to underline that the evaluation plan describes what will be done during the evaluation process (future). The evaluation report describes what was done (past).

BOX 19.7 TEMPLATE FOR AN EVALUATION MANAGEMENT PLAN

		Data Collection				
Questions	Indicators	Sources	Methods	Sample	Timing	Person Responsible
What was the level of satisfaction of the participants?	Percentage of participants who were satisfied?	Question-naire	Survey/ interview	100% of participants	At the end of the last training session	External evaluator

---

BOX 19.8 SAMPLE EVALUATION REPORT OUTLINE

- Executive summary
- Program description
- Evaluation methodology
- Findings
- Interpretation and reflection
- Recommendations

PROGRAM EVALUATION AND PERFORMANCE MEASUREMENT

Program evaluation includes performance measurement to assess overall organizational effectiveness. The term "organizational effectiveness" refers to the extent to which an organization achieves its vision and mission. In the for-profit sector, effectiveness is mainly measured in terms of profit. In nonprofit organizations, effectiveness cannot be measured exclusively in financial terms, because the raison d'être of nonprofit organizations resides in the achievement of their social purpose (vision, mission). Inputs, outputs, and outcomes are examples of indicators that are used for performance measurement in nonprofit organizations.

Performance Measurement

Performance measurement refers to the ongoing collection and reporting of data regarding the efficiency, quality, and effectiveness of programs, projects, and activities of an organization in the context of its vision and mission statements. As a process of regular data collection and reporting, performance measurement provides nonprofit organizations with unique opportunities to monitor progress and take corrective actions when necessary.

Efficiency: Efficiency assesses the relationship between the outputs of a program and the inputs used to produce them. Efficiency measures whether a program makes the best use possible of its resources. In other words, efficiency measures the level of productivity or the best value of a program. Efficiency is measured through (a) a ratio of inputs divided by outputs (e.g., cost per unit of services; dollars spent per client) or (b) a ratio of outputs divided by inputs (e.g., average case load per case manager; number of clients served per $100).

Quality: Quality measures the extent to which the outputs of a program meet a level or standard. Quality is always viewed in comparison to other similar programs and is based on criteria that are conventionally accepted. The quality of a program is measured through the number or proportion of outputs that meet or exceed a standard related to the implementation or operation of such a program (e.g., percentage of requests or applications processed within a standard timeline of 30 days; percentage of clients who completed treatment according to program guidelines).

Effectiveness: Effectiveness measures the extent of achievement of the organizational mission through program outcomes. Effectiveness is about whether a program has produced the best result possible. Effectiveness is measured through the ratio of outcomes to inputs (e.g., cost per client for job placement; total staff hours per ex-offenders transitioned to normal life in the community).

PROGRAM EVALUATION AND FINANCIAL SUSTAINABILITY

Program evaluation is conducted to measure the performance of an organization on various factors related to its mission, goals, and objectives. Program evaluation concerns input, output, and outcomes. The input includes the financial resources used to implement a program or project. Performance indicators from program evaluation are an integral part of effective strategic planning and financial decisions of nonprofit organizations. Therefore, program evaluation is directly related to decisions that will influence the financial sustainability of an organization.

Program evaluation confirms whether the programs of an organization are efficient and effective or not. Findings from program evaluations are used in strategic planning and in budgetary decisions. Analysis of findings from program evaluation reveals the performance of specific programs and helps make evidence-based financial allocation decisions to either continue or discontinue a program. For example, if an underperforming project or a program run by a nonprofit organization no longer helps satisfy a critical need and is not included in a key programmatic area, there is no justification for allocating resources to it. However, such decisions must be based not on assumptions or anecdotes, but on objective performance data obtained from program evaluation reports.

Program evaluation provides information that can help strengthen the commitment of board members and staff, and the support of external stakeholders, such as donors, public officials, and community members. Commitment of internal stakeholders and support of external stakeholders can serve as positive seeds for the financial sustainability of a nonprofit organization.

QUESTIONS AND ACTIVITIES

1. What is program evaluation?
2. What is a logic model?
3. What are the benefits of program evaluation for a nonprofit organization?
4. What are the types of program evaluation that you are aware of?
5. What are the key items to consider when planning a program evaluation?
6. What is performance measurement?
7. What are some key performance measures?
8. What is the relationship between program evaluation and financial sustainability?

CASE STUDY: HOPE

Significant numbers of Hispanic children under age 3, in Hillsborough County, have shown developmental delays (Fox, Dunlap, & Powell, 2002). This is often related to minority language status and low maternal education, as explained by Zill and West (2000). A recent needs assessment revealed that many children in the Hispanic community are at risk of abuse and neglect. Their parents are not willing to participate in prevention programs that involve the state for a variety of reasons, including their nondocumented immigration status, the fear that the state will take away their kids, their language barriers, and their national cultural backgrounds. They prefer interacting with people who speak their language and

(continued)

CASE STUDY: HOPE (continued)

know their culture. However, when their kids are involved in declared abuse and neglect, the county necessarily endorses the related costs. As a matter of fact, a recent study concluded that child abuse costs the United States about $94 billion annually (Prevent Child Abuse America, 2001). The same study explains that for every dollar spent on child-abuse prevention, at least $2 are saved that might have been spent on other child-welfare services (From, 2001). It is worth it to invest in prevention of child abuse, especially because of other costs, such as academic underachievement, violence, substance abuse, low productivity as adults, teen pregnancy, juvenile delinquency, and adult criminality, which every society must address by any reasonable means.

The program is intended to strengthen families and communities with a better learning and development environment. More specifically, the PECA (parent early child awareness) will help:

■ Increase parental skills and understanding of early child development
■ Improve a child's behavioral, emotional, and social development
■ Promote positive parent and child interaction
■ Encourage appropriate use of the health care system and medical resources available to families
■ Improve the safety of the home environment of the participants
■ Reduce chances for child abuse and neglect

The program targeted 200 low-income parents in Tampa, Florida, with children ages birth to 10 years old. Because we will have at least one child per parent, the program will have at least 400 direct beneficiaries (parents and children). The HOPE will hire a well-qualified project director with at least a bachelor's degree in behavioral sciences, an office assistant, and two outreach workers with credentials in early childhood education. The project director will provide ongoing support and training for outreach workers assigned to the program.

Questions

Draft a program evaluation plan by answering the following questions:

1. What is the purpose of this evaluation?
2. What are the questions that the evaluation will help answer?
3. Describe how you plan to collect data to answer the questions.
4. What instrument (s) will you use to collect the data? Explain.
5. How do you plan to analyze the data?
6. Prepare a work plan detailing the questions that you want to answer, the indicators, and the data-collection procedures (source, method, sample, timing, and the person responsible) used.

REFERENCES

Fox, L., Dunlap, G., & Powell, D. (2002). Young children with challenging behavior: Issues and consideration for behavior support. *Journal of Positive Behavior Interventions, 4*, 208–217.

Prevent Child Abuse America. (2001). *Total estimated cost of child abuse and neglect in the United States: Statistical evidence*. Chicago, IL: Prevent Child Abuse America.

Royse, D., Thyer, B. A., Padgett, D. K., & Logan, T. K. (2006). *Program evaluation: An introduction*. Belmont, CA: Wadsworth Publishing.

Yuen, F. K. O., Terao, K. L., & Scmidt, A. M. (2009). *Effective grant writing and program evaluation for human service professionals*. Hoboken, NJ: Wiley.

Zill, N., & West, J. (2000). *Entering kindergarten: A portrait of American children when they begin school. Findings from the condition of education, 2000* (ERIC Document Reproduction Service No. ED448899).

Community Relations and Financial Sustainability

OBJECTIVES

At the completion of this chapter, the reader will be able to:

1. Define the terms "community relations," "outreach," "partnership," "advocacy," and "public relations" in relationship to nonprofit organizations.
2. Describe the different facets of community relations.
3. Discuss community outreach, partnership, advocacy, and public relations as facets of community relations.
4. Explain the relationship between community relations and financial sustainability.

This chapter introduces the institutions and processes that constitute the external environment of nonprofit organizations. The chapter examines the role of community-relations approaches, such as partnership, advocacy, outreach, and public relations, in the financial sustainability of a nonprofit organization.

DEFINE "COMMUNITY RELATIONS"

Community relations combine an organization policy and process used to develop and implement community outreach and awareness about programs and activities in order to promote the organizational vision and mission in a community-oriented manner. As a policy, community-relations programs and activities are intentional. Such programs and activities are part of a strategic intent to promote a positive image of an organization. Community relations involve a process. As such, all internal stakeholders are an integral part either through a strategic decision, the planning, implementation, or assessment of the possible outcomes of community outreach and awareness activities.

Community relations are an expression of how an organization translates its social responsibility. It shows an understanding that an organization is part of a larger environment, which can be a local community or a larger society. In that context, the practice of engaging in community relations by an organization sends a message that the organization values the surrounding community. Individuals and institutions tend to react positively to such signals.

FIGURE 20.1   Facets of community relations.

Community relations involve various outreach, partnership or collaboration, advocacy, and public relations activities with internal and/or external stakeholders in order to further the vision and mission of an organization. Community relations involve four pillars that are not mutually exclusive, and that are based on the organizational culture, the community context, and the challenges faced. As Figure 20.1 illustrates, community relations include various activities related to public relations, advocacy, partnership, and outreach events.

OUTREACH

Simply put, the word "outreach" means reaching people from the outside to bring them inside. In other words, outreach implies a process from the inside to the outside in order to foster a reciprocal process from the outside to the inside. The assumption is that people in a given community, which constitutes outsiders in regard to what is happening in a group, do not necessarily understand what is going on inside an organization. Therefore, they may ignore, despise, resist, or fight what is coming from inside of such a group, organization, or institution. What is going on from the inside can be a vision, a mission, or a purpose that is potentially beneficial to the larger community. However, they may not grant their appreciation or support. It is the responsibility of the insider to inform, educate, increase awareness, and convince the outsiders about the nobility of a particular purpose. Outreach has several basic implications.

■ An acknowledgment that a certain purpose, vision, or mission exists within an organization
■ An authentic confirmation of such purpose from the insider as an authorized source
■ A recognition and validation that the insider counts for the outsider in its purpose
■ A request for some form of collaboration in the context of a clear purpose

Outreach can be initiated to implement actual delivery of services; educate or inform the target population, increasing their knowledge and/or skills; help expand access to services, practices, or products; educate or inform people who interact with the target population or establish beneficial connections between people and/or organizations. Outreach contributes to increase the willingness of a community to collaborate with a nonprofit organization, use services that are available, and contribute monetary and nonmonetary support to the activities offered by the organization. The reason is because outreach serves as evidence that an organization commits to meeting the target population on the population's turf. When an organization leaves its comfort zone and goes to meet people where they are, it makes it more difficult for them to turn down an offer of services or a request for collaboration or support. Outreach involves one-on-one interactions that enable better understanding of the wants, needs, experiences, and perceptions of the target population. Sometimes, outreach is even a must for healthy community relations if an organization wants to help a target community overcome barriers, such as lack of transportation, disabilities, marginalization, or cultural beliefs that deter them from using readily available community services. Outreach can be used to reach target populations through people who influence their decision-making process or change in their behavior. For example, an organization may reach out to religious leaders and in turn access their members. Similarly, an organization may develop outreach with the school principals and the teachers in order to reach out to their students. Outreach can be done indirectly through an organization's printed materials, social media (e.g., Facebook, Twitter, or Myspace). Organizations can organize educational events, such as fairs, workshops, seminars, conferences, retreats, open forums, or other similar events, to reach people in their target communities. It is easier for people to form their own opinions about an organization when they have direct experience or they benefit directly from such an organization. A nonprofit organization may be suffering from the bad reputation of another nonprofit agency. Community outreach that provides people opportunities to experience your organization, ask questions, and observe without filters may be very effective at gathering support for programs and activities. Support to programs and activities may seem obvious for a nonprofit organization that is attempting to meet the needs of a target community. However, it is not always automatic. Sometimes, the bad reputation of a program may reach the target population before your information gets there. This will negatively affect their willingness to collaborate even if they need the service that is offered. Other times, the target population may not collaborate because people do not know what is available or whether their support is necessary. Outreach can help address such challenges. At the end of the day, if an organization offers services that are needed and the community does not use such services, the organization will not be sustainable. Donors and the community at large might start questioning the relevance of such an organization. As ironic as that may sound, it is possible. An organization cannot be financially sustainable without the collaboration that community outreach can provide.

Planning Outreach

In other to be effective, community outreach efforts must be systematically planned. A community outreach plan should take into account items such as:

- *Purpose, goals, and objectives*: What do you want to accomplish through your outreach initiatives? What are the goals? What are the objectives?
- *Human resources*: What staff will be sent to meet the target population? What skills and competence do you want them to have (e.g., communication, interpersonal)? What type

of cross-cultural competence is necessary? Do you have a curriculum to ensure that your staff meets the prerequisites before they start to engage the target community? How will you monitor your staff to ensure that problems or issues that may emerge during contacts with the community can be addressed in an effective manner?

■ *Location*: Where will your outreach activities take place? Will it be in your own facility? Will it be in community settings, such as churches, mosques, synagogues, temples, schools, clinics, public markets, or community centers? Will you need to rent facilities? How accessible will any facility be that is used for an outreach event with respect to transportation and people with disabilities?

■ *Assets*: What are the community assets (e.g., individual, associational, institutional, environmental) that you can use for your outreach activities? What is your plan to benefit from such assets?

■ *Action plan*: What is your implementation plan? Who will do what (activity and person responsible)? When will it be done (timeline)? What outcome will document that a specific outreach activity was completed? What messages will be communicated to the target groups? How will you customize the message for each specific group, based on their cultural backgrounds and experiences?

■ *Continuing evaluation*: Outreach is a continuing effort and must be evaluated continuously.

■ *Budget*: What are the expenses related to your activities? How will you measure the return on investment of your outreach initiatives?

Benefits of Outreach

In order for nonprofits to stay around, they need to inform the community about what they have to offer. Nonprofits must use their core values to define their mission, their work, their professionalism, and their success so that people know what the organization is all about. Nonprofits also need a good mission statement that informs everyone about their priorities. They also need to be effective at delivering services to clients and keep the staff up to date with changes that occur in the field.

Outreach can involve clients, allies, funders, volunteers, public officials, and the general public. Outreach to clients may secure their participation in using an organization's resources and services. Outreach to allies may generate support for the overall purpose and activities of an organization. Outreach to funders may generate financial support. Outreach to volunteers may bring to an organization the generous skills and talents of community members. Outreach to public officials may gather legal and official legitimacy for the purposes of the organization. Outreach to the general public may secure public support for an organization and its activities.

PARTNERSHIPS

Partnership is a form of collaboration whereby two or more partners discuss and agree on a formal or informal term of reference in order to implement an activity or project for a common purpose. Many businesses develop partnerships because they want to be seen as good citizens in the community and nonprofits show them how to do it. A common example is a nonprofit organization asking restaurants to donate a percentage of their net returns on a special day to the nonprofit. In return the nonprofit will advertise this event and tell their clients and friends to go to the restaurant that day. A partnership can be tactical or strategic.

Tactical partnership: Tactical partnerships occur on a specific project or activity in order to respond to a conjectural challenge.

Strategic partnership: Strategic partnership is an intentional collaboration intended to achieve long-term goals and large-scope activities. A partnership can take the form of *cooperation* (i.e., short-term informal relationships that exist without a clear purpose or structure), *coordination* (i.e., longer term formal agreement for a specific project or program), *collaboration* (i.e., formal agreement to achieve a common goal within the context of shared funding), *strategic alliance* (i.e., contractual agreement between or among nonprofit organizations for mutual supports), and *merger* (i.e., formal partnership that transforms two or more nonprofit corporations into a new entity). Partnership among nonprofit organizations to implement projects and programs is required as a condition for funding by some grant-maker agencies and is strongly recommended by others. However, collaboration between nonprofit organizations does not happen naturally, unless there is a common interest to either tackle a challenging issue that unites one or more entity or funding that provides an opportunity to benefit from shared resources. There is no denial that organizational partnership can positively affect the quality and efficiency of partners involved in a formal collaboration. On the other hand, collaboration can fail and negatively affect the partners involved if the partnership was not based on a shared purpose and did not include adequate resources and guidelines for making shared decisions and addressing conflicts.

Planning Partnership

Effective partnership must be intentional. In other words, it must be planned and involve key stakeholders of a nonprofit organization. The process of developing a partnership should consider the following items:

Purpose: What is the purpose of the partnership? What is the common vision that will be pursued?

Fitness: How does the purpose of the partnership fit with your vision and mission statements? How do you document such fitness? Is there an agreement among the majority of members that the proposed partnership passed a fitness test?

Mandate: Is the proposal for partnership approved by the board of directors? Is there a partnership policy developed and adopted by the board to monitor fitness, adequacy, and progress of organizational partnership?

Risks and benefits analysis: Was there an analysis of the risks and benefits of the proposed partnership? Was there evidence that the benefits outweighed the risks of being involved in such partnership?

Mechanics: How will the partnership be structured? What will be the decision-making process? Where will the resources come from? How will the resources be shared? What will be the rights and responsibilities of each partner? How will disagreements and conflicts be managed?

Financial sustainability: What will be the total cost for the proposed partnership? What will be the expenses? What will be the financial return from the partnership? Will there be a net financial return from the partnership?

Agreement: What is the process of developing the partnership agreement? Who will be involved in drafting the partnership agreement? What will be the documentation requirements?

Approval: What will constitute a legitimate approval of the partnership agreement? When will the partnership be effective?

Implementation: How will the partnership agreement be implemented? Who will be accountable for specific activities? What will be the process of data sharing? What is the calendar of implementation? What are the deliverables at each stage of the implementation process? Who will be responsible to report the deliverable for each partner involved? What are the benchmarks and outcomes?

Oversight: Who will oversee the development of the partnership? Will the board create a special committee? What information will be collected to monitor and evaluate the benefits and liabilities of the partnership? What will be the reporting requirements and the frequency of reports?

Box 20.1 contains a sample partnership agreement.

ADVOCACY

The French philosopher of the Enlightenment, Jean-Jacques Rousseau, wrote in *The Social Contract*, "The problem is to find a form of association which will defend and protect with the whole common force the person and goods of each associate, and in which each, while uniting himself with all, may still obey himself alone, and remain as free as before" (Rousseau, 2014, para 1). This statement about the principles of a democratic society by the people and for the people is closely related to the Elizabethan Poor Laws of 1601, revised in 1834, in England. These Elizabethan Poor Laws, which planted the foundation of the social welfare system and the emergence of social work, constituted by the same account an appeal to advocate for the powerless and the disadvantaged. Yet the term "advocate" has a lexical sense that many people might agree on. However, the word "advocacy" as a social sciences concept may have a broader meaning than the simple lexical meaning.

Rektor (2002) defines advocacy as " the act of speaking or of disseminating information intended to influence individual behavior or opinion, corporate conduct, or public policy and law" (p. 12). In other words, the term "advocacy" implies the act and process of supporting, pleading, or defending a cause on behalf of oneself, someone else, or a group of people. Advocacy is not a single action. It is a continuum of activities. Advocacy implies research, public education, and increasing awareness on an issue.

According to Jansson (2003), "advocacy aims to eradicate or mitigate some of these factors in hopes of creating a more favorable environment for specific subgroups. It also aims to provide resources to assist professionals, agencies, community groups, and citizens to empower people and communities caught in structural discrimination to mobilize and use their strengths and assets" (p. 23).

Actually, personal advocacy occurs every time someone has to defend his or her interests or rights that are in jeopardy. Advocacy can be done in the form of negotiation, clarification, or a speaking out to make people hear your point. Professionally, advocacy implies using academic and professional approaches, tools, or resources to support, defend, or pledge a cause, an idea, or a principle. Advocacy includes activities with public policy implications that an organization strives to change for its target population and community.

ADVOCACY, LOBBYING, AND THE IRS

Nonprofits support changes in laws, policies, regulations, and appropriations in ways that will help their consumers and their programs. Nonprofits should not endorse candidates

BOX 20.1 SAMPLE PARTNERSHIP AGREEMENT

PARTNERSHIP AGREEMENT—MEMORANDUM OF UNDERSTANDING

CALIFORNIA COMMUNITY FOUNDATION AND OAKLAND COMMUNITY COALITION

This memorandum of understanding (MOU) describes the responsibilities and expectations between California Community Foundation (CCF) and Oakland Community Coalition (OCC) for the YOUTH EMPOWERMENT PARTNERSHIP (YEP). The purpose of this partnership is to build our capacity to address youth violence issues in our community. CCF is partnering with OCC to carry out the YEP program. The partnership contains three components: (1) community needs assessments; (2) training and technical assistance provided by CCF to OCC for the purpose of capacity building to meet the needs of youth who are at risk of being involved with gang activity, youth violence, and/or domestic abuse and neglect; and (3) financial assistance provided by CCF to OCC to implement capacity-building activities.

Responsibilities and Expectations

For the YEP program, CALIFORNIA COMMUNITY FOUNDATION serves as the "lead" organization. As the lead organization, California Community Foundation is responsible for the following:

- Ensuring that the program activities and finances of the partnership are in compliance with YEP requirements and federal regulations
- Providing direct technical assistance and training services to OCC by CCF staff professionals, as needed for OCC capacity building
- Providing "financial assistance" (YEP grant funds) to OCC, to be used by OCC to finance capacity-building activities
- At OCC's request, and with regard specifically to the "financial assistance," acting as fiscal agent for OCC for purposes of contracting technical assistance and training services or undertaking other procurement actions on behalf of OCC
- Serving as the coordinator for the multiple community assessments and evaluation activities for the partnership
- Reporting the results of the partnership activities and accomplishments

Under this Agreement, OAKLAND COMMUNITY COALITION agrees to:

- Actively participate in the community assessments and evaluations
- Complete an organizational self-assessment, with CCF support, to determine the priority capacity-building needs for OCC and its partners as they relate to youth at risk of becoming involved in gang activity, youth violence, and/or domestic abuse and neglect
- Develop a detailed capacity-building plan based on the organizational self-assessment, including timelines, budgets, sources of technical assistance and training, clearly defined anticipated outcomes, and specific indicators to measure results
- Arrange for and ensure participation in capacity-building activities by staff and board members of OCC and its partner organizations

(continued)

BOX 20.1 SAMPLE PARTNERSHIP AGREEMENT (*continued*)

■ Provide monthly reports to CCF on OCC capacity-building activities undertaken in pursuit of YEP program objectives, using the sample format in Attachment A

■ Comply with all local, state, or federal laws and regulations regarding the use of funds provided through the Partnership (per Attachment B)

■ Submit a final report at the end of the MOU period listing OCC's major accomplishments and outcomes attributable to the YEP program

Disbursement of Funds

For direct technical assistance and training services provided to OCC by CCF professional staff, CCF will cover all costs directly.

For "financial assistance" (YEP grant funds made available by CCF to OCC pursuant to the YEP program), funds will be administered in two ways:

a) Advance/liquidation of funds: When needed and requested by OCC, CCF will advance funds to OCC. OCC will submit to CCF a monthly advance liquidation invoice, including a description of expenditures incurred with detailed back-up and/or receipts. Additional advances will be made by CCF to OCC as needed, covering anticipated OCC requirements for the succeeding month.

b) Funds administered by CCF on OCC's behalf: At OCC's request, CCF will act as OCC's fiscal agent to administer the "financial assistance" funds. CCF will contract for technical assistance and training services, and undertake other procurements, per instructions from OCC. In these instances, CCF will be solely responsible for the accounting and administration of the relevant expenditures.

Time Period

This Agreement covers the first year of the YEP program, corresponding to the period from October 1, 2010, through September 30, 2013. If the YEP program is extended for a second and third year, as currently anticipated, the time period of the Agreement will be modified subject to amendments signed by the two parties.

Termination

CALIFORNIA COMMUNITY FOUNDATION may terminate this Agreement, in whole or in part, with or without cause, with a seven (7) day written notice of termination. Such notice shall be given in writing to OCC and shall be sent via certified or registered mail with return receipt requested.

Signatures of Authorized Representatives

> ### BOX 20.2 IRS, LOBBYING AND NONPROFITS
>
> In general, no organization may qualify for section 501(c)(3) status if a substantial part of its activities is attempting to influence legislation (commonly known as *lobbying*). A 501(c)(3) organization may engage in some lobbying, but too much lobbying activity risks loss of tax-exempt status.
>
> *Legislation* includes action by Congress, any state legislature, any local council, or similar governing body, with respect to acts, bills, resolutions, or similar items (such as legislative confirmation of appointive offices), or by the public in referendum, ballot initiative, constitutional amendment, or similar procedure. It does not include actions by executive, judicial, or administrative bodies.
>
> An organization will be regarded as attempting to influence legislation if it contacts, or urges the public to contact, members or employees of a legislative body for the purpose of proposing, supporting, or opposing legislation, or if the organization advocates the adoption or rejection of legislation.
>
> Organizations may, however, involve themselves in issues of public policy without the activity being considered lobbying. For example, organizations may conduct educational meetings, prepare and distribute educational materials, or otherwise consider public policy issues in an educational manner without jeopardizing their tax-exempt status.

Source: IRS (2013a).

for political offices. Some may wonder whether it is legal for nonprofit organizations to be involved in advocacy or lobbying. This is a legitimate concern that is fortunately addressed by the Internal Revenue Service (IRS), as described in Box 20.2.

As you may notice, nonprofit organizations can participate in lobbying activities by trying to influence legislators with the potential to affect their constituents positively or negatively. If legislators will the potential affect the constituents negatively, the organization will attempt to prevent passage of such legislation by lobbying their local, state or federal representatives. The opposite will be done if legislation may have a positive effect on the welfare of a nonprofit organization's constituents. The only thing that constitutes a red line is involvement in partisan politics. Lobbying for a public policy issue is different from advocacy for a political candidate or taking sides in electoral campaigns. The issue is not whether a nonprofit organization can lobby or advocate, but how much such activity represents the agenda of a nonprofit organization. There is no specification in terms of percentage, but the language says "too much lobbying activity risks loss of tax-exempt status." The right amount of lobbying activities done by a nonprofit organization is at the discretion of the IRS based on how much an organization spent on lobbying activities.

According to the IRS (2013a, para 1), "Organizations other than churches and private foundations may elect the expenditure test under section 501(h) as an alternative method for measuring lobbying activity." This election provides a nonprofit an opportunity to engage in lobbying activities for the equivalent of expenses that do not exceed $1,000,000, as indicated in Table 20.1. The IRS used what is called the expenditure test to make such determination. Expenditures information is found in the reporting of Form 990, which nonprofit organizations have to submit to the IRS. Table 20.1 provides specifics related to the expenditure test.

Under the 501(h) expenditure test, public charities may spend:

■ On direct lobbying:
  ● 20% of the first $500,000 of its exempt purpose expenditures
  ● 15% of the next $500,000, and so on, up to $1 million a year

TABLE 20.1 Expenditure Test Under 501(h)

If the Amount of Exempt Purpose Expenditures Is:	Lobbying Nontaxable Amount Is:
≤ $500,000	20% of the exempt purpose expenditures
>$500,00 but ≤ $1,000,000	$100,000 plus 15% of the excess of exempt-purpose expenditures over $500,000
> $1,000,000 but ≤ $1,500,000	$175,000 plus 10% of the excess of exempt purpose expenditures over $1,000,000
>$1,500,000	$225,000 plus 5% of the exempt purpose expenditures over $1,500,000

Source: IRS (2013b).

■ on grassroots lobbying:
- 5% of the first $500,000 of its exempt purpose expenditures
- 3.75% of the next $500,000, and so on, up to $250,000 a year

Direct lobbying refers to attempts to influence legislation by stating a position on specific legislation to legislators, government employees participating in the formulation of legislation, or urging members to advocate for a position on specific legislation. Grassroots lobbying is conducting lobbying on specific legislation before the general public and suggesting the organization's advocacy position to the general public. It is important to underline that the term "lobbying" does not include activities such as:

■ Providing examinations and discussions of broad, social, economic, and similar problems
■ Updating the members of your own organization on the status of legislation, without a call to action
■ Providing technical assistance or advice to a legislative body or committee in response to a written request, making available nonpartisan analysis, study, or research
■ Communicating with a legislative body regarding matters that might affect the existence of the organization, its powers and duties, its tax-exempt status, or the deduction of contributions to the organization

A nonprofit organization that elects for the expenditure test under section 501(h) must file Form 5768, Election/Revocation of Election by an Eligible IRC Section 501(c)(3) Organization to Make Expenditure to Influence Legislation. However, there is a risk that a nonprofit organization might lose its tax-exempt status if engaged in excessive lobbying activities over a period of 4 years.

PUBLIC RELATIONS

Public relations involve the communication of intentional messages to the public in order to influence the opinion or perception of an organization by the public at large. According to the Public Relations Society of America (PRA, 2012, para 1), "Public relations is a strategic communication process that builds mutually beneficial relationships between organizations and their publics." Coombs (2004) argues that public relations have a function to "manage the relationships between an organization and its stakeholders" (p. 106). For Botan and Taylor

(2004), the function of public relations is to build "relationships with publics that constrain or enhance the ability of the organization to meet its mission" (p. 654). Cheney and Christensen (2001) argue that public relations encompass:

■ *Organizational communication:* Communication in organizations and between organizations to further the organization's goals
■ *Rhetoric:* Study of audience adaptation, situation analysis, and message content in order to craft appropriate, effective messages
■ *Interpersonal communication:* Building and maintaining relationships between the organization and the public, and consequently emphasizing the importance of the making or breaking of those relationships
■ *Intercultural communication:* Study of how messages are crafted and interpreted in different cultures and, as a result, crafting messages that are appropriate for various cultural audiences

Public relations is a key communication practice for organizations, including nonprofit organizations. According to Gibson (1991), effective public relations imply that "organizational or individual needs are identified as informative, persuasive, or refutative, and when appropriate strategies and tactics are implemented based upon socially responsible, theory-based professional communication" (p. 177). Some of the common public relations communications include, but are not limited to press releases, media advisories, public service announcements, and press conferences, which are used as strategies to present information to the public, including constituents. Public relations may aim to persuade the public in order to change attitudes, beliefs, and behavior on a particular issue. Public relations can be in the form of refutation to mitigate the damage of a crisis or situation that can generate negative perception or a bad reputation about an organization or entity.

As previously indicated, nonprofit organizations are publicly supported entities. They have a responsibility of accountability, which is for organizations to use their resources as promised to the constituencies or donors (e.g., individuals, groups, institutions). One aspect of accountability is to build and maintain good relationships with constituents and the public. From a public relations perspective, maintaining good relationships with constituents and the public implies that people experience a positive image of a nonprofit organization. A positive image is more likely to generate monetary and nonmonetary support to further the mission of a nonprofit organization. Maintaining a positive image is a challenge for a nonprofit organization because people's perception and experiences can change rather quickly based on what Vasquez and Taylor (2001) call "situational perspective of publics." They argue that the public is not "a permanent collection of individuals with enduring characteristics; rather, it is viewed as a collection of individuals, identified by social-psychological variables, that emerges in response to a problem" (p. 144). The outcry when the Susan G. Komen Foundation decided to cut funding for Planned Parenthood illustrated how quickly public perceptions can change about an organization.

Some constituents are apathetic about what nonprofit organizations do. Others are concerned only about some facets of a nonprofit organization's activities. Some people are concerned about every aspect of the management and operation of a nonprofit organization.

Public relations can be used as a means to implement advocacy initiatives that aim to mobilize individuals, organizations, and the media to participate in support of matters of social or political importance. Public relations communications can help increase community awareness, build coalitions, and increase lobbying on an issue that is of interest to both a nonprofit organization's vision and the welfare of its constituents.

PLANNING PUBLIC RELATIONS PROGRAMS

Kelly (2001), Ledingham and Bruning (2001), Wilson (2001), and Woodward (2000), suggest the following in planning public relations programs or activities: research, planning, implementation, monitoring, evaluation, and stewardship.

Research

Research is the first phase of public relations planning, and aims to identify the needs of the community in the organization's area of expertise. At this phase, a SWOT (strengths, weaknesses, opportunities, and threats) analysis of an organization's environment is required. Ledingham and Bruning (2001) advise creating a list of all key constituencies, circulating the list throughout the organization to gain insight into the relationships between the organization and the key publics identified, and identifying the needs of the community. The research phase should target all internal (e.g., employees, board members, and volunteers) and external (e.g., donors, clients, government officials, and members of the media) stakeholders, and should help identify the relationships between the stakeholders and the organization.

Planning

Information gathered during the research process is used to further the second phase: planning. The planning phase will specify problems related to communication (e.g., image problems, lack of community or financial support, or crisis management). This makes it possible to define the audience, the communication effect, and the message. The planning will identify necessary funding expenses related to printing, mailing, and labor costs. A public relations budget should be cost-effective.

Implementation

The implementation aims to design activities related to the objectives stated in the planning phase. This is the phase during which a public relations campaign is being launched to raise awareness on key topics or issues of interest.

Monitoring

At the monitoring phase, organizations carefully observe and track behavioral, environmental, and attitudinal changes through surveys, questionnaires, or observation, to measure community response regarding the public relations plan. For example, nonprofit organizations may monitor whether there is correlation between the implementation of the public relations plan and increase in monetary and nonmonetary supports received from the overall community.

Evaluation

During the evaluation phase, organizations assess the effectiveness of a public relations plan. Evaluation can include facets of planning, process, and outcomes.

Stewardship

The last phase is stewardship, which is the opportunity for organizations to prepare the foundation for future interactions with stakeholders. As Kelly (2001) explains, steward-ship "not only ensures continuity in the public relations process but also promotes ethical behavior by practitioners and their organizations" (p. 283).

COMMUNITY RELATIONS AND FINANCIAL SUSTAINABILITY

Community relations programs aim to show how an organization practices its social responsibilities. These programs are targeted at the macro level, the community at large, and specific segments of it. The micro level is focused on the individual, client, or patron. These programs start with the organization's strategic plans and values. Program values guide the strategic planning, assist in recruiting, help with preparing grant proposals, and fund-raising. Community relations programs and activities should be based on mutual benefits, value and worth, long-term viability, and return on investment.

OUTREACH AND FINANCIAL SUSTAINABILITY

Outreach can be used to develop collaboration with intermediary entities that have influence over the decisions made by the target population. For example, an organization may lack direct access to high school students for a program about underage drinking. However, the organization can contact the entities working with high school students, such as school districts and high schools. Outreach can be done by sending representatives to meet and engage with school board members, school principals, and teachers. Outreach of that nature may not only provide direct access to the target population, but also generate additional monetary and non monetary resources for the organization. For example, the school board may provide financial support to a program that is in alignment with their core strategic goals. The school board may allow the organization to use their facilities and equipment to implement aspects of the program. This in turn will save the organization money that can be spent on other activities or put in a contingency fund.

PARTNERSHIP AND FINANCIAL SUSTAINABILITY

Grønbjerg and Curtis (2004) conducted a study on interorganizational relationships among nonprofit organizations and found that partnership contributed to the capacity-building of the organizations involved. The study found that partnership contributed to enhancing the visibility of partner organizations, helped them meet the needs of their members or clients, helped them to obtain funding, and helped them recruit and retain volunteers and board members. These factors are contributors to the financial sustainability of nonprofit organizations. They were fostered by interorganizational partnership. It is clear that partnership has the potential to contribute to the financial sustainability of nonprofit organizations.

PUBLIC RELATIONS AND FINANCIAL SUSTAINABILITY

Nonprofit organizations can experience crises that have the potential to damage their reputation and legitimacy, as well as their funding, and lead to their dissolution. According to Coombs (2004), crises can threaten or challenge organizational legitimacy; cause an organization to fail to meet the social norms and expectations of stakeholders; experience financial damage, injuries, loss of life, or reputational damage. The Association of Community Organization for Reform Now (ACORN) is a classic example of an organization that was destroyed by a crisis. The Susan G. Komen Foundation had seen its funding decrease quickly as a result of a crisis over allocating money to Planned Parenthood. Crises can negatively affect the relationship between an organization and its stakeholders in a manner that potentially threatens the relationships. As Fearn-Banks (2001) argued, a crisis may interrupt "normal business transactions and can, at its worst, threaten the existence of the organization" (p. 480). Public relations help identify crisis clusters and crisis management strategies (e.g., resolution) that can prevent a crisis from having devastating effects on the sustainability of an organization to continue to generate necessary financial and nonfinancial supports to further its vision and mission. For example, public relations can equip nonprofit organizations to use accommodative crisis management strategies, through which an organization "accepts responsibility, admits to the existence of problems, and takes actions to remedy a situation" (Marcus & Goodman, 1991, p. 286). This is in contrast to a defensive signal image that is fostered when an organization "insists that the problems do not exist, tries to alleviate doubts about the firm's ability to generate future revenue, and takes action to resume normal operations rapidly" (Marcus & Goodman, 1991, p. 286).

QUESTIONS AND ACTIVITIES

1. What does the term "community relations" mean?
2. What is a partnership in the context of nonprofit community relations?
3. How would you define "community outreach"?
4. What does the term "public relations" mean?
5. How do you think partnership, outreach, and public relations are effective community relations strategies for nonprofit organizations?
6. What is the relationship between community relations and the financial sustainability of a nonprofit organization?

CASE STUDY: JOSHUA COMMUNITY HOUSE

You have just been hired as Outreach Manager for Joshua Community House. Your organization provides foster care services. Your supervisor asks you to develop a network of collaboration among community partners in your area of intervention.

1. Make a list of organizations that you plan to contact for that collaboration and explain each choice.
2. Write a letter to invite them to a meeting to explore collaboration opportunities.
3. Write a proposal of the agenda to accompany the letter.
4. How do you plan to follow up on the letters?

CASE STUDY: NETWORKING ACTION PLAN

Consider that you are working for an organization in your community and are asked to develop a networking action plan. Write a networking action plan using the following template:

1. Name, mission, and goal of the organization
2. Objectives
3. Programs and/or services provided
4. Beneficiary population
5. Justification of the networking action plan
6. Collaboration framework

    6.1. Responsibilities of my organization
    6.2. Responsibilities of the partner agencies

7. Strategies to develop collaborations
8. Evaluation (How will you evaluate the effectiveness of the collaboration?)
9. What specific information will you collect in order to make that evaluation?

REFERENCES

Botan, C. H., & Taylor, M. (2004). Public relations: The state of the field. *Journal of Communication, 54(4)*, 645–661.

Cheney, G., & Christensen, L. T. (2001). Public relations as contested terrain: A critical response. In R. L. Heath (Ed.), *Handbook of public relations* (pp. 167–182). Thousand Oaks, CA: Sage.

Coombs, W. T. (2004). Impact of past crises on current crisis communication: Insights from situational crisis communication theory. *Journal of Business Communication, 41(3)*, 265–289.

Fearn-Banks, K. (2001). Crisis communication. In R. L. Heath (Ed.), *Handbook of public relations* (pp. 479–485). Thousand Oaks, CA: Sage.

Gibson, D. (1991). The communication continuum: A theory of public relations. *Public Relations Review, 17*, 175–183.

Grønbjerg, K. A., & Curtis, C. 2004. *Indiana nonprofits: Affiliation, collaborations and Competition.* Bloomington, IN: Indiana University School of Public and Environmental Affairs.

Internal Revenue Service. (2013a). *Lobbying*. Retrieved from http://www.irs.gov/Charities-&-Non-Profits/Lobbying

Internal Revenue Service. (2013b). *Measuring lobbying activity: Expenditure test*. Retrieved from http://www.irs.gov/Charities-&-Non-Profits/Measuring-Lobbying-Activity:-Expenditure-Test

Jansson, B. S. (2003). *Becoming an effective policy advocate: From policy practice to social justice*. Belmont, CA: Brooks/Cole.

Kelly, K. S. (2001). Stewardship: The fifth step in the public relations process. In R. L. Heath (Ed.), *Handbook of public relations* (pp. 279–290). Thousand Oaks, CA: Sage.

Ledingham, J. A., & Bruning, S. D. (2001). Managing community relationships to maximize mutual benefit: Doing well by doing good. In R. L. Heath (Ed.), *Handbook of public relations* (pp. 527–534). Thousand Oaks, CA: Sage.

Marcus, A. A., & Goodman, R. S. 1991. Victims and shareholders: The dilemmas of presenting corporate policy during a crisis. *Academy of Management Journal, 34*(2), 281–305.

Public Relations Society of America. (2012). *Public relations defined: A modern definition for the new era of public relations*. Retrieved from http://prdefinition.prsa.org/

Rektor, L. (2002). The sound of citizen's voices. In *Advocacy*. Ottawa, Canada: Advocacy Working Group.

Rousseau, J. J. (2014). *Social contract and discourses*. Retrieved from http://www.bartleby.com/168/106.html

Vasquez, G., & Taylor, M. (2001). Research perspectives on "the public." In R. L. Heath (Ed.), *Handbook of public relations* (pp. 139–154). Thousand Oaks, CA: Sage.

Wilson, L. J. (2001). Relationships within communities: Public relations in the new century. In R. L. Heath (Ed.), *Handbook of public relations* (pp. 521–526). Thousand Oaks, CA: Sage.

Woodward, W. D. (2000). Transactional philosophy as a basis for dialogue in public relations. *Journal of Public Relations Research, 12*, 255–275.

Information Technology and Financial Sustainability

OBJECTIVES

At the completion of this chapter, the reader will be able to:

1. Define "information technology."
2. Explain the purpose and benefits of information systems for nonprofit organizations.
3. Discuss the dimensions of information systems.
4. Discuss the most common types of information systems in organizations.
5. Discuss the relationship between information technology and the financial sustainability of nonprofit organizations.

This chapter emphasizes the role of information technology as support for financial sustainability in a nonprofit organization. The chapter introduces the reader to concepts related to technology and various aspects of management and financial management of a nonprofit organization. The reader will learn how to use computer and information technology to support a path toward financial sustainability.

INFORMATION TECHNOLOGY

Information technology refers to the means of access to information and related services that combine various support and devices, such as telephone, computer, software, and the Internet. In other words, information technology includes all computer-based information systems and related technology used by organizations in the operation of their programs, activities, or services.

INFORMATION SYSTEMS

When individuals make donations to a nonprofit organization during a fund-raising campaign, information about these donors is collected. Whether manually or online, information is processed in a form (e.g., name, address, telephone, e-mail, donation amount, and other information). Information is transferred to fund-raising or public relations staff who will either call, e-mail, or send a letter to thank donors. Information is also transferred to accounting staff who will record donations as a financial transaction and deposit them in either a restricted or unrestricted fund. Staff can go back to information collected to verify accuracy or make corrections of mistakes made when data was transferred. Information about donors can be classified and analyzed to make decisions about fund-raising planning and monitoring. Data can help monitor fund-raising practices and effectiveness, and assess which fund-raising strategies worked and which ones did not. The process that I just described is an information system. The term "information system" is used to designate the network, support, and devices that organizations develop and maintain to collect (or retrieve), process, store, and distribute data or information to support their decision-making and control processes. Information systems of organizations are usually managed by a chief information officer (CIO) or a chief technology officer (CTO) or a chief operating officer (COO) or someone with a dual role to carry the duties of a CIO (Box 21.1).

BOX 21.1 SAMPLE JOB DESCRIPTION FOR CHIEF INFORMATION OFFICER

- As the chief technology expert of the organization, guides senior management in understanding IT initiatives and represents the company's technology needs and interests at all levels.
- Is responsible for developing and maintaining the IT budget, assuring quality assurance, business continuity solutions, and managing all centralized and distributed technology, including voice and data communication.
- Offers solutions to enhance the organization and know when to be decisive on IT matters after fully considering input from stakeholders.
- Develops and executes the direction and delivery for the technology systems to maintain performance, stability, reliability, recoverability, and application execution.
- Stays abreast of emerging technologies and makes appropriate recommendations regarding their applicability and implementation.
- Drives the creation and implementation of an IT strategy (planning, performance management, IT effectiveness, benchmarking, operating model, etc).
- Develops, implements, and monitors IT policies and controls to ensure compliance with laws and regulations, data integrity, availability, security, and confidentiality, including systems documentation.
- Establishes policies, procedures, and practices to operate at full capability, while supporting continuous expansion and multisite facilities.
- Provides guidance to the organization's program staff on the technological aspects of implementing policy goals.
- Leads and manages the architecture, design, and implementation of the systems and network infrastructure to provide low-latency, high-performance solutions.
- Ensures timely and accurate technology budget analysis and financial review.
- Gains immediate credibility with senior leadership and the IT staff by listening, creating relationships, and developing IT plans that align with business goals.
- Delivers continuous improvement in the identification and resolution of problems.
- Develops escalation procedures to ensure reliable operations and response to incidents.
- Meets regularly with executive teams to ensure all aspects of technology operations advanced are clearly defined and executed in a continuous and timely fashion.
- Develops and maintains an appropriate IT organizational structure that supports the needs of the business.

The development of an information system starts with an investigation to understand problems and needs; analysis of options; selection of the options and design of the system; execution of the design plan; and the monitoring, assessment, review, and maintenance of the information system. Information systems are multifaceted because of the different specialty interests and functions that exist within the structures of an organization. Information needs exist at the strategic (executives, leaders), management (managers), and operational (staff) levels. Some organizations develop and maintain:

- *Executive information systems* to satisfy the needs of executives and leaders to address strategic issues and make long-term decisions
- *Management information systems (MIS)* to help managers to make planning, implementation, control, and performance measurement decisions
- *Transaction processing systems* used by operational staff for data inputs, processing, and transfer

As I indicated in previous contexts, an effective information system must meet at least five criteria:

1. *Accuracy*: There is an internal control and check of information as well as a uniform procedures manual, which enables the production of accurate information.
2. *Completeness*: Summarized information from the system provides pertinent data that can be considered complete enough to inspire decision making.
3. *Consistency*: The system provides reliable, consistent, and uniform information.
4. *Relevance*: Information obtained from the system is relevant, appropriate, and trustworthy.
5. *Timeliness*: The system must be able to receive, process, edit, summarize, and adjust information in a timely manner, according to the needs of the users of your business.

Benefits of Information Systems

As you may have noticed from the illustration on fund-raising, information systems matter to nonprofit organizations in almost the same way they do to for-profit businesses. Obviously, nonprofit organizations do not have the luxury of for-profit businesses to make large capital investments in information technology. However, even modest investment in information technology can be beneficial to nonprofit organizations, because information systems:

- Redefine the way business is being done in the world, including nonprofit organizations that have to compete for fewer financial resources with more nonprofit competitors;
- Help organizations achieve greater productivity, efficiency, and effectiveness, thus contributing to enhance their path toward financial sustainability;
- Provide strategic opportunities and competitiveness to organizations that differentiate themselves from competitors based on new options and services linked to the use of new technologies;
- Provide real economic value to the operations of an organization through cost reduction, increases in revenues, strategic positioning, and access to data and networking that help make better decisions to improve process.

Dimensions of Information Systems

An information system is articulated around technology, but is also linked to organization and management.

Technology: As previously indicated, technology is at the heart of an information system. Organizations use computer hardware (e.g., central processing units, storage devices, and physical media), computer software (e.g., operating system, application and enterprise software, and Internet platforms), storage technology (e.g., database management systems, data warehouse), and communication technology (e.g., network, Internet) to create information technology infrastructures (ITI) that help cope with change in their external environments. In that context, technology is at the core of an information system, because the information infrastructure serves as the foundation on which any specific information system can be built to serve particular needs of the organization. In other words, once an ITI is built, any unit in the organization can create a micro-information system that can inform data-driven decision making to improve processes, services, efficiency, or effectiveness.

Organization: An information system does not exist in a vacuum. It is part of an organizational structure that includes people, politics, culture, and process. Therefore, the creation of an information system must take into account the internal and external environments of an organization. An information system is not an end in itself. It is a system of support. Therefore, its development or transformation must be collaborative and integrative, and consider the overall mission or purpose of an organization. A well thought-out information system is an asset for any organization, including nonprofit organizations. A nonintegrative information system can turn into a disaster that costs an organization its existence. This applies also to nonprofit organizations. In other words, organization is an important dimension of information systems.

Management: The role of management is to support an organization in making decisions and developing action plans that can support strategic foci and help organizations overcome current and potential challenges. Part of management's responsibility is to initiate organizational change whenever it is necessary to further the interests or the mission of an organization. The development and maintenance of information systems is part of management's roles. Further, information systems are essential to helping managers gather data to make strategic and operational decisions. For example, the development of new products, programs, or services by an organization can be disruptive unless it has an information system that can not only inform the decision-making process, but also provide the flexibility to integrate new initiatives into the system without destroying existing assets. It is the role of management to facilitate changes and transitions in the information systems of an organization. Management has a key role to play in deciding which technology investments to pursue.

INFORMATION TECHNOLOGY AND NONPROFIT ORGANIZATIONS

As with other organizations in society, information technology has influenced the way in which such entities are led, managed, and administered. Video, audio, computer, photography, computer, Internet, software, open-source software, microblogging, wiki, telephone, mobile phone, and online social networking are examples of technological resources or support used by nonprofit organizations to support programs and activities that can further their vision and mission.

According to data publicized by Techimpact (2013), social media, especially social networks like Facebook, Myspace, Twitter, Webo, LinkedIn, and others, enable nonprofit organizations to design peer-to-peer campaigns that influence people to donate and volunteer their time to support their issue of interest. Additionally, nonprofit organizations use cloud computing to implement advocacy and fund-raising campaigns in a way that was not possible two decades ago. Techimpact (2013) reported that a large majority of nonprofit organizations worldwide use the cloud not just because it of its technology, but also and especially due to its cost-effectiveness.

Technology constitutes an asset for nonprofit organizations to disseminate information that helps people understand their relevance in their communities, and raise money to support their activities. Technology is involved in the strategic planning of nonprofit organizations either as support to conduct the process or as part of strategic programming areas. Technology is also involved in management, administration, fund-raising, and service delivery facets of nonprofit organizations.

INFORMATION TECHNOLOGY AND ASSET MAPPING

The geographic information system (GIS) is used by many nonprofit organizations to conduct asset mapping. The GIS is a "powerful set of tools for collecting, storing, retrieving at will, transforming and displaying spatial data from the real world" (Burrough, 1986, p .6). With GIS, assets in a community can be located based on their geographic boundaries, addresses, service locations, and surrounding residences and workplace facilities. It is basically like any traditional database program, except that it involves spatial data that can be translated into a map.

The GIS provides better visuals about the dispersion of the target population of a particular organization. GIS can be integrated into needs-assessment and asset-mapping activities to develop better tools for planning, community development, and fund-raising efforts. In fact, the ability of a nonprofit organization to address the needs of its target population resides in the capability of such an organization to capture needs, desires, and expectations that reflect the neighborhood trends where the target population resides. The GIS can organize information in layers, and create a more customized or targeted view from that. The organization of information on communities and target populations in a comprehensive manner can facilitate better decision making that can contribute to the overall sustainability, including financial sustainability, of a nonprofit organization.

INFORMATION TECHNOLOGY AND SERVICE DELIVERY

Information technology is an added value to services, including services that nonprofit organizations provide to children, families, and communities. According to recent information published by Pew Research Center (Duggan, & Smith, 2013), 91% of American adults have a cell phone, 55% have a Smartphone, 32% own an e-reader, and 42% own a tablet computer. This is not just the reality of the United States. For example, the Australian Bureau of Statistics (ABS) reported that 79% of Australians aged 15 or older have access to the Internet (ABS, 2013). Most people use their phone and/or computer as their primary means for communication or consumption of services. Special Effect (2013) is a charitable organization based in the United Kingdom. The organization is dedicated to using technology to enhance the quality of life of people with disabilities. Their programs help children and young people with disabilities access mainstream video games and leisure technology. They have occupational therapists who work with their clients in their facilities. If a client has a major disability that prevents travel, they reach out at home. This organization has clearly used technology not just as a support to service delivery, but as a service in itself.

With information and communication technology, services that some nonprofit organizations provide are becoming more accessible to clients. There have been initiatives to develop mobile phone applications to help individuals living alone at home, people with disabilities or living in rural or remote areas, and people at risk of violence or intimidation. For example, the National Network to End Domestic Violence maintains a 24/7 phone line, and the National Safe & Strategic Technology Project helps in prevention of domestic violence against women living with dangerous partners or in abusive relationships.

Technology provides flexibility that enables nonprofit organizations to reduce face-to-face time for some activities, and use their staff for more urgent needs to help clients who need special attention. This flexibility may help build better rapport with clients and increase their level of satisfaction with the assistance they receive. This has a cost-saving application for service delivery. With flexibility to help more clients at the same time, the cost of service delivery can be reduced considerably.

INFORMATION TECHNOLOGY AND HUMAN RESOURCES MANAGEMENT

Information and communication technology has been useful in all aspects of job analysis, recruitment, interviewing, hiring, orientation, staff training and talent developing, performance appraisal, and compensation and payroll, which are all related to human resource management and development. Technology has enabled organizations to create IT-based workplaces that foster talent development, which in turn contributes to the sustainability of an entity. With technology, organizations are able to design opportunities to attract more talented staff, motivating and retaining their existing staff, and strengthening staff commitment.

INFORMATION TECHNOLOGY AND FINANCIAL MANAGEMENT

Information technology may have provided more effective support to finances and financial management of organizations than any other factor one can imagine. Information technology enables financial managers to input financial data quickly and efficiently, perform statistical analyses that would otherwise require much time and manpower, develop financial reports in an expedited manner, and negotiate and make decisions on urgent financial matters.

With information technology, organizations can make electronic transfers of money, and secure transactions that can generate high rates of returns. This applies to both for-profit and nonprofit organizations. Technology provides convenience to the contributors of nonprofit organizations. For example, it is easier for some donors to make a contribution to an organization that offers them the opportunity to make secure transactions online as opposed to writing and mailing a check or making a cash donation. This does not mean that traditional ways of income generation do not matter because of technology. However, this means that people who like the convenience of using technology to make their contribution may be less inclined to do so if that opportunity does not exist with an organization, or they may contribute to a competitor. At the end of the day, whatever makes it more convenient for a donor to give, that's what an organization should do. The point is the convenience that technology provides to clients, contributors, or even the public can only strengthen financial management practices in nonprofit organizations.

INFORMATION TECHNOLOGY AND FUND-RAISING: DONOR MANAGEMENT SYSTEM

A donor management system (DMS) is an application, a group of applications, or a system that nonprofit organizations use to record, track, and report fund-raising activities. A DMS helps collect and generate information about types of donors, correspondence, relationships with constituents, gifts received, proposals submitted, grants awarded, pledges, volunteers, events, and other similar information that can be used for reporting and accountability (Leslie, Berry, Quinn, & Bernard, 2011). Nowadays, there are several DMSs that are available to nonprofit organizations to streamline their operations and improve their fund-raising performance (Blackbaud, 2013; Leslie, 2013). A DMS enables a nonprofit organization to maintain a centralized fund-raising operation and thus improves their ability to generate and share information that is critical to increasing fund-raising performance. In fact, more and more donors put greater pressure for accountability on organizations receiving their donations. Donors want to know the purpose of a request for a donation, how the money will be spent, and what the reporting will be on the use of donations. A DMS helps satisfy donor emphasis on performance and accountability (Saxton & Zhuang, 2013). A donor management system helps an organization gather information to justify its purpose to donors, its identity, its commitment to stewardship, and its level of accountability.

INFORMATION TECHNOLOGY AND FINANCIAL SUSTAINABILITY

Emerging technologies, such as neutral networks, geographic information systems groupware, and Internet applications, are vitally important for nonprofit organizations managers to catch up and keep up with IT. IT supports communication and collaboration, cornerstones of today's nonprofit organization environment. Technology integration provides a method for nonprofits to achieve better service delivery, fund-raising, outreach, and communication outcomes. Nonprofit organizations can use technology uptake to reduce the time it takes to complete services and the cost of conducting them. Technology provides opportunities to reach more clients, advocate for the creation of joint innovations, initiate collaboration with donors and the private sector, and strengthen the ability of an organization to continue to provide vital services over time.

Nonprofits can use information technology to engage in planning, budgeting, staffing, training, or collaborations for IT-related activities and materials. Nonprofit organizations can also use information technology as an asset for grant-seeking efforts and external and internal market research. However, small- and medium-size nonprofit organizations tend to have limited abilities or flexibility to invest in information technology, especially when dealing with restricted funds. One of the strategies that can be used is to (a) identify and use free or low-cost technology resources that are available to nonprofit organizations, and (b) seek technical-assistance and capacity-building grants that would enable them to improve information technology infrastructures and systems. It is always possible to convince donors or even some businesses how technology can best serve their purposes. It is up to nonprofit leaders to convince others to support IT investments for internal efficiency gains, better service delivery, and staff development.

QUESTIONS AND ACTIVITIES

1. What is information technology?
2. What is an information system?
3. What are the benefits of information systems for nonprofit organizations?
4. What are the dimensions of information systems?
5. What the relationships between
   a. information technology and asset mapping
   b. information technology and service delivery
   c. information technology and human resources management
   d. information technology and financial management
   e. information technology and fund-raising
6. What is the relationship between information technology and financial sustainability?

REFERENCES

Australia Bureau of Statistics. (2013). *How Australia accesses and uses the internet how Australia accesses and uses the internet.* Retrieved from http://www.abs.gov.au/ausstats/abs@.nsf/Lookup/by%20Subject/1301.0~2012~Main%20Features~How%20Australia%20accesses%20and%20uses%20the%20Internet~175

Blackbaud. (2013). *Raiser's edge fund-raising software.* Retrieved from https://www.blackbaud.com/fund-raising-crm/raisers-edge-donor-management

Burrough, P. A. (1986). *Principles of geographical information systems for land resources assessment.* Oxford, UK: Clarendon Press.

Duggan, M., & Smith, A. (2013). *Cell internet use in 2013.* Retrieved from http://www.pewinternet.org/2013/09/16/cell-internet-use-2013/

Leslie, J. (2013). *Trends in donor management.* Retrieved from http://www.idealware.org/articles/trends-donor-management

Leslie, J., Berry, A., Quinn, L. S., & Bernard, C. (2011). *Low cost donor management systems.* Retrieved from http://www.idealware.org/sites/idealware.org/files/IdealwareDonorMgmt2011.pdf

Saxton, G. D., & Zhuang, J. (2013). A game-theoretic model of disclosure-donation interactions in the market for charitable contributions. *Journal of Applied Communication Research, 41,* 40–63.

Special effect. (2013). *Special effect: The games charity.* Retrieved from http://www.specialeffect.org.uk/

Techimpact. (2013). *20 insightful nonprofit technology and social media.* Retrieved from http://blog.techimpact.org/20-insightful-nonprofit-technology-and-social-media-stats/#sthash.solmjghk.dpuf

Social Marketing and Financial Sustainability

At the completion of this chapter, the reader will be able to:

1. Define the concept of social marketing.
2. Identify some of the common areas for the use of social marketing by nonprofit organizations.
3. Describe the contents of a social marketing plan.
4. Establish the relationship between social marketing and financial sustainability.

This chapter is designed to provide an introduction of the principles and practices of social marketing and their applicability to nonprofit organizations. It emphasizes the need for strategic planning in the marketing, not only of products, but also of programs and services. It is intended to enable nonprofit managers to manage their social marketing efforts strategically.

DEFINE "SOCIAL MARKETING"

The term "social marketing" has been used for several decades to refer to a systematic process of using marketing strategy to influence current behaviors of a target population into a desired behavior in order to positively change a social or community issue. As the two words "social" and "marketing" imply, social marketing is modeled on commercial or business marketing principles and techniques used to induce changes in behavior that have the potential to contribute to the well-being of a target population. According to Weinreich (2011), social marketing uses marketing principles and techniques to influence a target population in the adoption of behaviors that can help improve health and community outcomes. As you may notice, this definition emphasizes health outcomes, because social marketing has been used considerably in public and community health. There are a variety of definitions for the concept of social marketing, as illustrated in Table 22.1. All of them have the commonality of being rooted in marketing principles and techniques.

TABLE 22.1 Sample Definitions of "Social Marketing"

Author (Date)	Definition
Andreasen (2006)	The application of commercial marketing technologies to the analysis, planning, execution, and evaluation of programs designed to influence voluntary behavior of target audiences in order to improve their personal welfare and that of society (p. 7).
Smith (2000)	Process for influencing human behavior on a large scale, using marketing principles for the purpose of societal benefit rather than commercial profit (p.12).
Donovan (2011)	Social marketing is the application of commercial marketing principles and tools where the primary goal is the public good (p. 9).
French (2011)	Social marketing is a set of evidence- and experience-based concepts and principles that provide a systematic approach to understanding behavior and modifying it for social good. It is not a science but rather a form of "technik" [sic]; a fusion of science, practical know-how, and reflective practice focusing on continuously improving the performance of programmmes aimed at producing net social good (p. 155).
Lefebvre (2011)	Social marketing is the application of marketing principles to shape markets that are more effective, efficient, sustainable, and just in advancing people's well-being and social welfare (p. 55).
McKenzie-Mohr (2011)	Social marketing is a process that involves (a) carefully selecting which behaviors and segments to target, (b) identifying the barriers and benefits to these behaviors, (c) developing and pilot testing strategies to address these barriers and benefits, and, finally, (d) broad scale implementation of successful programs (pp. 8–10).

ABOUT SOCIAL MARKETING

Social marketing dates back to the late 1950s and early 1960s with the emergence of the use of mass media in business as a strategy to use commercial marketing principles for social issues, and evolved to become more of a behavior-change approach during the 1990s (Andreasen, 2006). The term "social marketing" itself was coined by Kotler and Zaltman (1971) to refer to a strategy that would make it possible to promote a customer's welfare, using the most effective marketing mix, (i.e., product, price, place, and promotion). Contrary to commercial marketing, social marketing was designed to create social change through education and increased awareness (Coffman, 2002). Social marketing focuses on client wants and needs to implement community-based projects and programs. The approach is integrated, rooted in the client's community, social, and cultural experiences. This inside-out approach can be very well received in struggling communities and target groups dealing with challenging issues. The use and integration of the overall client behaviors and experiences can provide knowledge and information that can be essential to the success of a community program intended for behavior or social change. As Andreasen (2006) indicated, social marketing uses an "upstream application" of client social behaviors that focuses on the source of behaviors and appropriate strategies to influence the change of such targeted behaviors. For example, in a campaign on alcohol, commercial marketing would focus on a downstream approach to identifying factors that influence people to buy alcohol and use such knowledge and infor-mation to sell more alcohol products. On the other hand, in social marketing, an upstream approach is used to identify factors influencing alcohol consumption and abuse behaviors, and use such knowledge to influence positive change or modification in such behavior, and thus cause people not to buy or abuse alcohol. Although Hornik (2001) had questioned the

---

BOX 22.1 ISSUES THAT CAN BE TACKLED WITH SOCIAL MARKETING

- Obesity
- Binge drinking
- Breast-feeding
- Breast cancer
- Prostate cancer
- Colorectal cancer
- College campus suicide
- Domestic violence
- Bullying
- Teen pregnancy
- HIV/AIDS
- Drinking and driving
- Wildlife habitat protection

---

isolated effect of social marketing in behavior change, various studies found that the use of social marketing has been very effective at positively influencing social and community changes (Stead, Gordon, Angus, & McDermott, 2007).

USE OF SOCIAL MARKETING

Box 22.1 illustrates some issues for which nonprofit organizations can use a social marketing strategy for the most effective impact possible.

SOCIAL MARKETING PLAN

A social marketing plan is a document that justifies the needs for a social marketing campaign, as well as the process of implementation by outlining a SWOT (*strength, weakness, opportunity, threat*) analysis, a description of the target population, the goals and objectives, an impact statement, the marketing mix strategies, an implementation plan, an evaluation plan, and a budget. A social marketing plan includes an executive summary that synthesizes key aspects of the plan so as to provide a brief overview.

Justification

The justification should provide a description of the social or community issue to be addressed by the social marketing plan. The problem-tree technique can be an effective approach to use when writing a good justification. The problem-tree technique asks the questions:

- What is the problem being taken into consideration?
- What is the impact of the problem on the target population and the larger community?
- What is the cause of that problem?

The justification should also include a purpose statement that explains how a successful social marketing campaign can help positively influence the behavior that is at the root of the problem and be beneficial for the overall community or society (Box 22.2).

BOX 22.2 SAMPLE PARAGRAPHS FROM A JUSTIFICATION SECTION*

Alcohol use constitutes one of the most serious public health issues for young people in the United States. According to the National Youth Risk Behavior Survey (YRBS) released in early November 2012, more that 70% of high school students have used alcohol, resulting in a high rate of underage drinking in communities across the United States. The YRBS further indicated that about 6,000 young people under the age of 21 die every year due to underage drinking. Underage drinking cost the tax payers more than $60 billion in 2012.

Underage drinking results primarily from binge drinking, which is the excessive consumption of alcohol by a group of young people, especially high school youth. During binge drinking, students may have five or more drinks of alcohol within a couple of hours. Binge drinking is the most common pattern of alcohol consumption among high school youth who drink alcohol and is strongly associated with a wide range of other health risk behaviors, such as unprotected sexual intercourse, use of illicit drugs, and suicide.

Researchers found that underage drinking cause serious problems, including homicide, suicide, traumatic injury, drowning, burns, violent and property crime, high-risk sex, fetal alcohol syndrome, alcohol poisoning, and need for treatment for alcohol abuse and dependence (Francois, 2010; Jean, 2011). About 40% of underage drinkers have experienced black-out spells in which they could not remember what happened the previous evening because of heavy binge drinking. Frequent binge drinkers were 10 times more likely than nonbinge drinkers to miss a class, fall behind in schoolwork, get hurt or injured, and damage property. Binge drinking is also associated with mental health disorders, such as compulsiveness, depression or anxiety, or early deviant behavior (Francois, 2010). Further, there is great potential for alcohol poisoning as a result of binge drinking. Alcohol poisoning is a severe and potentially fatal physical reaction to an alcohol overdose, which can deprive the brain of oxygen. Even moderate binge drinking carries consequences in the form of risky behaviors, such as

■ *Sexual violence and unplanned and unprotected sexual activity:* like adults, youth are most likely unable to think clearly under the influence of alcohol; alcohol abuse leads to increased unplanned and unprotected sexual intercourse.

■ *Drinking and driving:* Alcohol-related highway death rates have significantly increased among drivers under the age of 21. Fatal vehicular accidents due to drunk driving are the number one cause of death among people 15 to 24 years old (Ellea, 2011).

■ *Alcoholism:* Research shows that drinking at an early age predisposes kids to addiction (Ann, 2010).

■ *Brain development:* Early alcohol exposure negatively affects adult brain functioning and behavior (Jung, 2009).

Several studies have documented the effectiveness of specific school-based strategies (Al, 2004). Research also found that the benefits of school-based drug prevention outweigh the costs (Chen, 2002). Schools constitute the primary setting with access to youth under 20 years of age. It is important that schools actively participate in activities to educate students about the dangers of underage alcohol use and implement programs to prevent underage drinking. Therefore, school-based prevention is an effective strategy to influence youth alcohol consumption behaviors, and prevent risky behaviors regarding underage alcohol use.

* Authors and statistics cited are fictitious.

As you may have noticed in the example in Box 22.2, the first paragraph briefly describes the problem with statistics coming from identifiable sources. It is important that the justification for a social marketing project find support in the literature. The second paragraph outlines the cause of the problem. Although it is important to describe a problem, it is also important to explain what causes such problems. For a social marketing campaign to be effective, the strategies for behavior modification must target the root or the cause of a problem in others. The third paragraph explains the impact of the problem on the target population and the overall community. This section of the justification is critical to convincing people to support a social marketing campaign. Finally, the last section makes a case for the approach that will be used, as well as a preview of what the social marketing program will help accomplish.

Purpose and Focus

The purpose is a statement that describes the benefits that will result from the implementation of a social marketing campaign. The focus states the main priority of an upcoming campaign. In other words, the purpose reflects what overall change will take place in relation to a targeted social issue. The focus specifies where specifically such change will be observed. For example, the purpose can be to reduce underage drinking in the Atlanta metropolitan area. The focus may be underage drinking of high school students in the city of Atlanta.

SWOT Analysis

A social marketing should be based on a SWOT analysis to ensure better understanding of internal and external factors that can influence positively or negatively the implementation of a social marketing plan. SWOT stands for *strengths, weaknesses, opportunities*, and *threats*. The findings from a SWOT analysis can help maximize organizational strengths, minimize identified weaknesses, outline strategies to use existing opportunities, and develop contingency plans for threats (Box 22.3).

BOX 22.3 SWOT ANALYSIS	
Strengths	**Opportunities**
■ Interdisciplinary programs/collaboration	■ Quality improvement
■ Access to diverse populations	■ Regional satellite network
■ New organizational structure and reporting	■ Outreach
■ Strong community support	■ Federal support
Weaknesses	**Threats**
■ Limited fixed support/funding	■ Economic downturn
■ Outdated accounting systems	■ Political changes (federal, state, local)
■ Relatively small development programs	■ Competition
■ Small clinical program	

Target Population

A social marketing campaign aims to change the behavior of a target population, in order to improve the overall well-being of a community or society. Therefore, it is obvious that this target population must be described as accurately as possible, with as much detail possible. Some of the factors that must be taken into account in describing the target population include, but are not limited to demographics, geography, psychographics, patterns of behaviors, readiness for change, and social network (Box 22.4).

Goals and Objectives

A social marketing plan should set clear goals and objectives in relation to behaviors of the target population that must be changed. The goals are broader-targeted behavior changes that you want to occur in the target population. The objectives set narrower focuses that will help achieve the goals. The objectives can be behavior oriented and focused on knowledge (what you want your audience to know), beliefs and feelings (what you want your audience to believe and how you want then to feel), action (what you want your audience to do) See Box 22.5 for sample goal and objectives.

BARRIERS, BENEFITS, COMPETITORS, AND INFLUENCERS

This section aims to identify factors that influence behavior adoption by the target population. The factors can be:

■ *Barriers*: Perceived or real reasons (e.g., knowledge, beliefs, skills, abilities, infrastructures, culture, technology, socioeconomic status) that may influence the target population not to adopt the behavior that will be promoted in a social marketing campaign. For example, some people may not participate in an event because they do not have access to transportation or feel that such an event promotes ideas that violate their religious beliefs.

BOX 22.4 PARAGRAPH ON TARGET AUDIENCE

TARGET AUDIENCE

The primary target audience consists of children, ages 5 to 11 years who are in kindergarten through fifth grade. The secondary target audience includes parents, children, school cafeteria, school physical education, and after-school programs. Data published by the County Planning Bureau (2012) revealed that Hispanic and African American children are most affected by the issue. Young children are still developing food preferences. Therefore, they are most likely to change behavior. Parents, teachers, school counselors, and school lunch staff are most likely to be able to shape circumstances relevant to the problem.

BOX 22.5 SAMPLE GOAL AND OBJECTIVES	
Goal	Objectives
Reduce by 30% the rate of excessive consumption of alcohol among high school students in Wisconsin.	*Knowledge objective:* Increase awareness of high school students about the risks associated with excessive alcohol consumption.
	Belief objective: High school students will share with peers that excessive consumption of alcohol causes risky behaviors that threaten their health, safety, and academic performance.
	Action objective: High school students will adopt talking points to reject peer pressure when invited to participate in excessive drinking activities.

■ *Benefits*: Perceived benefits that may influence the target population to adopt the promoted behavior. For example, participants may be eager to participate in a fair about breast cancer because they want more information to help a family member.

■ *Competitors*: Other agencies or entities that promote behavior that counters behavior promoted in a social marketing campaign. For example, potential participants in an alcohol prevention program may receive competing messages from advertising about beer or alcohol.

■ *Influencers*: Other people or entities that may have some bearing on influencing the behavior of the target audience. Influencers can be family members, friends, community leaders, religious leaders, a social network, or opinion leaders.

FORMATIVE RESEARCH

Social marketing is a systematic process that should be based on reliable information collected from the target population and from relevant literature. The research process in social marketing should be community based. In other words, community members or the target audience should be trained in basic principles used to collect and analyze data, and participate in gathering pertinent information that can contribute to the project design. Formative research will make it possible to better understand the target audience, receive useful insights from key members of the target population, make decisions that are client oriented, and refine the social marketing plan to ensure the success of the program. The formative research process includes the following phases:

Developing a gap analysis: To decide which gaps to keep and which ones to dismiss.

Developing research questions: These are broad questions whose answers will help fill gaps and inform decisions about the social marketing program. Research questions are conceptual questions about key variables related to the purpose of the social marketing campaign (e.g., what influences do peers exert on high school students to participate in excessive alcohol consumption? What are the biggest challenges facing clinics serving women at risk of being diagnosed with breast cancer?) They are not survey questions to ask members of the target audience.

Selecting a data-collection method: How will you collect data? Will you conduct a survey? Will you conduct individual interviews of participants or key informants? Will you use focus group sessions with members from the target audience?

Developing or selecting instruments of data collection: Depending on the method selected, instruments can follow an interview guide, a focus group moderator's guide, a questionnaire, or an observation checklist.

Recruiting participants: How will you contact the participants in your formative research? It may be through community centers, local churches, community markets, or referrals.

Collecting data: Will you personally collect the data? Will you contract with a professional agency to do it on your behalf? Will you approach a college or a university for assistance from volunteer graduate students?

Analyzing and reporting the findings: Who will analyze the data collected? What will be the criteria for the analysis? How will the data be reported?

Impact Statement

The social marketing plan is a challenge to behaviors that are rooted in a target population. As a result, there can be resistance to change. The social marketing must outline the benefits and the impacts of the social marketing interventions on the lives of people in the target community or society. The benefits and impacts must be expressed in concrete and measurable ways that outweigh the benefits of the status quo. In other words, an impact statement must put the benefits or impacts of existing behaviors of the target population side by side with the benefits of behavior change that can result from a social marketing campaign. The impact statement should define the benefits of the *promoted behavior* with the *consequences* of the *competing behavior* for the *target population*. In other words, the impact statement must explain the benefits of the promoted behavior for the target population while emphasizing the consequences of the competing behavior. See Box 22.6 for a sample impact statement.

Strategic Marketing Mix

As suggested in the beginning of the chapter, social marketing is based on commercial marketing principles and techniques. Consequently, a social marketing plan should include the Four Ps of commercial marketing: Product, Price, Place, and Promotion.

Product

In commercial marketing, the product refers to the good or service that will be at the center of a transaction between a provider and a client or customer. The purpose of the marketing endeavor is to have as many transactions as possible. In social marketing, the product

---

BOX 22.6 SAMPLE IMPACT STATEMENT

We want high school teenagers *(target population)* to see planned parenthood *(promoted behavior)* as a more responsible decision for their future and as more important and beneficial than unprotected sexual intercourse *(competition)*, which can lead to unwanted pregnancy *(consequences)*.

is the specific, concrete outcome that will result from a campaign. Depending on the purpose of a social marketing campaign, product can be very easy or very difficult to define. For example, in a social marketing campaign about driving under the influence, it is easy for people to understand what it means to have fewer deadly car accidents on a particular highway. A social marketing campaign that involves discouraging youth to use illegal drugs might pose more challenges in defining the outcomes. There may be a need to develop an augmented product, such as guaranteeing anonymity to participants or people who want to assist.

Price

In commercial marketing, there is an explicit expectation of monetary return on investment. In social marketing, the price involves the monetary and nonmonetary costs that the target population will pay. On the other hand, the price can include the monetary and nonmonetary benefits that the target population will receive as a result of a social marketing campaign.

Place

Place refers to the location where the behavior of the target population can be observed. The place is linked to the delivery system of a social marketing campaign.

Promotion

Promotion is about communication strategies and messages that will be used to influence the behavior of the target population. See Box 22.7 for sample strategic marketing mix strategies.

Implementation Plan

The implementation plan is the translation of the goals and objectives of a social marketing plan into who will do what, how, and when. In fact, the achievement of the goals depends in large part on an effective, efficient implementation plan and its execution (Box 22.8).

Evaluation Plan

The evaluation plan aims to assess whether the goals and objectives were achieved. Assessment and documentation of outcomes of behavior change will result from the evaluation plan (Box 22.9).

BOX 22.7 SAMPLE STRATEGIC MARKETING MIX STRATEGIES

PRICE

Cost: Free digital rectal examination and PSA blood test.

PLACE

Community clinics: Participate in screening tests in an atmosphere that is convenient and safe that guarantees your privacy!

PROMOTION

Key message:
- You can win the fight against prostate cancer!

Key messengers:
- Lay health agents
- Community leaders
- Religious leaders

Key media channels:
- Print materials: Brochures, fact sheets, posters
- Videos: Videos on prostate cancer
- Advocacy: Local groups targeting families
- Special events: Cancer fair

Budget

A social marketing plan requires some expenses. These expenses must be explained and justified in a budget.

SOCIAL MARKETING AND FINANCIAL SUSTAINABILITY

Social marketing campaigns provide nonprofit organizations with a unique opportunity to use an inside-out technique that allows the target audience to be directly involved in programs, projects, and activities that aim to further their vision and mission. This approach increases the level of involvement of the target population and allows for a sense of ownership in the programs of a nonprofit organization. Social marketing has a built-in mechanism for assessment of the wants and needs of the target population because of its goal to influence behavior change. Continuing evaluation processes help a nonprofit organization understand its target audience's cultural norms and local knowledge. Through social marketing, organizations develop unique abilities to identify the

BOX 22.8 SAMPLE IMPLEMENTATION PLAN

Activity	Person Responsible	Outcomes	Period
Assign a social marketing coordinator	Executive director	Assignment letter	January 15
Conduct asset mapping	Social marketing coordinator	Asset mapping report	March 30
Develop formative research proposal	Social marketing coordinator	Formative research proposal	April 15
Conduct formative research	Social marketing coordinator	Research report	July 30
Organize special events	Social marketing coordinator Special event committee		September 1 to December 31
Evaluation of social marketing activities	Consultant	Evaluation report	May 15

popular and accepted behaviors that may be competing for those promoted by a campaign. Consequently, a nonprofit organization can foster a space of awareness within the community, and in turn allow clients to re-evaluate their current behaviors against the benefits and repercussions of those being promoted. The integration of a nonprofit program into the lives and culture of a community to the point of a sense of ownership is a key for program sustainability. Effective integration means that members of the target population receive training that enables them to take over partly aspects of programs that used to be managed by a nonprofit organization. A sense of ownership not only increases the level of community participation, but also constitutes evidence of success that can attract new donors to contribute to support the activities of nonprofit organizations that show evidence of efficiency and effectiveness through social marketing. Further, social marketing can provide opportunities for a nonprofit organization to develop fee-based services and position itself for contracts and other unrestricted or restricted monetary contributions that can help diversify its revenue stream, and consequently contribute to its financial sustainability.

BOX 22.9 SAMPLE EVALUATION PLAN

The evaluation will measure outcomes related to the community leaders and participants in our social marketing campaign. A post campaign survey will be used to measure community leaders' change in knowledge about risk factors of prostate cancer, change in their health beliefs about screening for early detection and treatment for prostate cancer, and change in their motivation to educate people in their local community about prostate cancer. Further, the evaluation will measure whether there were increases in requests for prostate cancer screening, number of PSAs completed by program participants, and number of prostate cancer treatments completed by participants in our outreach activities.

QUESTIONS AND ACTIVITIES

1. What is social marketing?
2. How does social marketing differ from commercial marketing?
3. How do you think social marketing can be used by your nonprofit organization?
4. What does the strategic marketing mix mean?
5. How can social marketing contribute to the financial sustainability of a nonprofit organization?

REFERENCES

Andreasen, A. R. (2006). *Social marketing in the 21st century.* Thousand Oaks, CA: Sage.

Coffman, J. (2002). *Public communication campaign evaluation: An environmental scan of challenges, criticisms, practice, and opportunities.* Prepared for Communications Consortium Media Center by the Harvard Family Research Project.

Donovan, R. (2011). Social marketing's mythunderstandings. *Journal of Social Marketing, 1*(1), 8–16.

French, J. (2011). Why nudging is not enough. *Journal of Social Marketing, 1*(2), 154–162.

Hornik, R. (2001, June 22). *Remarks on the occasion of the Andreasen fellowship.* Lecture paper presented at the Social Marketing and Health Conference, Clearwater, FL.

Kotler, P., & Zaltman, G. (1971, July). Social marketing: An approach to planned social change. *Journal of Marketing, 35,* 3–12.

Lefebvre, R. C. (2011). An integrative model for social marketing. *Journal of Social Marketing, 1*(1), 54–72.

McKenzie-Mohr, D. (2011). *Fostering sustainable behavior: An introduction to community-based social marketing* (3rd ed.). Gabriola Island, BC: New Society.

Smith, W. A. (2000). Social marketing: An evolving definition. *American Journal of Health Behavior, 24,* 11–17.

Stead, M., Gordon, R., Angus, K., & McDermott, L. (2007). A systematic review of social marketing effectiveness. *Health Educ., 107*(2): 126–191.

Weinreich, N. K. (2011). *Hands-on social marketing: A step-by-step guide to designing change for good* (2nd ed.). Thousand Oaks, CA: Sage.

Leadership and Financial Sustainability

At the completion of this chapter, the reader will be able to:

1. Define the concept of leadership.
2. Describe the most common leadership theories.
3. Explain the relationship between leadership and community relations.
4. Discuss the role of leadership in strategic planning.
5. Explain the relationship between leadership and financial sustainability of nonprofit organizations.

This chapter examines leadership from various perspectives with an emphasis on the influence of particular leadership styles on the financial sustainability of a nonprofit organization. The chapter integrates theory-based and practice-based approaches, and thus provides tools to better understand and influence the leader–follower dynamic in the nonprofit setting.

ABOUT LEADERSHIP

Most scholars agree that leadership is a key component of organizational effectiveness (Borman & Brush, 1993; Chemers, 1993). For a long time, management was synonymous with leadership, until Zaleznick (1986) clarified the systematic difference between leadership (leader) and management (manager) in organizations. In fact, employers tend more and more to look for leadership skills or leadership potential in the hiring process of applicants (Hollenbeck, 1994). However, the hiring of a manager is not necessarily the hiring of a leader. The inverse is not necessarily true. The leader at least "manages" people or human behavior.

Studies tend to agree that a leader has followers, whereas a manager has subordinates (Blank, 2001; Martin, 1997). In both cases, the term used suggests implicitly that the manager or the leader holds the power while the subordinate or the follower is the "influenced subject." It seems obvious, then, that the leader or the manager influences, motivates, empowers, inspires, serves, or transforms the subordinate or the follower. Although this sounds like a one-way process, there is evidence of the existence of at least two parties in the process. Although the subordinate or the follower seems to play a rather passive role in the process through which the leadership influence occurs. However, the followers can also influence the leader in specific contexts. As the negotiational leadership approach argues, there is a likely interaction between the leader and the follower that takes the form of an implicit negotiation of interest and commitment between the leader and the follower (Jean Francois, 2005).

The very range of definitions of leadership and the absence of consensual agreement between the definitions make the concept of leadership an issue in itself. However, most definitions involve a process of social influence over the cognition, affect, and behavior of others to structure the activities and relationships within a group or an organization (Bass, 1990; Rauch & Behling, 1984).

"Leadership" had been considered a synonym for "management" until scholars from the Harvard Business School addressed systematic arguments about the differences between the two concepts (Kotter, 1990; Zaleznick, 1986). Variables, such as personal thinking, personal history, and motivation, distinguish leadership from management. Zalenick (1986) argues that contrary to management, which implies impersonal and even passive attitudes toward goals, leadership involves an environment of personal and active attitudes to accomplish goals. He noted also that management is a combination, an interaction between people and ideas to establish strategies and make decisions. Leadership is a process of influence through high risk and even danger. Similarly, Kotter (1990) sees management in terms of its complexity, which means plans, rigid organizational design and structures, and outcome monitoring. However, leadership is coping with change through vision, direction, and inspiration. Other variables may be embodied when talking about leadership. For example, McGregor (1966, p. 73) noted that:

There are at least four major variables now known to be involved in leadership:

■ the characteristics of the leader
■ the attitudes, needs, and other characteristics of the follower
■ the characteristics of the organization, such as its purpose, its structure, the nature of the task to be performed
■ the social, economic, and political milieu

Leadership is sometimes also confused with power. Yet people in all positions of authority exert some type of power and authority on followers. However, as Etzioni (1965) explained, leadership is not just a matter of influencing people's behavior, but also a matter of enhancing the voluntary compliance of followers. Thus, influence in a leadership context is different from influence in power (Gibb, 1969; Kochan, Schmidt, & De Cotiis, 1975). Power and authority are most likely related to a position or a status in a formal organizational structure, but leadership is an influence process that goes farther than simply the exercise of power and authority. Leadership exerts power and authority through motivation, not merely through status or position.

EARLY LEADERSHIP THEORIES

Great man theory: A great deal of leadership research has been undertaken over the years, which has led to a variety of leadership theories. The earliest studies on leadership started with the "great man theory," which stated that world progress results from individual achievements of great persons (Carlyle, 1910). This theory was questioned for its intentional sexism, linking leadership exclusively to men.

Traits theories: The questioning of the great man theory led to the formulation of the leadership traits theories. Innumerable studies have been undertaken to examine physical, personal, social, and personality traits in individuals who are leaders (Stogdill, 1974). According to advocates of the leadership traits theories, these traits could determine whether an individual is a leader or not (Gardner, 1989). Most studies conducted to show the consistency of the relationships between the traits associated with leadership and organizational effectiveness have failed to convince (Jennings, 1968; Yukl & Van Fleet, 1992). Wright (1996) said there were "no difference between leaders and followers with respect to these characteristics" (p. 34).

Behavioral theories: The limitations identified in leadership traits theories led researchers to look at the behaviors of leaders. Research projects in behavioral theory have attempted to identify relationships between patterns of leadership behavior and performance of groups within organizations. Douglas McGregor's (1966) theory X and theory Y, Rensis Likert's (1967) Michigan studies, Blake and Mouton's (1978) managerial grid, and Lewin's studies (Megginson, Mosley, & Pietri, 1989) are among the best known behavioral leadership theories. Many critiques have been leveled against behavioral leadership theories, especially because of a lack of consideration for the situational factors that influence leadership interactions between the leader and the followers. As Robbins (1996) wrote, "Situations change and leadership styles need to change with them. Unfortunately, the behavioral approaches don't recognize changes in situations" (p. 419).

Contingency theories: The inability of behavioral leadership theories to take into account the situation where the process of influence is occurring facilitated the emergence of contingency theories, prompting researchers to turn to the context of leadership style. Fiedler (1967) studied the effectiveness of the leader based on the leadership style and the degree to which the situation or the context gives control and influence to the leader. Hersey and Blanchard (1977) stated that leadership style is contingent on the situation, which means the level of followers' readiness or maturity. The successful leader, according to Hersey and Blanchard, chooses the appropriate style for the particular situation. In short, situational leadership theories promote the idea that the leader must understand his/her own behavior, the behavior of the followers, and the situation before deciding to use any particular leadership style (Fleishman, 1973). Other approaches, such as the leader–member exchange theory (Duchon, Green, &Taber, 1986), the path–goal theory (House, 1971), and the leader–participation model (Vroom &Yetton, 1973), have also considered the interaction between the process of leadership and the situation or the context. However, the contingency or situational theories of leadership have focused mainly on the relationships between the leader and the immediate followers. Very little consideration has been given to the structure, politics, or symbols that constitute a leadership environment (Bolman & Deal, 1997).

Attribution and charismatic theories: Further research has contributed to more recent approaches to leadership, such as the attribution theory, which associates the performance of an organization to the leader (Pfeffer, 1992) and the charismatic theory in which the followers attribute the observed leader's behaviors to heroic or extraordinary leadership abilities (Conger & Kanungo, 1988).

RECENT LEADERSHIP THEORIES

Servant leadership: In the tumultuous periods of the 1960s and early 1970s characterized by the involvement of the United States in Vietnam, Greenleaf (1967), a retiree of AT&T, introduced the theory of servant leadership. For Greenleaf, serving is the first priority of a leader who is obligated and responsible for the moral environment of his group, organization, or society. In other words, the premise of servant leadership is that the leader is one for whom serving and the search for serving are natural components of the leader (Farling, Stone & Winston, 1999; Greenleaf, 1977). Greenleaf (2002) believed that a leader earns the right to lead only when people's needs are satisfied. Servant leadership is based on the virtues of love, humility, altruism, vision, trust, empowerment, and service (Harrison, 2002; Kaplan, 2000; Patterson, 2003; Veronesi, 2001; Wis, 2002). The servant leader focuses on the followers whom he or she leads and serves in such a way as to exemplify a servant's attitude. Spears (1995) has identified 10 principles of servant leadership, which are listening, empathy, healing, awareness, persuasion, conceptualization, foresight, stewardship, commitment to the growth of people, and building community. Servant leadership was promoted by Greenleaf (Prosser, 2007) as a way of leading others through a desire to serve. In practice, servant leadership is translated through an approach of collaboration and integration with others. The secret of servant leadership resides in the ability to build bridges and persuade others by earning their trust.

Like other leadership theories, servant leadership is not exempt from criticisms. Boje (2003), for example, said that "The servant leader is a bureaucratic authority and at the same time a servant to the social welfare. It is not clear that the servant leader decentralized authority" (p. 9). The real question raised by Boje (2003) is whether the servant leader is authoritarian or egalitarian? Boje (2003) underlines the fact that:

> Greenleaf makes the point that while at AT&T, his servant leadership included at times a "Machiavellian strategy to maneuver within it and to make any contribution to it." Does this means that sometimes the Prince is a servant leader, asks Boje? (para 22)

This is a relevant question whose answer could elucidate how truly "servant" the servant leader is. Weber (1947), who used the concept of "servant" before Greenleaf, said:

> The fact that the chief and his administrative staff often appear formally as servant or agents of those they rule naturally does nothing whatever to disprove the authoritarian character of the relationship.

Therefore, the answer to the question of whether leaders, such as Castro, Gandhi, Martin Luther King, Jr., Mao Tse-tung, and Perón, were servant leaders can be very subjective for each of the above leaders.

In addition, Boje (2003) argues that servant leadership can be seen as "a learned behavior, since Greenleaf tried to train managers to serve, while at AT&T" (p. 10). This is in contradiction with the Greenleaf definition of servant leadership, which indicates that servant leadership begins "with the natural feeling that one wants to serve, to serve first. Then conscious choice brings one to aspire to lead " (Greenleaf, 1991, p. 6). This implies a supraeducational foundation of servant leadership, which is more a trait that someone can "catch" than a skill that can be taught.

Another critic (Bradley, 1999), has pointed out the fact that a leader focusing on being a servant can distort the task of leadership. Bradley also states that servant leadership can be perceived as being weak or indecisive and "the servant-leader idea underestimates the need for accountability in leadership, the wide variations in human conceptual abilities, and the general aggressiveness of people in the workplace (p. 52)

Despite the criticisms, many scholars have supported the servant leadership theory (Harrison, 2002; Kaplan, 2000; Patterson, 2003; Veronesi, 2001; Wis, 2002). However, Bowman (1997) explains that the concept of servant leadership lacks the support of well-designed and published empirical research. Bowman argues also that the many examples of servant leaders in organizational settings offered by the servant–leader concept writers are mostly "anecdotal."

Transactional and transformational leadership: Other scholars opt for leadership theories, such as transactional and transformational leadership. For example, Bass (1997) states, "Since 1980, general findings have been assembled that the best of leaders are both transactional and transformational" (p. 132). Transactional and transformational leaderships have been approached through a comparative model that Burns (1978) and later Bass (1985) called the "Transactional-Transformational model of Leadership." Nevertheless, these two styles of leadership are different in several aspects.

In fact, transactional leadership influences and motivates toward short-term performance and transactional role models (Wofford &Goodwin, 1994). The transactional leader motivates followers by clarifying desired outcomes into a contract, defining task requirements, consulting, monitoring, providing feedback, and rewarding in exchange for successful performance (Avolio, Bass, & Jung, 1995). Transactional leadership can increase performance within an organization, especially in promoting persistence to accomplish tasks. However, some critiques have found that rewarding can negatively affect intrinsic motivation and creativity. They believe also that transactional leadership is not capable of building the trust and motivation that are needed within an organization to make followers achieve their full work potential (Avolio, Bass, & Jung, 1995).

Transformational leadership, then, seems to offer more insight for organizational effectiveness than transactional leadership. Wright (1996) argues that transformational leadership inspires and motivates followers toward self-actualization needs and higher organizational goals that neglect self-interest. Bennis and Nanus (1985) describe a transformational leader as one who "commits people to action, who converts followers into leaders, and who may convert leaders into agents of change" (p. 3). Avolio, Bass, and Jung (1995) see also transformational leadership as a process of influence that entails changes in belief, values, and attitudes of followers. Furthermore, they argue that in transformational leadership, the followers feel trusted and respected by the leader; they feel empowered, not controlled.

Based on studies outlined in the preceding paragraphs, transformational leadership has evidence of superiority over transactional leadership. However, as Bass wrote, transactional leadership and transformational leadership are two "distinct dimensions rather than opposite ends of a continuum" (Doherty & Danylchuk, 1996, p. 294). Bass also noted that "all leaders are transactional, to some extent, exchanging rewards for performance, but some leaders are also transformational, going beyond simple leader-subordinate exchange relations" (Doherty & Danylchuk, 1996, p. 294). Yet transformational leadership includes behaviors associated with other leadership styles, especially transactional, but it does offer a dynamic of leader-followers relationships.

Transformational leadership certainly offers several theoretical perspectives to better comprehend the leader (Bass, 1990; Pawar & Eastman, 1997; Yukl, 2002). However, some scholars believe that the transformational leadership theory has serious limitations. For example, Keely (1995) has questioned the ethics of transformational leadership, stating that it can be exploitative and manipulative by encouraging followers to go beyond their own self-interests to accommodate the self-interest of the leader on a primrose path on which they lose more than they gain. Also, Carey (1995) argues that while transformational leadership can promote the values of equality, honesty, loyalty, fairness, and justice, it can also be subverted to endorse evil values, such as racial superiority, submission, and social Darwinism. Another criticism of transformational leadership is the issue of impression management. Gronn (1995) believes that when transformational leaders engage in impression management, they tend to project a greater image of confidence, strength, decisiveness, and mental accomplishments than what their reality is. Gronn (1995) also argues that transformational leaders engaging in impression management present a fantasy picture of the future and try to be more inspirational in order to give the followers a false impression of ideal leadership. Transformational leadership is also questioned for its lack of checks and balances between the leader and the followers, such that the followers may be transformed against their own interests (Keely, 1995). In fact, transformational leadership has left many questions unanswered for scholars. Yukl (2002) says there is vagueness in transformational leadership that allows for an "almost anything" interpretation.

Other contemporary leadership theories: Contemporary leadership theories include but are not limited to emotional intelligence and negotiational leadership. The emotional intelligence theory, promoted by Goleman (1998), argues that intrapersonal and interpersonal skills (self-awareness, self-regulation, motivation, empathy, social skills) are necessary for individual adjustment in today's world. Their application in the leadership context makes it possible to establish better and healthier relationships with workers or employees. Negotiational leadership refers to an approach that founds its principles on the basis of a learning and reflecting process of negotiation of interest and commitment through a social interaction of influencing, serving, and transforming each other, between leader and follower, to achieve a shared vision (Jean Francois, 2005).

Jean Francois (2005) asserted that negotiational leadership is based on a series of assumptions or propositions, such as:

■ Leadership involves a learning and reflecting process of negotiation of interests and commitment through a social interaction between leader and follower to achieve a shared vision.
■ There is a bright side of explicit and conscious negotiation of interest and commitment, and a dark side of implicit negotiation of interest and commitment between the leader and the follower.
■ Negotiational leadership creates a shared vision, through modeling (leading by example), motivation (inspiration), discussion (build consensus), context (accounting for circumstances), and mind-set metamorphose (rejuvenation).
■ Negotiational leadership is governed by the principles of interest (shared vision), co-sufficiency (explicit or implicit acceptance by a leader and follower in which neither the leader nor the follower is sufficient alone to carry out a vision), cooperation (working together), commitment (persistence, resilience), trust (co-reliance), responsibility (role clarification), and accountability (implicit rewards and consequences).
■ Negotiational leadership has the potential to contribute to subordinate's commitment, sustainable achievement, retention, and consequently affect organizational growth and effectiveness.
■ Negotiational leadership can help foster a learning, reflecting, and inclusive organizational climate.

LEADERSHIP AND COMMUNITY RELATIONS

Leaders who manage financial institutions or whose responsibilities include the oversight of the financial management of an organization are referred to as "financial leaders." The chief executive officer (CEO) and the chief financial officer (CFO) of a nonprofit organization are accountable to the financial management of the organization before the board of directors and the external stakeholders. The members of the finance committee of the nonprofit organization can be considered financial leaders, depending on the extent of their involvement in the finances of a given organization. Financial leaders of nonprofit organizations develop community relations that can generate great financial returns. In difficult times, cultivating transparent and accountable relationships with donors and clients can turn out to be the equivalent of a line of credit for a nonprofit organization. A proactive relationship with stakeholders always plays well, because this sends the signal that an organization is relevant in the lives of others. This sends the signal of an organization that one cannot let dissolve, given the important community functions that the organization shows it is performing.

LEADERSHIP AND STRATEGIC PLANNING

Obtaining financial resources has become more competitive for nonprofit organizations. With long-term planning, an organization has better opportunities to cope with change and prepare for unforeseen events that would threaten the existence of the nonprofit organization. In that sense, long-term planning can strengthen the financial sustainability of a nonprofit organization. Smart strategic planning and attractive service models can help a nonprofit organization position itself to generate needed revenue even when the economic environment is challenging. This is not possible for an organization that is operating on a day-by-day mind-set. Obviously, the day-by-day operations are important, because this is the very purpose of a nonprofit organization: to provide expedited assistance to people who need urgent help that they will not find elsewhere or from a for-profit business. However, this mission must not stand in the way of a nonprofit organization as it carries out consistent long-range plans that include funding projections and revenue creation.

Stid and Bradach (2009) highlighted the need to follow up on projections of income and revenue creation. Likewise, the use of strategic funding options, such as bonds, can help nonprofit organizations improve their financial position and allow them to take advantage of situations that previously they had not been able to leverage given their financial position (Brinckerhoff, 2009).

FINANCIAL LEADERSHIP PREVENTS POOR FISCAL MANAGEMENT

Further, a nonprofit organization can be well funded, and still find it difficult to continue to provide services over time if there is poor fiscal management and a lack of financial stewardship. This illustrates that although leadership does not necessarily rhyme with money or finance, it plays a key role in the financial performance and sustainability of a nonprofit organization. It is important to remember that an effective leader oversees the overall financial management activities of a nonprofit organization, including fund-raising, budgeting, spending, and reporting. These four functions have almost everything to do with financial sustainability. If a leader is committed to being as effective as possible in being a good steward, a great deal of difference can be easily observed between a nonprofit organization with effective financial leadership and another that does not. This in turn will make a difference as to whether or not an organization engages on a path for financial sustainability. Financial sustainability is an aspiration. It takes visionary leadership for a nonprofit organization to make decisions—sometimes tough decisions—that can further a commitment toward financial sustainability.

LEADERSHIP IS ESSENTIAL TO FINANCIAL VIABILITY AND SUSTAINABILITY

The survival of a nonprofit organization depends on its financial viability. Part of being a financially viable nonprofit organization is the ability to make long-term strategic-planning decisions to anticipate financial challenges and develop strategies to neutralize or adapt to them. Leadership is key. I mean leadership will make a difference. Effective leadership undoubtedly influences the strategic thinking of an organization. Strategic planning definitely contributes to the ability of an organization to survive times of hardship. In fact, the inability to make long-term strategic decisions has caused many nonprofit organizations to fail. Nonprofit organizations that fail to practice long-term planning and fiscal stewardship tend to have poor performance and very few outcomes to document. A strategic leader contributes to the financial viability of a nonprofit organization by building an organization on sound fiscal principles.

With reduction in either federal or state funding, nonprofit organizations can find themselves under a lot of financial stress. In fact, it is easy for a nonprofit organization to dissolve due to a lack of liquidity. The nature of leadership in a nonprofit organization can make a big difference on that front. Effective and skilled financial leaders can foster a climate that strengthens fiscally healthy and future-focused nonprofit organizations. For example, a skilled leader can develop and promote a culture of flexibility and creativity in her or his nonprofit organization by encouraging all internal stakeholders to feed the organization with new a creative ideas that can lead to development of new packages of service opportunities within the broad framework of the vision and mission statements. A culture of flexibility and creativity is inherently linked to continuous quality improvement. In other words, the leader ensures that the organization is continuously assessing its service packages and service delivery systems. This ensures that an organization measures the success or failure of previous plans, adjusts, and adapts to new realities without abandoning its vision and mission. This not only helps uncover issues early or at least on time, but also exposes the organization to the latest advances and opportunities in the sector. It is undeniably a recipe for a competitive nonprofit organization that can be very attractive to donors and contributors, and in turn influence a nonprofit organization's financial viability and sustainability.

QUESTIONS AND ACTIVITIES

1. How would you define "leadership"?
2. How would you differentiate leadership from governance?
3. What is your preferred leadership theory, if any? Why?
4. Describe your worst experience with an organizational leader! What makes you consider this experience the worst one? What have you learned from that experience?
5. Describe your best experience with an organizational leader! What makes you consider that experience the best one? What have you learned from that experience?
6. What are the key characteristics that you would be looking for in an effective leader? Why?
7. To what extent, if any, do you think leadership can contribute to the financial sustainability of a nonprofit organization?

REFERENCES

Avolio, B. J., & Bass, B. M. (1985). *Transformational leadership: Charisma and beyond.* Working paper, School of Management, State University of New York, Binghamton.

Avolio, B. J., Bass, B., & Jung, D. I. (1995). *MLQ multifactor leadership questionnaire: Technical report.* Palo Alto, CA: Ming Garden.

Bass, B. M. (1985). *Leadership and performance beyond expectations.* New York, NY: Harper.

Bass, B. M. (1990). *Bass and Stogdill's handbook of leadership: Theory, research and managerial applications.* New York, NY: Free Press.

Bass, B. M. (1997). Does the transactional/transformational leadership paradigm transcend organizational and national boundaries? *American Psychologist, 52,* 130–139.

Bennis, W., & Burt, N. (1997). *Leaders: Strategies for taking charge.* New York, NY: Harper Collins.

Bennis, W. G., & Nanus, B. (1985). *Leaders: The strategies for taking charge.* New York, NY: Harper & Row.

Blake, R. R., & Mouton, J. S. (1978). *The new managerial grid.* Houston, TX: Gulf.

Blank, W. G. (2001). *The 108 skills of natural born leaders.* New York, NY: Amacom.

Boje, D. (2003). *Traits: The journey from will to power to will to serve.* Retrieved from http://business. nmsu.edu/~dboje/teaching/338/traits.htm#servant

Bolman, L. G., & Deal, T. E. (1977). *Reframing organizations: Artistry, choice and leadership* (2nd ed.). San Francisco, CA: Jossey-Bass.

Borman, W. C., & Brush, D. H. (1993). More progress toward a taxonomy of managerial performance requirements. *Human Performance, 6,* 1–21.

Bowman, M. A. (1997). *Popular approaches to leadership: Theory and practice.* Thousand Oaks, CA: Sage.

Bradley, Y. (1999). Servant leadership: A critique of Robert Greenleaf's concept of leadership. *Journal of Christian Education, 42,* 43–54.

Brinckerhoff, P. (2009). *Mission-based management: Leading your nonprofit in the 21st century* (3rd ed.). New York, NY: Wiley.

Burns, J. M. (1978). *Leadership.* New York, NY: Harper Collins.

Carey, M. R. (1992). Transformational leadership and the fundamental option for self-transcendence. *Leadership Quarterly, 3,* 217–236.

Carlyle, T. (1910). In P. C. (Ed)., *Lectures on heroes, hero-worship, and the heroic in history.* Oxford, UK: Clarendon Press.

Chemers, M. M. (1993). An integrative theory of leadership. In M. M. Chemers & R. Ayman (Eds.), *Leadership theory and research: Perspectives and directions* (pp. 293–319). San Diego, CA: Academic Press.

Conger, J. A., & Kanungo, R. A. (1988). Charismatic leadership in organizations. Thousand Oaks, CA: Sage.

Doherty, A. J., & Danylchuk, K. E. (1996). Transformational and transactional leadership in interuniversity athletics management. *Journal of Sport Management, 10*(3), 292–309.

Duchon, D., Green, S. G., & Taber, T. D. (1986, February). Vertical dyad linkage: A longitudinal assessment of antecedents, measures, and consequences. *Journal of Applied Psychology, 71,* 56–60.

Etzioni, A. (1965). Dual leadership in complex organizations. *American Sociological Review, 30,* 688–698.

Farling, M. L., Stone, A. G., & Winston, B. E. (1999). Servant leadership: Setting the stage for empirical research. *Journal of Leadership Studies, 6,* 49–72.

Fiedler, F. E. (1967). *A theory of Leadership effectiveness.* New York, NY: McGraw-Hill.

Fleishman, E. A. (1973). Twenty years of consideration and structure. In E. A. Fleishman & J. G. Hunt (Eds.), *Current developments in the study of leadership* (pp. 1–40). Carbondale, IL: Southern Illinois University Press.

Gardner, J. (1989). *On leadership.* New York, NY: Free Press.

Gibb, C. A. (1969). Leadership. In G. Lindzey and E. Aronson (Eds.), *The handbook of social psychology* (Vol. 4). Reading, MA: Addison-Wesley.

Goleman, D. (1998). What makes a leader? *Harvard Business Review, 76*(6), 93–102.

Greenleaf, R. K. (1977). *Servant leadership: A journey into the nature of legitimate power and greatness.* New York, NY: Paulist Press.

Greenleaf, R. K. (1991). *The servant as leader.* Indianapolis, IN: The Robert Greenleaf Center.

Greenleaf, R. K. (2002). *Servant leadership: A journey into the nature of legitimate power and greatness.* New York, NY: Paulist Press

Gronn, P. (1995). Greatness re-visited: The current obsession with transformational leadership. *Leading and Managing, 1*(1), 14-27.

Harrison, W. H. (2002). Prudence and custom: Revisiting Hooker on authority. *Anglican Theological Review, 84,* 897.

Hersey, P., & Blanchard, K. H. (1977). *The Management of organizational behaviour* (3rd ed.). Upper Saddle River. NJ. : Prentice Hall.

Hollenbeck, G. (1994). *CEO selection: A street smart review* (Rep. No. 164). Greensboro, NC: Center for Creative Leadership.

House, R. J. (1971, September). A path-goal theory of leader effectiveness. *Administrative Sciences Quarterly, 16,* 321–328.

Jean Francois, E. (2005). *Negotiational leadership and influence strategies.* Tampa, FL: Springfield College.

Jennings, E. (1968). *An anatomy of leadership: Princes, heroes, and supermen.* New York, NY: McGraw-Hill.

Kaplan, S. (2000). Human nature and environmentally responsible behavior. *Journal of Social Issues, 56,* 491.

Keely, M. (1995). The trouble with transformational leadership: Toward a federalist ethics for organizations. *Business Ethics Quarterly, 5,* 67–95.

Kochan, A. K., Schmidt, S. M., & De Cotiis, T. A. (1975). Superior-subordinate relations: Leadership and headship. *Human Relations, 28,* 279–294.

Kotter, J. P. (1990). What leaders really do. *Harvard Business Review, 68*(3), 103–111.

Likert, R. (1967). *The human organization.* New York, NY: McGraw-Hill.

Martin, C. (1997). *Looking at type: The fundamentals.* Palo Alto, CA: Consulting Psychologist Press.

McGregor, D. (1966). *Leadership and motivation.* Cambridge, MA : MIT Press.

Megginson, L., Mosley, D., & Pietri, P (1989). *Management: Concepts and applications* (3rd ed.). New York, NY: Harper & Row.

Patterson, K. A. (2003). *Servant leadership: A theoretical model* (Doctoral dissertation). Regent University, Virginia Beach, VA. AAT 3082719.

Pawar, B. S., & Eastman, K. K. (1997). The nature and implications of contextual influences on transformational leadership: A contextual examination. *Academy of Management Review, 22,* 80–109.

Pfeffer, J. (1992). *Managing power.* Boston, MA: Harvard Business School Press.

Prosser, S. (2007). *To be a servant-leader.* New York, NY: Paulist Press.

Rauch, C. F., & Behling, O. (1984). *Functionalism: Basis for an alternate approach to the study of leadership.* New York, NY: Pergamon.

Robbins, S. P. (1996). *Organizational Behavior: Concepts, controversies, applications.* Upper Saddle River, NJ: Prentice-Hall.

Spears, L. (1995*). Reflections on leadership. How Robert Greenleaf's theory of servant-leader influenced today's top management thinkers.* New York, NY: Wiley.

Stid, D., & Bradach, J. (2009). How visionary non-profit leaders are learning to enhance management capabilities. *Strategy & Leadership, 37*(1), 35–40.

Stogdill, R. M. (1974). *Handbook of leadership: A survey of theory and research.* New York, NY: Free Press.

Veronesi, J. F. (2001). Producing a caring environment for staff: Forging old paradigms. *Nursing Administration Quarterly, 25*(3), 69.

Vroom, V. H., & Yetton, P. W. (1973). *Leadership and decision making.* Pittsburg, PA: University of Pittsburg Press.

Weber, M. (1947). *The theory of social and economic organization.* Glencoe, IL: Free Press.

Wis, R. M. (2002). The conductor as servant leader. *Music Education Journal, 89,* 17.

Wofford, J. C., & Goodwin, V. L. (1994). A cognitive interpretation of transactional and transformational leadership theories. *Leadership Quarterly, 5,* 161–186.

Wright, P. (1996). *Managerial leadership.* London, UK: Routledge.

Yukl, G. (2002*). Leadership in organizations.* (5th ed.). Upper Saddle River, NJ: Prentice Hall.

Yukl, G.. & Van Fleet, D. D. (1992). Theory and research on leadership in organizations. In M. D. Dunnette & L. M. Hough (Eds.), *Handbook of industrial & organizational psychology,* (2nd ed., Vol. 3). Palo Alto, CA: Consulting Psychologists Press.

Zaleznik, A. (1977). Managers and leaders: Are they different? *Harvard Business Review, 55,* 67–78.

Organizational Transformation and Financial Sustainability

At the completion of this chapter, the reader will be able to:

1. Discuss the life cycles of organizations.
2. Reflect on the life cycle of nonprofit organizations.
3. Identify factors affecting the organizational transformation process of nonprofit organizations.
4. Discuss the elements of an organizational transformation initiative.
5. Explain the relationship between organizational transformation and financial sustainability.

This chapter argues in favor of organizational transformation as a strategy for financial sustainability. The chapter discusses the history, context, and applications of organizational development, adaptation to change, resistance to change, and transition management.

ORGANIZATIONS HAVE LIFE CYCLES

Organizations have life cycles. They are created. They grow. And sometimes, they die. Other times, they transform themselves into something new, or into a different organization. The process for an organization to survive its cycle by transforming itself is called organizational transformation. Daft (2007) argued that the life cycle of an organization includes four stages: entrepreneurial, collectivity, formalization, and elaboration.

Entrepreneurial: The entrepreneurial stage (birth) is characterized by a need for leadership. At this stage, an organization is relatively small, with almost no bureaucratic structures, and a simple overlapping division of labor. At this stage, everything is centralized around the leader or the founder like a one-man show. There is little to no formalization, administrative structures, and internal coordination system.

Collectivity: The collectivity stage (youth) occurs with a need for delegation. The organization has grown and started to develop some form of bureaucracy and a more formal division of labor. There is the presence of at least another leader involved in decision making. More formalization is taking place. The organization creates needed administrative processes and systems for coordination.

Formalization: The formalization stage (midlife) is the period during which the organization experiences some form of midlife crisis involving too much red tape. The organization has become relatively large and has maintained a bureaucracy within several units or departments led by leaders who share more responsibilities. There are more policies and procedures, administrative systems, and coordination structures in place.

Elaboration: The elaboration stage (maturity) is the period during which the organization feels a need for revitalization. At this stage the organization has become too bureaucratic. Multiple units or departments are involved in decision making. This may delay the ability of an organization to move quickly on important issues. There are strong administrative and coordination structures in place. However, the organization may experience frequent breakdowns in its bureaucracy.

I will caution that this life cycle has its limitations. For example, not every organization or company starts small. In the case of a merger, for example, you may have two experienced organizations that start a brand-new organizational venture without their individual dissolution per se, but they develop a new identity. Two colleges can merge and adopt a new university name, but they still operate under some autonomy. Or a large institution may have an internal unit that they allow to operate with great autonomy for the purpose of funding or accreditation. In these cases, you have technically brand-new organizations that have been through an entire life cycle. These organizations simply renew or transform themselves. This stage of transformation or renewal is lacking in Daft (2007).

LIFE CYCLE OF NONPROFIT ORGANIZATIONS

Stevens (2001) argues that nonprofit organizations evolve from vitality to regeneration, through seven stages, encompassing idea, start-up, growth, maturity, decline, turnaround, and terminal.

Idea: At this stage, a founder may have a burning desire to make a difference regarding a particular need being observed. The only thing that may exist is a purpose. There are no board members involved yet. There might be some supporters of an idea. The idea may start from a personal experience. For example, someone visited a new place or a country, saw a need, and wants to make a difference. An idea can emerge from a personal loss as well. For example, someone may want to start a nonprofit organization after the loss of a loved one from cancer, smoking, drunk driving, domestic violence, HIV/AIDS, or other similar situations.

Start-up: The start-up is basically the passage from idea to action. The organization is incorporated. The vision is put in writing. A board is created. However, this is the period of little to no budget. There tend to be no strong administrative systems in place.

Growth: During the growth stage, the organization starts implementing programs and offers opportunities to stakeholders. There is more and more need to expand and add further structure. The board develops a sense of ownership about the organization. Activities are rooted in strategic plans. The organization sets more ambitious goals.

Maturity: At the maturity stage, the organization develops its identity and recognition for services provided. The activities have become more focused on the vision and the clients. The organization receives funding from multiple sources of income. The organization is relatively stable.

Decline: This is the stage during which the organization becomes comfortable with the status quo and afraid of change. Decisions are focused primarily on the interests of the internal stakeholders rather than the clients. External stakeholders are losing faith in the credibility of the organization. Projections of opportunities and challenges reflect past experiences rather than current realities. The board is in denial and refuses to admit that there is something wrong.

Turnaround: An organization in decline can turn things around. This choice is made when there is self-awareness about the decline of the organization, and a determination to change course. In that case, a turnaround leader may emerge. Programs are re-assessed in light of current reality. Changes are made in policies and processes. Decisions are made, and concrete steps are taken to restore organizational integrity.

Terminal: An organization reaches the terminal stage when there is no evident reason for the organization to continue to exist. At this stage, programs are underfunded and become unreliable. Staff cannot get paid. The organization is out of money and has accumulated debts. The organization has to dissolve.

It is important to note that there is no set timetable as to when a nonprofit organization may reach a particular stage. Some nonprofit organizations have started and dissolved before they even reached a level of maturity. Some organizations have reached a stage of maturity in a relatively short period while it takes years for other organizations to get there. The fact is there is no rigid stage of evolution of nonprofit organizations. There are key factors, such as the strength of leadership, the commitment to the vision, the diversity and reliability of funding, the unforeseen consequences of internal and external factors, which determine whether a nonprofit organization moves from one stage to another.

ORGANIZATIONAL TRANSFORMATION

The organizational transformation of a nonprofit organization includes factors that are antecedent to the process and other elements that are part of the process (see Figure 24.1).

Antecedent Factors

Organizational transformation does not occur in a vacuum. It is the consequence of other factors or elements, which must be taken into consideration in future plans of action.

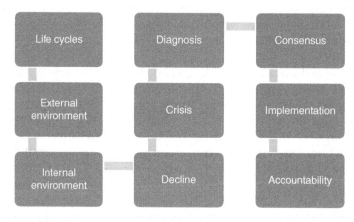

FIGURE 24.1   Process of organizational transformation.

These factors include, but are not limited to, life cycles, internal environment, and external environment.

Life Cycles

As the previous paragraphs indicated, organizations go through life cycles. Organizational life cycle theories explain that the characteristics of an organization may change based on life-cycle stages (Merchant, 1997; Moores & Yuen, 2001). One of these cycles is decline. Therefore, an organization can experience a normal stage of decline, which must be addressed in order for such organization to survive.

External Environment

The external environment of a nonprofit organization encompasses the external stakeholders, such as clients or customers, suppliers, partners, donors, and the community or the public. The external environment also includes the social, political, and economic events that have the potential to affect the life of an organization as an entity in a community or society. The external environment can be a source of decline in an organization. For example, if the external stakeholders lose faith in the vision of an organization, they will withhold their support, and this can trigger a decline or a crisis.

Internal Environment

The internal environment includes the board of directors, executives, managers, staff, and volunteers, as well as the administrative and coordination systems. The lack of a transparent and participative decision-making culture, the level of stewardship and accountability, and the mismanagement of resources can be sources of decline for a nonprofit organization. In fact, an organization can become so attached to its own status quo it fails to anticipate or recognize the need for a change.

Decline

In one form or another, decline is a constant in almost all theories or conceptual frameworks on organizational life cycles. Decline can happen for various reasons. It can be triggered by the inability of an organization to anticipate, recognize, neutralize, overcome, or adapt to internal or external factors that constitute a threat to its survival. Other organizations may experience a decline because they grew too much or too fast or both, and were not able to control the implications of their growth. A nonprofit organization in decline may find it more difficult to make strategic decisions, because key members or leaders are looking in different directions. A nonprofit organization in decline may see its expenses increasing and income decreasing in a consistent way, because donors are not as excited to donate or there is not enough diversification in revenue streams. A nonprofit organization in decline might see a significant decrease in positive outcomes that can be reported. A nonprofit organization in decline might see increasingly negative reports in the press about its reputation and credibility in the eyes of the community or the public.

Crisis

According to Seeger, Sellnow, and Ulmer (1998), an organizational crisis is a "specific, unexpected, and non-routine events or series of events that [create] high levels of uncertainty and threat or perceived threat to an organization's high priority goals" (p. 232). As this definition suggests, a crisis is an event or a series of events that are out of the ordinary, and which constitute a threat to the core of what an organization aims to accomplish. In other words, a crisis has the potential to completely destroy an organization, if not solved in time. As Venette (2003) argued, a crisis usually puts an organization in a situation where something has to change. A nonprofit organization is in crisis if, as a result of an event, the organization

- Cannot make strategic or operational decisions
- Cannot conduct normal operations of business in a peaceful atmosphere
- Cannot meet its regular financial obligations
- Sees either internal or external stakeholders or a combination of both turn against key decisions made by the leadership

Any combination of two or more of these factors or similar elements would be a sign of an organizational crisis or an imminent organizational crisis.

ORGANIZATIONAL TRANSFORMATION ELEMENTS

Organizational transformation is a radical rethinking of the overall structures of an organization in order to start afresh with new or modified structures and processes and new energy and commitment that are rooted in the current reality and linked to a sense of renewed purpose for organizational effectiveness and sustainability. Organizational transformation is another way to say organizational reengineering or organizational change through new mind-sets, approaches, strategies, and behaviors. If a nonprofit organization is in decline, or experienced a major crisis or continuing minor crisis or conflicts, the organization must go through some process of transformation. As Figure 24.1 illustrates, a generic organizational transformation process should involve diagnosis, action plan, consensus, implementation, and accountability.

Diagnosis

A diagnosis consists of gathering all possible information about a problem in order to determine what is/are the cause(s) of such problem. Without a diagnosis, it is impossible to adequately solve a problem. I said "adequately" because temporary solutions can sometimes be found for a problem without any systematic diagnosis. Obviously, such a solution will not be sustainable. Organizational transformation that does not involve a diagnosis can only be superficial. As a result, I argue that organizational transformation can be superficial, transitional, or transformational.

The transformation is superficial if it addresses only the apparent aspects of decline or crisis, and does not deal with the core issues that may constitute a threat for organizational sustainability or financial sustainability. For example, an organization may experience a negative perception with some internal stakeholders who are not satisfied with core aspects of how programs are being implemented. The leader of the organization may decide to organize a meeting, listen to the staff, make an inspirational speech, give a small raise to the staff, and think that the issue is solved. It will not take too long for the organization to have to deal with the same issue again if the problem is structural.

A transformation is transitional if the process did not take into account all the factors that are sources of decline or chronic crisis for an organization. For example, a process of organizational transformation might involve some minor changes in policies and the service delivery system, but not investigate why these changes were needed, and whether the changes made will be sufficient to prevent this problem from affecting the survival of the organization.

An organizational transformation process is transformational if it starts with a thorough diagnosis of the organization that accounts for the internal and external environment, including the core values, strategic areas, and leadership. Diagnosis is a critical step for organizational transformation.

A proper organizational diagnosis should be conducted by an outsider, an external independent consultant hired with responsibilities to look at aspects of decline, have access to all relevant information, and make recommendations that explore all options, including change in leadership behavior or even leadership personnel. An effective organizational diagnosis is a review of all political, economic, social, and technological (PEST) aspects that directly or indirectly contributed to a decline or crisis. It also includes a SWOT analysis that explores the current *strengths, weaknesses, opportunities,* and *threats* related to the organization. Finally, an effective diagnosis analyzes an organization readiness to change.

Action Plan

The diagnosis must be followed by an action plan. The development of an action plan for organizational transformation must be rooted in a participatory collaborative approach, which involves transparent deliberations. All stakeholders should be given opportunities to provide their inputs, ask questions, and suggest changes. The development of an action plan should include a set of strategies to communicate the need for organizational transformation, a clear process, a comprehensive timeline, a list of measurable benchmarks, and contingency items needed to deal with the politics of transformation. Box 24.1 illustrates the generic items that should be included in an action plan.

Consensus

Change is always difficult, because the change agent faces a challenge to beat the odds. Organizations that are mature tend to be very comfortable with the status quo, and are afraid of changes that may seem too radical. In fact, radical change can be frightening, because it promises the unknown compared to what is already concrete. Radical change is threatening because it may take away opportunities or privileges that are good for a few, but will not serve the effectiveness and sustainability purposes of an organization. The main challenge is that it may be difficult to find out who will be individually affected

BOX 24.1 ACTION PLAN

Call for Action	
(A justification of why change is needed: Decline? Crises? Changes in PEST?)	
PEST	
Report of findings about the political, economic, social, and technology changes and implications for organizational decline or crisis)	
SWOT Analysis *(Report finding from SWOT analysis)*	

VISION STATEMENT

Current	Potential Changes
(Describe current organizational vision statement; describe potential issues with the mission statement in light of PEST/SWOT)	*(Suggest possible changes in vision statement)*

MISSION STATEMENT

Current	Potential Changes
(Describe current organizational mission statement; describe potential issues with the mission statement in light of PEST/SWOT)	*(Suggest possible changes in mission statement)*

VALUES STATEMENTS

Current	Potential Changes
(Describe current organizational values statements; describe potential issues with the mission statement in light of PEST/SWOT)	*(Suggest possible changes in values statements)*

ORGANIZATIONAL STRUCTURES, PROCESSES, AND CAPACITY

Current	Potential Changes
Structures	
Leadership (People/Behaviors)	
Management/Staff (People/Behaviors)	
Clients	
Partnerships	
Funding	
OUTCOMES AND BENCHMARKS	

(continued)

BOX 24.1 ACTION PLAN *(continued)*

Timetable	Timetable Should Include:			
	Action step	Person in charge	Required resources	Completion date
Communication Strategies				
(What message will be communicated? When? How? Who will be responsible? How will feedback be collected? ...)				

the most if an organizational transformation occurred for the financial sustainability of an entity and for the benefits of the clients. It turns out that it is not difficult to realize who will be affected individually the most, because these individuals will be the most resistant to change regardless of the long-term benefits that an organizational transformation can bring for the clients. The solution is not to ignore individuals with personal interests in the organization, because they play a key role and may be vital for the future success of a change process. As a matter of fact, people who have individual interests in organizations tend to have a higher level of commitment, which is essential for organizational sustainability. The solution is to identify individual interests, find areas of compromise, and develop a consensus with all internal and external stakeholders, so that the organization can engage in a transformational process as a whole. Obviously, consensus does not mean total surrender to individual interests at the expense of the strategic interests, vision, and mission of a nonprofit organization. Consensus is made with everyone who wants to make a consensus, and at least concedes something. If a stakeholder cannot concede anything for the strategic interests of a nonprofit organization, the stakeholder must go and cannot be part of any organizational transformation project. Sometimes, an organization has to separate from some of its funders, some of its leaders, and some of its key members, and then start with new energy, if this is what is needed to prevent the organization from dissolving in a manner that may significantly affect the clients.

Implementation

Even with the most effective diagnosis possible and a well-designed action plan, organizational transformation does not happen until it has been implemented. The implementation is critical, because it will test the real commitment of an organization as a whole to go through a process of transformational change. The implementation phase should be based on the outcomes, benchmarks, and timetable set in the action plan. There should be a system of ongoing reporting about progress being made, challenges encountered during the implementation, and strategies adopted to overcome them. The implementation is an opportunity to provide evidence of a new or continuing culture of accountability.

Accountability

Accountability is very important for organizational transformation. In addition to the action plan and implementation strategies, an organization should develop a specific calendar for accountability, specifying what information will be communicated to internal and external stakeholders, when such information will be shared, what feedback will be collected, and how such feedback will be used for continuous improvement of the organizational transformation process.

ORGANIZATIONAL TRANSFORMATION AND FINANCIAL SUSTAINABILITY

Organizational transformation can be used as a strategy for financial sustainability because it leads to long-term organizational changes. When an organization goes through a transformational change process, a new identity is developed. The organization tends to have new or more targeted vision statements, streamlines processes that foster organizational effectiveness, client satisfaction, and more accountability to stakeholders. This in turn helps create a new sense of purpose and commitment to support the organization's vision from all stakeholders, including the donors.

QUESTIONS AND ACTIVITIES

1. How would you define organizational transformation in your own words? How does organizational transformation differ from strategic planning?
2. You are hired as a consultant to conduct a diagnosis for an organization that is supposedly in decline. What information will you collect in order to document evidence of (a) organizational decline, (b) financial decline, (c) decline in program outcomes, and (d) credibility deficit?
3. Suppose you conduct a SWOT analysis for a nonprofit organization, and realize that there must be radical change in leadership and management of the organization. Write a step-by-step argument to convince the people who hired you as an independent consultant that such change is necessary. What information will you present first? What actions will you recommend them to take? How would you suggest that they lead the change? What resources will you recommend to them?
4. You are the executive director of a nonprofit organization. The organization has developed an action plan for change. Some of your staff members are trying to boycott the plan. Write a step-by-step plan to identify their concerns and develop a consensus with them!
5. What are some examples of situations that would convince you to recommend each of the following changes:

Change	Fictitious Situation
Information management and communication system	
Performance reviews	
Operations tracking and scheduling procedures	
Facilities management systems	
Counseling and employee assistance program	
Mandated diversity training	
Across-the-board salary adjustment	
Hiring freeze	
Job reclassification	
Remove a complete layer of organizational hierarchy	
Replace equipment and technology	
End existing partnerships	
Redefine conditions of eligibility for clients	
Rename an existing program	
Consolidate two programs	
Open a contingency fund	
Start a new social enterprise	
Rewrite the vision and mission statements	
Hold a burial for the past	
Secure newspaper and television coverage	
Organize a quarterly event to celebrate champions of strategic change	

REFERENCES

Barry, B. W. (1984). *Strategic planning workbook for nonprofit organizations*. St. Paul, MN: Amherst H. Wilder Foundation.

Berkowitz, W. R. (1982). *Community impact: Creating grassroots change in hard times*. Cambridge, MA: Schenkman Publishing.

Bryson, J. M. (1991). *Getting started on strategic planning: What it's all about and how it can strengthen public and nonprofit organizations*. San Francisco, CA: Jossey-Bass.

Daft, R. L. (2007). Organizational size, life cycle, and decline. In R. L. Daft (Ed.), *Organizational theory and design* (9th ed., pp. 319–356). Willard, OH: Thomson South-Western.

Fawcett, S. B., Claassen, L., Thurman, T., Whitney, H., & Cheng, H. (1996). *Preventing child abuse and neglect: An action planning guide for building a caring community*. Lawrence, KS: Work Group on Health Promotion and Community Development, University of Kansas.

Fawcett, S. B., Paine-Andrews, A., Francisco, V., Richter, K. P., Lewis, R. K., Harris, K. J., ..., in collaboration with Vincent, M. L., & Johnson, C. G. (1992). *Preventing adolescent pregnancy:*

An action planning guide for community-based initiatives. Lawrence, KS: Work Group on Health Promotion and Community Development, University of Kansas.

Lord, R. (1989). *The nonprofit problem solver.* New York, NY: Praeger.

Merchant, K. A. (1997). *Modern management control systems: Text and cases.* NJ: Prentice-Hall, Englewood Cliffs.

Moores, K., & Yuen, S. (2001). Management accounting systems and organizational configuration: A life-cycle perspective. *Accounting, Organizations and Society, 26*(4–5), 351–389.

Olenick, A. J., & Olenick, P. R. (1991). *A nonprofit organization manual.* New York, NY: The Foundation Center.

Seeger, M. W., Sellnow, T. L., & Ulmer, R. R. (2001). Public relations and crisis communication: Organizing and chaos. In R. L. Heath (Ed.), *Handbook of public relations* (pp. 155–165). Thousand Oaks, CA: Sage.

Stevens, S. K. (2001). *Nonprofit life cycles: Stage-based wisdom for nonprofit capacity.* Wayzata, MN: Stagewise Enterprises.

Unterman, I., & Davis, R. H. (1984). *Strategic management of not-for-profit organizations.* New York, NY: CBS Educational and Professional Publishing.

Venette, S. J. (2003). *Risk communication in a high reliability Organization: APHIS PPQ's inclusion of risk in decision making.* Ann Arbor, MI: UMI Proquest Information and Learning.

Wolf, T. (1990). *Managing a nonprofit organization.* New York, NY: Prentice Hall.

Index

Made in the USA
Middletown, DE
16 January 2020